Queen of ICE
Queen of SHADOWS

The naive American public knew her as a blonde bundle of energy who won Olympic gold medals and world figure-skating championships and whose first film for Darryl Zanuck established her as a top box-office attraction. The Norwegian papers called her "pro-Nazi" and a "female Quisling." She called Adolf Hitler "my dear friend." Only those closest to her saw the Sonja possessed by an insatiable passion for money, diamonds, furs, and men. Lawsuits and hysterical attacks against her family were brought on by alcoholic binges; friends and business associates were spied upon, abused, and alienated; at her second divorce she staged a midnight raid with a moving van on the posh estate she had occupied with her husband—she stripped it bare, taking even the toilet tissue. Sonja took dozens of lovers, from among Hollywood's biggest stars and lowliest extras, and three husbands, but there was only one man she ever loved, Tyrone Power.

When she died of leukemia in 1969, her multi-million-dollar fortune was intact, but she had disinherited her blood relatives, left her faithful secretary of twenty-six years with nothing, and had left instructions that her jewelry be permanently displayed as if they were the Crown Jewels of England. This book could have been called *Sonja Dearest*.

Also by Raymond Strait:

Mrs. Howard Hughes
The Tragic Secret Life of Jayne Mansfield
This for Remembrance (The Rosemary Clooney Story)
Star Babies
Lanza: His Tragic Life
Lou's on First (The Lou Costello Story)
Hollywood's Children
Alan Alda: A Biography
James Garner: Hollywood Maverick

Queen of Ice
Queen of Shadows

*The Unsuspected Life of
Sonja Henie*

Raymond Strait
and
Leif Henie

SCARBOROUGH HOUSE

Published by Scarborough House
4720 Boston Way
Lanham, Maryland 20706

First Scarborough House paperback edition 1990.
Originally published in hardcover by Stein and Day Publishers.

Distributed by National Book Network

Certain quotes from Sonja, prior to 1940, come from her autobiography,
Wings on My Feet, published by Prentice-Hall, Inc. (1940).

Library of Congress Cataloging-in-Publication Data
    Strait, Raymond.
        Queen of ice, queen of shadows: the unsuspected life of Sonja
    Henie / Raymond Strait, Leif Henie
        p.   cm.
    Reprint. Originally published: New York: Stein and Day, 1985.
    Includes filmography and index.
    ISBN 0-8128-8518-X (pbk.)
        1. Henie, Sonja, 1912-1969.   2. Skaters—Norway—Biography.
    I. Henie, Leif.   II. Title.
    GV850.H4S77 1990
    796.91'092—dc20   90-42152
                                                   CIP
    ISBN 0-8128-8518-X (pbk. : alk. paper)

The paper used in this publication meets the minimum requirements of
American National Standard for Information Sciences—Permanence of
Paper for Printed Library Materials, ANSI Z39.48–1984.
Manufactured in the United States of America.

It is regrettable that so much of the story of Sonja Henie's life will be painful to her public, but this is not a fairy tale on ice. It is a factual biography. I loved the sister I grew up with, and it is to the memory of that lovely child that I dedicate this effort.

Leif Henie

and

To Frances Ross from whom I learned much about celebrities and their frailties.

Raymond Strait

Contents

Illustrations

Acknowledgments

Biography involves not only the life of the subject but the many who were part of that life. This was particularly true of the preparation of *Queen of Ice, Queen of Shadows*. We therefore wish to express very special thanks to Dorothy Stevens, who was Sonja Henie's loyal secretary for twenty-six years. Her extraordinary memory made it possible to provide intimate details of Sonja's life far beyond the slim substance of newspaper columns and Hollywood gossip. Without her help this book could never have been satisfactorily completed.

We also wish to thank Sherwin Goldstein for bringing the two of us together and inspiring us with a common purpose. Additionally, we acknowledge the valuable contributions of the following: Dr. Terry Robinson, Miss Kitty Kelley, Belle and Robert Christy, Gloria and Michael Mikeler, Jack and Liz Pfeiffer, Gerd Weldon, Fred de Cordoba, Milton L. Dixon, Patte Barham, Marshall Beard, Emily Cole, Danny Simon, Twentieth Century-Fox Films Corp., Buff McCusker, Mary Healy Hayes, Sheila T. Cluff, Cesar Romero, Milton Sperling, Cornel Wilde, Rudy Vallee, Bruce Humberstone, Dick Lochte of the *Los Angeles Times,* Hank Grant of the *Hollywood Reporter,* Jules Levine, Claude Terrail, the Library of the Academy of Motion Picture Arts and Sciences, the Library of the University of California at Riverside, the Oviatt Library of California State University at Northridge, and most certainly our agent, Miss Teresa Chris of Thompson & Chris, San Francisco.

R.S. and L.H.

Leif Henie died in San Francisco on August 13, 1984, shortly after the completion of this book.

Ascent

1

" "**B**ULLSHIT!" she screamed. "You tell that sonofabitch Zanuck to get his ass off the polo ponies and meet me on the set. I show that sonofabitch he don't fool with Sonja."

Darryl Zanuck was not the only person who learned you didn't fool with Sonja. The little, dimpled darling whom Americans had taken to their hearts could be as hard as her skate blades and as cool as the ice on which she skated. Film producers crossed her at their peril, and lovers who were less than loyal chanced the fate of her second husband, Winnie Gardiner, whose house she trashed by moonlight, stripping it down to the toilet paper and only leaving the carpets behind because there were too many tacks to pull up.

Sonja was a woman of awesome talent and Napoleonic ambitions. The passage of her life from child prodigy to aging Hollywood queen was a roller coaster ride packed with bumps and jolts. Those who would follow her in her journey would do well to fasten their seat belts.

It isn't supposed to snow in Oslo in April, but when Sonja Henie was born on April 8, 1912, a freak snowstorm was raging. It lasted for two days and abated only after the Wilhelm Henie family had welcomed a new daughter into the world.

Sonja was a warm, cheerful, cuddly, and vivacious child with a winsome smile that would eventually capture the hearts of millions around the world. Her brother, Leif, was five years old when she was born, and he was delighted to have a baby sister. He loved her intensely and so did everyone else in the family, but it was clear that Wilhelm Henie loved her most of all. In her father's eyes Sonja never did any wrong, and during his lifetime he spoiled her outrageously.

After Sonja's motion picture career was launched, rags-to-riches stories about her were occasionally concocted by Hollywood publicity flacks. Those tales made good copy. But none of the Henies had ever had money problems. Sonja would have lived comfortably all her life if she had never earned a nickel. She came from "old money" that her father's mother had inherited. By the time it was handed down to Wilhelm, it was third-generation wealth, and he had the acumen to make the fortune grow.

Wilhelm's philosophy was that money didn't just get lost in a deal—someone lost it. He made it a point never to be that "someone." He had no known enemies, and it was said of him that the whole world was his friend.

Wilhelm Henie, the son of Niels and Catinka Jordan Henie, was born in Oslo in 1876 when the city was still called Kristiana. Catinka's fortune was inherited from her mother, who was the sole owner of Jordan's factories in Oslo—a firm similar to the Fuller Brush Company in the United States.

There was other "old money" in the family as well. Wilhelm's father left a fur business to him, and over the years he expanded it into an internationally respected firm that placed furs on the backs of reigning monarchs throughout Europe.

Wilhelm's wife, Selma, was the daughter of a Captain Nielsen, who came from Risor, Norway, and who commanded a fleet of lumber schooners that transported Norwegian timber to foreign ports. Although the captain's wealth was not so great as that of the Henies, he left his daughter financially comfortable.

This was the lap of luxury into which Sonja Henie was born. She never wanted for anything material as a child, nor as an adult. Sonja wore wealth like a full-length Russian sable.

Wilhelm Henie was an excellent sportsman, abounding in energy and endowed with a leprechaun's sense of humor. Perhaps that accounts for his immense popularity. Both Leif and Sonja inherited his athletic prowess, and Sonja fell heir to his financial wizardry as well, becoming a shrewd, tight-fisted businesswoman.

During the 1890s cycling was the number one sport of the era, and Wilhelm twice won the world bicycle championship. He also excelled in speed skating, ski jumping, and cross-country racing, winning medals in these events and setting records that were not bettered for years.

Wilhelm Henie owned both the first automobile and the first private airplane in Oslo. His two-cylinder 1905 Horch was banned from the city streets every week or so on the complaints of citizens angry that their horses were being frightened by that "damned fool Henie and his contraption."

The Henies were a tightly knit family. They became even more so after Sonja was born. Not that they didn't have friends—they had many. Had it been left to Wilhelm, the parlor would have been overrun in the evenings with his business associates and drinking companions. After work, he liked to raise a glass or two with a few friends, and he certainly would have invited them home to continue in that spirit had not his wife put her foot down. She wanted no riffraff littering her immaculate parlors, which were designed for aficionados of bisque and Wedgwood rather than for her husband's aquavit-happy friends with their loud laughter and cigars.

16

Because of their immensely successful fur business, the Henies not only lived richly but counted among their personal friends many titled and crowned heads. The Henie label in a fur coat was treasured by all, royalty and commoner alike.

When Sonja was about two years old, just as World War I was breaking out, Wilhelm decided that it was time to invest in a luxurious summer estate for his family. He found just such a location on the west coast of Denmark and purchased five thousand acres of Jylland by Vesterhavet, facing the North Sea. It provided all the privacy that they would ever need. There was little chance of visitors dropping in without invitation, and the family could live a close, happy, and secluded life together, just the four of them. They entertained themselves hiking, swimming, fishing, and enjoying nature on the vast acreage.

The Henies were a musical family. Wilhelm played piano, accordian, and cello; Selma, who was considered one of Norway's greatest beauties, sang and played piano; Sonja was adept at both drums and piano. Leif took piano lessons, but after his teacher caught him improvising in American jazz style instead of playing the classics, he was dropped from the class. He switched to banjo and continued to enjoy jazz.

As a family, they enjoyed a special quality of togetherness. Leif remembers that although his mother was the cook of the family, his father insisted on fixing certain dishes. Sometimes everyone else had to pitch in and help him. Of course, the Henies had many servants, and there was no need for family members to lift a finger to do anything unless they wanted to, but Selma Henie loved her kitchen.

Sonja's father handwrote all of the menus for the family, and her mother encouraged everyone to participate in home affairs. "My mother," Leif states, "only wanted to be around Sonja, my father, and myself—immediate family only. She never wanted me to marry. My father, however, was exactly the opposite. When he heard that I wanted to get married, he gave me the family fur business as a wedding gift."

Sonja idolized her older brother, and as soon as she was old enough to toddle she was never far behind him. This created a few problems for Leif as he grew older, for he was popular with his classmates, and the girls competed for his attention.

Although Sonja's mother did not share her family's enthusiasm for sports, the Henies owned a hunting lodge at Geilo, a mountain village that was popular for winter recreation. From the time Sonja was four, as soon as the first snow fell, the family went there for weekends and holidays. Of her early childhood experiences there, Sonja, in 1940, wrote:

I was crazy about Geilo, even about going to Geilo. Father, round of figure and jolly to go with it, and wholly the pleasantest person I have ever known, would bundle us all under big fur

17

rugs, mother quiet but missing nothing, the firm pillar of the family as always, and Leif and I very unruly in our enthusiasm. I was born just too late for the thrills of long distance rides in horse-drawn sleighs. By the time I appeared the family was well into its third generation of cars. So I had to wait for later years in smaller places to learn the sleigh bells' myriad music.

Once in Geilo, no one walked. Feet out of doors were feet on skis. Sonja was given skis the first winter she accompanied the family to the lodge. She followed along behind Leif, trying as always to keep up with him. Sonja loved speed, seeming never to get enough of it. She remembered later that "Brilliant winter days always went to my head anyway, and when I could add speed that I made myself to the natural whip of the wind, I wanted never to go indoors."

Occasionally, when a blizzard was forecast, Sonja and Leif would stay out long enough to worry their parents—and even themselves—then rush downhill to home, often reaching the house in tandem with the advancing snowstorm.

From these beginnings Sonja acquired a feeling for balance and rhythm in movement that served her well when she took to ice skates. Everyone marveled that the young child was so graceful on skis. She said, "I don't know about that. What I do know is that Geilo meant skiing, and skiing was like flying, and this flying made me winter-drunk, an affliction I have never got over."

Sonja later switched her earthbound wings from wooden runners to steel blades, but her love affair with speed never changed. During those early years, she gained enormous confidence in her ability to conquer anything she chose.

It was Leif who first put her on skates and who witnessed her first triumph. "I was playing ice hockey at the time in Oslo," he remembers. "My sister was about five years old and running after me all the time. I discouraged her as much as I could, telling her to go home, but it was impossible to get away from her. She was so fast. She tagged along with a pair of my old skates—not hockey skates, but the kind that clamp onto the shoes. All of a sudden there was a championship event for kids, and my God, she went up and won—at five years old. Her prize was a little pearl-handled silver paper cutter, for first place."

That little silver knife became one of Sonja's most cherished possessions, and she kept it all her life. It now rests, along with her hundreds of professional trophies, in the Sonja Henie-Niels Onstad Museum in Oslo.

When her father was told of Sonja's feat, he went out and bought her a new pair of expensive shoe skates.

Sonja had been dancing since she was about the age of two, and all of her life she credited that activity with being her initial motivating force.

18

"I absorbed so much," she once said, "that it has marked everything I have done since. It was never forced on me. The ballet was my first love, skating my second."

Leif recalls her training in ballet. "My mother took her to Pavlova. 'She should study ballet,' the great dancer advised, and so it was done. She was entered in ballet classes."

Sonja had the best teachers available and was an exhibitionist from the beginning. When the Henies had guests in their home, Sonja's dancing was always a part of the entertainment.

She seemed to have theater in her blood, showing signs of that bent at a very early age. It was not unusual for Sonja to invade her mother's unguarded closets, picking out the soft formal dresses for "play acting."

"I casually took what I wanted," she said. "The more perishable, the better, put it on, tied it up off the floor, and went downstairs to give a 'dancing recital'."

When the damage threatened to grow serious, Sonja's mother gave her young thespian some old dresses and scarves in order to protect her wardrobe from the "artiste's" passion. With a new wardrobe all her own, Sonja's recitals became even more frequent.

Costuming, more than theater, played a major part in Sonja's performances. She had a feeling for costumes and was, by her own recollection, "deadly earnest about setting a formal atmosphere for the occasions. But the actual seat of the disturbance was the dancing itself. When I heard music, I wanted to do something in motion about the way it made me feel."

Through dancing Sonja learned different tempos and moods and developed a taste for particular types of music. She said, "I found that reflecting the quality of the music in movements that were fast or slow, smooth or jerky, was so fascinating an occupation that it took a mass walkout of my audience plus a firm hand leading me off to bed to make me stop."

Her audiences were indulgent. She was allowed to group the living room chairs into "boxes," which she numbered, and then she made out tickets, ushered in the "customers," turned on the gramophone orchestra, and proceeded to perform her interpretation of the dance. Her father and mother dutifully applauded each number. Leif, often bored with these sitting room theatricals, would doze off, leave the room, or simply not show up at all. Love Krohn, her teacher—a famous ballet mistress who had taught Pavlova at one time—often came to these shows and offered suggestions to Sonja in private.

"For all I know," Sonja later confessed, "I might have remained content as Love Krohn's pupil, hurling featherweight challenges at the great Pavlova, if it hadn't been that Leif had skates and I didn't. He was tall and well-built, in a slender way, with a lean-cheeked look and slow-waving blond hair. All his likable traits, internal and external, however, did not prevent his being just one blur of enviable brother to me. Leif had skates, went places, and had fun. I didn't have skates, couldn't go to Frogner with him, but detected he had fun because he always came back in a glow and usually later than he should."

Sonja always wanted what she didn't have. Even after she had her own skates she wanted more than that: She wanted to be with Leif and to share whatever he did. One morning when Leif went up to his room to get his skates, Sonja went up to her own room, pulled on a heavy sweater, grabbed her skates, and dashed downstairs again to find him sitting on the sofa, reading a newspaper.

"What's the big rush?" he growled, never taking his eyes away from the print.

"I thought you were going skating," Sonja stammered.

"Well, I'm not," he curtly answered, "and Mother wants you upstairs to help her plan lunch."

"That's not true," she said, feeling hurt that he didn't want her with him and angry that he would lie to her. "Lunch is four hours away, and you know it. Besides, Mother doesn't plan serious lunches unless there are guests and even Father won't be here for lunch." Leif shifted on the sofa and she caught sight of a metallic glint from behind the edge of a cushion. Sonja ran over and yanked on the cushion, revealing Leif's glistening skate blades.

Furious, but defeated, he took his sister along with him to Frogner Stadium. Leif had his own friends, all older than Sonja and all better skaters. She knew that, but her argument was always, "I'm learning."

Although she insisted on chasing him everywhere and acting like the spoiled brat that, indeed, she was, Leif had a great deal of patience with his younger sister, actually taking time to teach her the rudiments of skating.

The first time she had gone with him, he started out onto the ice ahead of her. It looked quite simple to Sonja, so she did what was natural to her—headed for the middle of the rink where all the better skaters congregated. She came to a jolting halt with her skates airborne and her bottom planted fiercely on the cold hard ice. After everyone had a good laugh, Leif skated over to help her up.

"If you're going to skate, you're going to fall," he counseled.

Fearful that he would tell their parents and that her excursions to Frogner would end just as they were beginning, she started to cry.

"Don't worry," he said, "and for God's sake, stop crying. Who do you think you are, to believe you can learn to skate without falling? Ten years from now you'll still be falling—maybe less often." Sonja listened to Leif and watched him and his friends closely. Not only did she practice on the

20

ice, but she went through the motions with Leif at home in order to perfect her balance.

And as for falling she soon learned "It was just as Leif said, all a matter of letting go completely, bending at the ankles, sagging my knees, doubling up in the hips as though I were going to sit down, and so going down to the ground in easy stages with my hips taking the major portion of the weight. Untrained people falling stay rigid. That hurts."

Before long, dancing as a career was forgotten. Skating was everything. Sonja soon appeared at Frogner before the stadium opened for the day and often forgot to come home for supper. Her parents worried little about their young daughter. They always knew where to find her if she wasn't at home with them.

When there was an amateur competition in which Sonja was allowed to compete, she did—and always won. By the time she was six-and-a-half, she was skating alone and enjoying it. Later, that same year, a member of the private club at Frogner took notice of the blonde youngster who seemed to be born with skates on her feet. Hjordis Olsen observed Sonja peeping inside the section that was roped off expressly for club members who were experts at skating. Sonja wanted to be with the grown-ups. She was beginning to become bored with her peers, and even with Leif's friends, who seemed to stay the same rather than improve. She marveled as she gazed into the special area of ice where the better skaters went through their spins and jumps, undeterred by the misadventures of boisterous children and inept adults.

Hjordis Olsen took an immediate notice of Sonja's enthusiasm and ability, and one day she asked the youngster, "Would you like to come and be my guest?" *Would* she? Indeed she would.

"I felt as if I had died and gone to heaven," Sonja said, of crossing into the exclusive territory on the other side of the ropes.

Miss Olsen took Sonja through some simple routines. Within months she had taught Sonja what she knew, and the youngster was easily the best of her age. Sonja was her own hardest taskmaster. She practiced school figures until she could etch the same figure ten times and leave only one single unblurred tracing behind her. She was already the perfectionist she would remain throughout her career. Miss Olsen suggested that Sonja be allowed to enter serious competition, and the proposal was quickly approved by Wilhelm and Selma Henie.

When she was eight years old, Sonja won the Junior Class C competition. She so soundly beat out her competitors that it was decided that she would skip Junior B and A, Senior C and B, and enter the Senior A—the national championship of Norway. That competition was held the following winter when Sonja was nine years old.

The Henie family efforts moved into high gear for this event. If Sonja won, she would be the number one amateur in the country. Her father, looking ahead as always, could see European tours and higher levels of competition in Sonja's future. Perhaps one day, the Olympics.

Of course there would have to be a professional teacher for Sonja. Hjordis Olsen had given all she had to give. Her student had outdone her. Miss Olsen recommended Oscar Holte, Norway's leading ice skating instructor. And since money was no object, Wilhelm easily obtained his services. Sonja was immediately put into a rigorous training program and held to a strict diet.

Mother and Father Henie closely supervised Sonja's training. One or the other was with her at every practice session, and they both became expert critics who could spot the slightest flaw in her performances. All of this began a year before the national competitions were to take place.

Sonja practiced for two sessions a day: three hours in the morning and two in the afternoon. After she became a professional, she kept to her three-hour morning practice, preferring to start at 6:00 A.M., when no one else was at the rink.

Her dietary regimen required her to eat only nutritious foods and to eat at the right times. Oscar Holte told her that eating must be precisely orchestrated, just like skating. Sonja meekly reported for breakfast, lunch, and dinner at the appointed hours. She no longer skipped meals to skate at Frogner, and the dining hours were set so that Sonja would have no meals in the two hours before she skated. Her mother rearranged the entire household's schedule to accommodate Sonja's needs. Even business trips were postponed or eliminated if they interfered with her practice schedules. Neither parent expressed any misgivings about giving up a more sedate private life for the excursion their daughter was taking them on. If there was inconvenience involved, they kept it to themselves. Their love for Sonja was totally unconditional.

Nonetheless, Wilhelm Henie did have business to attend to, and when he was absent on the Continent, Selma assumed his place in the training program. Nothing could have pleased her more. She had her beloved Sonja all to herself, and she took over the complete supervision of all her activities. In Hollywood Sonja once said in an interview, "She has been my closest counselor in all the years since, going with me everywhere and giving me the soundest advice I've ever had."

During the spring Sonja was sent back to Love Krohn for more ballet lessons, and these were followed by a trip with her mother to London for a quick, but concentrated, course under Mademoiselle Karsavina, who had been associated with Pavlova, the prima ballerina of Russian ballet for many years.

With the advent of her career on ice, Sonja's school days were over. For the rest of her years of formal education she was tutored privately—when the time was available. She later reflected that "If my family had not had the means to give me my schooling on a tutor's flexible time schedule, I would have had no schooling, or else no championship career."

The fact that the family could afford to travel abroad also allowed Sonja to have the benefit of the best foreign instructors and coaches available.

Having the ability is one thing; having the means and opportunity to develop it, however, can make the difference between becoming a champion or just a good athlete.

Sonja had it all.

2

WHILE the family focused on Sonja's ice skating exploits, Leif was also aggressively participating in sports. During this period he won two speedboat championships and an important tennis tournament, and he played on championship ice hockey and soccer teams. Now, with the family concentrating on Sonja's amateur career, he was in a position to enjoy a little private life for the first time since Sonja's birth.

Yet, with the Norwegian national skating championship competition drawing closer, Leif temporarily put aside his own activities in order to be of whatever help he could to Sonja. The truth was, however, that she had all the help she could possibly use.

The day of the Norwegian championships finally arrived. By the time the Henies reached Frogner Stadium, a large crowd had already assembled in the grandstand—thousands more than had witnessed Sonja's earlier competition in the children's and Junior C events.

Sonja's parents fidgeted nervously, and while some of the girls who would be competing giggled and tittered, Sonja's composure was placid and as cool as the ice on which she would be skating.

When it was time for her to perform, Sonja's name was called, and there was polite applause. At that point, she experienced her only bout of nerves: "I felt as though all Oslo had risen to swallow me up." The feeling passed, though, the moment she reached the ice. She knew the mandatory routine better than her competitors, and that gave her the confidence she needed. Sonja went through her preliminary figures to applause from the grandstand; it sounded like a symphony to her. It was at that point that she fully realized how much she loved being watched and applauded for her efforts. She would remember that day all her life.

When Sonja returned to the ice for the freestyle segment, she was applauded as she came into the arena. With her flashing smile and the blonde locks of her hair clinging to her face, she was quickly a favorite of the spectators. They saw that she was not just a child playing at games that were beyond her. Sonja flew across the stadium ice, whipping up unbelievable spins and jumps and coming down from her highest leaps in a graceful swanlike glide across the surface. These were the choreographed routines she had never done before in public. The crowd gasped, cheered, and jumped to its feet in approval. When the cheering stopped, Sonja was ice skating champion of all Norway.

At the award presentation ceremonies, the head of the national championship committee prophesied, "Miss Henie is on her way to becoming the greatest ice skating champion in history. It is only a matter of time, and not too much of that will pass before it happens."

Sonja was awestruck. But this was only the beginning. There were new vistas and new challenges ahead. Sonja's board of mentors sat down to map out her future with an eye beyond just the next championship. They knew there would be larger stakes and greater recognition to come.

Oscar Holte, Hjordis Olsen, and Wilhelm and Selma Henie all agreed that Sonja would have to leave the country in order to prepare herself fully. She needed more lessons, and she needed experience with a class of competitors against whom she had never vied. Sonja was pleased with their decision. It presented an opportunity to receive a brand new wardrobe, as well as a chance to travel. Above all, it was an opportunity to encounter new ice rinks and new audiences.

In the fall of 1923, Sonja and her entourage of family and instructors embarked for St. Moritz and Chamonix. St. Moritz seemed a fairyland to Sonja. There was lots of snow for skiers, and the ice was firm, smooth, and sparkling. Hotel life abounded with international sports enthusiasts and competitors, along with vibrant personalities, winter events, and jealousies. Sonja was hardly affected by the last of these, but as she climbed the ladder of competition she would be.

At St. Moritz Sonja made her first non-Norwegian skating friend, Gillis Grafström, the internationally recognized Swedish skating champion who, at the time, was riding the crest of his fame. Sonja, of course, posed no threat to him, and he was generous with suggestions and friendly criticism. She adored him and listened avidly to what he had to say. Indeed, she may have developed a mild crush on the handsome Swede, but then, of course, she was only eleven years old at the time.

Some people (including Sonja) have felt it was a mistake for her to enter the 1924 Olympic Games at Chamonix. There was little chance for her to gain much more than general exposure because compared to her competitors she was a novice. Still, perhaps the experience was useful. She met the world's greatest champions and learned things from them that would benefit her in 1928. She was required to perform exactly as the other competitors. The competitions were divided into two sections: school figures and free skating. School figures involved basic skating moves such as figures 8 and 3 and all the variations of those numbers. The important thing—it was the basis of scoring—was to make sure that the blade cuts in the ice were exact and the repetitions were done over the exact track of the original figure. There could be no wavy lines or overlapping blade marks. Free skating involved spirals and the waltz jump, loops, hoops, and original variations. In Sonja's case, her original variations tended to be a form of dancing on ice.

Herma Planck-Szabo won the gold medal in figure skating and became the new reigning Olympic champion. Sonja placed eighth and last, and her father was furious with the decision. One judge had rated Sonja first in free skating, and Wilhelm felt his daughter should have been awarded a higher position. Of course, her first defeat left Sonja disappointed, but she knew she'd do better in the future. In 1925 she again defended her Norwegian championship and kept her title, and there was no reason to believe that she would not remain number one in her native country as long as she chose to compete. She was not only the darling of Norway but the hope and delight of all Scandinavia.

In 1926 it was announced that the 1927 world championship ice skating competitions would take place in Oslo. It seemed logical that if Sonja won Norway's championship in 1926, she would be selected to represent her country in the world championships. However, Sonja had some misgivings. In spite of her many skating accomplishments, she was still considered only an upstart child by many who had worked long and hard over the years for a chance to compete for the world title.

Sonja would be fourteen, and she was worried that people might think her presumptious. Many world sports officials, including some from Norway, hadn't been enthusiastic about her appearance in the 1924 Olympics. She was too young and inexperienced, they said. There was much concern expressed that the world championships in Oslo might turn into "a Norwegian skater's farce." They wanted to avoid that happening. Wilhelm Henie was ready to take on those officials. Sonja, he asserted, was the national champion of Norway and therefore entitled to enter any international contest she chose. But by pressuring the sports bureaucracy he also put a great strain on his teenaged daughter.

Should Sonja enter the competitions, presuming that she would be the national champion again, or should she wait for the 1928 Olympics? The cases for and against her entry were heatedly debated, both in the family and among Sonja's increasing number of tutors, instructors, and advisors.

"We will never have another chance like this," Wilhelm Henie argued. "To fail to enter Sonja on our own ice would be an insult to our country and would certainly be thought strange by the rest of the world." In the end, the temptation was overwhelming and the decision was made. Sonja would compete for the world title. It would be the first of Sonja's ten consecutive entries into the world competitions.

Now the pressure was on Sonja and the entire Henie household. The family was determined that their honor would be upheld on the ice of Oslo.

Sonja knew her capabilities and believed she could win. Her chief excitement derived from the prospect of being able to compete once again with world-class stars, as she had done in Chamonix.

The Henie clan settled into a new winter home just outside of Oslo in order to be closer to Frogner Stadium and to Oscar Holte, who would be helping to prepare Sonja for the world championships. To the already long list of advisors was added the name of Martin Stixrud, an internationally acclaimed skating instructor.

Selma Henie took a very active part in preparations for Sonja's participation, even designing her daughter's costume, a tight-fitting outfit with no folds or frills that would clash with Sonja's movements. "If I never remembered anything else," Sonja said, "I would remember that trim, white velvet dress with its bell skirt. It was a revolution from the clumsy skating dresses that were currently standard costume for female skaters."

Sonja's mentors decided that she shouldn't go abroad to train for the event. She was more familiar with the Oslo facilities than any foreign instructor could be, and she might as well continue to train on her home ice. Sonja spent hours every day at Frogner, concentrating on balance, limbering, and muscle tone.

Sonja later recalled the extensive preparations for her first world championship competitions. She had planned, with the help of her numerous coaches and advisors, to present the most impressive free-skating program she dared to perform. "I hoped I would be startlingly different without falling on my face. My skating hours were curtailed to prevent me from over-tiring myself. But no one, not even my parents, could control how hard I worked during the hours I had." Sometimes she felt as though her muscles were bundles of live wires that would electrocute her if she made the wrong move.

When Sonja climbed into bed at night she often felt that her body "had turned into a mass of lead that would sink lower and lower through the bed all night; I couldn't move it if I tried." But she kept up the pace.

In the dead of winter of 1926-27, the skaters and their entourages began to descend upon Oslo. Many came early. The champions and would-be champions moved into the city in twos and threes; later by the dozens. They all showed up at Frogner, and Sonja found she no longer had the stadium to herself.

On the day the championships were to begin, Sonja stood on the sidelines at Frogner and watched the various national champions go through their paces. They seemed confident and sure of themselves, and Sonja thought they were brilliant. The section of boxes reserved for honored guests was draped with flags and surrounded by silk ropes, with a long red carpet leading to the area. The royal box was in this section;

King Haakon and Queen Maude of Norway, as well as their many attendants and guests, would sit there.

Sonja would be the youngest skater ever to compete in a world championship, and she knew it would be difficult to perform better than all the more experienced young women. She was full of anxiety the night before and noted it: "I suddenly thought of what it would be like to fail before all of Oslo and the whole skating world. I thought of falling and prayed that if I did I would break a leg so that I could be carried out and not have to skate my way off to disgrace. There was an endless night to be waited through. I went home and put the pearl-handled paper cutter I had won in my first competition under my pillow for luck."

In the morning, at Frogner, Sonja remembered how the pearl handle had glinted the night before with the reflection of her bed lamp, and how cold the blade had felt in her hand. "Superstitions," she said, "give one courage that is like a fake boost. Maybe the paper cutter saw me through that first world championship event. No skating trophy has ever meant as much to me as that first simple one."

The afternoon of the championships was bitingly cold, with a strong wind. Sonja remembered how it cut into her as she swept across the ice and completed the final spin of her free-skating segment. She had done what she could. She had finished on her feet. It was up to the judges to decide.

Moments later she was being presented to her king and queen as the youngest world figure skating champion in history. She had never met the royal family before and had only viewed them from the sidewalks during parades and national holiday events. "They were smiling directly at me," she recalled with warmth, "congratulating me and saying nice things, especially noticing my being the youngest girl ever to win the world championship. I lost all my self-consciousness, curtsied many more times than I needed to, and became ardently patriotic."

The king expressed his pride that she was Norwegian and presented her with bouquets of giant pink carnations. He continued to send her these over the years before her competitions, as well as cablegrams and telegrams of good luck on opening nights throughout her career.

After winning the world championship in Norway in 1927, it was clear that Sonja would be entered as Norway's representative to the 1928 Winter Olympic at St. Moritz. Sonja was about to begin nine years of incessant competition and whirlwind travel. Her training began almost immediately following the world competitions. She was able to train at Frinse, near Oslo. The location was suitable because the ice was excellent early in the fall, making it totally unnecessary to go abroad. Besides, her father's theory was that "It is good to train far away from your rivals."

National championships and world championships require intensive training, but they demand less than Olympic preparation. First, Sonja would work diligently on each of the eighty school figures, polishing them to perfection so that she would be prepared for any that might be selected for the Olympic test that year.

Second in importance was exhibition experience. Her father busied himself booking Sonja into every exhibition possible so that she could retain her poise while facing all sorts of audiences and conditions. Sonja also put on informal exhibitions at Frinse, her own private training grounds, attracting large crowds from the neighborhood who were, of course, all staunch supporters. Two formal exhibitions at Bergen brought out more than thirty-five thousand people, both surprising Sonja and forever endearing the Bergeners to her.

The third, and, to her, the most important part of her preparations was recalled by Sonja in later years:

> During the summer between my first world championship and the fall when I started working toward the Olympics, I went to London and saw Pavlova. She had, for me, what all great artists have—the ability to give you something you had not been able to imagine in advance. She was a dancer whose performance went beyond dancing, transcending technique to such an extent that the onlooker was unaware of technique.
>
> So she became my idol more than ever. The influence she had on me was twice as great as anyone outside my own family. My old and constant passion for dancing burst into new flame.

Returning to Norway in the fall, Sonja wanted more than anything else to make her free-skating program a blend of dancing and figure skating. She wanted a choreographed form of ballet solo on ice. Martin Stixrud became her mentor in this; he suggested that she could incorporate into her number jumps and spins to show the judges her stylized skills in a pattern and sequence that would reflect the mood of dancing, not just skating.

Arriving in St. Moritz for the Olympics, Sonja was filled with confidence.

For the first time, Maribel Vinson, the United States champion, would be competing. She was one of a new breed of skaters from North America who were gaining world acclaim. Sonja already recognized that in winter sports Europeans would have to share the limelight with the newcomers.

Sonja was brilliant. No one came near her performance, and she won the gold medal easily. Her recollections were vivid:

> My first Olympic victory meant so much to me that I broke right down and wept in the locker room after I knew the results. It

seemed to me then I had worked my way uphill a long time to get there. It was a very short time, as I see it now, but the first hundred weeks are undoubtedly the longest.

Following the competition, in the evening, Sonja was chosen to open the Olympic Ball in the Palace Hotel with the Grottumsbräten. Norwegian skiers were being wined and dined as champions in their field. Sonja wore some of the pink carnations that had been sent to her by her king. She wished he could have been there to share her victory that day.

Sonja stepped into the world of real international fame that night. She crossed a magic line she would never have to recross again. She also became acutely aware of the incessant rivalry of international sports; it created an atmosphere in which jealousies bred and temperaments flourished. There were many acquaintances and few firm friends. It was a world of trunks, suitcases, fast express trains, steamships, hotel suites, parties, balls, fetes, music, costumes, spotlights—and amidst all of this, it was still necessary to sleep long hours, to eat regularly and correctly, and to train constantly.

Wilhelm Henie continued to spend large sums on his daughter's career, while her mother never seemed to tire of accompanying Sonja to all sorts of functions, and of watching over her physical well-being. After the 1928 Olympics, Sonja began to dabble in prophecy about herself. "You know," she told her parents, "I have decided to become a movie star."

That ambition was nothing new. From the time she was a small child she had dreamed of appearing in films, and only the year before she had been in a Norwegian silent movie entitled *Syv Dager for Elisabeth*, which has long since disappeared from the motion picture archives.

Not only did she win the Olympics in 1928 but also the next World Championship in London. She would go on to win ten in a row—the last one in Paris in 1936, the same year she won her third and final Olympic gold medal. This came at the end of her amateur athletic career.

At St. Moritz Sonja climbed aboard a merry-go-round with no idea whatsoever of getting off anytime in the near future. Afterward, she said, "If you start to go the rounds of the competitions, you can't stop unless you are quitting for good. If you skipped a year, you would get out of touch with developments, and, more important still, if you slackened training because of a loss of the incentive of competition, you would find yourself far behind when you tried to reenter." Sonja had no plans to "reenter" anything.

No sooner had the competitors folded their tents at St. Moritz than it was time to pitch them again on the banks of the Thames in London. The first thing Sonja noticed was that the British attitude toward figure skating was different from that on the continent. The British focused more upon the entertainment and recreational appeal of skating than upon its competitive aspects.

The setting was different, too. Continental rinks were rather austere, while London rinks were lined with marvelous restaurants and shops. The mood of the seasoned skaters was also more relaxed than it was when they were on the Continent.

The night before the competitions, the royal family expressed a desire to meet personally the athletes who'd be performing. The skaters gave an informal exhibition before the royal assemblage, which included King George V, Queen Mary, the Prince of Wales (later Edward VIII), and the Duke of York (who would become George VI upon the abdication of Edward VIII when he chose a divorcée for a wife and gave up the throne).

Sonja was elated at meeting the British royal family, especially the handsome young Prince of Wales, who particularly charmed her. They would become friends in the years ahead.

During the early part of the skating exhibition, the two young daughters of King George and Queen Mary were allowed to view the skaters, and the royal children were presented with ice skates by the performers.

Sonja never forgot her first meeting with Queen Mary, known to be a very proper lady and as austere as the image of old Queen Victoria.

> It was the worst faux pas of my career. I responded to her disarming expression of interest in the sport with a suggestion that she might take up roller skating. Nobody knows how I spent the night after that, asking myself over and over how I could have done it. I only meant that roller skating would be a less dangerous form, that the Queen had been so gracious as to make me forget that she was a person for whom many sorts of activities are impossible, and that I had a genuine impulse to make a helpful suggestion. The instant's pause that followed my remark will be ringing in my ears to my final hour. Queen Mary broke it, saying, "I will think about what you have said."

Following the command performance Sonja prepared for the next day's events, buoyed by a feeling of royal approval. She again won the world championship; Maribel Vinson placed second, Fritzi Burger of Vienna was third, and Constance Wilson from Toronto was fourth.

Sonja had brought some innovations to London, and the British audiences cheered her spins on flat skates and her double-revolution jumps. They had never seen such acrobatics on ice. They also gasped at the skimpy costumes that Sonja had made famous at the Olympics and that set the style for the costuming of ice skaters from them on. She enjoyed shocking audiences.

Invitations for Sonja to skate in exhibitions came from all around the world. The first offer accepted on her behalf by her father came from Berlin. Sonja had been asked to perform the ceremony opening a six-day bicycle race. A former bicycle champion himself, Wilhelm responded to the invitation with pleasure. Although the family was exhausted from the Olympic Games and the London competitions, they quickly packed and crossed the English Channel, where they boarded the Berlin Express.

Once the cyclists were officially on their way, the Henies left for Oslo, where Sonja's own club (she was now a member of the private club at Frogner) had asked her to compete in the Norwegian national championships. It was actually a step down for Sonja, but the sponsors felt that having an Olympic gold medalist in the competition would guarantee a much healthier "take" at the box office.

The ice was bad at Frogner on the night of the event, and Sonja was very displeased with the situation. Still, she won her fifth consecutive Norwegian championship, and the sponsoring club was delighted with the ten thousand people who attended on the final night.

Skating had been fun for Sonja until then, but now she was an international figure and her schedule reflected that. There were demands upon her time that she'd not had to contend with before. Now *she* was the big event. Everybody wanted to see and admire Norway's child prodigy.

3

*A*NY hope of resting up after Oslo was dispelled by an invitation from Prince Heinrich of the Netherlands; Sonja was to be a guest of honor at the 1928 Summer Olympic Games in Amsterdam.

Instead of being one of the competitors, Sonja was a celebrity in her own right, sharing a box with royalty and being sought after for autographs. People seemed never to get enough of Norway's darling. It was heady business for a starry-eyed teenager.

Sonja's first real taste of how enthusiastic crowds become mobs came in Gothenburg, Sweden, during the fall of that year. Sonja had been invited to perform in an exhibition there, and her father had accepted, although the rest of the family would much rather have gone back to Oslo and locked themselves up at home for a brief respite. It had been a long time since the Henies had enjoyed the privacy of family life they so valued.

Arriving at the rink, Sonja and her parents found spectators milling about. When the crowd spotted her, they took up a chant, "Sonja! Sonja!" and they began to press in on the young star. Sonja, believing that all she had to do was ask them to move back and make room, did just that. She was ignored as the crowd moved even closer. She was starting to feel the squeezing mass of human flesh around her, and for the first time in her life she became frightened of her fans.

"I was naive about crowds before that," she recalled, "but never afterward!" She learned in a few horrifying moments just how dangerous people can get—and how quickly. Wilhelm Henie, who had been talking to an official up in the stands, heard Sonja cry out for help and bounded down to the rink, his ample body gyrating like a runaway bowling ball. He yelled out, "I am Sonja's father! Let me through! I am the father of the girl who is giving this exhibition!"

Those on the outer fringe of the crowd disbelieved him, and he had to unfold a long sheath of papers, including his passport, before they would be convinced. But only after the officials came down on the ice was a wedge formed to get Sonja away from the dangerous, albeit affectionate, mob of surging humanity. Once out of the arena, Sonja and her entourage were mobbed again by the crowds that surged toward their chauffeur-driven automobile, shattering the windshield and windows and, after they reached their hotel, the plate glass front windows of that building. The militia had to be called out.

The exhibition was to take place at Peblinges Island, where the ice isn't always solid at that time of year. Arrangements had been made in expectation of a few thousand people. Thirty-five thousand appeared and their combined weight caused long, running cracks in the ice. Sonja's father left the ice in a gesture designed to encourage others to do the same. With more room, Sonja was able to skate, but she hardly dared look where she was going. The crowd went wild with enthusiasm, and Sonja wondered if it was her performance they were applauding or the spurts of water that geysered in her wake. It was, for Sonja, a lesson in professionalism: The show must go on, no matter what the distractions.

Sonja was young, healthy, vibrant, and better able than her parents to withstand the rigors of her frenetic schedule. Still, they kept pace with her. Selma and Wilhelm poured all their energies and the overflow from their enormous financial reservoir into accomplishing whatever was necessary for Sonja's future.

Meanwhile, the young skating sensation wanted to have fun. No matter where she went, parties were arranged in her honor. She was expected to attend them all, and she usually was able to oblige. It seemed that partying went hand in hand with exhibitions. During the 1928-29 season, covering only the winter months, Sonja might as well have been a whirling dervish. She attended and won the Norwegian, European, and World championships. The last of these was held in the old city of Budapest, where Sonja was crowned by acclamation, and in all these places, she enjoyed the delights of fame.

Sonja wasn't getting enough sleep. She was like a little pauper who'd been thrust into a candy store and allowed to gorge herself without restraint.

Sonja tried to insist that the parties in her honor be held early in the evening so that she would be able to retire early, but it rarely happened that way. Later in life, Sonja became totally a night person. These amateur tours probably had planted the seeds of that life-style. During her amateur days, particularly while she was a teenager, Sonja didn't drink so much as a sip of champagne, and she never smoked. She developed a very firm but polite way of saying, "No thanks, my parents do not approve." Her diet restrictions set the pattern she would follow throughout her adult life as a film star.

The 1930 World Championships were going to be held in Madison Square Garden in New York City. The Henies had never been to America, and the last-minute preparations for the trip were exhausting since

Sonja was appearing almost daily somewhere in Europe right up until the moment of their departure.

Although it was vehemently denied by the Henies, Wilhelm was known to demand "expense money" whenever Sonja appeared at exhibitions. Bruce Jenner, the Olympic decathlon gold medal winner at Montreal in 1976, recently acknowledged in an interview that many amateur athletes today are receiving hundreds of thousands of dollars annually. That no longer shocks anyone since it is common knowledge throughout the sports world that amateurs are being paid in one fashion or another for their participation in sports. Although technically it is against the rules, officials of amateur sports choose to ignore it.

This was also the case, although perhaps not quite so blatantly universal as it is now, in the days when Sonja was competing. From the beginning she was a "big draw" at the box office and was much in demand throughout Europe and, eventually, in America as well. Rumors were rampant that she was "the richest amateur in sports," and that her father was demanding and receiving astronomical fees (for the era) to assure Sonja's appearances. Wilhelm Henie was a clever man, and there were never any checks or bank drafts. Cash was the policy, and the money that exchanged hands never appeared on official ledgers or tax reports. With his tremendous wealth, it was not difficult to conceal large sums of money within his business transactions.

Formal complaints were never lodged against Sonja or her father, even though the rumors persisted throughout Sonja's amateur career. It is possible that charges were never brought simply because those who might have done so were afraid of being put on some secret blacklist and effectively barred from competition. Technical reasons for disbarring troublemakers are usually not difficult to find.

The Henies sailed from Oslo in early December of 1929 aboard the Norwegian liner *Stavanger Fjord*. Sonja and Leif were filled with choking excitement, standing on the first-class deck watching their homeland fade into the distance. When they turned to look ahead, the western horizon beckoned invitingly. All her life Sonja had dreamed of going to America. It was the land of skyscrapers and movie stars—where all of her childhood fantasies could be lived out in larger-than-life fashion.

From her arrival in New York until her departure for Norway, her days and nights were one gigantic ceremony. New York's mayor, the celebrity-conscious Jimmy Walker, met the Henies at the pier, as did the United States Figure Skating Association representatives, together with Maribel Vinson and Beatrix Loughran, who had competed with her at the St. Moritz Olympics.

Prior to the World Championships, the New York Skating Club invited

Sonja to participate in an ice show dedicated to her homeland. It was called *The Land of the Midnight Sun*. The ice spectacle was to take place in January, about a month before the 1930 world competitions. The club maintained a permanent ice rink on the third floor of Madison Square Garden. It was a small rink and not what Sonja was accustomed to, except when practicing. Sonja's father quickly concluded that the club officials knew very little about show business. He, on the other hand, knew quite a bit about it; everything his daughter did would be as theatrical as any Broadway stage production.

The president of the club had planned to hold the event on the third floor rink. Wilhelm Henie was aghast. "My daughter," he declared, "will not skate on such a small rink. Where will you seat the thousands of people who will come to see the show?"

The man laughed. "Mr. Henie, you don't understand the American public. They're not skating enthusiasts. Even in the third floor rink it's difficult to fill all of the seats."

"That," Wilhelm said, "was before my Sonja came to America. The seats will be filled this time. I assure you. No, I think the show will be done downstairs in the main arena."

"You must be jesting, Mr. Henie," the club official replied. "You're talking about an arena that accommodates over fifteen thousand people. Skating is not the same as prizefighting, sir. There is no way that an ice skating event will attract that many people in New York, or any other place in America. Take my word for it. It will be embarrassing not only to your daughter but also to everyone else involved."

"You take *my* word," Wilhelm countered. "My daughter will pack the place to the rafters." The opportunity-conscious Henie went further. "I tell you what," he said. "Just let me have the main floor of the Garden and I'll fill it my own way."

The man hesitated. "I don't know, Mr. Henie."

"Okay," Henie said, taking a new tack, "just rent the Garden to me, and I'll print and sell my own tickets—and keep the profits." Awed by such confidence, the official changed his mind and decided to put the ice show in the main arena. Tickets were printed and placed on sale, and twelve thousand sold the first day. In no time the event was a sellout, and on opening night the main floor of Madison Square Garden was filled with cheering spectators waiting for a glimpse of the Norwegian champion.

Wilhelm Henie hadn't left the selling of tickets purely to chance. He had information to which the club officials were not privy. He knew there were nearly fifty thousand Norwegians living in Brooklyn; moreover the Norwegian-American Gale Borden, of the Borden milk family, was a personal friend of Henie's. Borden's appeal to New York's Norwegians helped assure that Madison Square Garden would be filled to capacity for the *Land of the Midnight Sun* ice carnival. He made them feel that national pride was involved, and Norwegians are fiercely patriotic.

The press often came early and stayed late during Sonja's stay in New York. It did not take her long to recognize the differences between the American and European press corps. "The American press," she contended, "has its interest in the little things that single one person out from another." A great deal of interest was expressed in the skates Sonja favored. "The papers made a to-do about my pet pair of skates. I had ten pairs with me, but naturally there was one pair I favored over the others—skates I had worn in my most important competitions."

They became Sonja's "lucky skates" in most of the stories that were written about her. More was printed about the fact that her father took special care of Sonja's skates than about her technique and skating background. Her two dozen skating outfits were described by the newsmen, down to the last stitch and spangle. She was upset that her costumes were considered "frivolous." Since this took place when the Great Depression was getting underway, the suggestion could be damaging.

Sonja said nothing publicly, but privately she complained bitterly to those who had access to the major newspapers, and the stories were toned down thereafter. "My costumes are necessary," she said in defense of her lavish wardrobe. "They are not foolish expenditures. Each one is different and unique and serves a specific purpose in my routines. Remember, I will be here for three months while I am appearing in both public and private exhibitions and championship competitions."

She stood in the wings at the entrance to Madison Square Garden on opening night, waiting to dash out onto the ice for the overflowing crowd of seventeen thousand who had come to welcome her. There were butterflies in her stomach. "It was an awesome sensation," she confessed, "and years later, with a veteran's experience, I still felt that way sometimes when I was about to skate onto the ice on opening nights."

By now she was universally known as the "Pavlova of the Ice." Even though her part in the pageant was fatiguing, it was excellent practice for the championship to be held in that rink two weeks hence. Sonja felt the carnival was rather long, sober, and pompous—almost professional in its commercialism, but the standing ovations she received assured her that she was a welcome guest in New York City. "My number," she said, "was the finale. I was really the star and it was during the New York Carnival that I realized the importance of structuring the sequence of acts so that the star came on at the end to highlight the show." Sonja had learned to save the best for last.

"The late and irregular hours," Sonja explained in print later, "were bad for my training, but the compensation of becoming acclimated to the Garden ice and, for me, to the American crowd, more than made up for it."

The Carnival had been a success; now it was necessary to think of the World Championships. Sonja's father, besides accompanying her, was part of the official committee to help put the American competitions together; he had his own ideas to promote those 1930 World Championships. He remembered what the club president had said about not being able to fill the third floor rink with spectators and, being a practical man, he understood that with the somewhat boring school-figure competition in the championships, his host might be correct. To assure that his daughter wouldn't play to an empty house, he made admission to that phase of the event free and took the fifteen hundred tickets, which would fill the place, and gave them to Norwegian sailors docked in Brooklyn.

During the preliminary school-figure competitions, Wilhelm sat in the balcony and every time Sonja finished a figure, he would take his cane and hit the paneled wall as hard as he could, and the sailors applauded madly. Selma Henie was mortified when she turned to see who the boisterous spectator was who was making all the racket. The judges probably weren't influenced by Wilhelm's theatrics, but his behavior added verve to what might otherwise have been a dull event.

The following day on the main floor of Madison Square Garden, thirteen thousand people turned out to watch the World Championship primary competitions. Sonja's appearance in the carnival, and the overwhelming acceptance by hard-nosed New Yorkers, had much to do with the turnout. Warmth and hospitality flowed from the grandstands, bringing tears to Sonja's eyes. She was thousands of miles from home and nowhere had she received such a welcome as in New York.

"Galleries of spectators indoors," Sonja commented, "seem somehow so much more intimately around you than the grandstands do out under the sky. Vast as Madison Square Garden is, one of the two largest indoor arenas in the world, the crowd seems closed in with you, and to be closing you in, as you stand in the spotlight at the bottom of that well of people. When I made my debut in the carnival, I had never had any experience like it, and it was good to get the distraction of the strangeness over with before the day when I needed all my concentration to retain the world title."

That wasn't easy. Sonja was getting to know her competition better and learning a very important lesson; it's more difficult to stay on top than to work up from the bottom. The challengers in 1930 all had excellent programs to offer, each with unique specialties. During the school-figures competition at the Ice Club rink on the third floor of the Garden, a critic watched and took notes. They appeared in *The New York Times* and Sonja clipped them for reference:

Cecil Eustace Smith of Canada, "studied and determined."
Maribel Vinson, American champion, representing Boston,

"spirited." Constance (Wilson) Samuel, Canadian and North American champion, "vigorous and determined." Melitta Brunner, Austria, "careful and exact." Sonja Henie, Norway, "delicately graceful."

Sonja's years of ballet training were showing up in her performances, enhancing her public stature. She felt that the critic's words made her execution sound frail, but they gave her confidence. She knew that school figures counted 60 percent of each skater's total score and standing in the competitions.

New Yorkers turned out in droves to view Norway's greatest export since sardines. Sonja, in the wings, checked every detail carefully, as she always did: her boots, the sharpness of her blades, whether her gloves were fastened and the ornaments in her hair were firmly in place. Loose hairpins or combs can cause disaster for a skater.

She knew that some of the other skaters had already tasted misfortune: Constance's skates had been sharpened incorrectly, causing her to have an accident in the final training period and putting her out of the running. Cecil Smith, through some minor irregularity in the ice, had a fall during her performance, in full view of the audience and judges. She was lucky, however, for she had done so well with school figures and her recovery from the spill was so smooth and sophisticated, her long swan glides superbly controlled, that the judges gave her second place, in spite of the disastrous fall.

Sonja appeared last among the six women competitors in the singles, showing the same pleasing appearance and skills that had won for her in Budapest the year before.

Ever aware of costuming, Sonja was dressed in brilliant salmon-colored velvet edged with fluffy fawn-colored fur. The outfit was topped off by a fawn-colored turban that clung close to her head; it was to become a Sonja Henie trademark. Her short-cropped curls popped out from under the turban around her face like unruly blonde springs seeking freedom from confinement.

Her four-minute stint on the ice began with a running glide, ending in a daring one-foot jump. She then swung into a flowing waltz to a waltz-march time. The thunderous applause was reassuring, since it indicated from the onset that she had caught the fancy and hearts of the audience as she moved swiftly and gracefully around the huge rink, concentrating on the more awe-inspiring intricate pinwheels, spins, and swirls that were natural audience pleasers.

Her "nerves of steel" reputation had been enhanced that night when she nearly fell while starting a jump spin only seconds after entering the arena. She quickly caught herself on the tips of her fingers, smiling all the while to the crowd as she straightened up. To let the crowd know she was about her business, she brought them to their feet by quickly executing a series of back glides, inserting sudden and unexpected pivots and swirls. The audience stamped their feet and went wild, not only for her expertise, but for her courage in the face of what could have been devastating adversity.

The most sensational exhibit from her bag of tricks was saved for last when she went into her double pinwheel, the execution of which gave the illusion of a flaming torch being rapidly spun in the air. Sonja was a showwoman and she knew it. So did the judges, when they awarded her the championship again.

Experts who analyzed her technique said that "her success is due to the fact that her figure skating is essentially dancing on ice. Sonja performs the hardest feats with the utmost ease." The Axel Paulsen, believed to be the most difficult jump known to skaters at the time, seemed so simple for Sonja that spectators didn't understand its difficulty and many couldn't understand the big fuss made over it.

Norwegian-Americans mobbed the Henies' Biltmore Hotel suite following the competitions, spilling out into the hallways and into other guests' rooms, where the party atmosphere seemed to spread like water seeking its level. Many of them remembered Wilhelm from his cycling days at the Bygdöy track in Oslo and, much to his pleasure, recognized him in spite of the girth he had acquired since. Throughout the ensuing tour, the Henies were met by Norwegians, Swedes, and Danes. It looked as if half of Scandinavia had moved to America, which caught the Henies totally by surprise. Wilhelm was aware of the Brooklyn Norwegians, but he'd no idea so many of his fellow-Scandinavians had settled in America's heartland, too. So, the tour involved many reunions and reminiscences for Wilhelm, with the traditional tipping of glasses of aquavit. Selma Henie was put out when Wilhelm went too far with his drinking companions. "But Mother," he would counsel, "they are old friends. It is just for a little time."

Not only was it Sonja's first North American tour, but the first time ever that such a tour had been conducted through the United States. The European caravan was making its debut in America and the United States Figure Skating Association, which had been trying futilely for years to generate domestic interest in the sport, wanted as many people as possible to have an opportunity to see these European show skaters.

Karl Schaefer from Austria (who succeeded Gillis Grafström, who had chosen not to defend the men's world championship) accompanied Sonja on the tour; they didn't get along at all. Each of the two champions was highly opinionated and had a personal style, and although the Association wanted to pair them in numbers, each absolutely refused to skate with the other. Consequently, they contributed to the peace and unity of the tour by sticking to solos and not speaking except at press conferences.

The tour was successful beyond anyone's expectations. It was also important to a nation entering a depression to find a new and relatively inexpensive form of recreation to divert its attention from poverty and soup lines.

The New York Times's John Rendel gave Sonja her finest press clipping to take away with her when she returned to Norway:

> Anyone wishing to tie her record, is advised to start early, work hard and live in a cold climate. Sonja did and the results were excellent. Though less than 18 years old, Miss Henie's performance has all the beauty and verve of the great dancer Pavlova, to whom she has been likened.

He went on to describe Wilhelm Henie's custodianship of Sonja's skates.

> Mr. Henie may forget his wallet, his keys, his railroad tickets, even his broad smile, but never will he forget those precious, irreplaceable skates.
>
> If those favored by fortune are born with silver spoons in their mouths, it can be said with equal truth that Miss Henie was born with skates on her feet.

By the time Sonja and her family boarded the SS *Bremen* for their trip back to Oslo, they were a physically and emotionally exhausted group. For the first time since she had become Norwegian national champion in 1924, it was decided that she would not go for that title again. She didn't need it any longer and by not competing she would have time to rest up for future exhibitions and competitions. She had to think of the European Championship that was only months away. There was an invitation from King George V and Queen Mary of Great Britain to skate in a big charity gala in early March, that was sponsored by the royal family in London—and another exhibition in England at which the Duke of York would preside.

Even at parties given for Sonja, she felt it her duty to perform, if asked. The night before sailing from New York for Europe, the Norwegian Turn Verein society in New York threw a farewell ball in her honor, and she performed on an improvised rink that was only twelve by twelve. Sonja was always a trouper.

"No air ever seemed fresher," she sighed, "nor decks more peaceful than the Atlantic breeze and the sweep of the *Bremen* on our way back home. The luxury liner was new then, and the swimming pool, tennis courts, and other facilities made it a wonderful recreation spot, entirely new to me, with my limited transatlantic experience, and so it was doubly appreciated."

Sonja had every reason to feel tired. Since 1924, she had captured five more Norwegian singles crowns, the Norwegian doubles title three times with Arne Lie, the all-Scandinavian championship, four world figure skating championships, and the 1928 Olympics. She had also taken the time to become the third-ranking woman tennis player in Norway, an excellent swimmer, a daring equestrienne, and a capable ballet dancer. These accomplishments brought her the first medal ever bestowed on a woman by the Norwegian government for versatility and achievement in sport.

She had earned a rest, as had her family.

4

SONJA had a delightful cruise across the Atlantic. She was going home, and she was happy to leave the hectic rushing and the interminable traveling behind. With America, however, she had had an instant love affair. En route to Norway she told Leif, "I will make my home in America. I know it."

"But why would you want to leave Oslo?" her brother asked.

"Because I want to be a movie star. Hollywood is in America, not Norway."

Her memories of America had been less of the concrete cities than of the warmth of the American people. Within seven years she would apply for American citizenship.

One of the showplaces of America that impressed her was New York's famous Roxy Theater. It was glamorous and built on the grand scale, and, in years to come, all of Sonja's motion pictures would have their New York premieres there.

Sonja's summer of 1930 was the first one in several years that she could really call her own. She had insisted that she was tired and wanted to rest for a while. She was only eighteen years old and since the age of six had worked harder than most adults.

During the warm months Sonja relaxed, soaking up the sun and playing tennis with Leif and his friends. Growing up Sonja had only one close friend and that was Lilyba Nelson. She and Sonja had been childhood friends since the age of five. Lilyba's family owned a beautiful estate near Landoën, the Henie's country house, just outside Oslo. The two had played with dolls together and swum in the fjord by the Henie estate. Lilyba had also taken ballet with Sonja from Love Krohn. Their childhood fantasies had Lilyba holding Sonja and lifting her high in the air, just as the ballet dancers in the films they had seen together. Both had dreamed of becoming ballerinas and dancing with the Russian ballet.

Wealth, of course, was another common bond between these two young ladies. Lilyba's father had a large sailboat anchored near the Nelson house. Sonja and Lilyba, as they grew older, enjoyed sailing and hiding out on the boat to talk and share girlish secrets.

During that summer of 1930, Sonja saw a great deal of Lilyba; it would

45

be the last of their good times together because soon Sonja would be too busy for childhood friends. It was also the only time anyone can remember the teenaged Sonja going out with boys—and even then she was always in the company of Leif and his friends. Her brother believed she was simply too interested in her career to care much about the opposite sex.

School friends and associates she had met at Frogner all began to wonder if Sonja wasn't working too hard. They wanted to know when she was going to give up competition and settle down in Oslo, like the other girls they knew. Sonja was conscious of their concerns. "Friends repeatedly asked me if I wasn't getting tired of traipsing around the world on ice skates. They even confided their fears to my parents, that I might be overdoing it. I think the power of suggestion had an effect on me. For the first time I actually began to wonder if one day I might get tired of the eight-month pace, year after year, that was part of the competitions."

Sonja very quickly decided that the answer was an emphatic "No." Skating was her life, and she wanted to continue. The thrill of competing with and winning over skaters with more experience than herself was an addicting challenge. She realized, "You get so used to whirling from place to place and challenge to challenge that the idea of being at a standstill looks lifeless, colorless, pointless. The merry-go-round has the power of hypnotism."

Sonja didn't want to give up competitions unless and until she had a vocation more desirable to which she could turn. Film studios weren't pounding on her door, though becoming a movie star was her ultimate aim. However, she was now receiving more notice in America, and her father had received many offers for Sonja to turn professional and skate in the United States. One film company even proposed she do skating "shorts," but that was totally out of the question. If Sonja did films, she wanted to be assured that they wouldn't be mere skating exhibitions. She expected to have star billing, story lines, and lots of dialogue. It never occurred to her that her thick, difficult-to-understand, Norwegian accent would in any way hinder or prevent her from being as romantic as Mary Pickford or Clara Bow.

It was a summer of rest but also of crisis in Sonja's thinking. There would have to be a future. She knew what she wanted, but loathed the American idea of "professionalism." "I have," she later recalled, "seen where professionalism may lead. I have seen players like Fred Perry and Ellsworth Vines forget the sincere competitiveness that inspires amateurs to keep their ability at its best and growing better. I did have the knowledge of these examples in the summer of 1930, but I had picked up a feeling that more often than not there was something tarnished about the sports of athletes turned professional, and I believe that if I had not

46

waited until I had run my full amateur course, if I had turned prematurely, my form in skating might never have reached its peak."

The Henie family enjoyed their first long stay at home in several years that summer and fall. It was not until December that Sonja's exhibition schedule was resumed. Late in November or early December the Henies packed up for another trek down to the Continent. En route, they traveled to London where Sonja took some lessons from Howard Nicholson, just then coming into his own as an international figure skating master. An American from the Midwest, Nicholson decided to open up shop in London, hoping to be centrally located for most of the world's ice centers.

Nicholson's instruction was invaluable for Sonja, giving her more confidence. Sonja acknowledged, "His training methods had the remarkable double-barreled power to spur on not only my technical development but also my attitude. Each day he had a new program of work to offer, an integral part of the whole training but an important bit in itself."

By the end of Sonja's two weeks with Nicholson, even her parents could see the additions to their daughter's packet of specialties. "He taught me," Sonja recalled, "how to use my arms to keep the attention of the public, what freshness means, and how to sustain verve throughout a program."

She credited Nicholson for her incredible performance in the Austrian capital on December 13. One critic said of Sonja's exhibition there, "Miss Henie exhibited soft and graceful turns coupled with figures never before seen in Vienna." The Viennese had expected Sonja to execute a difficult program in the style of Mademoiselle Planck-Szabo, a Viennese favorite and the lady who had bested Sonja in the 1924 Olympics. The difference was, in Sonja's opinion, that her skating had dancing in it. The Associated Press said, "In Vienna, as in America, Miss Henie impressed local critics with her grace and faultless execution, and became a favorite immediately."

From Vienna Sonja made a quick trip back to Oslo to give an exhibition at Frogner Stadium with Karl Schaefer, the man who would become the next Olympics singles champion. And, if Sonja was virtually a national treasure in Norway, she was just as dear to the hearts of Germans, especially in Berlin where the seeds of Hitler's Third Reich were being sown. Between 1930 and 1932 the National Socialist German Workers' Party (NSDAP), under the leadership of Adolf Hitler, came from almost nowhere to become the largest political party in the country, partly as a result of the effects of a worldwide depression. Sonja Henie was a favorite of Hitler's and although he had never met her, he felt she epitomized his vision of a pure, blond Aryan race.

Although Sonja had, as an amateur, performed all over Continental Europe, her career received its greatest boosts at the Berliner Sports

Palast. Her popularity in Berlin spread her fame throughout all of Europe. When Sonja performed in the German capital the building was always filled to capacity. So beloved was she to Berliners, they affectionately called her *Häschen,* the "little rabbit." It was a nickname that came about because she always performed in Berlin during the Easter season.

In January 1931, before her annual sojourn in Berlin, the skating world was stunned by an announcement out of Copenhagen, Denmark, that was carried on the Associated Press wire service. The story read as follows:

> International skating events probably will no longer see the flashing figure of Miss Sonja Henie, the Norwegian schoolgirl who wears the laurel of the 1928 Olympics in figure skating.
>
> The local press quote her parents as saying they are tired of following their daughter around to tournaments and want to settle down in a Norwegian home.

Selma Henie wanted Sonja to retire from competition, and she convinced her husband that a joint announcement would be the best way to let the world know, so no one would believe there was a division in the family. But there was Sonja to be convinced. Leif tried to take a neutral position. If Sonja stayed in Oslo, married, and raised a family, then he would be able to pursue his own life without his every move depending on Sonja's current situation. Sonja would, she argued with her parents, quit the competitions if they would permit her to go to America to pursue a film career.

"Never!" her father shouted, in a rare explosion. "If you go to America, it will be with your family and under the right circumstances. I have made commitments for you and you will keep them. If you still feel the same way, then we will discuss that afterward." He also chastised his wife for pursuading him to make rash statements to the press that neither he nor Sonja really agreed with. Selma withdrew her complaints, and Sonja and her father planned for her entrance into the world title championships to take place on March 1 at the Berliner Sports Palast.

In Berlin, for the fifth straight year, Sonja was crowned the female world champion figure skater. She shared the crowd's enthusiasm and applause with Maribel Vinson from the United States and with a young woman who must have seemed to Sonja an upstart—thirteen-year-old Hilda Holowsky from Vienna. It hadn't been very long since Sonja herself had been an upstart. Again, Associated Press, without mention of Sonja's earlier retirement plans, carried the story from Berlin:

> The greater international experience and smoothness of Miss Henie gave her a victory over little Miss Holowsky, whose

flashing grace and skill came near wresting the title from the Norwegian star. Miss Vinson was placed fourth by the judges, but the award was little indication of her popularity with the onlookers, who shouted and stamped on the floor and all but raised the roof in appreciation.

It was one of the few times when Sonja was seriously challenged. Perhaps, however, the near fall from grace prompted another announcement out of Berlin on December 16, two weeks after the championship competitions. In a special cable to the *Chicago Tribune*, Wilhelm Henie made one of what was to become a long series of similar statements:

Miss Sonja Henie . . . has decided to enter the ranks of the professionals, Wilhelm Henie, her father and manager, announced today.

Complaining [that] the Norwegian sports authorities had never helped, only formed obstacles for himself and his daughter, Mr. Henie declared that Sonja will abandon amateurism.

She will not, however, make the change until after next winter, so that she will be able to compete in the 1932 Olympic championships in the United States.

Sonja had already begun to prepare for the Olympics. She'd been shaken by the events in Berlin, not expecting a serious challenge to her crown:

"I had gone to Berlin expecting Fritzi Burger to be my closest rival, but as the days of practice went by, Hilda Holowsky became the one whose skating I admired above all and whom I feared the most. . . . She was just thirteen years old and her specialties were only partly developed. But her work was fresh and courageous and she was full of joie de vivre and eagerness. Berlin loved her, and it was no wonder.

When she placed second, uncomfortably close on my heels in points, beating three far more experienced stars, Fritzi, Maribel, and Vivi-Anne Hulten, then Sweden's rising national champion, I anticipated that she would be a very serious rival in the 1932 Olympics at Lake Placid, and I also had an intimate realization of the insecurity of crowns.

Lake Placid would never see Hilda. She died unexpectedly before the year was out, and her death devastated Sonja. She locked herself up and cried for days over the loss of such a young, vibrant athlete. It taught Sonja that life, like fame, is precarious at best.

In Berlin one of Sonja's tour friends asked her about her impending switch to professional status. She denied it and quickly excused herself. Back at the hotel she vented her feelings about the rumors and press she considered irresponsible. Her father tried to soothe her and her mother looked at her daughter with fear. She'd never heard such vehemence from Sonja.

"Everybody is talking about *Sonja's retirement*. I told everyone that I am not retiring." Sonja was fuming and there was nothing to do but hear her out. "My amateur career is in jeopardy. Gossip like that can ruin me forever. I told you before, the only way I will give up competing is when I become a movie star." She slammed the door behind her, tears of anger streaming down her face as she raced to her own room, locked the door, and threw herself across the bed.

"It is the pressure," Selma Henie assured her husband. "Sonja has been under a lot of stress. I don't know how she does it. It had to happen eventually. It will pass."

Wilhelm shrugged his shoulders. "This doesn't worry me. She is a star. Stars are entitled to temperament." He knew that the rumors stemmed from his angry outburst over the way Norway's Skating Association had behaved during the preceding year and a cable he'd sent to an American newspaper. The affair had, he felt, been badly handled and the results were unfair to his daughter.

It was several days before Sonja recovered from her loss of control, but when she did, she apologized for her behavior. She wasn't always aware of the things her father said that got into print, sometimes exaggerated or twisted out of context. Sonja wouldn't dignify the story with an explanation. Her father had his eyes on the future, as always, and even if he didn't make a lot of noise about it, he wanted Sonja to have her chance in the movies as much as she wanted it. He was sending out signals to first one reporter and then another. If a film company was interested in Sonja, certainly such stories would only enhance their interest. The problem was that it was a bit too early for such a gambit.

Practice for the 1932 Olympics at Lake Placid soon commanded all Sonja's attention. Her lazy summer was over. By fall, Sonja was practicing morning and afternoon, back on a strict diet and getting plenty of sleep every night.

Sonja knew that every year new skaters were arriving on the scene, and that, thanks in part to her ground-breaking efforts, many of them were smarter and more sophisticated than the skaters of the past. Not only was Europe sending its best, but Britain and America were taking the Olympics more seriously than ever before, and national pride in gold medals was just beginning to take on that impassioned quality that characterizes Olympic competition today.

The future seemed more clouded to Sonja than it had been before. "My newfound enemy," she recalled dismally, "rumor, reappeared in the months that followed, and before the year was out I came to realize that my skating life had taken on a new color. It was no longer a simple, fresh matter of hope, effort, and excitement. The mature phase was to be clouded by envy and jealousy of rivals and their supporters. My skating no longer belonged to me. It was a public thing. I should have to watch not only my skating, but my step."

Sonja was growing up. She realized that being dimpled, blonde, cute, and talented wouldn't be enough to sustain her much longer. She had to have something new and different every year. She was facing the same audiences more often than in the beginning and the paying public, fickle as it is, would demand more from her. Otherwise someone else would replace her as number one and to Sonja that prospect was out of the question.

The early part of the 1931-32 winter season was almost Sonja's Waterloo. She described it as "the Gemini syndrome—satisfaction and also trouble." Once again the family packed their bags and in August left Oslo for Paris, where Sonja would begin a series of exhibitions interspersed with her already ongoing intensive training with various teachers. Never did Sonja go onto the ice without her mother nearby, watching every step, every twirl, every turn and run. Her mother was her most severe rinkside critic. "Sonja," she would cajole, "your leap wasn't high enough today." Or, "Sonja, you're dropping your arms. Are you tired today?"

Her father managed Sonja's amateur career, but it was Selma who helped her with day-to-day decisions, supervised her wardrobe and her diet, and made sure she rested at the right times. Sonja was her life, and she never hesitated to sacrifice her own well-being in order to assure her daughter's comfort.

Sonja loved Paris in the fall and winter. "For all the charm of Paris in the spring," she declared during a visit there, "it is doubly charming in a snowfall." She adored the ornamented buildings, which glowed luxuriously behind a curtain of snowflakes like a bejeweled and brocaded dowager behind her fan.

Sonja left Paris for the United States in February of 1932 to participate in her third Olympic Games. For most Norwegians the 1932 Olympics in Lake Placid were disastrous. The weather proved totally unpredictable and this cost the Norwegian ski team its title. Only the figure skating events saved any portion of the Norwegian national pride.

For the American public, the games were a festival. It was only the third time that Americans had seriously participated in the winter Olympics and the first time they were held in the United States—in 1932 both the winter and summer games would take place in America. It was also the advent of winter Olympic sellouts. It was no secret that Sonja's appearance had much to do with attracting the crowds. Except for a few minor events every single ticket was sold early. According to *The New York Times,* the ticket situation became so acute at the arena on the night Sonja was competing for the figure skating championship that officials began selling standing-room-only tickets at $5 per person. That price was unheard of, given the economic conditions existing in the United States. Sonja was the big draw.

The 1932 Winter Olympics were still a novelty—and a fragile one at that. Prior to 1924, largely because of political squabbling, there had been no separate winter games. Even at Lake Placid there was no assurance that winter sports would continue to be part of the Olympic program in years to come.

The ancient Greek Olympics, from which the modern games developed, didn't include winter sports. It was only at the 1908 Games in London that figure skating was added to the normal summer festivities. It was an experimental affair that featured only men's and women's singles, pair skating, and an event called "special figures." Londoners didn't take to figure skating and consequently it was dropped from the Games until 1920 (there were no Games in 1916 because of the war), when it was revived as a companion feature for ice hockey, which was added that year.

By 1924, skiing was generally accepted throughout Europe as a winter sport (although it was just starting in America), and it was well organized by the Federation Internationale de Ski (FIS).

The International Olympic Committee, known for its conservatism, initially rejected the inclusion of skiing or skating in the Games, in spite of a growing popular demand. The committee argued that the original concept of the Games was as a summer event.

With more national and international winter sports competitions being held all over Europe, pressure was brought to force the committee to include these sports in the 1924 Games. France led the fight, agreeing to set up separate facilities at Chamonix for the winter events. The committee agreed to an experiment, and besides skating and skiing, contests were held in ice hockey, speed skating, bobsledding, and a form of biathlon, as well as a demonstration of curling.

So successful had the Winter Games been—with no little credit to Sonja, who captured imaginations because of her youth—that the committee relented and gave official sanction to permanent Winter Games. Yet, there were conditions. Both the Winter and Summer Games must be held in the same host country in the same calendar year. That was fine in 1924, but in 1928 when the Summer Games were hosted by the Netherlands, which had no facilities for winter events, the rule was dropped and the Winter Games were moved to St. Moritz, where Sonja won her first gold medal.

Thus, 1932 was a milestone for the Olympic Games and Sonja was an integral part of that historic occasion. Scandinavian countries, particularly Norway, objected to the Games being held in the United States. America, they argued, had no expertise in such things, and they felt that amateurish arrangements might set back the Winter Games after they had worked so hard to convince the Olympic Committee to sanction them.

Sonja would be coming into Lake Placid favored to win a second gold medal. The choice of Lake Placid had been disputed, and California and Lake Tahoe had offered to spend three million dollars to bring the Winter Games to the Golden State, but without success.

President Herbert Hoover was invited to preside over the opening of the first Olympics to be held in America. He declined. He felt that with the country struggling through a depression it was no time for the president to be officiating at what many people considered an ill-advised and frivolous event. Franklin Delano Roosevelt, then the popular governor of New York, and already off and running toward the 1932 Democratic presidential nomination, accepted the Olympic Committee's invitation to do the honors at Lake Placid. Roosevelt correctly saw that it would be a feather in his political cap, and that it would give him national news coverage.

Lake Placid was known to be cold in winter, and generally several feet of snow fell, a good percentage of that in late February when the Games opened. However, in 1932 an unseasonal warm spell descended on the resort and the snow and ice were slushy and difficult to perform on.

Although Sonja did not have tiny Hilda Holowsky to detract from her popularity, she nevertheless had plenty of competition. Fritzi Burger, Maribel Vinson, and Constance Samuel were in the field and eventually placed second, third, and fourth behind Sonja, in that order. Some newcomers also came into their own. Vivi-Anne Hultén, Sweden's popular favorite; Yvonne de Ligne from Belgium; and two youngsters from England, Megan Taylor and Cecilia Colledge.

Lake Placid was a personal disappointment for Sonja, even though she won her second consecutive gold medal in figure skating. "Apart from the stiff skating competition," she complained, "the Games left us Europeans with few memories. Lake Placid was far removed from our ice world. It was utterly unlike Garmisch-Partenkirchen in 1936, where the scene of competition was at the center, the burning point. Too many outsiders at Placid reduced the Games to tameness."

At Lake Placid there were more ill-tempers flaring and more commercialism than Sonja had ever witnessed before. Now the winter caravan was moving out of the Adirondack Mountains of New York to the colder climes of Canada. The next World Championships were coming up within a week. More pressure would be placed on Sonja to defend again.

Thirteen other stars were challenging her this year for her World Crown, including the Lake Placid pack she had just defeated.

Sonja arrived in Montreal and was greeted by a friendly press with a flurry of flashbulbs. Before she departed a black mark would be indelibly etched on her life, no matter the outcome of the competition.

5

SEVERAL Canadian clubs had requested that Sonja skate at their exhibitions and carnivals, and two of these Wilhelm had declined on behalf of his daughter. Ordinarily his custom was to accept all offers, or nearly all, but Sonja's European temper tantrum had indicated that perhaps she was performing too close to her breaking point. Wilhelm had, however, agreed to accept an invitation from the New York Skating Club for an event to be held later in March.

Before Sonja was even in their country, two of the Canadian clubs that had invited Sonja to perform were already advertising her appearance. When he learned what had happened, Wilhelm Henie flew into a public rage. He had been adamant in his refusing any appearance by Sonja, he said, and he hadn't changed his mind by the time she arrived in Montreal.

The Canadian clubs grew angry in turn and insisted that he had committed Sonja to appear, and that they expected her to live up to his word.

Sonja recalled it with bitterness. "It was another outrage against me. I would appear. I would not. And then rumor, gossip and downright libel began spreading all the way down the American continent, creating ill-will towards me. It seemed that everyone was becoming jealous of my success."

Once again the ugly specter of under-the-table expense money returned to haunt Sonja. Both American and Canadian newspapers carried dark accusations on their front pages that Wilhelm, as Sonja's manager, had made exorbitant demands for appearance money and, for that reason, Sonja would not appear in either of the Canadian carnivals as advertised. One paper went so far as to say that Sonja's attitude was "scandalous," and that she was merely "pretending to be an amateur."

With the conflict swirling around her, Sonja held her head high as she skated out onto the ice to defend her world championship. Number four on the program, she followed Vivi-Anne Hultén of Sweden. Sonja wore a brown skating dress with a rabbit's foot pinned to it for luck.

One paper chronicled her performance, in the face of adversity:

> Miss Henie skated with the confidence of a champion, and on completion of her figures remained to watch her rivals.

She had determined before the competitions started that she would stay to the end, no matter what happened. She felt that all of the gossip about her and her father was too malicious to ignore, and she wasn't about to run away and hide from it. She would be out front where everyone could see her at all times.

Then Sonja was crowned World Champion Women's Figure Skater for the sixth consecutive time, but it was a bittersweet victory. "I was sick," she confessed, "without any physical cause."

Angry and disappointed, she left Montreal, swearing never to return to Canada. Her words were spoken on impulse and, ironically, many years later, down on her luck and seemingly washed up as a skater, a meeting in a Canadian hotel room with skating entrepreneur Morris Chalfen would reestablish her career.

Arriving in New York, the family was ready to spend as little time as possible before boarding the *Ile de France* for Europe and home. Of course, rumor had preceded the party, and reporters mobbed Sonja, asking both relevant and irrelevant questions so quickly that she had difficulty understanding what they were asking. Her tentative responses combined with her thick accent caused much of what she said to sound like gibberish.

She recalled her feelings upon meeting with the press: "I found statements that I had turned professional preceded me. I didn't know what to do. I finally got it across to the press, I think, or at least to some of them, that I was still an amateur. Some of them appeared to be open-minded and not out to 'get Sonja'."

She said that if she intended to turn professional she would have done so the year before when lucrative offers were being made; that neither she nor her family wanted any money paid to them for her competition or exhibition appearances; and that her father was an independently wealthy man and didn't have to stoop to such low levels of business practice. "We never received a nickel," she explained, "other than the usual expense coverage allowed all contestants."

One reporter wanted to know if it was natural to have her entire family with her and who was paying their expenses. Sonja replied, "The fact that I have my mother and father with me seems like the natural thing for an eighteen-year-old girl to do. Girls of eighteen don't go on half-year foreign junkets without chaperonage and guidance, even if they are skaters!"

The American press has always loved the underdog, and although she was the reigning champion, it seemed to some of them that Sonja was definitely being picked on. Those writers and their newspapers rallied to her side and defended her from the accusations. She never forgot those who took her side in the fray.

"The New York press and the people there were kind to me," she recalled. "Kind and understanding, and before the final evening at Madison Square Garden the whole matter had faded into the past."

It had been an experience, however, that left its mark on Sonja. Such lessons were to hold her in good stead in years to come, when she would have to be hard to be successful in business. The day would also come when she would be even harder on those who loved her most.

En route to Norway, there was a stopover in Paris, where Sonja made a brief appearance at a sold-out exhibition at the Palais des Sports, one of her favorite skating arenas. All her life Sonja loved Paris and its audiences. "I could hear each person clapping warmly, accepting me just for my performance and no more."

The Henies arrived in Oslo early on an April evening. The boat train carrying Sonja and her family docked at the East Railway Station to the roar of thousands of voices. It seemed that most of the capital had come to welcome their champion home. For Sonja it was one of the warmest memories of her life.

She was glad to be home. The Norwegian Olympic Committee honored her at the Hotel Bristol with a big party and, at least in Norway, it looked as if bygones were bygones.

During the summer of 1932 Sonja dreamed of skating for fun instead of competing. She also, for the first time, had serious reservations about continuing as an amateur. If the rumors continued to abound, perhaps she would give up her amateur standing. At least, she'd be able to accept the money she had been accused (falsely, she thought) of taking. She never acknowledged that her father was demanding sums for her appearances, although there can be little doubt that eventually she knew about it, since Leif knew. She discussed with her family at some length the notion of turning professional.

They all wanted whatever was best for Sonja. If she turned professional, then she would need similarly professional advisors, not family, in that role. Leif enjoyed traveling and meeting new people, especially the girls who seemed to flock around this handsome, blond Scandinavian with the winning smile, but he was already in his twenties, and his sole function in life seemed to be attending to the needs and desires of his sister. Perhaps that was all right for his parents, who had raised their children to maturity and who enjoyed catering to Sonja, but her brother didn't plan to live his entire life for her benefit.

Sensing that Leif wasn't enjoying himself as much as he might, Wilhelm allowed him to mix business with pleasure. He was sent to Germany to learn languages and on to Austria and Czechoslovakia to study the fur business. For three years he was away from the family, except on holidays and vacations. He spent two of those years in Berlin, where he saw the rise of Hitler from rabble-rouser to chancellor of Germany.

In August, Sonja's preoccupation with the question of her skating was interrupted. She was invited to participate in a race for amateur automobile drivers in Stockholm. Although she had been driving her own car for some time, she was taken by surprise by the invitation. Wilhelm believed it would be great publicity and that, if Sonja was really serious about being a professional, she should make the most of the opportunity.

Initially the prospect didn't appeal to Sonja. "They want to make fun of me," she cried. "I will not be the subject of practical jokes." She wondered what had given them the idea that she would accept such an offer. Wilhelm said nothing further about it but let Sonja dwell on it for a while. He knew that in the end she would do it, if only for the challenge.

What at first had seemed ridiculous, now became a game. Sonja suddenly felt that perhaps she could *win* the race. Her father had given her a Chrysler roadster, and she loved dashing about the countryside in it. Teasing her along, Wilhelm claimed to have second thoughts and suggested that perhaps she shouldn't go after all. Sonja teetered, delaying her decision. Then the officials sent her a telegram saying that she could ship her car ahead and make up her mind at the last minute, if she needed more time to think about it.

A chartered plane was sent for Sonja, and she had the time of her life. It was a cross-country race that lasted three days, with time out for meals and sleeping. Although she had never been involved in such a venture, she came in second and was almost as proud of that as she was of her Olympic medals.

Leif accompanied her to Stockholm for the race. "She took me for several rides while I was home visiting and scared the hell out of me. It is a wonder they didn't take her license away from her."

Back in Oslo, Sonja, who seemed to have given up the idea of dropping her amateur status, immediately began, along with her father, to plan the new season beginning in September. Within days she was on her way to Paris and then to Milan. The charming old Italian city was to be the site of the most daring innovation in the history of ice skating.

For months Sonja's practice sessions had been more private than before. She still permitted visitors to watch her practice the various figures and specialties she'd performed previously, but now something new and exciting was being added to her repertoire. For a long time Sonja had been referred to as the Pavlova of the ice, because she incorporated ballet steps and routines into her ice skating performances. Now she felt it was time to go well beyond those tentative first steps.

She was never more secretive and never more intense in her work, and she never forgot her opening night in Milan. "There was a moment when I stood before the mirror in my dressing room, looking at the white feather wings on my arms, counterpart of the ballerina's costume, and felt consumed with pride and humility. I was about to put ballet on ice in recognizable form, after all those years of only imagining it."

The appreciative Italian audiences quickly understood what she was doing. They cried out, "Brava!", stamped, and cheered. That night a new era in skating opened for Sonja. It was the debut performance of her soon-to-be world-renowned ice version of Pavlova's transcendent solo. It became more popularly known as "Sonja's Swan Number." From that moment on, all her solos were designed to clearly feature both dance and theater.

Following that masterful coup in Milan, even the championships, which included her seventh world competition in Stockholm, appeared tame by comparison.

In December 1933 Sonja introduced her Swan entrance to her Parisian fans. She was greeted by a chorus of tin-whistle blasts from the top gallery. The clapping of enthusiastic spectators in the grandstands drowned them out, but it was a disconcerting moment for Sonja, and she almost took a fall. It had been totally unexpected. Parisians had always given her more support on the ice than any other audiences and she had been certain that the Swan number would take them by storm.

Early the following morning Monsieur Berretrot, the rink announcer (and a good friend of the Henie family), headed up a group of Palais des Sports officials to investigate the cause of what became known as "the tin-whistle affair." Their probe revealed that the current French figure skating champion (a bitter rival of Sonja's) had purchased and distributed balcony tickets, provided the tin whistles, and furnished instructions to the rabble, specifying precise times for the blasts to occur. Monsieur Berretrot announced the commission's findings at the opening of the next evening's show. The French champion sued, but, after witnesses from the balcony were paraded before the magistrate during the preliminary hearing, the case was never brought to trial. The young lady gained only national embarrassment.

Sonja swept from success to success. In February 1934 she retained her world championship in Oslo. Her old friends King Haakon, Queen Maude, Crown Prince Olaf, and Princess Martha attended every event in which Sonja competed. Oslo was crisp and cold. Frogner Stadium, filled to capacity, boasted a packed grandstand of fifteen thousand, and another three-to-five thousand spectators with binoculars dotted the surrounding hills for a view of Sonja, who now came close to rivaling the royal family as the focus of popular attention.

Sonja's performance, once again, was flawless. The American champion, Maribel Vinson, who seemed always to be just behind Sonja in competitions, fell during a spin in the free-skating portion and was forced into a disappointing fifth place. Sonja retained her title by acclamation.

The World Championships had been preceded by another European championship in Prague, and now the offers were pouring in once again from across the Atlantic where Sonja Henie fever was reaching new highs. It was inevitable that she would do another American tour. Wilhelm patched up their differences with the Canadians and accepted an invitation for Sonja to appear with other international skating stars at the Toronto Skating Club's seventh annual carnival. She would be appearing again with Karl Schaefer, the reigning men's champion of Europe, the world, and the Olympics. The group also included tiny Hedy Stenuf of Austria.

Upon her arrival in New York accompanied by her parents, as she descended the gangplank of the Cunard Lines' *Berengaria* Sonja was greeted by the Norwegian consul general, Wilhelm Morgenstierne, who boasted that "Miss Henie is the best ambassador Norway could send to America."

Sonja gave a rather impromptu press conference in which she spoke in what she considered her "flawless English." Several of her answers to questions had to be repeated before she was thoroughly understood by the reporters. Although Sonja had previously denied all reports suggesting she would turn professional, she now fed the rumors herself. Journalists were treated to a rare public display of Henie family differences of opinion. While Selma and Wilhelm were saying that they hoped "Sonja will limit her skating to exhibitions" Sonja seemed to imply more: "Well, I don't think now I will skate in championships anymore, but by next summer I might change my mind." Pressed to elaborate on her statement, she shrugged and said, "Make of it what you will. Skating is not limited to competitions and exhibitions." Most reporters present took her to mean that she was seriously considering professional offers.

Attired in a smart black velvet coat with a silver fox neckpiece and a black toque hat with a bill that partially hid her famous blonde curls, she provided a perfect image of success and serenity for the dozen or so still photographers who took advantage of the moment.

Other rumors were beginning to surface, now involving Sonja's private life. Was it true, she was asked, that she might surprise the world by announcing her engagement? Already learning to play games with the American press, she coyly asked, "To whom?" Several names were tossed at her, including a couple of eligible royal bachelors.

Sonja laughed. "Why, the papers have me engaged every week, but the worst thing is that I don't even know most of the men they mention."

Was she looking forward to her five-week tour of America? Her answer lent even more credence to the idea she might be turning professional. "Oh yes," she responded quickly. "I like exhibition work so much better than competitions. There are no worries, and it is so much more fun."

At the Waldorf-Astoria, her headquarters in New York, she was faced with another battery of photographers and newspaper people. What were her immediate plans, she was asked. "Oh, I just want to see if they'll let me skate today for a while in the Garden." Although the ice

60

was being prepared for a hockey game that evening, Sonja was permitted to work out before the game to the pleasant surprise of a few early arrivals. Sonja added a little something to her workout for the benefit of these hockey fans. Posing in the center of the rink, with a spotlight shining down on her, she executed a series of spins, went from those into dance steps and jumps that *The New York Times* later described as "an impromptu performance of superb grace and control." It was a publicity coup for the world champion.

The following day, in Toronto, Sonja was warmly received by the Canadian press, and her apprehensions that she might be interrogated about the debacle in Montreal the year before proved unfounded.

A five-week whirlwind tour of the United States followed her smashing Toronto success. She played ice carnivals and exhibitions almost nightly and always to packed houses. In Chicago she appeared before more than eighteen thousand spectators during a two-night exhibition stand. The Chicago Stadium was second in size only to Madison Square Garden. She went on to Minneapolis, where they take their ice skating more seriously, playing to enthusiastic standing-room-only crowds—and to other midwestern sites, with the tour coming to an end in Muskegon, Michigan, where Selma and Wilhelm decided to take a break from the tour so that the family could visit with friends from Norway who had settled there.

Sonja welcomed the recess. She felt she had learned to know Americans better, and the better she knew them, the more she was determined that America would soon become her home. She told her father, "I believe that there is an enormous interest in figure skating in this country. I can make a lot of money in this country when I turn pro." Wilhelm agreed.

Of course Madison Square Garden, as always, was to crown her tour. At an ice carnival held at the Garden to raise money for the Bellevue Hospital Social Service Fund, more than sixteen thousand contributors came to watch Sonja skate. There were other skaters on the program, but it was Sonja the cheering throng wanted. *The New York Times* feature writer Lincoln A. Werden reflected on her magic:

> Not only did Miss Henie captivate the distinguished gathering ... but the 21-year-old girl who has been world's champion for the last eight years, scored a personal triumph in the magnificent swan dance number. Under the lights that transformed the famous rink into a rippling lake, Miss Henie skated like a premiere danseuse of a ballet.

Attired in an orchid-colored costume, with orchids pinned to her shoulder, Sonja had treated the crowd to a spectacular display of jumps, spins, and spirals, before the fifty-piece orchestra finally played "The

61

Swan" of Saint-Saëns. For that featured number she wore a white costume trimmed with downy feathers, and she electrified the audience with her interpretation.

Karl Schaefer received plaudits as well. He was described as giving "a true Schaefer program of steps to tango time that was distinctly of his own creation." Everyone loves a child performer, and eleven-year-old Hedy Stenuf paired up with Schaefer in a duet that received as much acclaim as Sonja's performance. Nevertheless, it was Sonja's Swan that would be remembered past closing day, not Karl Schaefer or the Austrian child skater.

Both Sonja and her father intended to return to the United States the following winter for another tour, making her name more familiar to average Americans and, they hoped, to the film producers in Hollywood. Now, complaints about the financial arrangements became so loud that the International Skating Federation (ISF), still unable to confirm any wrongdoing on the part of the Henies, finally took limited steps.

In November 1934, the ISF announced from Stockholm that Sonja Henie would not be permitted to give any "exhibitions" in the United States unless the Amateur Skating Union of America agreed to pay a percentage of her "performance receipts" to the international organization. Sonja was shocked and angered at the decision. Wilhelm was irate.

Joseph K. Savage, a former president of the American Amateur Skating Union and in 1934 a member of the executive committee of the United States Figure Skating Association, acting as its spokesman, prepared a response that was delivered the following day. He declared that he was "perplexed" by the ISF action. He said that Sonja had never skated in the United States in any type of performances other than competitions in which "receipts" were barely adequate to cover the expenses of running the affairs, and in ice carnivals in which whatever was left after paying production bills went to the sponsoring charity. He asked what such moneys had to do with ISF. He was further baffled, he stated, by the announcement coming from Stockholm, since no official meeting of the ISF had been held in that Swedish city.

The hullabaloo became an international affair. Norway, quick to defend the honor of its most famous citizen, stepped in and announced that Sonja had the Norwegian Skating Federation's approval, permission, and backing to skate in America in any way she chose, so long as she limited her appearances to competitions and charities.

There is little doubt that the decision of the ISF was a form of backroom politics designed to satisfy Sonja's rivals who were neither as colorful nor as newsworthy as she. Sonja knew it, but there was little she could do as long as she remained in the amateur ranks. It was ironic that the United States Figure Skating Association hadn't even expressed any public interest in having Sonja return that winter for appearances, although in private conversations with her father, the FSA had asked if he would consider doing just that if the organization should decide to present another formal carnival in New York then.

Before things settled down, the American organization did formally ask Sonja to return and participate again that winter, but the invitation was too late. She had already made commitments in Europe for events there and to have canceled those would have only enlarged the furor caused by the ISF's Stockholm decision.

The perpetrators of the earlier rumors now were whispering that Sonja was too temperamental in the demands she made on her American "friends." She was sure that Americans knew better. "Incidents of this sort," she said, "are sometimes foolish enough to be amusing, but they certainly don't contribute to a feeling that retirement would be very peaceful."

Sonja's often-felt concern about her ability to remain at the top was justified. Amateur competitions could be vicious and destructive. She might be adored as that "sweet little girl from Norway" by millions of skating aficionados, but to her competitors she was just another obstacle to be overcome.

6

A vivacious young woman like Sonja inevitably sparked rumors of romance. She was an international celebrity, and men were attracted to her for many reasons. Some, of course, would have liked to use her position to enhance their own careers. Others knew she came from a monied background and was certain to become wealthy in her own right once she turned professional.

There were still others who found her physically attractive and her personality appealing. Most of these suitors were rejected by Sonja. However, there was a skater with whom she appeared quite frequently and to whom she responded. His name was Jackie Dunn. Sonja suggested that too much was made of their friendship and, at a slightly later stage in her career, stated that, "I am a public figure. People make up romances about me. In Hollywood such things are to be expected, but in the amateur skating paths of Europe for two years these stories have been tailing me. It is hard on Jackie to be involved in my schooling in the ways of a film player." But although she denied that she and Jackie were anything more than friends, the truth was that they were a great deal more than that.

Sonja declared that any idea "of an engagement between us gives us both a good laugh along with the headache." The fact was that she was crazy about him and her parents were concerned that she might elope with him and lose her career. It was understandable that the two of them would be attracted to one another. Sonja was small, fair, and blonde. Jackie was masculinely handsome, with dark hair, and he bore a strong resemblance to Tyrone Power—who would later figure prominently in Sonja's life.

Sonja had met Jackie in England and had been brought in closer contact with him during the European and World competitions. He had placed second in the World Championships behind Karl Schaefer; Sonja felt he should have been first. This may well have contributed to the friction between herself and Schaefer. Even though her parents frowned on any romantic ideas she might have had about Dunn, she made every effort to see him. They would eventually skate together for two years after she came to America, until his untimely death in 1939 of rabbit fever.

The winter of 1934-35 brought other rumors about Sonja, and she began to feel a real sense of paranoia that had never before been a part of her personality. Her feuds with other skating personalities were beginning to become public knowledge now as many newsmen focused more on her romances, her temperament, and her verbal exchanges with others. Perhaps some reporters had simply become bored with Sonja's athletic perfection. At least that is what an incident at St. Moritz suggests.

Sonja seldom fell during her amateur career. Judges often looked upon a fall, no matter what caused it, as a sign of the skater's weakness or inadequate control. In exhibitions tumbles aren't so important because there's little at stake. Sonja took such a fall during an afternoon of exhibition skating at St. Moritz, where she was training for the European championship.

She might as well have taken a spill in the Olympic finals. Sonja said, "My fall resulted in my finding out just how cruel and bitchy people can be, if they wish you no good. I already had the European title for a seventh year and was moving on to the World Championships in Vienna. I arrived there expecting a warm welcome. The Viennese had always been kind to me in spite of my disagreements with Karl Schaefer. On this occasion I found the press extremely cold. They seemed to think . . . that I was washed up."

Some of her friends in Vienna unfolded the story for her. Sonja was stunned. The Polish tenor Jan Kiepura, she was told, who had been a staunch supporter of local skating groups, was supposedly behind the anti-Sonja press. "I thought he was my friend, too," she protested. "I had no reason to think he would do me harm." As the story was pieced together, it seemed that Kiepura had made it one of his goals to boost little Hedy Stenuf of Austria toward the World Championship at Sonja's expense.

"Jan," she related later, "was at St. Moritz and saw my fall. He quickly scurried back to Vienna with the story that my fall indicated the end of my career as a skater. He made it sound like I was a has-been, and the press believed him because he was supposed to be trustworthy—what we today call 'a good source'."

Sonja had to control her anger. All of Vienna made Hedy the favorite to beat Sonja for the World title. "There were a few other obstacles in Hedy's path besides me," she recalled. Those obstacles came from England, Sweden, and central Europe and included another fine young Austrian competitor, Liselotte Landbeck. Still, the press made Hedy the odds-on favorite to win.

The competitions were held at the Engleman Rink, where many important skating events had taken place. On the day of the competitions it was bitterly cold, and the ice was rough.

The zero-degree temperatures did not prevent the fans from turning out in record numbers to cheer Hedy Stenuf, whose appearance preceded Sonja's. The crowd went wild when Hedy skated out onto the ice. So strong was the spectators' bias that it was hard to believe they would allow anyone else to be crowned World champion.

There was no doubt that Hedy's performance was brilliant, but her trainers and advisers had given her a program that was beyond her. "It was so obvious," Sonja said. "From the moment I saw her I knew that, no matter how popular she might be with the crowd, I had nothing to fear from her as a competitor. Actually, I felt sorry for her once I got over my sense of relief. I believe she and her people took Kiepura's story to be the truth and she became overconfident. She fell right at the climax. This was not a fall in St. Moritz for the people who came to watch practice. This was the world championship competition. She simply lost control. The public's enthusiasm fell with her as did the judge's ratings of her performance, or lack of it."

Suddenly, Sonja was on the ice with only one thought in mind. "I must not fall!" She knew the ice was wavy and dangerous and she had to make allowances for that as she drifted across the rink. She knew that her best performance would be at the corners, since the ice at the center of the arena was too risky. Sonja's program was up to par, and once again she was adjudged champion female figure skater of the world. Vivi-Anne Hultén of Sweden came in second. Hedy placed a disappointing fourth.

Of all her amateur championships, Sonja savored that one the most, and declared that "No other gave me such elation." The press, embarrassed, said little of Hedy but gave Sonja her just due. They didn't mention, and seemed to have forgotten, the fall at St. Moritz that had been so much in their thoughts before she arrived.

Wilhelm, Selma, and Sonja departed for Oslo, and Jackie Dunn accompanied them as far as Holland. Later he joined the Henie family in Norway. Sonja always denied that there was any romance. "I had no secret affair with Jackie Dunn. I was going home to rest, but the rumors were again running rampant. Now they were positive that Jackie and I were engaged and would soon elope. It was so utterly ridiculous. When you travel in a caravan from one competition to another you acquire numerous acquaintances but one simply doesn't have time to develop that kind of relationship."

Sonja contended that the press was looking for a reason to smear her name again. No matter how much she publicly denied a romance, however, she couldn't deny it to her parents. Wilhelm cautioned his daughter to proceed carefully. "Be discreet my child. Remember your name and who you are." He did not lecture. He loved Sonja beyond all reason and wanted her happiness. Wilhelm and his daughter were like partners. Besides, it would have done little good to chastise her too strongly, because Sonja was already beginning to do largely as she pleased—with parental approval more and more frequently but a rubber stamp. Sonja told the public that because she and Dunn skated together in doubles numbers, they were necessarily together more than with others.

At one point, Sonja lost her temper in front of the reporters. "If you are determined to print something about marriage and me, you may be interested to know that I receive offers of marriage from all sorts of people. I get them by letter from people I've never seen. Furthermore, I have had a few from people I really like. Jackie Dunn has not proposed marriage to me. Now make of that what you like!" Sonja left the questioner stunned, and she was elated.

The preceding weeks had taken a toll on Sonja. She'd been nervous and had snapped at people around her. During the unbearable lull preceding the 1936 Olympics, Sonja had finally made up her mind to turn professional. The pressure of amateurism had become too much for her, and, besides, during her stay in St. Moritz temptation had presented itself in a tangible form. The amazing thing was that none of the press "spies" had picked up on a visitor who hounded the Henies while they were in St. Moritz—a man who presented himself as an "entrepreneur" who would help Sonja turn professional and make millions. Although he had no contracts in hand, Sonja was entranced by his tales of Hollywood glitter and of millions of dollars. He was telling her that he could make her a movie star, present her with her own ice show, and more or less give her America.

Despite her father's admonishments that Dennis Scanlon was "a fraud" and should be "ignored," Sonja kept an open mind. "But I like him, Papa. He makes me dream of Hollywood. There's nothing wrong with that, is there?"

Wilhelm said there probably wasn't any harm in it, but she should be careful what she said to the man. "Make no statement that sounds as if you really take anything he says seriously." Mr. Henie didn't concern himself too much with Scanlon, since they would soon be leaving for Vienna and the pest would be left behind. He quickly put the offensive man out of his mind. However innocent Sonja's encouragement of Scanlon might have been, it would prove costly. He was to reappear in years to come, and he would fulfill Wilhelm Henie's worst premonitions.

In Oslo Sonja sat down with her parents and discussed her feelings about becoming a professional. Leif, who was back from his stay in Germany and Czechoslovakia, joined in the discussions. Her father felt it would be better to wait until after the Olympics to make any formal announcement. After all, he pointed out, there had been several premature announcements already, and he, admittedly, was guilty in at least one instance. There was general agreement that the entire family did not wish to give the international press any reason to pounce on Sonja, as the European newspapers had done in Vienna.

It was left up in the air just when the formal announcement would be made. Wilhelm wanted to make contacts in America, totally off the record, to see what could be lined up for his daughter when she did make her announcement. It would be much more newsworthy, as well as profitable, if he could present a long list of professional commitments—and it would certainly silence Sonja's critics.

Sonja later reflected on her life that summer. "Swimming in the calm summer sea, letting the sun beat my skin hot on the beach, cooling off with long rides in the . . . Cord roadster the Norwegian-Americans had given me, I leisurely looked over the past nine years since I became a World champion, and I looked ahead. Taking it quietly like that, I grew certain I would feel satisfied I had run my amateur course to its end if I could round out a decade of ten World Championships and three Olympic titles. No one else had done that in any sport. Whatever might come after, if I went on, would inevitably seem anticlimax."

It was presumptuous of Sonja to preordain herself World and Olympic champion once again, but it was characteristic of her self-confidence. It would not, of course, be easy. She had her toughest time in competitions yet ahead of her, and perhaps it was wise of her to withdraw from amateur competition when she did.

Wilhelm's summer calm was disrupted by the appearance of Dennis Scanlon in Oslo. Arriving in a luxury automobile, he made every effort to impress the Henies with his wealth, position, and influence. Sonja was awed by this man who promised her everything for the asking. Her father wasn't impressed. He discovered, upon investigation, that the car was rented. Before Scanlon left Oslo, Mr. Henie made it quite clear that he would have no business dealings with him, nor would anyone in the Henie family. As Sonja's manager, her father wanted to have absolute control over her activities. He felt that he would be the best judge of what was in her interest.

In private talks with Sonja, who had stars in her eyes, Scanlon was encouraged to tell her more of America and her chances for fame there. Whatever transpired beyond that between the two would later be disputed. It could have been only a matter of misinterpretation or Sonja may have actually asked the man to make inquiries for her. After his departure, she assured her father that nothing important had been said. After all, she wanted to know more about America and the way things operated in that country. She told Wilhelm she had let Mr. Scanlon know that only her father could speak for her in business matters. That she was only a performing artist, not a businesswoman. Once again, after Scanlon left for America, Mr. Henie thought they had seen the last of him.

69

The Henies's previous statement that Sonja would retire from competition after the 1936 Olympics and World Championship competitions was just that—a statement. Such announcements had been made in the past. Nothing was set commercially. In spite of her ambition to become a Hollywood movie star there were no film offers.

"Vaguely," Sonja reflected, "I was aware that I would never quit skating entirely, that I should like in some way to go on with my efforts at developing the ballet on ice, and that a new desire had been born in me during my trips to America—a wish to help more of the energetic, enthusiastic people of that country become interested in skating. I had been impressed with the fact that few Americans realized the fun of skating, compared to the tremendous number who would love it if they were ever introduced to the ice. What to do with all these impulses was a pleasant mystery I didn't bother to unravel at the time."

There is no doubt that preparations for the dual championships of 1936 were the most strenuous of her career. She wanted to go out in a flash. Both she and her father felt that such a brilliant finish to her amateur career would pay off when Sonja became a professional.

She was anxious to begin training by late summer for the Winter Olympics that would be held in Garmisch-Partenkirchen in February 1936. This was now Hitler's Germany, and Sonja was the darling of the Reich. She was neither Jewish nor dark; indeed, she seemed the very archetype of Hitler's concept of an Aryan woman.

The 1935-36 skating season included, besides exhibitions and charity affairs, the European Championship contest in Berlin and the World Championships in Paris, and, of course, the Olympics. It was to be a grinding schedule for all the Henies, and Sonja felt that she must be successful to assure the attention of those wealthy American showmen who, she knew, liked nothing better than a winner.

She began her conditioning in London, where British competitors Megan Taylor and Cecilia Colledge were already at work. The two fifteen-year-olds had gained polish since Sonja had seen them the previous season and would add excitement to the tour. Howard Nicholson, the American, now boasted quite a stable of young skaters eager to topple Sonja from her thrones. She knew it. "I felt like a veteran watching them," she mused. "So wise in the ways of the ice world, but too wise to be overconfident." She was surprised to see that these younger skaters were now using training methods that she had originated.

Perhaps it was all the youthful challengers that caused Sonja to set up too rigorous a practice schedule for herself. Her reward for overdoing it was aching muscles. Nicholson, under whom she was also training, slowed her down and she felt better. Her tour and her Olympic skating program were beginning to take form. Within weeks every detail, turn, and jump were rehearsed dozens of times, until she could do it perfectly.

While in London Sonja was asked to take a part in an instructional film. Not since her 1927 appearance in a Norwegian silent film had she been before a motion-picture camera, and she welcomed the opportunity to refamiliarize herself with that art and its techniques. Karl Schaefer appeared with her in the movie, which was soon completed.

Nicholson's instructional talents were in high demand during the months preceding the Olympics, and he did not want to devote his time entirely to Sonja. But Sonja wanted him, and her father convinced him. Nicholson probably came at a very high price, which Wilhelm could well afford.

The Henie entourage left London for Paris in mid-October and spent scarcely more than two or three days in one spot until February 1936. Their home, it seemed, was a railroad car crisscrossing the national borders of Western Europe. They went first to the Palais des Sports in Paris, and then the exhibition route took them to Brussels, Basel, Bern, Zurich, Munich, Prague, back to Oslo, and then on to Berlin.

Sonja encountered Jan Kiepura in Munich, where he was making a film, and he could not have been more charming—swearing that the Vienna incident had all been a misunderstanding and that he had completely forgotten it. Sonja visited him on the set of his picture and accepted his apology.

Prague, which still had several years of freedom left before Nazi storm troopers arrived, opened its arms to the touring ice skaters. Sonja was charmed by the old university city and touched when eight thousand students attended an afternoon performance. During an autographing session, she lost her hat and other pieces of her clothing, and was fortunate to escape more serious damage at the hands of the eager fans who surrounded her. She was easily the most popular skater on the tour in Czechoslovakia, and before she left she was received at the palace by President Thomas Masaryk.

The family had a brief respite in Oslo before the Berlin appearance. Sonja's father was on the telephone most of the time, checking out various possible deals in the United States and hoping that these preliminary inquiries would not be ferreted out and speculated upon by the press. Since Sonja had to retain her amateur status for the time being, no money would change hands and no contracts would be signed prior to the completion of the Olympics. But Wilhelm wanted all options open the minute Sonja picked up her gold medal, which he was sure she would.

The family arrived in Berlin feeling fresh and full of confidence. The historic Adlon Hotel, where they stayed, was filled to capacity with skaters and their entourages. Sonja, like a child, ran up and down the creaky old staircase that had once borne the heavy boots of aristocratic Prussian militarists.

Berlin was important. Make a good showing there at the European

Championships and one would go on to represent one's country in the Olympics. But if she failed there, Sonja felt she could forget the Olympics and World Championship competitions.

Sonja sensed the crackling tension that pervaded the Sports Palast where the international group practiced together. "It was difficult for all of us; especially for me. There was so much at stake—the finale of all my years of skating. I cared more in advance about winning then, than in any other winter of my life."

Where usually a few hundred people might come early in the morning to watch the skaters practice, thousands came daily, now, to the Sports Palast. Although it was not said aloud, many felt war in the air; it might be Berliners' last chance to see and mingle with people from all over the world. The crowds came, too, reflecting the fact that Berlin had long been one of the ice skating capitals of the world. Germans take their skating seriously, just as they do all winter sports. They took good care of their arenas, spending large sums every year to ensure that the ice was perfect for skating.

Sonja had a definite advantage over the other skaters. The Sports Palast had been her springboard to amateur stardom; it was an indoor rink, with lights, and she had always worked better with spotlights. And she was no stranger to the faithful fans who always packed that arena to see her. She felt at home and had little reason to be nervous. She knew the German press would be favorable, since the influence of Hitler and his propaganda minister, Joseph Goebbels, would come to bear on them if any event occurred that might otherwise call for newspaper criticism. Sonja was a favorite with the Nazi hierarchy.

The European Championship competitions were held in Berlin on January 25, 1936. On January 24, Sonja herself made a formal announcement that, win or lose, her amateur career would come to a close at the end of the Olympics in Garmisch-Partenkirchen. She had now burned her bridges behind her and stood, as she said, on the brink of "Only God knows!"

The German press, as expected, treated Sonja with kindness and respect. On the evening before and on the day of the competitions in Berlin, they printed her past record, listing in detail all of the championships and trophies she had accumulated during her amateur career.

Sonja was delighted with the newspaper account of her past victories. "It was no longer just I who knew that this was to be my farewell season. The eyes of the whole skating world would be peering to see how I'd make my exit," she said.

In the wings the day following her announcement, she went over the same four-minute program that she would perform at both the Olympic and World competitions. Sonja's parents and many of her countrymen sat near the entrance of the rink, where they could wave encouragement to her before she went on. Wilhelm shouted, "No one can take the title from you, girl. No one!"

It was an odd situation. For years Sonja had been applauded in part because of her youth. Now in Berlin she was the eldest competitor. Almost all of her challengers were teenagers, the youngest, Etsuko Inada, an eleven-year-old Japanese, finished ninth in the field of seventeen skaters.

Cecilia Colledge, the sparkling British skater, came quite close to taking the Berlin meet. Sonja won with a point score of 434.6. Cecilia finished with 417.2. The 17.4 spread was Sonja's smallest ever. Her perfect performance of the required turns enabled her to win the title for the ninth time.

Many high-ranking Nazis attended, including Joseph Goebbels, Reich Minister of Propaganda and Public Enlightment; Air Minister Hermann Göring; Reich sports leader Hans von Tachammer-Osten, and others. It was a first-class Nazi display of pomp and splendor, although Hitler was absent.

"It is one down and two to go," Sonja told her jubilant parents. Wilhelm gave his daughter a hug and whispered almost wickedly, "It will only get better."

Sonja took another lasting memory from Berlin. Before she left the city, she attended a reception and was introduced to Crown Prince Wilhelm. His charm captivated Sonja. "I was surprised that he was so well informed on skating matters and quite an enthusiast." She counted among her most cherished possessions the Hohenzollern crest stickpin that he gave her as a memento. "He apologized," she recalled, "that he had not sent flowers and hoped I would accept the pin in their stead. 'My God,' I cried, 'flowers die. The pin will last forever!'" Sonja was overwhelmed by his grace and manners.

Although Paris would follow Garmisch, the Olympics would be the big event of the year. The World competitions would be anticlimactic. Sonja wished the order were reversed. She would have preferred her send-off to the professional world to take place after she had won her third gold medal, rather than after a lesser event. But she accepted the situation.

7

$\mathcal{N}$O other sports pageant compares with the Olympics. The Games are the supreme test of athletic prowess, and four years is barely enough time to prepare for them. Many athletes take even longer, passing up Games in order to be better prepared for the succeeding Olympiad.

The Henies, along with Howard Nicholson, arrived three weeks before the Games in Garmisch-Partenkirchen, a Bavarian village in the Alps on the Austrian border, south of Munich, less than a hundred miles west of Adolf Hitler's mountain retreat at Berchtesgaden.

Sonia's event would take place at the Olympia Eis Stadion, about ten minutes walk from the center of town. It was a Christmas-card setting with lots of snow, the sound of sleigh bells ringing, and local shops overflowing with Olympic souvenirs. The onslaught of competitors and tourists would swell the population of six thousand many times over.

The Olympia Stadion was one of the most efficient and modern winter sports arenas in the world. It had everything from ice-making machinery (if needed) to a giant electric time clock; it accommodated more than ten thousand people and, much to the delight of the Fourth Estate, had perhaps the most modern press tower in the world, reaching six stories into the sky.

The comfort of the athlete was ministered to with locker rooms custom-tailored to the competitors' needs—and dreams.

Checking in at the Alpenhof Hotel, an inn Sonja described as having "more fame than facilities," they found other advance parties already settling in. The picturesque old hotel would soon become one of the centers for the Olympic athletes and their followers and fans.

The figure skating championships would be held at the main rink, while speed skaters performed far to the south of the big Olympia Stadion. Sonja did most of her training at a small rink on the outskirts of the village. She would, from time to time, inspect the stadium rink to keep herself apprised of its condition.

Rumors seemed to be as frequent as practice as the area became more and more congested. Tension mounted. Sonja, as one of the "old ladies" of the Olympics, came in for a great deal of scrutiny by competitors and press alike. This was, after all, her fourth Olympics, and several observers commented that her stamina must have diminished after twelve grueling years of competition. She was aware of their opinions.

The judges were also a favored subject of gossipers and were of special importance to the Henies. "In Berlin there had been no Norwegian judge," noted Sonja. "I had been entitled to a judge of my own nationality on the panel. No matter how impartial judges are supposed to be, they are human, and biases do occasionally raise their ugly heads. For a while it seemed possible that there would be no Norwegian judge here either. I had some bad moments, wondering about this. I worried whether my rivals were getting in better training than I, and if I would be able to round out twelve years of Olympics, nine of them on the crest, spanning three titles. I was faced with the real truth that no one had ever accomplished that feat."

Cecilia Colledge and Megan Taylor were there, as was the American champion, Maribel Vinson, whom Sonja feared more than the youngsters. Maribel, she knew, was not only a great skater but extremely popular with crowds. Sonja had seen the rose-violet dress Maribel planned to wear, with a violet corsage, and she envisioned how enchanting the American would look in that with her raven hair. Sonja would stick to her traditional white, which had served her well over the years.

Her other competitors included the diminutive Etsuko Inada of Japan; Vivi-Anne Hultén from Sweden; Hedy Stenuf of Austria (wiser, she was sure, after the Vienna fiasco); Constance Wilson Samuel of Canada; Liselotte Landbeck, also from Austria; a total of twenty-three stars, from twelve countries.

The stadium lay in a pocket of Alpine peaks. Above the rink the grandstand, village, and mountains rose like a succession of terraces. Sonja remembered that "at the bottom it seemed as though the whole world were looking down on our little piece of ice. Everything was blue white but the small overhanging houses that broke into brilliance at night. The road from the village swung up a shoulder of hill towering directly above the stadium, and on that hill the Olympic fire was to be lighted and to flame there throughout the . . . competition."

The director of winter sports preparations, Max Werneck, was known for his military-style organizational efficiency. Housing, transportation, and food catering, always problems at such events, were handled superlatively. More than a hundred thousand people descended on the small village, fifty thousand on special trains from Munich alone. Army field kitchens littered the countryside. This was the organizers' practice for the Summer Games in Berlin, which much of the world would call "Hitler's Games" (although it would be an American runner, Jesse Owens, who would make history there).

The entire operation was a miracle of logistics. During the daytime everyone was fed the same diet: hot soup, thick and full of meat and vegetables. At sundown there was an exodus. Only the athletes, Olympic officials, and reporters were allowed to remain within the village at night and there, to the extent their training allowed, they partied—eating their dinners, drinking their beer, and eventually collapsing into the billowy featherbeds for which alpine villages are so famous. The visitors to the Games had been packed back at evening into their trains and routed out to Munich, Innsbruck, and the Brenner Pass.

Teams garbed in their national colors lined up in columns on opening day, before they started their parade up the hill for the altar-lighting ceremony that would officially open the 1936 winter Games.

"As we all stood in line," Sonja recalled, "and started the march, snow flurries dusted down on us, hushing the scene. Hardly anyone spoke on the way up the hill, and from the moment the flame shot up in the altar, and brasses blared the Olympic anthem, I doubt that any contestant was quite right in the head until it was all over."

The first hurdle for figure skaters was the school-figure competitions. Sonja's lead was small, with Cecilia Colledge closer than ever before in second place. The gauntlet was down. There was little or no room for error. Sonja didn't have the usual margin of points from the school figures that she had managed in the past. It would be a head-on competition with Cecilia and Maribel Vinson in the free-skating finale. That would be where Sonja's third Olympic crown would be won or lost, and she knew it.

It was the final night of the Games; scheduled for dinner time, the next to last event of the entire Olympic program. Sonja, again, was to be the last contestant to perform. She followed a relaxing procedure that had served her well in the past and would do so again prior to an important performance.

"To eliminate unbearable waiting," Sonja explained, "I stayed soundly asleep in bed until father telephoned from the stadium that there was only an hour. That way I could go from the hotel right out on the ice, fresh and rested, without having to stand around through introductory events, and the nerve-straining challenges of my rivals."

Sonja left the hotel in early evening. Below was the brilliance of the diamondlike glittering ice stadium. Above was the velvety blue night sky. This was the moment.

The music rose while Sonja waited at the edge of the rink for her cue. Two hundred thousand spectators, from within and without the stadium, in the grandstands and gathered on the mountainsides above, looking down on the skating arena, awaited the appearance of the miniature dynamo from Norway—Berlin's "Häschen." Among the grandstand spectators were most of the Nazi high command, including the German Führer, Adolf Hitler. They could all see her, but there was too much reflection from the spotlights on the ice for her to see any of them. She knew they were there. Acutely aware, she had cause to pause and remember her past experiences with the dictator of Germany. It had brought considerable criticism down on her head. Even more was ahead.

The controversy stemmed from an exhibition in Berlin at the Sports Palast, one of Sonja's favorite rinks. One evening, very unexpectedly, Hitler, Göring, Goebbels, and other important Nazis came to see Sonja perform. Sonja was told of Hitler's presence only seconds before she entered the rink. She asked where the German leader and his party were seated. When she entered the ring, she shot out full speed across the ice, coming to an abrupt ice-spraying halt in front of the Führer's box, gave the Nazi salute, and in loud voice, her German perfect, shouted out, "Heil Hitler!" The stadium went berserk. Hitler rose from his seat and tossed her a kiss. She brought down the house—and almost the roof. It was her night in Berlin, and she sealed a friendship that would last for many years and do much to help her family during the war years to come.

The following day, however, the Norwegian papers denounced Sonja in bold headlines: *"IS SONJA A NAZI?"* It was a universal cry throughout not only Norway, but all of Scandinavia. America was not at that time taking Hitler very seriously, and one would have been hard-pressed to find an account of the event in the U.S. press, much less any criticism.

Sonja was furious with her countrymen. "How can they say such things," she demanded, angrily shaking the newspapers in the faces of her family. "Nazi-schmatzy," she spat, "Hitler is the German leader. I was honoring Germany, not the Nazis. I don't even know what a Nazi is." The furor died down eventually, but she and Hitler remained friends, until his troops invaded Norway.

Now, going for her third Olympic skating title, Sonja decided she would not make any overt gesture to Hitler's group that night. He had already spoken to her on the phone and wished her luck in the competitions. She didn't know if he had done the same with others, but there is no evidence that he did.

Sonja did some other calculations before entering the arena to defend her title. "I shut everything out of my mind but three things. I led in points, the ice was not too good, and I had to be careful. From somewhere in the distance, chords vibrated in crescendo. I moved out onto the ice."

She had trained all her life for this, it seemed. Yet, at that moment she felt it was the first time she had ever entered an ice rink. So much depended on the perfect execution of every spin, whirl, and jump. Sonja recalled it as "Without a doubt the longest four minutes in my life. I cannot remember anything beyond skating onto the ice that night and later the official announcement. Everything in between has remained a total blank in my mind."

Four minutes later it was over. There was cheering, the likes of which few people ever hear in a lifetime. The Scandinavian competitors descended on Sonja, mobbing her and showering their heroine with acclaim. No one cheered louder than the members of the Nazi hierarchy, led by Adolf Hitler. Then, a hush, as the announcement was made, along with history. Sonja Henie was the winner—champion for an unprecedented third time. Sonja's victory had not been an easy one. It was her most difficult ever. She outdistanced Cecilia 424.5 points to 418.1; Maribel was third with 388.7. Sonja's last Olympics. Her record stands almost fifty years later.

Again, the torches glowed as the double procession from the village made its way up the hill to where the Olympic flame was about to be extinguished, and then the procession came back down. The gigantic crowds of spectators milled about. The skiers, with the Olympic flag between them, had been the last to descend from the temporary Mount Olympus.

Before departing for Paris and the World Championship competitions, Sonja and her parents accepted an invitation from Hitler to lunch with him at the Eagle's Nest, his mountain aerie near Berchtesgaden. It was not her first visit to Hitler's hideaway in the mountains. She had at one time given a charity exhibition for the Nazi organization *Kraft durch Freude* (Strength through Joy), in Munich. While there, Hitler had personally thanked Sonja and invited her and her parents to Berchtesgaden for lunch to show his appreciation. Following lunch, he walked over to his desk, brought back a large photograph of himself in a silver frame, and wrote a lengthy inscription underneath his picture. Although it seemed only a compliment at the time, it would later prove more valuable than gold to all the Henies.

It was rumored from time to time, before Sonja turned professional, that she might have had more than a passing acquaintance with Hitler. She never commented on it one way or the other, but the allegations are doubtful because during that period of her life she was heavily chaperoned by both her parents, and they had no use for the Nazi dictator. However, Sonja did share some of his ethnic and racial views. When she was later reported to have had a romance with a black American prizefighter, she was infuriated by the allegation.

Paris and the World Championship won by Sonja for the tenth consecutive time, was an anticlimax. Few of the Olympic stars showed up. When it was over, Sonja and her family, with Jackie Dunn in tow, departed for Oslo where Sonja immediately collapsed and was ordered to bed for several weeks by her doctors, who announced that she was suffering from total exhaustion as a result of her heavy schedule of the preceding few months. All her engagements were canceled. The family and Jackie Dunn stayed close, allowing her the rest she needed. Sonja would not perform again until she reached the United States several weeks later.

After recuperating, Sonja was ready to sit down with her father and discuss the future. He ran every detail of her business life. Meanwhile, the fact that she and Jackie Dunn were lovers was kept a very private matter, hidden from public and family alike. Sonja's late-night trysts with Dunn, while he was a guest in the Henie home, were carried out long after her parents had retired to their bedroom and were sound asleep.

Jackie accompanied Sonja and her parents when they sailed from Le Havre to America on March 5, 1936, on her way to a new life. Leif remained in Oslo to take care of the fur business for his father. There was no fanfare when she boarded the luxury liner *Ile de France*. No press. This was unusual for Sonja and her father, who loved to have the reporters crowding around.

A great deal of speculation was generated among skating enthusiasts on the Continent, but Sonja later explained her quiet departure at a press conference:

> **Q.** Why did you board the ship so quietly?
> **SH.** I'm amused at the question. I was tired after five weeks of solid competitions and decided to cancel all appearances at exhibitions that had been previously arranged by my father in Norway and elsewhere. Consequently, I saw no reason to make a big press production of my departure.
> **Q.** Yes, but why did you wear dark glasses on the trip from Paris to Le Havre? Was there any special reason for that?
> **SH.** I did not want to be bothered. I was tired.

Five days with Jackie aboard the *Ile de France* gave Sonja's spirits an additional boost. Although she would announce in New York that Dunn was "considering" turning pro, it was already a matter signed, sealed, and consummated with a kiss aboard ship. They would band together as skating partners. Sonja, by now, was madly in love with him and wanted to be sure that he was always close to her.

Sonja admitted to certain qualms as the big ship steamed into New York harbor on Tuesday, March 10. It seemed to her that the skyscrapers looked down and asked: "What makes you think you can scale the walls of success as a professional in America?" Sonja mentally tossed back the challenge. "What makes you think I can't?"

Never before had she encountered such a gathering of press and photographers as when she, her parents, and Jackie Dunn descended the gangplank. Among them were also skaters, skating officials, old friends from Norway, and Dennis Scanlon. The press conference that followed was hardly informative. Reporters spoke simultaneously and Sonja was hard pressed to understand their questions, much less answer them. Whom was she marrying? Where was she going? What plans did she have? How long would she stay?

Sonja responded as well as she could. Her aim? Hollywood, of course. Her plans? Also Hollywood. Marriage? Not yet. No interest—yet, even though she posed for anyone who cared to snap a picture, arm in arm with Jackie Dunn. That picture appeared on front pages across America the following day.

Her old friend Lincoln Werden of *The New York Times* acceded to her wishes and did not make an issue of romance. "Also on the liner," he wrote "were Jack Dunn, 19-year-old English skater, visiting this country for the first time."

Metro-Goldwyn-Mayer, from its New York office, also issued a statement to the press. Yes, they said, they would be meeting with Miss Henie's representatives the following morning concerning the prospects of a movie contract. The MGM spokesman was quick to add that although negotiations had been under way for some time, they recently had been held in abeyance to protect Miss Henie's amateur standing.

So far, in spite of her announcements to the contrary, Sonja had not lost her amateur status. She was still an amateur until professional money changed hands, and MGM pointed that out in its statement. "The mere signing of any such proposal does not automatically alter Miss Henie's amateur status." The matter, they said, would depend largely upon the contents of any contract, whether or not the terms would call for her skating in motion pictures.

Sonja, seeming to contradict her earlier positive statements, appeared to have been coached in the matter. She stoutly denied that she had given up her amateur position. "I am still an amateur," she said, "but I have retired from competitive skating."

She certainly looked smart, dressed in a brown wool suit and a below-the-calf-length mink coat, which adequately protected her from the brisk March winds that whipped about her. She held a bouquet of orchids and wore a hat, to which was attached a custom-made diamond brooch that read "Sonja Henie."

Dennis Scanlon fielded questions alongside Sonja. Wilhelm was privately furious but there was little he could do, especially in public.

Without his knowledge or permission, Sonja had apparently authorized Scanlon to speak for her with MGM officials. She would later deny this. Scanlon appeared knowledgeable as he referred to film contracts that had been offered not only by American producers but also from German and English film companies—and the money offered, he stated, had been substantial. Sonja stood by his side, silently nodding what seemed to be her concurrence.

There was some doubt about Sonja's availability to skate in an upcoming ice carnival at Madison Square Garden. As an amateur, she would have to be sanctioned by the Norwegian Figure Skating Association, and that sanction had not been obtained. A reporter suggested that she turn professional for the Garden event and make that her debut performance as a pro.

An official of the New York Skating Club, when asked about such an arrangement, responded that as far as he knew, Sonja had not even been invited to appear in the carnival. Jackie Dunn announced that his skating plans in the United States were indefinite. He neglected to add that he was more or less at Sonja's service.

The following day Dennis Scanlon issued a statement:

> Metro-Goldwyn-Mayer will make a screen test of Miss Henie in New York this coming Monday morning. I have already made arrangements.

Again, Sonja didn't deny that Scanlon was her representative, nor did Wilhelm Henie. Sonja and Jackie were having fun skating together at the Ice Club, holding hands, and sipping chocolate sodas from the same glass.

Rather than embarrass the Henies or be embarrassed themselves, the New York Skating Club quickly secured the necessary clearances from Norway and announced that Sonja, along with Jackie Dunn, would head the carnival at Madison Square Garden on March 22 and 23, which was being held to raise funds for the Bellevue Hospital Social Service Relief Fund and the Carroll Clubs, another charity.

Within a week Sonja's amateur status was behind her. Her father had been working feverishly behind the scenes, and he saw no reason for her to appear at the Garden and receive nothing more than an amateur's "allowance" when she was ready to turn pro at the scratch of a fountain pen. Why Wilhelm said nothing about Scanlon's appearances at press conferences or in discussions with MGM executives, remains a mystery. He did not like the man. It can only be assumed that he and his daughter "used" Scanlon and dumped him after he had served their purpose. Some evidence of such a ploy exists. When contracts were to be signed and money was at hand, Scanlon was not advised, nor was he later able to reach any of the Henies by phone or in any other way.

With or without Scanlon, the MGM deal was never consummated. The studio wanted Sonja as a skater, not an actress. She was determined not to have "also featuring" billing in films. She wanted stardom or nothing.

Sonja agreed to keep her commitment to the Bellevue charity carnival. It didn't matter now what money openly changed hands. Sonja would never again enter an amateur competition.

The reception for Sonja at the International Skating Carnival was described by *Time* as "extravagant." A professional tour contract that made Sonja a partner of Chicago real estate genius and entrepreneur Arthur Wirtz was signed with full press and photographic coverage. It was a show business alliance, which would endure for many years and prove exceptionally beneficial to both—especially to Sonja, because it gave her a solid foothold in the entertainment world of her newly adopted country.

Sonja was to receive $70,000 up front, plus a hefty percentage of the gate receipts, which eventually swelled her take to well over $200,000. At the contract signing, Sonja was once again asked why she had turned professional at that particular time. She made no excuses, and her response reflected what others had been saying for quite awhile.

"If I have to practice two times every day, cannot smoke or drink, and have to put up with the stares of total strangers, then I might as well get something out of it besides silverware and entertainment." That brought guffaws from the reporters, appreciating her sharp sense of humor. She continued. "Also, I have an all-consuming desire to become a movie star—and nothing will stop me in that effort."

The *Time* article reaffirmed Dennis Scanlon's involvement in Sonja's career:

> Last summer at the neat Henie country place just outside Oslo, she discussed with her parents her longtime ambition. They heartily approved the idea. Wary of professional managers, . . . they made contact with a longtime friend named Dennis Scanlon. Mr. Scanlon, who runs a surgical-instrument factory in Sweden but lives in Manhattan, promptly set to work to bally-hoo Sonja to Hollywood by way of a U.S. skating tour.

Time described Sonja arriving in New York, "squired by her watchful father, whose fur business seldom receives his attention, and her morose, dour-faced mother." Jackie Dunn was described as "her most persistent companion."

Sonja, beaming brightly as ever, stated that her father had spent untold thousands of dollars to make her the greatest amateur athlete of all time. "I owe him, and I wish to earn enough to pay him back every penny he ever paid out for my benefit." Loving words and seemingly good intentions, but she would never repay any money at all. The only money Wilhelm would ever make from Sonja's professional earnings was the percentage he kept as her manager. It didn't really matter to him; he had more than enough in his own Norwegian coffers. But within a year he would be dead, and Sonja would assume control of her own destiny.

It was Maribel Vinson, Sonja's old nemesis on the ice, who wrote *The New York Times* story that reviewed Sonja's professional debut at Madison Square Garden before ten thousand cheering spectators. Officially billed as "Sonja Henie Night," it was evident from the beginning that Sonja would savor many such evenings during her maiden year as a pro.

Sonja made sure Jackie Dunn also had a contract. He was her opening act. If Sonja was unhappy that Jackie received a glowing report from Maribel, she did not express it. Later in her career, a skating partner who received such a review would subsequently receive shorter time on the ice and less glamorous numbers to perform. In love with Jackie, she allowed him all the ice he wanted. Maribel critiqued Sonja's now most-famous number:

> The crowd settled quickly into a receptive mood for Sonja's famous interpretation of the Dying Swan of Saint-Saëns. With spotlights giving the ice the effect of water at night, Miss Henie, outlined in a blue light, performed the dance made immortal by Pavlova.
>
> Whether one agrees that such posturing is suited to the medium of ice, there is no doubt that Miss Henie's rendition is a lovely thing. Too much toe work at the start leaves the feeling that this does not belong to skating, but when she glides effortlessly back and forth, she is free as a disembodied spirit and there is an ease of movement that ballet never can produce.

Maribel might well have had an axe to grind considering that Sonja's Swan had kept her from ever beating the Norwegian in competition. But she didn't choose to spoil the American debut of the queen of ice. She also lauded other parts of Sonja's performance.

Although Sonja had originally agreed by contract to give only ten performances, the pot was sweetened by Wirtz (his own pot benefiting heavily from Sonja's shows), and her tour was expanded to cover a total of seventeen performances between March 24 and April 15, traveling as far west as Minneapolis, where she was wildly acclaimed.

Sonja had stories planted with some of her favorite gossip columnists suggesting she might turn out to be as fast a money-maker as Red

Grange, Bill Tilden, and Suzanne Lenglen—other recent converts from amateur to professional sports status.

Sonja was learning quickly how to manipulate the press to her advantage. She would eventually become so accomplished at it, that few celebrities before, or since, have equaled her.

Peak

8

ONJA never looked back. Her interest in competition had been superseded by a lust for money and Hollywood stardom. Offers were pouring in, and Wilhelm sifted through them, discarding the less attractive ones. Tour skating was in the hands of Arthur Wirtz. Endorsements, films, and other types of personal appearances were the domain of Sonja's father.

Both Sonja and her father were certain there were millions to be made from ice skating. Sonja knew her appeal. "There was an audience in nearly every civilized country for good figure skating. This public could be increased enormously if skating were presented more attractively than rules of competition and small budgets of club exhibits permitted. There was a public waiting for dancing on ice, for ice spectacle. The cinema would be a perfect medium to give skating this scope, and the cinema thus far had no figure skating worth noticing. The big indoor arenas in American cities would serve well as theaters for a touring ice show. There was a place for a skating star."

Sonja hoped and prayed that the big tour would bring her into contact with motion picture executives. By now the prospect of becoming a movie star had become an obsession. "Plenty of motion picture people did come to see my performances in Madison Square Garden," she recalled. "All of my numbers were in dance form, and nicely costumed. I had a white satin dress, designed by Patou, that I wore with a Juliet cap, for my fox-trot-tempo solo; a gay peasant bodice dress for a Mazurka, and my classic ballet dress with the wings for the Swan. Jack did a rhumba, and it all went off quite brilliantly. But there was not the response we had expected from the cinema forces."

The prelude to Sonja's big film break came through Arthur Wirtz when the tour played Chicago. Wirtz knew all the big stadiums and ice arenas in the country, as well as their owners. He actually controlled most of them, which made it easy to set up his original deal with Sonja. (Arthur Wirtz had not only a partnership with Sonja, which provided her with her own ice show, but he also became a second father to her, advising her on her investments and pointing out new ways to make and save money. After the death of her father, their relationship was even closer.)

Wirtz, hounded by Sonja about a film career, sat down with Wilhelm, Selma, and Sonja and made a suggestion. "If you put on a show in Hollywood, you're sure to attract the right people."

Sonja wanted to know how she could get into Hollywood with an ice show; she realized that ice sports were foreign to Southern California.

"Your father is a salesman. He'll sell you to Hollywood—with your help, of course."

Sonja agreed. It had never been Sonja's plan to go to Hollywood and like so many star-struck young girls, offer to "do anything" to get into pictures. She'd been on the amateur circuit long enough to know that couches, casting or otherwise, had one thing in common—they were designed for seduction, not stardom.

Sonja felt she had something to offer that was missing in Hollywood. "I was certain," she said, "that the method of knocking on doors and presenting myself with nothing but words and theories to show for what I believed could be accomplished, would get nowhere. We were all certain that it would be useless to go to Hollywood unless we either went on a likely sounding call from the fortress or at least were sure there was some ice in Hollywood to prove our theories on, to an audience."

With the assistance of Arthur Wirtz and his good name, Wilhelm was instrumental in renting the Polar Palace Ice Rink for a few days. The plan would be to complete the current tour and than have a splashy opening in Hollywood. Sonja was convinced that the film capital had never seen anything like her and that film producers would be fighting each other outside her dressing room door for the chance to make an exclusive deal for her services. There was never any doubt on her father's part, either. Arthur Wirtz took a middle of the road position. "You'll either knock 'em dead or they'll bounce you on your keister," he said, but predicted the former.

Sonja's debut tour as a professional in the United States had been successful beyond her wildest dreams. Her father went to the West Coast to see the Polar Palace and, although it wasn't exactly to his liking, it was an ice rink and would suffice. He hoped to pack it for two days the same way Sonja had been playing to standing-room-only houses all over the country.

When the tour closed in Detroit on April 15, Sonja and her parents took a train to Chicago, where they transferred to The Century Limited, the number one cross-country train of the time, and settled in for the two-day ride across America. She could hardly keep her eyes off the scenery as the luxury passenger train raced across the vast expanse of country. Through the plains and up over the great mountain ranges, she was spellbound by what she saw, but never more than when the train descended from the mountains into the lush orange grove country between San Bernardino and Los Angeles. This was what she had dreamed of all her life—this was it. Hollywood!

90

May 7 and May 9, 1936, had been selected as the two nights for Sonja's show. There was no problem with choreography or skaters; she had already built a show from the tour, and it was transported cross-country with her.

Upon their arrival in Los Angeles the Henies were met by associates of Arthur Wirtz and taken to their hotel. Wilhelm set out immediately for the Polar Palace to meet with the managers, while Sonja and her mother unpacked. Then, wanting to see the rink for herself, with her mother at her side, Sonja hailed a taxi outside their hotel and said, "The skating rink, please."

After several minutes the taxi pulled up in front of a building in Hollywood and stopped. "Here y'are, lady." Sonja stuck her head out the cab window and looked up at the sign urging pedestrians to get off their feet onto "roller skates." It was a terrible moment for Sonja. Was this the great ice rink of Hollywood—part-time roller skating, part-time ice skating?

The driver had never heard of the Polar Palace. So much for the appeal of ice skating in Hollywood, Sonja thought. But thanks to the telephone directory they found its address. She was almost as disappointed at the ice rink as she'd been at the roller rink.

There were only four people on the ice when she and her mother entered the Polar Palace, and the manager explained that this was "practically the rush hour." The denizens of Hollywood were not exactly taking to the ice like penguins. It was immediately obvious that a lot of promotion had to be accomplished, and quickly. With no more than three weeks to prepare, Sonja and her father put their heads together to plan their approach.

Wilhelm paid for advertising and to have tickets printed. The response was tepid. Orders for tickets trickled in, and it looked as though Sonja's debut in Hollywood would destroy her hopes of becoming a movie star if, indeed, she had a debut at all.

But her father had some ideas. He knew that charity affairs had a tendency to bring out celebrities. His plan was to find a suitable charity that would guarantee Sonja a packed house on opening night and assure press coverage the following day. A bit of research at the public library, and rummaging through old newspaper stacks, produced the required results. William Randolph Hearst, head of the giant publishing empire, was both lover and benefactor of Marion Davies. Miss Davies owed her film stardom more to the money poured into her career by Hearst than to talent. Hearst, Wilhelm discovered, often arranged for Marion to host charity balls that resulted in favorable publicity for the actress.

Ordinary advertising in the paper was obviously not going to fill the arena so, armed with the results of his research, Sonja's father went downtown to the offices of the *Los Angeles Examiner,* a Hearst newspaper. Sitting in the publisher's office he advanced his plan to publicize

Sonja's ice show. "I will personally donate $5,000 to a charity of your choice if you will promise us a full page ad to run seven days, for which I will pay the going rate." He suggested that Miss Davies might be the ideal one to host the affair. With the nation still struggling through a depression, it was a generous offer. Some phone calls were made, and after brief conversations with the parties on the other end, a deal was consummated. A big plus for Wilhelm and his daughter was that they not only had Miss Davies as a sponsor, but they also were given access to her mailing list. It was a coup for the Henies.

Invitations were sent out to major celebrities and film executives, as well as to all the news media, including the international wire services. Wilhelm's ingenuity assured Sonja a star-studded, jam-packed, sold-out house on both nights. With the audience problem solved, Sonja turned her attention to her show. She packed all the dance and sparkle she could into the program, checking each detail personally. It opened with the chorus doing a tango; then, an apache pair, followed by Jackie Dunn's rhumba—and then Sonja.

During the course of the evening, Sonja performed all of her three tour solos, ending with the Mazurka from *Coppelia*. With exclusive access to the rink for several days preceding the big night, she was able to supervise the local workmen and teach them the art of putting a perfect surface on the ice. Sonja's father instructed the lighting men, and the best available orchestra was hired to provide music.

Although the rink was smaller than those to which the skaters had been accustomed on the tour, they somehow managed to whip all their numbers into shape for the more-compact arena.

The audience assured, one question remained uppermost in the Henies' minds. Would those sun-blessed Southern Californians appreciate what Sonja was doing?

She would soon find out. The night of May 7 arrived and stars came in droves, shoving past each other in front of the cameramen's barrage of popping flashbulbs at the curbside at the Polar Palace. The biggest names were out in force: Mary Pickford, Douglas Fairbanks, John Barrymore, Spencer Tracy, Clark Gable, Myrna Loy, Robert Taylor, and what seemed to be the entire roster of Metro-Goldwyn-Mayer, where Louis B. Mayer boasted of having more stars than there were in heaven.

Jeannette Meehan, Hollywood correspondent of the *New York World-Telegram*, recounted the evening in her dispatch:

> People shoved—cars jammed—parking prices had been put up another twenty-five cents. Limousines were parked in the tumbleweeds in a vacant lot across the street, and stars got their hose ruined trekking through to the sidewalk. The whole thing

had the standing, staring, curbstone-sitting look of an old-fashioned Hollywood premiere.

Inside there was bedlam. The bleachers were packed. There were chairs in the aisles, people standing behind the orchestra, others seated in chairs on the floor boarding. A squad of hefty cops kept people from crowding on the rink itself. Everybody was there—society, Main Street, Hollywood's great and near-great. Carole Lombard, Jeanette MacDonald and Gene Raymond, Ginger Rogers, James Stewart, Jean Arthur, Bette Davis, Gary and Mrs. Cooper, Norma Shearer. . . . Every production boss in the business. But the people weren't there to see Hollywood.

One could sense [as the program got under way] a current of tense anticipation. Thousands of eyes kept glancing up to the gray curtain at the far side where the name of the evening's star performer was spelled in glittering letters four feet high. Again the lights went out. Excited voices hushed. Suddenly a single spotlight broke through the smoky atmosphere and flattened out on the ice. Into its gleam floated a small white figure—Sonja Henie.

She had the audience in the palm of her hand. They wouldn't let her go. "Encore! Encore!" people jumped up and down. Stars forgot themselves in her performance and yelled themselves hoarse. Producers eyed one another and fervently prayed that the other fellow wasn't thinking in terms of a contract. Pandemonium continued. When Miss Henie finally withdrew, the rafters complained of the applause.

The next morning, Hollywood had elbow bruises on its ribs, and Sonja Henie was the talk of the town. Studios were cooing at her. Universal, Paramount, M G M wanted her. It has been a long time since Hollywood's producer contingent has devised as many attractive contracts for one person.

Every producer was there except the one Sonja really wanted to come a'courting. Darryl F. Zanuck was not in the star-studded audience. Zanuck had a reputation for recognizing new talent. Sonja had her watchdogs at the door and throughout the rink at strategic points, but none of them reported seeing the short, mustached film mogul.

The papers were filled with praise for Sonja Henie, and there were so many requests for interviews that additional secretarial help was hired to accommodate the onslaught and filter the more important ones through to Sonja's father.

May 8 was a day of rest for Sonja and her family. They celebrated with a night on the town; everywhere they went Sonja was mobbed by autograph seekers. Even in posh Hollywood night spots, accustomed to celebrity and its trappings, tuxedoed magnates and mink-clad ladies in expensive evening gowns pushed one another aside, hoping to get a glimpse—and if they were lucky, an autograph. The crowds grew larger at each stop. Obviously someone had phoned ahead that the new sensation of Hollywood was en route.

The second night's show was just as successful—even more so for Sonja, because Darryl F. Zanuck, in the flesh, appeared to watch and applauded her performance as loudly as anyone. Mary Pickford sent flowers. Sonja was assured by one and all that she and her skates would be the next Hollywood craze.

It was a whirlwind three days that Sonja found the most exciting in her young life. She had always dreamed of coming to Hollywood, but she never imagined that overnight she would be the toast of the town and one of its most sought-after attractions ever.

Zanuck, sure of himself, sent for Sonja and her parents. When Sonja and her father arrived, they were ushered into an executive suite. A number of the Fox top brass were seated around a conference table. Zanuck was not present. His absence annoyed Sonja, and she let it be known that she felt snubbed. They made excuses for Zanuck and proceeded with their offer.

One of Zanuck's stand-ins, sporting the prototypal big cigar, said, "Mr. Henie, we are prepared to offer your daughter $75,000 for one picture." Sonja looked at the man and then at her father. She shook her head no, and shortly after that Sonja and Wilhelm picked up their papers and belongings and prepared to leave. As they exited, Wilhelm Henie turned and said, "Thank you, but no thank you!" The executives were aghast that anyone would turn down a movie contract.

Sonja wanted stardom, but on her terms. She did not want to be a flash across the screen on ice skates. It wasn't the money so much as the chance to be a legitimate film actress that excited her.

In the studio limousine that returned them to their hotel, Sonja asked her father, "Well, what do you think? Did we blow the deal or will I be a star?"

He patted her jeweled hand and said, "You will be a star, darling. A big star. Mr. Zanuck will call again—and he will see you personally. He wants you more than you want him."

Sonja was worried but hoped her father was right. Otherwise the big splash at the Polar Palace had been for nothing. If the other studios found out that Fox wouldn't take her, then she might not get in anywhere. She knew thay had just taken a reckless gamble, but she trusted her father's judgment. He'd never been wrong in important business matters before, and there was no reason to think he was wrong now.

Nor was he. A summons came from Zanuck. This time Wilhelm

decided to send Sonja with her mother instead of going himself. He had already thrown down the gauntlet. Zanuck had a reputation for liking young ladies, and the Henies could count on Sonja's charm to work its magic. And yet, she was, after all, their daughter. She had been trained in business and Selma would lend moral and ethical support.

Zanuck stood up to greet the beaming Sonja, as well as her mother, whose face never changed expression. Selma had the facial expression of an old-time poker player in a high-stakes game. She rarely smiled except with family and friends—never in business offices or at public affairs.

Sonja and her mother sat on a settee in Zanuck's office. He tapped a riding crop on the top of his desk throughout their conversation, which annoyed Selma enormously. At times she actually glowered at the movie mogul, which seemed to amuse him.

"I understand you are not pleased with our offer," he began. "Of course we want you to be happy at Fox."

"My daughter is not at Fox yet, Mr. Zanuck," Selma said stiffly.

"Yes, yes," he responded, "but we will correct that situation I am sure. Right, Miss Henie?"

Sonja wanted so much to say, yes, yes, yes, but she had been coached thoroughly by her father and so she merely smiled mysteriously.

"Now what is it that you want, Miss Henie?" Zanuck asked. "More money?"

Money, she assured him, was not the prime concern. "I want to be a star, Mr. Zanuck," she said in a low, thickly accented voice.

"Oh you will be. I'm sure of that, but we have to put first things first, don't we?" He spoke in a patronizing tone as if the World and Olympic champion sitting across from him were a small child asking for her allowance to be increased.

"What does that mean?" Selma asked.

"It means that we will feature your daughter in an ice skating scene in one of our major films—perhaps an Alice Faye musical. That will give the public a chance to see you at your best and if all goes well, which I am sure will be the case, we can expand your performance in future films." He leaned back in his chair and waited for Sonja's reaction, which he was sure would be immediate approval.

It was not. "I'm sorry, Mr. Zanuck. I don't wish to appear impudent, but I want star billing. I want a good story and dialogue. Everyone knows I can skate. I want to be a movie star, not an act in someone else's picture." She had said it. "My God," she thought, "I hope I did the right thing."

Zanuck grinned. He loved a challenge. He always won. Especially with women. This one was no different. "Now, Miss Henie—may I call you Sonja?" Sonja nodded assent. "Sonja dear, what you are asking is impossible. You have come from sports, from the field of athletics. You have no training as an actress. We will work with you after you are under contract and you will eventually become part of a story in a good picture and you will receive all of the training that every contract actress receives here at Fox. We are like one big family. Everyone works up through the ranks. It is not as though you came from Broadway or another studio."

Sonja shook her head and picked up her purse as if to leave. "Mr. Zanuck, I want the title role."

Zanuck laughed—or rather snorted. What an upstart. There were accomplished actresses who would get on their knees for this opportunity. This one couldn't even speak good English. But he totally underestimated the Henie family. They had more than the usual resolve. they were rock. "I can't give you that, Miss Henie. Not just yet."

"In that case, Mr. Zanuck, this meeting is useless. I have no desire to play supporting roles that would be carried only by my skating. I am ambitious. I want to go beyond today and tomorrow. My first film must be decisive for both me and the company I sign with. I have had other offers, you know."

Suddenly Zanuck was listening. No one ever stole his prospects once he had them in his office. Selma nudged Sonja's foot. Zanuck's tone had softened. He was no longer the hard-nosed producer talking down to a starlet. He was actually listening. He spoke softly. "Someone else must have the lead," he said, "but don't worry. You'll show them."

Sonja continued to be adamant. She was quick to recognize when she had the upper hand. "I want to have a real chance of it, Mr. Zanuck. I'll sink or swim, and if you don't want to take the chance, I'll go elsewhere."

"All right! All right!" He threw up his hands. "I know when I've been beaten. But I want a long-term commitment. A five-year contract. Seventy-five thousand dollars per picture."

"One hundred twenty-five thousand, Mr. Zanuck. One picture a year to be filmed during the summer months, which will allow me to go on tour with my own ice show."

"I thought money was no concern," he countered.

"It isn't, but you wouldn't want your biggest star to be underpaid, would you? What if word got around?"

Zanuck roared with laughter. He knew he had a tiger by the tail, but it looked like his little import might prove to be a lot of fun—and who could tell, maybe she knew what she was talking about. The terms of the contract were generally agreed to and a formal signing was set for a few days later when the red carpet could be rolled out for the Hollywood press corps who were gambling among themselves about who would manage to grab off the hot property. Most thought Metro-Goldwyn-Mayer would win out. Louis B. Mayer probably would have come up with a better offer, but Sonja wanted to work at Fox and for Zanuck. She later commented on her decision.

"From the day I put my name on that hard-earned line, I found in Mr. Zanuck one of the best advisers, a man with a fantastically sharp grasp of details and a surpassing instinct for knowing what the public wants."

It sounds as if she had a real love affair with Fox and Zanuck. That was not the truth. She loved the studio; hated Zanuck. Their battles would become juicy gossip, with new fuel added daily. Some of it true. Some of it manufactured. True or otherwise didn't seem to matter. Fact mixed with fiction has always attracted Hollywood hostesses more than the hard truth.

Zanuck had been the savior of Fox. When he came to the studio it was at the bottom of the industry and in danger of collapse. In 1933 Zanuck, after resigning from Warner Brothers because of policy differences with the famous brothers, particularly Jack, joined forces with Joseph Schenck and took over Fox, forming a new company to be known as Twentieth Century Pictures (later to become Twentieth Century-Fox Films).

It was Zanuck who believed that musicals would revive the studio. He had a proven record by the time Sonja Henie arrived on the lot, having made a major star of everybody's little darling, Shirley Temple—by way of the musical. So successful was the musical at Fox, that it was the vehicle that Shirley rode to the position of number one box-office attraction from 1935 to 1938. Sonja had signed with the studio at the height of Shirley's popularity. Alice Faye had been another of Zanuck's promotions. Her films, unlike Shirley's, had little story line. She sang, danced, looked romantic, and made room for a variety of comedians and vaudeville acts. Again, it was the genius of Zanuck that did much to make the star. The same was to be true of Betty Grable and Sonja Henie.

The biggest worry for Zanuck and his staff of trained experts who could turn buzzards into swans, was what to do with Sonja's virtually unintelligible English. Some of it could be looped in by experienced actresses, but not all. Sonja's problem was ice. There had never been a film that had as its theme an ice rink with the star spending most of her time in midair sailing across a sound stage. Since Sonja was under a long-term contract, it was decided that the best thing to do would be build an artificial rink on one of the sound stages—one that could be covered over when Sonja wasn't working and used as a dance hall or for any other suitable purpose that might arise. Zanuck did not like his talent drawing Twentieth Century-Fox money without earning it, so he immediately sent out a memo to various departments on the lot to find a project for Sonja Henie—and fast. He hoped to keep it simple. Find a story tailored to Sonja's talents and surround her with an outstanding cast. He believed that if she were put in the right setting the picture would be a hit, but that the trained actors would get most of the credit. That, he hoped, would keep Sonja in line. He had a strange feeling that this vibrant young lady was going to give him a lot of headaches.

Raymond Griffith was assigned to produce the picture and Sidney Lanfield to direct. So it started out with top talent behind the camera as well as in front. Lenore Praskins and Mark Kelly whipped out a quick script entitled *The Peach Edition*—as inept a movie title as there ever was, considering that the plot had Sonja playing a Swiss innkeeper's daughter who becomes an Olympic ice skating champion. Zanuck intended to keep Sonja within her proven milieu, whether she liked it or not.

Sonja was indeed surrounded by other proven talents. Handsome leading man Don Ameche was cast as Sonja's romantic interest, with supporting roles going to the Ritz brothers, Jean Hersholt, Ned Sparks, Arline Judge, Dixie Dunbar, Borrah Minnevitch and his Rascals, and Montagu Love. It was to be variety with a healthy blending of solid character actors who could be depended upon to carry a picture in spite of any acting deficiencies of its star.

With all her experience on ice, Sonja knew virtually nothing about the making of motion pictures. She was awestruck by the mechanics of putting films together, and from the outset decided to learn everything there was to know about the industry. Meanwhile, the Henies had to find a decent house to live in. Sonja was tired of hotels. She had been living out of a suitcase for practically all her life, and now she wanted her own home in Hollywood.

A young actor who had just made his own mark on Hollywood came to Sonja's rescue and took her house hunting. He had just completed a picture called *Magnificent Obsession*. His name was Robert Taylor. Taylor knew just the place for the Henies, a Spanish-style house with a pool in Holmby Hills. It delighted Sonja. Although she had stars in her eyes, those eyes were as sharp as an eagle's when it came to her finances or the fine print of a contract. Even on her first picture, she was about to test her will against Zanuck's. Her contract with Twentieth Century-Fox stipulated that she work only so many days on acting scenes and so many on skating numbers. Sonja was to receive an additional $7,000 a day for putting the ice portion of the show together. It was hard, meticulous work and required long and tedious hours. This extra time added up to sixty days at $7,000 a day. Almost half a million dollars. Zanuck was apoplectic, but Sonja confronted him.

"Mr. Zanuck," she beamed, "it is all in the contract. I am only obeying your orders. See!" She pointed to one of the subclauses in the lengthy document she held in her small hand.

Sonja learned about Hollywood quickly. Zanuck's worst fears about his new star were already coming true.

98

9

SONJA understood the trials and tribulations of skating. She knew all about early hours, late hours, quick lunches—often no dinners—and stress. Hollywood had its own brand of obstacles. She would later write, "If movie-struck girls could get a glimpse of what a Hollywood star's day is really like, there would be few who would not sit down and quietly thank heaven they were in peace behind a typewriter, a counter, or their boyfriend's Ford dashboard."

She pointed out that "the pictures of luxurious ease and spangled night life painted by story writers and the cheaper sort of publicity romanticizers are as fake as the old-time movie heroine's marcel waves in a thunderstorm."

Whatever the perils, Sonja did not follow her advice to others. If anything, her ambition had grown. Stardom wasn't enough—she wanted to be the number one box-office attraction in the world. Sonja's first year in Hollywood found her alarm clock jangling at five every morning. By eight she was at the studio. The three hours between were spent in elaborate preparations, which included shampooing, having her hair done, making up, and finally dressing for the scene that would be played that morning. She barely had time for a very light breakfast.

In addition to a maid to tend to Sonja's needs, Selma was by her side from the moment she got out of bed in the morning until she was safely asleep at night, and until her father died in 1937, the three of them would go over the day's expected problems while sipping a quick cup of coffee.

It wasn't an easy life she'd chosen for herself. "The moment I arrived at the studio," she later complained, "I was caught in a whirlpool of action that never let up until nightfall." By nine o'clock in the morning the studio was humming and there was work on every front. An actress playing a scene is constantly moving, not only in skating scenes but in the others as well. She learned quickly the art of using the camera to her own advantage. "Sometimes it seems as though you are obliged to shift positions a thousand times in one scene," she said, "because you find that somehow you're not quite within vision of the camera. Meanwhile, all around you architects, costumers, technicians, and a multitude of others are passing up and down, in and out, going about their apparently unending work."

Skating scenes were particularly lengthy, especially in Sonja's early films. One miscue and the whole scene had to be reshot with perhaps fifty or sixty skaters on the ice, plus all the technicians behind the cameras. It was an expensive process and tempers often flared. Sonja had a great deal of difficulty in the beginning, and her scenes sometimes had to be done twenty-five or thirty times before the director was satisfied. Her fuse would grow short.

It was not unusual for her to unload on a cameraman—switching back and forth between her native Norwegian and her adopted English, which was nearly as unintelligible to the untrained ear as her native tongue. The fact was that keeping Sonja in focus was difficult. Sonja didn't understand camera techniques and being a free-form skater she was all over the place. After a while, camera crews began to use three cameras when filming Sonja, so that if she skated out of range in one area, she was picked up elsewhere. It was a big money saver in Sonja's films.

Later, Sonja would devise a method whereby the studio technicians could place markers on the ice without creating a hazard, and Sonja would adhere to her marks in the same manner an actor or dancer does in a stage production or a motion picture. It was an innovation that would be used in all subsequent ice skating films.

Another fallacy about Hollywood was brought home clearly to Sonja in those early days. When she arrived on the West Coast she frequently visited the Mocambo, the Trocadero, the Cocoanut Grove and Ciro's. Once she went to work, she found that a visit to one of those was a once-a-week event—usually on a Saturday night (because many of the actors worked on Saturdays). "I soon discovered," she said, "that there is an unwritten agreement among Hollywood's film colony—they all must go to bed early. It is necessary for survival. An actress like Greta Garbo, whom we seldom see, works extremely hard and takes the rest she needs. That's why she is good."

Sunday was truly the day of rest and most of Hollywood slept. Sonja was no exception. She didn't go out a lot in those early days of her career. Small dinner parties at the homes of other actors were frequent, and Sonja reciprocated, but certainly not in the fashion she would become famous for once she was a major box-office attraction. She didn't smoke and at that stage of her life, rarely took a drink. She was concentrating on her career and didn't want to do anything that might interfere with it. "There is very little hard drinking," she said, "among the people who work in films. It doesn't mix with concentrated, clear-minded effort. In Hollywood, if in no other place on earth, you learn what work really means."

Work, yes, but Sonja was either being naive or defensive about the film colony. Alcohol was quite a problem in Hollywood. It simply wasn't discussed as openly as it is today.

Before her arrival in Hollywood, Sonja had never had a massage in her life. In an arena the fact that her legs were bulky with muscle wasn't as important as it was at Fox studios. The camera picks up everything and exaggerates it, and consequently, Sonja's legs left a lot to be desired. Zanuck, in one of his piques with her, once remarked, "Slap some keys on her and we'll have a grand piano."

Sonja decided to do something about the bulging muscles in her calves. She had to in any event because every night her muscles ached so badly she could hardly walk. A dancer under contract at Fox suggested that Sonja try her masseuse, which she did. Afterward massages became a daily part of her routine. "Massages," she contended, "helped keep my muscles soft and pliant, apart from making me feel more human. Another good method I found and put to use back then at the beginning was steam baths. These are not the type I remembered from home, nor the Finnish style either. They are very American steam baths, in which you sit in an electrically warmed box, with only your head sticking out, and let the heat make you sweat. You feel a little weak afterward, but your muscles have had a thorough going-over, and a few hours' nap brings back your energy."

Determined to learn everything there was to learn about making films, Sonja dogged the technicians from the lowest grip right up to the top camera and lighting men. She wanted to know their problems and what they were aiming for in a scene. She had also been interested in how the big indoor ice rink was going to be installed.

Because it sounded exotic, hack journalists and soppy fan magazine writers said Sonja's ice rink at the studio was frozen sour milk. It was actually artificial ice (which is made with water treated with chemicals) painted over with a special color that prevented the spotlights from making reflections that would mar the photography. It was easier to skate on and a great deal safer than natural ice for the choreography in Sonja's skating scenes.

Although she acquiesced to the experts in most cases of filmmaking, she refused to take anybody's advice when it came to putting music to her skating numbers. Sonja believed that the music was an essential adjunct to the skating, and she knew about skating. Naturally, the orchestra leader was constantly at odds with Sonja about the manner in which the music and the skating should be adjusted to each other. It was during that first film that workers and executives alike learned that Sonja had a vocabulary not unlike that of a drunken sailor in a foreign port.

During one episode Sonja skated off the ice and the director shouted, "Cut!" Sidney Lanfield walked over to Sonja who had headed for her dressing room with Selma close on her heels. "Sonja," he said softly, "what's the matter, dear?"

Sonja didn't answer. She kept going toward her dressing room, ever faster, her face set in stony fury. Lanfield followed along behind, saying nothing until he entered the dressing room behind her and Sonja was seated before the mirror at her dressing table with a powder puff dabbing at her nose.

She looked up into the mirror at Lanfield, standing behind her. "That sonofabitch wouldn't know a two-step from a rhumba. He stinks," she spouted, her words running together thickly.

"He's the best in the business," Lanfield said, trying to soothe his star.

"Then he is in the wrong fucking business."

The matter was eventually resolved, but everyone connected with *One in a Million* learned not to cross Sonja unless he was prepared to listen to a tirade. Sonja always denied that she was temperamental or difficult. Usually she wasn't with her fellow screen artists, but there was no one she loved to abuse more than executives and those she considered "sloppy musicians."

Although she developed the reputation of being "a bitch" while filming *One in a Million,* Sonja saw things differently. "I feel there are little things in the film, as well as larger ones, that were brought off much more professionally because I had the guts to speak up. I wish I had said more."

Any criticism from another actor was considered by Sonja to be "professional jealousy." She complained at home and in the privacy of her dressing room that "they are all jealous because I didn't spend years in those dreary actors' study groups to become a star." She was determined to be on her guard against any schemes to ruin her that might be produced by the envy and competitiveness of her fellow stars. She had managed to incorporate into her own personality all of the hard-nosed business ability of her father together with the iciness that her mother exuded without effort. Sonja's dimpled, almost coquettish, smile was a professional facade that she created for film and public appearances.

Veteran actor Jean Hersholt was more instrumental than anyone else in seeing Sonja through her first picture. She adopted him as another of her "second fathers" during the filming of *One in a Million.* Hersholt, a Dane, understood Sonja's fear of failure in the picture and, being Scandinavian, was able to lend the kind of support that bolstered her confidence.

It can cost twenty million dollars to "launch a star" in the 1980s. In 1936 it cost a million, which was a lot of money at the time. Sonja was terrified that the studio might regret spending so much money on an actress who had never acted. The daily rushes—shot the day before—were always screened that evening. Sonja kept her fear inside. "The big bosses," she recalled later, "didn't spend their money with a smile. Especially not Darryl F. Zanuck. That's why he didn't want to start me off as a star. I forced him to gamble."

102

Zanuck had acknowledged that she had engineered him into the high stakes investment. "I have signed Miss Henie and her skates," he said. "Even if she couldn't skate, I'd have signed her anyway, but not for so much money." Maybe.

The rushes weren't very good, except for Sonja's skating, which was sensational as always. Zanuck, after viewing the early rushes, insisted that Sonja spend "more time on the ice." His plan was to give the public what it wanted from Sonja and let the "real actors" act. The one place where he said that money was no object was in Sonja's costumes. He believed that Sonja's skating numbers should be "extravaganzas with scores of skaters wearing dazzling costumes," Sonja's to be the most dazzling of all. He was further convinced that her attraction on the ice had been due as much to music and costuming as it had to skating. "Anybody can skate," he declared at a production meeting. "Miss Henie has merely made it attractive. I want to keep that attraction in her pictures. That's what the movie-going public will pay to see."

Tyrone Power, who worked his way through romances at a fast clip, soon discovered the new girl at Fox Studios. Always a date but never a groom (until sometime later, after he was an established star), the handsome young contract player was photographed often with reigning movie queens or those who seemed headed in that direction. His name was linked to Loretta Young, Alice Faye, Janet Gaynor, Betty Grable, and Lana Turner. There was also Annabella, the French actress who eventually became the first Mrs. Tyrone Power. However, the real love of his life was not and did not aspire to be a star. He met her before arriving in Hollywood while appearing in a Katherine Cornell show on Broadway. She was a little girl from Buffalo named Eve Abbott.

Whatever ambitions Sonja had in Hollywood, she made a big mistake when she made Tyrone Power a part of them.

Sonja met Ty when he came onto the set of *One in a Million*. He invited her to lunch and they soon began a torrid affair. They saw each other before shooting in the mornings, at lunch, during breaks, and after work. Sonja felt no need to sit patiently through the preliminaries of courtship. When she saw something she wanted, she wanted it right away.

Romance wasn't the only merry-go-round Sonja was traveling on.

Her first film was finished and ready to be presented to the American, and then world, moviegoers. Time had flown so fast. During 1936 she had won three championships and was the world's best-known figure skater, then moved to America where she took everything from Madison Square Garden to Hollywood by storm. Almost overnight she was the most talked about new personality on the American screen, even before the first foot of film was shot.

Now, it was time to taste the pudding. Was she as good as they said, or as she thought? Summer came and went; and autumn, too. In December

103

she found herself aboard an eastbound transcontinental plane (airplanes were beginning to make inroads then into the railways' passenger travel monopoly) with her new lover, Tyrone Power, by her side. Columnists made much of Power's presence and there were rumors of marriage. Sonja had been through that sort of speculation so many times that she was scarcely annoyed. What the gossips failed to report was that Ty was en route to Cincinnati to visit his mother (and Eve Abbott, who was one of his better-kept secrets at the time) while Sonja's business was in New York where *One in a Million* would be the number one film of the holiday season, opening at the Roxy Theatre, where she had first dreamed of seeing her name in lights as a movie star.

She first sat, along with her parents and a small crowd of Twentieth Century-Fox executives in the Fox projection room in midtown Manhattan and watched her summer's work being screened for those critical eyes. She knew that it would be the theater-going public who would eventually decide her future in pictures, but it would be the studio's decision whether or not to schedule another film right away. She didn't want to think of the press and their opinions.

She need not have worried. *One in a Million* was the best Christmas present both she and the public could have had that year. It was declared a box-office success during Christmas week.

For all her frequent stinginess with money, Sonja didn't like to broadcast her generosities, and they were many. She enjoyed taking chorus boys and dancers nightclubbing or on vacations with her; she picked up the tab. When the studio tossed a "wrap party" at the end of filming on *One in a Million,* Sonja presented each of her supporting skaters in the film with genuine cashmere sweaters. It was an expensive gift, but throughout her career she liked to show her appreciation to those who helped her artistically or who helped make her look good either on the ice or the screen.

With *One in a Million* now a guaranteed success, Sonja had to look ahead. Success in motion pictures, if it is instant, is traumatic. Columnists and critics place a star in an exposed position. On any given morning or evening, a critic can make one's day or career, or destroy it. This wasn't the time for Sonja's destruction, although she could begin to feel the pressure of the demands that would be made upon her shortly after Christmas. A profile in the Sunday *New York Times,* written by B. R. Crisler, left no doubt that the hounds would soon be at Sonja's door:

> The world's greatest virtuoso in her own field, a Degas ballerina on ice skates, prettily and perilously winging along a dangerous rink at thirty miles an hour, or executing perfect figure eights or interlocking circles at 300 or so R.P.M., Miss Sonja Henie may surprise her Madison Square Garden public when she appears

at the Roxy Theatre on the day before New Year's in her first picture, "One in a Million," with the realization that she is also a highly competent movie actress. At least, Darryl F. Zanuck, who hardly ever backs a dark horse, is willing—on the strength of her work in this film—to trust Miss Henie with a straight dramatic role, without skating.

The attitude of Miss Henie, of course, is very much what we assume Heifetz's would be if someone wished to deprive him of his violin and to star him in a picture for his classic profile alone. . . .

Her really big scenes in "One in a Million" are skating scenes, of course, but there are certain sentimental passages on the strength of which Miss Henie may shortly become of more immediate world importance than her distinguished compatriot, Henrik Ibsen.

While in New York for the opening of *One in a Million,* Sonja answered many questions from the press—some silly and some intelligently inquisitive. She surprised the media with the fact that she didn't change skates often. Hers were specially made by John Strauss, a custom skate maker of Minneapolis with all the care and artistry formerly lavished upon Cremona violins. The leather tops, she advised, wore out before the blades, which were simply sharpened and resharpened.

She also informed them that in figure skating there are eighty championship figures and that in competition one never knows which of the eighty the judges will ask a contestant to perform. Consequently, each of them has to be letter perfect.

This was Hollywood stardom, and it was what Sonja had waited for all her life. Holding on to it wouldn't be easy. Surviving in Hollywood is perhaps even more difficult than getting in. Hollywood is a game; either one plays well and survives or becomes its victim and is destroyed. Success brings, as well, the legions of hustlers with slick con games by which they hope to relieve the star of his or her newfound wealth.

Sonja was a smart young woman. Wilhelm had always taught her to be wary of the silver-tongued and light-fingered types. She reflected on what had happened to her in less than a year. She had arrived in Hollywood almost a child never far from the shelter of her father's wisdom and her mother's watchful eye. Now she was confronting reality, and it was frightening.

Her new life wasn't just one of competition. She understood competition. Now she was a combatant in the professional battle for money. Next to image, she found that in Hollywood money is what it is all about.

It didn't take long for the trade papers to announce that *One in a Million* was headed for at least a two-million-dollar gross. Because of that, her phone and doorbell never stopped ringing. It would be someone wanting to take over the management of her contracts or her money, her daily itinerary, or just her whole life. "They track me down," she moaned, "and try by fantastic means to gain your confidence and a job with you; anything so long as it looks like an inroad to the bank account they think you're going to have." A novice, she would have to learn quickly to sidestep the leeches without stifling legitimate approaches. "Thank God," she thought, "I have Papa."

Sonja always said that Wilhelm was her luck. His shrewdness had assured the best possible contract from Zanuck. The contract had read like a landlord's lease—all in Sonja's favor. He had helped her through the tough times while she was making her first picture and had hammered out her lucrative skating tour agreement during an all-night planning session with Arthur Wirtz.

Sonja hadn't seen her brother, Leif, in some time. He'd been busy in Oslo rebuilding their father's fur business, which had suffered from Wilhelm's total devotion to Sonja's career. Sonja had been too busy to think of the good times she and Leif had had together. Now, she suddenly heard that Leif had a steady girlfriend and might even get married. Sonja considered it almost a personal affront that her brother would even think of doing such a thing without consulting her. She had always felt that she had a psychic ability that forewarned her of danger. She wanted to see Leif—right away.

Leif didn't travel to Hollywood or New York at Sonja's request. She was annoyed but not thoroughly angry. The Henie fortunes had to be tended, and she certainly didn't want to be the only family member earning money. Sonja had always loved money, but now that she was flirting with millions of her own, she'd no intention of sharing it with anyone—not even her father. This was a flaw in her personality that everyone, including her mother, learned to avoid aggravating. Sonja was still too young for her greed to be obvious and ugly, but the time would come when it would destroy the togetherness on which the Henie family had always prided itself.

She didn't return to Hollywod immediately. Her first tour, under the aegis of Arthur Wirtz and their new contract, wouldn't take place until the winter of 1937-38. In the meantime, Wilhelm arranged some paid exhibitions on the east coast. First, she skated during the intermissions between ice hockey game periods in New York and Boston. The exhibitions had a purpose beyond being mere paid performances. Actually they promoted *One in a Million*. Sonja found that whenever she appeared on ice in a city, ticket sales for her movie almost doubled. She was earning money and impressing Darryl Zanuck at the same time.

There were other exhibitions, too, and wherever she went the houses were sold out for her performances. It was obvious that the Henie name was the draw. Arthur Wirtz, in Chicago, read the reviews daily and kept in close contact with the Henies. Although he planned a big production tour for the coming season, he thought that he might slip her into Chicago for a trial run—if she were free and would agree to do it. Wirtz arrived in New York, where Sonja was resting between dates.

"I'd like you to come to my Chicago Stadium on your way back to California and star in a big extravaganza." That simple statement was the beginning of the most revolutionary change ever made in American ice skating. The future of "ice theater" was being prepared, and Sonja was on the verge of seeing her dream of combining skating, dance, costumes, music, and drama into one unified artistic form become a reality. Already a movie star, this was the other thing she had come to America to do.

10

SONJA called her 1937 Chicago Stadium performance the "pioneer show of all I ever did afterward." It was a two-hour extravaganza with Sonja as the prima ballerina, surrounded by seasoned professional skaters. The Chicago Stadium, Arthur Wirtz's home arena, had a seating capacity of over ten thousand, making it one of the largest in the world, if not the largest for an indoor show. Sonja gave five performances and there were never enough seats available. Lines of hopeful ticket buyers formed down the street for several blocks, four abreast.

So intense was the humanity crammed into the giant arena that Sonja couldn't see the customary aisle breaks in the stands when she came out onto the ice. There was only a massive sea of faces. Spectators jammed the aisles, screaming for all they were worth. Sonja thought she knew the reason for the outpouring. "I was a Hollywood star with a professional cast behind me—all on ice—and very obviously something the public had a taste for."

She was not drawing the usual ice skating crowd. These were movie fans. This was an early harbinger of the many theaters-in-the-round and dinner club showcases for movie and television stars that would appear decades later. Sonja was breaking new ground for more than just herself or ice shows.

The Henies returned to Hollywood elated at Sonja's new conquest. Tyrone Power met her at the airport and the two embraced unashamedly. Their romance appeared to glow as warmly as ever. The entire Henie family, with the exception of Leif, who hadn't met him, was extremely fond of Ty Power. Wilhelm would not have minded having this nice young man as a son-in-law. He had hoped for a long time that Sonja would find a good matrimonial prospect and settle the domestic part of her life. It needn't, he felt, interfere with her career. Sonja wanted love but she didn't know if she wanted marriage. She was a romantic and simply thought that she was in fairyland; Jackie Dunn or Tyrone Power was Prince Charming. Why should she think of marriage?

Wilhelm was thinking quite seriously of a wedding. Leif had informed him that he and his girlfriend, Gerd, were engaged. Marriage, he said, was at least a year away. He wanted his family's blessing. His father was so ecstatic at the news that he gave the entire fur business to Leif as an early wedding present.

Neither Selma nor Sonja was pleased. Mrs. Henie wanted only her family together—Wilhelm, herself, Leif, and Sonja. Outsiders weren't a part of her inner circle and she didn't want them to be. That circle, she hoped, would never be broken.

After returning to their home in Los Angeles, Sonja and her mother went over to Fox Studios to discuss her new film with Zanuck and with Raymond Griffith, who would be producing. It was to be called *Lovely to Look At,* which immediately created some controversy because it sounded so much like a Fred Astaire/Ginger Rogers dance picture. It was soon changed to *Thin Ice.* The story was only slightly different from that of Sonja's first picture. This time she was a skating instructor who falls in love with a visiting prince. One Hollywood publication said, "It is a light-hearted musical vehicle for Hollywood's newest novelty—a skating star."

Boris Ingster and Milton Sperling were assigned to write the screen play, which was based on the novel *Der Komet,* by European author Attilla Orbok. Since Sidney Lanfield had gotten along fairly well with Sonja on her first picture, Zanuck felt there was no reason to change what he called "the right chemistry." Robert Planck and Edward Cronjager handled the camera chores and one of the greatest Fox musical directors, Louis Silvers, was delegated the chore of keeping Sonja happy in her dancing-on-skates production numbers.

Once again, Zanuck built the film around Sonja, permitting her to be the diamond sparkling in a solid gold setting. Veteran character actors and comedy routines were injected liberally. Arthur Treacher, Raymond Walburn, Joan Davis, Sig Rumann, Alan Hale, and Melville Cooper made up the supporting cast. Zanuck wanted either Don Ameche or Michael Whelan to be Sonja's co-star. In fact, Fox wasn't known for its male stars. Warner's, Paramount, MGM, and Columbia had most of the young leading men under exclusive contract, and the only way it was possible to pry loose one of those studio's hot properties was to loan them an equally important star or pay an astronomical rental. As a courtesy, and only that, Zanuck asked Sonja which of the two men she might want to be her co-star in her next picture. "You'll have to admit," he kidded, "they're both dashing and handsome."

"Bullshit!" was Sonja's impertinent response. "Ameche is colder than a sardine in the wintertime. Ugh! No, no. They won't do. I want Ty Power."

Zanuck was well aware of the highly publicized romance between Sonja and Power. He had encouraged the publicity department to play it up. Better that she was romancing someone from Fox, where he had some control over his actors, than Metro. It was good for the studio. As long as there was no overt scandal, he didn't give a damn what they did. He had a morals clause in his contracts, if that ever turned into a problem, but who could ever complain of two young kids in love?

Tyrone Power had only recently completed *Lloyds of London* with Madeleine Carroll, in which he had fourth billing on the screen credits. There was no doubt in anyone's mind, though, that once the picture was released, Ty would be a star of major proportions—no one's mind except Tyrone Power's. He was a very uncertain actor in his early days, insecure in a profession known for insecurities. His father, a Broadway matinee idol, had dropped dead making a film in Hollywood. He had left his family without funds, and young Tyrone's own future at that time had seemed conspicuously shaky. He still had difficulty believing that he could make a living in motion pictures.

Darryl Zanuck didn't want to waste Tyrone Power, a serious dramatic actor, in a Sonja Henie picture. Sonja's films, he decided, should be ice, music, skating, and costumes. Use a tried dance formula script, set it to winter escapades, and let the cash register record the profits.

"Sonja, dear," he tried to reason, "why pick someone who might upstage you?" He knew Sonja had a monumental ego, and so it seemed reasonable to appeal to that. This time he was wrong.

"I want Ty!" She clamped her mouth shut and her jaw appeared to have been chiseled out of an iceberg.

"Well, you can't have Ty!" Zanuck was just as stubborn.

"In that case, we have nothing to discuss." She jumped up from the chair opposite his desk and quickly left his plush executive suite. She went directly to Tyrone Power's dressing room and plopped herself into a large overstuffed chair. "Would you believe that lousy sonofabitch said no?" She threw her hands up in total exasperation. "He said no. I don't believe it. I've got the biggest picture of the year behind me and a new one ahead and he has the fucking nerve to say no."

Power, touching up his makeup, didn't so much as bat an eyelash. "He'll come around. It's up to you to make sure that he does. I *want* to work with you in that picture." Ty got up from the dressing table and walked over to Sonja. He leaned over the chair and kissed her on the cheek. "I *want* to do that picture."

Zanuck was not only dealing with a love-struck ice skater, but with a young woman who was about to blossom into a real actress.

Sonja, listening to the advice of her lover, went home to let her father know what she was up to. "Good for you," he said, chortling at his daughter's audacity in speaking up to the head of her studio. "Don't let them push you around, little girl. If you allow them to do it now, they'll do it always."

Sonja was not to be moved by plea or threat. Zanuck threatened to suspend her. She said, fine. She would spend more time on the road with her ice show. Finally, accompanied by her father, she appeared by invitation at Zanuck's office. There had already been a lot of preproduction work done on her new picture and every day she held out for Tyrone Power was a day of overhead that had to be added to the picture's budget.

She was given a very cordial welcome by Zanuck, who saw them alone. Sonja didn't look like a girl in need of money. She wore a three-quarter length silver fox fur coat. Her fingers, wrists, throat, and ears glittered with diamonds and emeralds. A simple white silk dress added the elegant touch that gave her the look of royalty slumming in Hollywood.

"Sonja, Sonja, Sonja," Zanuck began, benevolently. "What are we to do? Hmmm?" Zanuck, known to be a charmer, had decided that that approach was the only way to get around Sonja's insistence on picking her own leading man. "You know," he purred, sounding more like a guard dog than a kitten, "that your contract does not give you choice of a co-star."

"It doesn't say I can't, either, Mr. Zanuck."

Zanuck hated being bested by a woman at any time and Sonja was getting to him too often. "I won't let you have Tyrone Power. That's final!"

Once again the two were at loggerheads. And once again Sonja stood up as if to leave. "I've got a suggestion for you, Mr. Zanuck. Why don't you teach Shirley Temple how to skate and let her do the picture with Mr. Ameche!" Sonja already knew that Shirley Temple's mother demanded and got whatever the toddler wanted.

Had Sonja not been so popular, Zanuck would have, based on his past decisions in such confrontations, fired her. But there were other considerations. The public saw Sonja as a grown-up Shirley Temple. To fire or suspend some one so popular with audiences could reflect badly on the studio, and Zanuck, despite his monumental ego, was first a businessman.

"We'll see what we can do," Zanuck said by way of dismissal and pretended to shuffle some papers on his desk. Before Sonja was out of sight he had begun dictating memos to all departments that Tyrone Power would be Sonja's co-star in the new picture. He hated the idea, but decided to turn it into a publicity coup in order to salvage what he could from a sour situation.

And coup it was. The papers were full of the news. Louella Parsons insisted on, and got, exclusive interviews with the two stars. Sonja, so taken with the handsome Power, was unable to see that she'd been used by the actor to further build his own career and not, as she thought, to be near his love.

Sonja's demands of the studio were not as outrageous as they might seem on the surface. It was 1937. The Depression did more for movies than all the stars in heaven or at Metro-Goldwyn-Mayer or Twentieth

Century-Fox. Even President Franklin Delano Roosevelt paused to give credit to the motion picture industry: "When the spirit of the people is lower than at any other time, during this Depression, it is a splendid thing that for just fifteen cents an American can go to a movie and look at the smiling face of a baby and forget its troubles."

He was speaking specifically of Shirley Temple, but more generally of the motion picture industry's contribution to the mental health, welfare, and, especially, economy of a nation down but struggling to get up off the floor.

About the time Sonja was ready to make her second film, Alice Faye was preparing to star in one of the largest color productions of the time, *In Old Chicago*. Not only would she have Sonja's "cold fish," Don Ameche, as a co-star, she would have Sonja's lover, Tyrone Power, as her love interest in the picture. Sonja was piqued on several accounts. She wanted her films to be in Technicolor. Zanuck refused. His theory, as presented to his skating star, was the ice looks better in black and white. Sonja's argument that her costumes looked too plain in black and white fell on deaf ears.

Rumors had it that Ty was having an affair with Alice Faye. Sonja grew jealous, but Ty denied it, and Miss Faye laughed at the idea. She had plans and Ty wasn't part of them.

Alice Faye was to be the beneficiary of an entire Chicago street that was being erected on the Fox lot to add authenticity to her new film. The street was built so that it could be altered to show the three phases of the city's growth. It would have the largest budget in Fox history, with $80,000 assigned to wardrobe and half a million in special effects to recreate the fire that was started, as legend has it, by Mrs. O'Leary's cow.

During the period of negotiations for her next leading man, Sonja had been quite busy on the ice. From April 29 to May 1, she appeared in a show at the Hollywood Polar Palace. As usual, it was a sellout. She now had her own movie star emcee, famous funnyman Leo Carrillo. Bert Clark, the manager of the Polar Palace, was featured in several numbers, one of which was the bullfight, for which he was quite well known. That was an act that Sonja would pick up as her own while on a South American tour many years later. She included, as always, the Dying Swan and the Mazurka. The studio assigned a regular Fox publicity team to cover the event with a photographer following Sonja and Tyrone Power (who was there every night) about, snapping candid shots to be disseminated among the newspapers and magazines.

A major change was about to take place in Sonja's life. In early May of 1937, shortly after the close of Sonja's triumph at the Polar Palace, her father became suddenly ill and was rushed to the hospital. He had worked very hard for her successful appearance in the ice show, and it was first thought he was suffering from exhaustion. At the hospital a team of doctors then diagnosed his condition as appendicitis. Both diagnoses proved to be incorrect. Wilhelm actually had a blood clot on his lung and died from complications three days after entering the hospital.

Sonja's grief was quite self-contained, considering the role her father had played in her life. Her actions following his passing were very prophetic as to her plans for handling her own future.

Leif hadn't even heard that his father was ill until after Wilhelm's death. Selma collapsed after the funeral and was sent to bed, where she stayed for the next few weeks. Leif immediately left Oslo, flying to France where he boarded the SS *Normandie* for New York, then flying on to Los Angeles where he was met at the airport by his sister and Tyrone Power. Leif had never heard of Tyrone Power and thought of him as just another of Sonja's actor friends.

The funeral was well publicized and paid for by Twentieth Century-Fox. Sonja's grief was also given thorough coverage in the press. What wasn't made public were Sonja's immediate actions following her father's death.

She and her father shared a safe-deposit box at a Los Angeles bank where it was Wilhelm's custom to cache large sums of money. Aware of this, and knowing that it would be taxed if the public administrator found it (during an inventory that is required of the contents of a safe-deposit box when an owner dies), Sonja devised a plan to get the money out before the box was sealed.

With Selma, she drove to the bank and asked to be admitted to the box. While the young man at the desk was consoling Sonja on the loss of her father, he noticed that both she and her father had joint ownership which, under the law, meant that the box couldn't be opened until it had been inventoried. But luck was with Sonja that day. First, the box hadn't yet been sealed, and second, the young man was so flattered by the friendliness of a movie star that he accepted the story she told him about there being an important contract in the box that she must have so as not to lose a great deal of money.

Apparently star struck, the young man turned his back while Sonja took $150,000 in cash from the box. Her mother was appalled at her behavior, and Leif, when he heard about it, felt that his father's share of the money should have been his mother's, not Sonja's.

Leif stayed in America for a time while Sonja worked to complete *Thin Ice*. Throughout the latter part of the film, she continued to get up at five in the morning and arrive home late in the evening. She and her mother planned to take a trip to Oslo when the film was completed. Leif had already returned. Both his mother and Sonja had been cool about his forthcoming marriage, but there hadn't been any real fireworks.

It was while making *Thin Ice* that outsiders began to catch glimpses of the inner workings of Sonja's psyche. Leif believed it was because she no longer had restraints. While her father was still living, Sonja hadn't dared to thoroughly indulge her temper or her lust. Once Wilhelm was no longer on the scene to keep his daughter in line, to manage her affairs, and to run interference when necessary, she became a different person.

Socially she was the epitome of tact, diplomacy, and charm, but with her family she could be selfish and totally lacking in compassion. Her moods fluctuated. One minute she would be nice to her mother and the next tell her she was lazy and shiftless. Wilhelm's death had let the poisons rise to the surface of Sonja's personality, along with a budding Napoleonic complex that inevitably began to affect her work at the studio as well.

Milton Sperling, a writer in his early twenties, was really a freshman when he was assigned to *Thin Ice*. His only previous film writing assignment was *Sing, Baby, Sing*—an Alice Faye musical, co-starring John Payne and Adolphe Menjou. Milton recalls quite well working with Sonja, both on *Thin Ice* and, later, *Sun Valley Serenade*:

> In those days writers were arbitrarily assigned. I was a junior writer on the lot and was teamed with Boris Ingster to come up with an original story for Sonja Henie. After *One in a Million* it was clear that she was going to be a big star, so Zanuck very cleverly said, "Let's make a series with her, playing this ice skater."
>
> He had great foresight. People were not skating in this country. Oh, there were people skating on ponds in New England during the winter, but that's no great reason to launch a career. Her first picture changed all that. She turned it into a national sport, and all over the country little girls learned to ice skate— trying to be Sonja.

There could hardly be better evidence for that than the fact that after she wore white shoe skates in her early pictures, every outlet in the country was mobbed for white shoe skates. It was a boon to the skating industry, which really hadn't even warranted that status. Now skates were moved from storeroom shelves into the display windows and onto counters.

Thin Ice was a location film, to be shot near Mount Rainier, where the panoramic background would enhance Sonja's sparkling screen personality. Setting can improve on a star's appearance or devastate it. Washington State during late spring is still crisp with plenty of snow on the mountains. Proper camera angles concealed any lack of snow at the lower levels. Young Sperling went along with the location company:

> Finding stories for Sonja in those days wasn't hard at all. She was very simple. A simple peasant girl, innocent, guileless—

115

with an ability to skate and no real experience with the world, with men or anything else—although that soon changed, the men I mean. The problem with all her pictures was whether she would be able to skate the big number at the end; also, would she wind up with the man of her dreams in the first one I did for her—which was Tyrone Power, the man of her dreams in real life, too.

Anyway, we finally found the right place to shoot the picture and went up there. Interestingly, there was no place to ski in the United States outside of Lake Placid until Averell Harriman built Sun Valley two or three years after Sonja arrived in Hollywood. Once we found a suitable spot to shoot the ski scenes, we had problems with Sonja. It was almost impossible to pry her out of her dressing room. She and Ty Power were conducting their passionate love affair throughout the filming of the picture. Getting them out of the dressing room was a problem. And when we did get them to the set, Ty always looked like he was about to collapse. Among other things, this guileless, simple girl was one of the most voracious sexy broads in town. She really loved to fuck.

She was a tough lady, but one must remember that she was an Olympic champion. She had to fight her way to the top in her field, so she got a lot of muscle doing that and a lot of bruises and callouses—emotionally as well as physically. Let there be no doubt—she was a tough woman through and through. What you saw at first meeting was not exactly what you got in Sonja. She was no naive child. She had worked her way through the athletic mill which is just as tough as Hollywood.

She wasn't naive with money, either. She was very frugal, and very rich from the beginning, and got richer all the time. She was a strong negotiator. I remember one instance on a picture when we had come back from location, perhaps it was the same film. We returned to do the interiors at the Fox studios and she was asked to do a number after the picture was finished. Zanuck had viewed the dailies and decided there was another production number needed. Sonja was being paid by the picture, not the number. Once the picture was finished—Sonja closed the page on that episode. So she said to Zanuck, "Sure, I do the number—for $25,000."

Zanuck said, "You're not going to get it. That's outrageous!" He was very angry with her, but his anger only bothered him— not Sonja.

"Then you don't get the number," was her response. "That's all!"

116

Fox finally agreed to pay her, and the terms of the deal were that she would come to work from nine to five (or whatever her working hours were normally) for one week only. In those days studios worked six days a week, Saturday being only a half day. Come noon on Saturday, the number wasn't finished and she quit.

She said, "That's it," and left the set.

Zanuck was called immediately and he asked, "Where's she going? What's going on down there?" The director explained what had happened, and Zanuck was incensed and panicky at the same time. "Don't let her off the lot. Stop her at the gate. Lock the gates!"

Sonja's car was stopped trying to leave the studio and she was brought back to Zanuck's office for a discussion. She faced him down. "Just because my father died doesn't mean I'm crazy. I don't work for free. I'll complete the number, but it'll cost you another five grand!" And Zanuck paid. She knew exactly what she was doing.

Sperling remembered that she truly was naive about some aspects of moviemaking. "Looking at this gigantic set they had built for her—the ice stage—where they invented studio ice rinks, she quite seriously said, 'Wouldn't it be pretty if there were some Chinese lanterns on the set?'

"Zanuck said, 'Jesus Christ! This set cost fifty thousand dollars and you want to put ten-cent paper Chinese lanterns all over the place? You crazy dumb broad, grow up!'"

Sperling remembered other things about Sonja. "Oddly, she was not physically an attractive person, although still shots were doctored to make her look glamorous. She was a little chubby, not pretty—very Scandinavian. She had a big broad face, bright brown eyes and the Scandinavian sense of humor, which is akin to zero. She didn't laugh too much. When she did laugh it was kind of 'puku caca' humor. Peasant jokes got to her. Subtle humor either didn't reach her or she'd pass it by."

Sperling's ability to assess her personality so well is unusual. Writers weren't deemed important in the thirties; they were much more a part of the film machine than individual creative entities. They were all housed in little cubicles. The late Harry Cohn, the mogul at Columbia Pictures, would walk down "writers row" and scream, "Write you bastards!" Writers at Fox were all confined to a Tudor building on the lot, jokingly referred to as the Shakespeare Building by the occupants of the tiny offices.

Sperling didn't see that Ty Power was using Sonja. "I went on location a lot and learned to ski during the Henie pictures. I got to know Ty Power and we became friends on *Thin Ice*. He was a newcomer who, like myself, had only one credible film behind him, and he was a wonderful man. Charming, well-educated, came from an acting family—like a Booth. I never understood the chemistry between the two. I can only speculate that it was all sex because she was absolutely insatiable.

Sonja did make lasting relationships from those early films at Fox. Jack Pfeiffer, a rehearsal pianist at the big studio, met Sonja when she started her second picture:

> Fox was involved in producing musicals and there were a lot of rehearsals, requiring a number of rehearsal pianists. I started out in legitimate musicals and was working in the pit on a Broadway show, *Anything Goes*. The conductor, Emil Newman, was brought to Hollywood and Fox Studios, and Emil took me along. I became what was called "first call," which meant I didn't have a contract at the time, but that was corrected within a short time.
>
> Harry Lossee, a very talented choreographer, began working on Sonja Henie pictures and was on *Thin Ice*. Harry wasn't an ice skater but a talented man in music with a thorough knowledge of the classics. He believed in the art of innovation and was incorporating classical music into the films as background for some of the ballets and things of that sort.
>
> Lou Silvers was head of the Fox music department then and Alfred Newman, Emil's brother, was at United Artists, moving over to Fox later on. It was a time of great excitement in films. We were only a few years into the talkies and Hollywood was still somewhat at sea and often a little wobbly on its artistic legs. The talking picture had the same effect on the making of a film as the tremendous pyrotechnic and special effects impact that came later and created the fantastic space films of today.
>
> Sonja was working on Stage 15, which was the ice stage. I received a call to come over to the stage. The wags in the music department were ready to give me a farewell party, because nobody thought I would ever get along with Harry Lossee. Working under him was supposed to be like being banished to Siberia. I surprised them all by getting along famously with the man.. . . . I also hit it off with Sonja and worked with her on every picture she made in the United States thereafter. She made one film in England in the sixties in which I was not involved.

Jack later became Sonja's personal music director and traveled the world with her and her ice show. It wasn't surprising that he and Lossee would get along together, nor that he would become close to Sonja. The common thread was classical music. Sonja had always included the classics in her routines.

"When we went onto the ice stage and Harry asked for dance music, I understood that as well. I remember one of the pieces we had to do in a

Henie film was Stravinsky's "Firebird Suite," a very complicated piece. I had never conducted an orchestra before, except dance bands. But to conduct an orchestra performing Stravinsky, even with all the rehearsals, was quite a challenge. Fortunately, we didn't do the whole ballet. We used a particular part of Firebird for a number called "Alice in Wonderland." It was a ballet in which all of the animals [chorus skaters] chase Alice [Sonja].

"We tried it out with Sonja's show at the Polar Palace, which was located by the old California Hotel at Melrose and Van Ness near Hollywood, and it became a part of Sonja's ice show later on. She was fabulous to work with in those early days—so filled with excitement and awe at being a movie star. Even then, however, she loved a party—and to party."

If Sonja took a liking to someone, the person's station in life didn't matter to her. Cooks, maids, stars, or chorus girls—she opened her heart, and often her purse, to those she befriended. She was by nature fiercely possessive of her friends. Belle Christy, a chorus girl in *Thin Ice,* became the object of Sonja's attention and beneficiary of her friendship. She recalls:

> I'd been dancing for about eight years in pictures and thought I'd better start looking for something else. It looked like dance pictures were on their way out. I mean, how many ways can you do Fred Astaire and Ginger Rogers? I'd worked for a choreographer, Harry Lossee, from time to time. Harry told several of us one evening over a cocktail that he was going to be doing choreography for Sonja Henie's next picture. We just laughed it off. He didn't know anything about skating.
>
> I dismissed it as drink talk and thought nothing further about it. About ten days before the interview date it came out in *Daily Variety* that Harry Lossee was going to choreograph Sonja's new film, *Thin Ice.* Well, boom! We were off to the rink. Harry knew what he was talking about and for whatever reason I was selected. Whatever skating I knew, I'd learned during those ten days.
>
> There was a big mob of us going around and they would pick this girl and that girl and then I was asked to come out. So I skated around behind him. I didn't know how to stop. My lessons hadn't been *that* complete. I tried to get in line with the rest of the girls and went right around it. I went around again. As I went by the second time I hissed at one of the girls, "Dammit! Stop me the next time." So, the next time she gracefully put her hand out and it looked like I knew what I was doing when I stopped. Of course, Sonja wasn't there or I might never

have got the job. She never bothered to come to any of those things. I'd never even seen her yet. But I got into the picture.

Suffice it to say, I was the worst skater of the lot, and although they didn't hold that against me, I think that's what drew Sonja's attention to me—my lousy skating. They had what they called a skeleton crew—three or four couples. Harry would try to work up routines with us. Well, if I could do them, anybody could do them since I was the worst skater, which was the point. I cannot overemphasize that I was outstandingly bad.

Sonja never mentioned my skating. She didn't even talk to me for a long time, and certainly not on that picture. I don't think she spoke to me even once while we were doing *Thin Ice*. And I certainly didn't expect to do another picture with her. To me, the whole thing was a big fluke. Sonja was never aloof. I never saw any of that sort of thing. She was so professional. Always so busy, thinking her things. I don't think she had time to talk to the people in the chorus. She gave us all gifts at the end of the picture—that was her style.

11

WHEN Sonja and her mother sailed from New York for Cherbourg in July on the *Queen Mary,* it was a journey that combined nostalgia with sadness. It was Sonja's first trip home since leaving Paris following the competitions the previous year. Then her father had accompanied them, and they were a happy family traveling to America. Now, the three of them made the journey back—Sonja, Selma, and Wilhelm's ashes en route to Oslo, where the ashes would be entombed.

Sailing on from France, she began to relax somewhat, glad to be going home again despite the painful memories such a return was sure to evoke. Although she was expecting some sort of official welcome, she wasn't prepared for the enormous greeting that awaited her as the ship came into the Oslo Fjord. A fleet of small boats sailed out to meet her, with pennants flying in the breeze. "It was," Sonja said, "as if I were somebody very special." The flotilla escorted the liner into port, where an official welcoming committee awaited their star-come-home. Behind them, hundreds of fans peered and waved at Sonja. They had come from all over Scandinavia to see one of their own come home an American movie star. Sonja wondered if they would think she had changed, if she was no longer "their Sonja." She felt she was the same person. "I wished they could understand," she said, "how good it seemed to me to be home."

She was surprised to discover that many Norwegians were very familiar with American films. Cinema magazines carried more stories about American stars than European. Gossip about Hollywood, it seemed, was on everyone's tongue, and they all had questions about their favorite American actors. While in Oslo, Sonja found an item quoting the *Motion Picture Herald,* one of Hollywood's trade journals, which indicated that just after the release of *One in a Million,* a poll of the American theater-going public indicated she was eighth on the popularity list. Sonja said, "It ain't first, but it ain't bad!"

As a gesture of good will toward Sonja, Zanuck had planned a lavish European premiere in Oslo of her first film. The event was equal to any held in Hollywood, attended by King Haakon and Queen Maud along with other members of the royal family. The theater was replete with klieg lights, the press, and dozens of unusual floral arrangements. The screening was interrupted with applause when Sonja appeared. No one could ever recall hearing applause in a Norwegian movie house before.

While visiting Oslo she ran into friends from Berlin shopping at Tastrup, the famous silver shop. They had come to Oslo for the premiere and couldn't understand why the film had not been shown in Germany where Sonja was so popular. Sonja shrugged her shoulders and said nothing as she continued shopping for silver plates with handcrafted enamel designs.

After the friends departed she went to the manager's office in the store and asked to use the phone. To the surprise and astonishment of the office personnel, she called Joseph Goebbels on his private line at his ministry in Berlin and asked, in perfect German, "Joseph, why isn't my *One in a Million* appearing in Berlin? Is there some problem?"

The minister of propaganda assured her that he knew of no complications and would do everything possible to get the film into the theaters. The picture was soon released in Berlin at the best theaters, with only minor cuts. It played to capacity audiences.

Although Sonja could influence Hitler's propaganda minister, she had less success with her brother regarding his intention to marry Gerd. Sonja was cordial enough to her future sister-in-law while in Oslo, but privately she expressed her negative opinion to her brother, while their mother nodded her concurrence. "She is not good enough for you, Leif." Leif, determined to marry his sweetheart, ignored their protests.

"You will love her once you know her better," he said. "She is a fine woman."

On a more positive note, Sonja wanted a new home, a permanent summer home on a wooded island in the Oslo fjord where she could rest when she made her annual summer sabbatical to Norway. "Perhaps," she told her family, "one day I will be able to spend half the year here and the other half in America."

Landoya, as Sonja's new house would be called, would be her shelter away from the world, her "rooted contact with my original home country."

Although Sonja was cool toward Gerd, she would later rely upon Leif's wife to oversee the construction of Landoya.

This return to Oslo and to Landoën, the old Henie homestead, may have dictated Sonja's decision to build Landoya. There were memories of Wilhelm everywhere. She remembered the crackling fires her father had built in the huge fireplace and his puttering about in the kitchen. It was even harder for Selma. She almost couldn't remember when she hadn't had Wilhelm in her life. While in Oslo, she urged Leif to move to America

122

to live with her and Sonja, to fill the gap in the family that was left by her husband's death. "We need you now, Sonja and I," she said. "I need you."

"It is something I'll have to discuss with Gerd," he insisted. "I will be getting married next year and whatever the decision is, it will be a joint one."

Thin Ice was breaking all records at the Roxy Theatre in New York when Sonja and her mother returned to America in the fall of 1937. The front cover of the *New York Sunday Mirror* was a full page photo of Sonja, in color. Sonja thought it was rather gaudy, but a Fox publicity person assured her it was a sign that she was "really getting somewhere."

"Hummph!" she snorted. "Maybe Zanuck will learn something from this. In New York I am in color. I am appreciated. In Hollywood I am still a black and white nothing." Then she sent a wire to Zanuck that read simply: "Next picture in color—Sonja."

Sonja's affair with Ty Power, meanwhile, was becoming a cause célèbre in the press, a tinseled guessing game. Would she or wouldn't she marry him? Generally overlooked by gossip columnists was the other question: Would Ty marry Sonja—or anyone else?

Both stars were evasive when questioned about their romance. Sonja's relationship with Jackie Dunn was totally ignored by a Hollywood press corps that wanted to know about pampered poodles, not insignificant consort skating partners. Sonja did everything possible to drain every ounce of juice she could from the print media. Ty did the same. Both were ambitious and determined to be major stars. That was the real romance.

Sonja's romance with Jackie Dunn had been ever so hot when she arrived in Hollywood. If Jackie had been a celebrity himself, he might have been able to hold Sonja's affections. After she met Power it soon became obvious that she would never marry Jackie Dunn, a possibility that had once given her parents cause for concern. Truthfully, Sonja wanted to be his friend, but she knew it would never be the same. She loved him but not in the way she had before. He had become more like family. Sonja replaced him in her ice show with a young Canadian Olympic skater, Stewart Reburn. It would be better, she felt, if she and Jackie were not at close quarters.

Ty met Sonja and her mother when they returned to Hollywood, and their hugs and kisses were blatantly passionate. Many magazines and newspapers detailed their romance regularly—sometimes even making up anecdotes that they regarded as plausible. One of the fan favorites, *Motion Picture* magazine, created its own version of their first meeting:

> The whole town is talking about them. Soon the whole country
> will be because they've got what it takes.... Sonja can perform
> minor miracles on skates.... Tyrone with the powerful heritage

of the theater . . . and the kind of good looks that has every Hollywood starlet on edge. But so far he has eyes only for the . . . vivacious little Scandinavian honey. . . . Engaged? They're not telling. It seems to be more a case of a couple of newcomers in a strange land finding their way together.

They met in front of the studio commissary—the publicity department wanted a still of them together. "Are you coming Friday night?" said Sonja. That was the night of her exhibition. Tyrone, thinking fast because he had not planned to go, said "I've had a terrific time getting tickets, but I'll be there," and he was—and that's the way it started.

Unbelievably romantic, and completely untrue.

While wags speculated, Power emphatically denied to the public that he would marry anyone, and to really close friends he added, certainly not Sonja Henie. "Marriage?" he responded to a questioner, "Certainly not! No! No! Not for a very long time. I have no serious romance. Some fellows seem almost constantly infatuated with one girl or another. I am like that, too. It is stimulating and very pleasant, but I have no intention of getting married now. Why I don't even know what kind of girl I'd want to marry. I like blondes, but I know some very nice brunettes, too. If I see the girl I want to marry, I'll know her, but that's a long way off. Sure, someday I'll build a house and have children and read them the funny papers on Sunday, but that's in the far far future."

The message to Sonja, and everyone else, was that Ty Power wasn't interested in marriage, just his career. His and Sonja's sexual activities, as Milton Sperling said, were passionate and constant. The two of them played a little game to keep others from knowing what was happening. They referred to one another's genitals by people's names. Ty's was known as "Jimmy" and Sonja's was "Betsy." If she hadn't seen him for a few days, Sonja would ask, "Is Jimmy sleeping well?"

Ty might respond, "He's having nightmares again."

During one of her trips to Europe Sonja read in the newspapers that Ty was romancing Janet Gaynor. It worried her, because she knew that his sexual appetite was as voracious as her own. Ty wrote to reassure her:

Janet Gaynor is supposed to be the newest flame, according to Miss Parsons. We have been out to dinner a few times, but I suppose if we dare go out again, we'll be getting married, or something. It's all so much nonsense, really darling.

I love you,
Tyrone.

Jimmy says hello. He misses you.

In another letter he ended with a PS: "Jimmy thinks I've died or something!"

Sonja's temperament and demeanor were the subject of constant Hollywood gossip. Some declared she was a combination of every star and her mother—a combination of Shirley and Mrs. Temple. She was said to be cute, cutsey, charming, domineering, demanding, and bitchy.

Sonja and Simone Simon, the French import, had arrived from Europe about the same time. Sonja hated Simone as much as she did Zanuck. Simone, a kitten-faced seductress, also had a romance with Ty Power. All the more reason for Sonja to despise her. Zanuck had a field day. He took delight in pitting Sonja against Simone. It was an opportunity to get back at his Norwegian star. He would often drop bits of information to Louella Parsons about Simone and Tyrone. It was one of the few moments of glee that he ever enjoyed at Sonja's expense.

Simone was never the go-getting businesswoman that Sonja was. One writer described Sonja as "a woman who has never sat back and waited for the world to come to her feet but one who has gone out and grabbed it by the short hairs, laid it down, and put one small boot, with a shiny skate attached, on its neck to keep it there. Whether she knows how to lose, neither she nor anyone else has ever found out."

With the runaway success of *Thin Ice,* Sonja was expected to ask for a new contract, and she did. It's never been revealed if she got a new agreement, but her price for a picture went up to somewhere between the $125,000 she had been making and $300,000, the exact figure depending on which columnist's "inside source" one wants to believe. What Sonja wanted more than anything else was to be filmed in color. If Alice Faye could have color, then why couldn't she? Zanuck refused to move an inch on that point. She requested that she be given straight dramatic roles. "I don't mind one skating scene," she said, taking her argument to magazine writers, "but I don't want to make pictures forever showing a tiny, dumpy Sonja always flying around on ice. I want to act and prove that I can be a great actress like Garbo."

She became convinced that Zanuck had made the sabotaging of Sonja Henie his principal interest. "The sonofabitch don't make me look good in publicity shots," she complained. "You know what happen to me? For a week the camera people from publicity come to my house and shoot great pictures. You think Zanuck okay them? Hell no. He send photographers to Palm Springs where they take awful pictures of me. They were terrible. The most awful things I ever see. Zanuck say, 'Fine. Use these.' That sonofabitch!"

In preparing to start a third film for Sonja, Zanuck followed the proven formula for making money in Henie films. Variety, songs, comedy, and Sonja on the ice. She was livid when the script, an original screenplay by Milton Sperling and Boris Ingster (Zanuck included these writers as part of his Henie "formula"), arrived at her house. The plotline was described as "amusing and glib," serving as the basis for "skating routines by Sonja Henie, and a variety of songs."

"I'm sure Mr. Zanuck knows best," Selma said, trying to ward off an outburst from Sonja. "He really has your interests at heart, dear."

"Bullshit! He thinks only of Zanuck and his stupid polo ponies. That sonofabitch Zanuck stinks!"

She immediately requested Ty Power as her co-star. Zanuck said that was impossible because Ty had already been cast opposite Loretta Young in *Second Honeymoon.* Don Ameche had been assigned the male lead for Sonja, and there wasn't anything she could do about it.

"I will not do the picture without Ty," she shouted at him. "Do you understand? I will not do the picture without Tyrone Power and that's final!"

Zanuck smiled knowingly across his desk at Sonja and her mother. "You will do exactly as you are told, Sonja, or I promise that you will never work in this or any other town in movies again so long as you live."

"You cannot do that to Sonja Henie!" she screamed, shaking her tiny fist at him, tears beginning to stream down her chubby cheeks as her anger overcame the usual placid composure. "You cannot do it. Do you hear me? You cannot do it."

"I can, Sonja. I don't want to. But I can. Don't force me to do something that neither one of us wants."

When Sonja and Selma left Zanuck's office that afternoon Zanuck felt he had won the round. However, he had not won the war by any stretch of the imagination. In the back of his mind was the question: what would Sonja do to get even? He was sure she would do something to make his life miserable.

Insisting that Sonja toe the line and live up to the conditions of her contract, Zanuck took an almost sadistic glee in knowing that apart from not getting Tyrone Power for her leading man, she was also upset that he was working with Loretta Young. Zanuck had allowed the Sonja Henie romance with Tyrone Power to happen. Now he encouraged a relationship between Ty and Loretta Young. He saw in those two the Fox answer to Metro's Jeanette MacDonald/Nelson Eddy pairing, carrying it one step further. Romance them on the screen, and off. Maybe, he thought, another Greta Garbo/John Gilbert pairing.

Sonja accepted the studio's edict. She would do the picture without Ty, without color, without decent dramatic dialogue—but she would "make that sonofabitch Zanuck wish he never hear of Sonja Henie!"

Sonja began to hear from Norway. It was only the start of years of controversy between Sonja and her native country. The Norwegian press was beginning to take shots at their prized daughter. Why, they were asking, were all of Sonja's films being set in other countries? She

126

had learned to skate and become a champion in Norway and yet, her pictures had no Norwegian flavor to them.

It didn't matter to Darryl Zanuck where the film was located as long as there were ski slopes and ice. Consequently, *Happy Landing* had a Norwegian locale. It begins in a small Norwegian village where some American fliers land by mistake. There were some familiar faces for Sonja. Don Ameche, of course, her "cold fish," and old friend Jean Hersholt, playing her father—almost as much off camera as on. This was also the first of several films in which Cesar Romero (who became Sonja's good friend over the years) would appear with Sonja. Rounding out the cast were singer Ethel Merman, Leah Ray, the Condos brothers (Nick Condos became even more famous as one of Martha Raye's husbands), the Ray Scott Quintet, and the Peters sisters.

Sonja was convinced that by now she had learned perfect English. During an interview with Jerome Beatty for *American Magazine,* she boasted of her language accomplishments. "I didn't speak so good English," she said, "when I first got here, but I practiced, and I thought I learned to speak youst like an American. Then I heard myself on the screen and, my, I was surprised! I think I still have a leetle accent. Don't ya think?"

Milton Sperling enjoyed the sparring between Sonja and Zanuck before a big confrontation. "They would do little things to irritate each other and you just knew that before too long one or the other of them was going to go one step too far and precipitate a head-on crash."

Whether Sonja liked Ameche or not was of no importance to Zanuck when he met with his writers and directors. "Zanuck felt that each group was a stock company," recalls Sperling. "In those days that could be done. It was very simple. Darryl used to sit behind his desk with a big chart laid out before him with all the contract players on the left hand side and titles of pictures on the right hand side. There were blanks where he didn't have stories but he would match actors with pictures.

"He would say, 'Well, we need another Alice Faye picture, another Betty Grable picture and another Henie picture.' He would then point to the producers and writers and say, 'You—you do Grable. You do Henie. Bring the stories in.' It was an assembly line."

It was easier to do that in the thirties and forties. They hired competent people who were dependable. They did the same with songwriters. Rarely did anyone wear more than one hat in a film. It was practically unthinkable for a songwriter to be a performer; and the idea of stars writing, directing, or producing, as they sometimes do today—was laughable. Many old-line Hollywood craftspeople believe movies were better when each individual was an expert in his or her own field and worked at it.

Sperling understands their point of view. "There were very few crossovers in those days. You did what your specialty was. Few exceptions. Zanuck knew, for instance, that Mack Gordon and Harry Warren would write the score for a film and there would be four or five hit songs coming out of that picture. Unbelievable. They would come in and play their score for the producer and the writers and whoever else was involved in the picture. Seven or eight songs, maybe, and Zanuck would say, 'I like this. This one is okay. I don't like that one.' And they had the score of the picture—that's all. In a sense he was in a position not only to make stars but to strongly influence the music being listened to all over the country. These songwriters were brilliant. They knew the script and wrote songs for the script. And how tuneful they were. Few musicals today have even *one* hit song. Every musical had several hit songs."

Sperling has his own opinion of Sonja's professional weaknesses. "She was a skater, not an actress, so direction to her was mechanical. It just meant, stand over there honey, and look at him. She would get the adoring expression on her face—she was very good at that—the innocent stare, and then an over-the-shoulder to the guy who's making the speech. I recall one scene, I believe it was in *Happy Landing,* in which she did the 'Mirror, mirror on the wall, tell me who's the fairest of them all.' She had to just look in the mirror and say that. That took about three hours to get just that one line out of her properly. I think she was embarrassed. To look at herself and say something. I think she was scared. She knew her limitations because she was very intelligent. A smart woman and a very worldly woman. She understood and knew where the power was by the time she was making *Happy Landing.* She knew where her strength was—where the authority was. She knew how to get along.

"Sonja usually did not have problems with directors. She understood the mechanism in which she was working and regarded the director as a traffic cop. He was a good traffic cop so far as Sonja was concerned and I never personally saw her argue with a director. I don't think she knew enough to argue with him. Not about directing. But when it came to her skating numbers, that was another piece altogether. She staged her own skating scenes and they were inserted into the pictures appropriately. She was known to tell a director, 'Don't tell me what to do on ice. Stick to your dialogue scenes. Just aim the camera at me and I'll do it. Just get the shot."

By her third film, both studio and star had a better understanding of what was expected from each. Sonja was an excellent showman on ice, and the studio had learned from previous experience always to have three or four cameras on her when she was performing on ice.

Busby Berkley had broken through with overhead cameras, and wonderfully imaginative numbers that were being shot at Warner Brothers, the studio that had spawned Darryl Zanuck. Zanuck came to Fox with a very good idea of how to make a musical; he could do it on stage, a dance floor, or an ice rink. He brought a team, the nucleus of his "stock company," with him from Warner Brothers. Among them was Roy del Ruth (who directed *Happy Landing*), a director with expertise in handling musicals. He had at one time been a writer for Mack Sennett and had gone on to direct such musical successes as *Kid Millions* (starring Eddie Cantor and Ethel Merman, a film in which Miss Merman popularized George Gershwin's Broadway song hit, "I've Got Rhythm"); "Broadway Melody of 1936;" and "On the Avenue."

Zanuck wrote, during that period of executive brilliance in the film world: "The producer of motion pictures like every other person engaged in large-scale creative enterprise should have, above all, the faculty of foretelling public taste."

He discounted critics as having little or no influence on what the moviegoing public would pay to see. If a critic believed that Sonja Henie was less than a good actress, Zanuck shrugged. "The public," he said, "loves ice skating, thanks to Sonja Henie. They are interested in what she does with her feet—not her mouth."

Zanuck preferred not to interfere with the shooting of a film unless there were production delays or serious problems with its budget. He depended largely on his coterie of professional experts to run the day-to-day set activities. Harry Lossee's temperament was perfectly suited to working with Sonja. Both considered directors incidental to their main tasks. The dance was the thing, whether on ice or on stage. Milton Sperling was awed at times by the harmony of the two.

"I used to watch them really work out a number together. Sonja might say, 'I think it would work better over there,' and Harry would say, 'I agree.' And the other way around. Much like a coach and player. They understood one another. So the director of the number was really the head cameraman. For the dramatic portions of the story the director was there for the rest of the cast, and to protect Sonja. The cast was there to protect her so she didn't look silly.

"Also, there was a dramatic coach on the set with her on every picture I ever worked on. It was always a big effort to get her to speak English better. She had a strange, almost unpleasant voice. A monotone; harsh and Germanic. It was the kind of voice that ruined the careers of many silent screen stars but that didn't seem to matter to Sonja's audience. The camera picked up a seeming innocence. A certain naivete."

According to Sperling and others who worked with Sonja after Wilhelm's death, Selma took a beating at the studio. "At times," Sperling recalls, "she rode roughshod over her mother. Mrs. Henie would take her abuse silently and pretend that she understood the star's temperament. I think at times she was quite hurt by her daughter's sudden outbursts. Sonja was always in charge. I recall that some people at the studio, seeing Mrs. Henie with Sonja at all times, were worried about another stage mother. But when Sonja opened up we all thought, 'The mother can't be any worse than the daughter.' Sonja knew what she wanted and she talked up for herself. She stood up to everybody. She was a tough girl off camera."

It was never given much publicity, but when the figures for the previous year came out in 1938, Sonja's income was listed at $210,000 and Darryl Zanuck's at $260,000. She was the highest salaried woman in show business and probably the world.

While filming *Happy Landing*, Sonja began to notice Belle Christy, who remembers, "Sonja invited a bunch of skaters from the picture over to her house one time. My girl friend and I started out but somewhere along the way we screwed up on our directions and never did make the party. It was on a Saturday afternoon, so on Monday morning I went up to her and started to explain why I hadn't come; that we were strangers to the area, absolutely lost, and didn't have Sonja's home phone number with us. She thought it was a funny incident. From then on, she began to talk to me a little every day. Also, they had to set up lighting for Sonja for some of her production numbers and she never came on the set for that sort of thing. It was always done by a stand-in.

"I had no idea why, but she arranged for me to be her stand-in for lighting. I was fitted with a duplicate of her costume and a blonde wig and directed to skate to all the places she would be when the film was shot, so they could have everything perfect when she arrived on the set. Sonja didn't like sloppiness or inefficiency."

Since it didn't come out of her own pocket, Sonja encouraged extra work and overtime for her skaters at Fox. Having Belle fill in for her during set-ups meant lots of extra money for the young woman who realized that she "had no future in skating."

Belle was the guinea pig. Harry Lossee loved to pressure the other skaters into doing difficult routines with his challenge, "If Belle can do it, anybody can." Instead of resenting Harry's remarks as a put-down, Belle felt that he really created a sort of miniature stardom for her. "I remember," she says of Sonja, "how our close relationship all began. We were at the Polar Palace working on a rather difficult routine. The picture was about halfway finished. Sonja came over to me one day at the rink and said, 'I go to Norway when this picture done. Next year I take you.'"

Before Germany invaded Norway, Sonja and her mother spent at least two months every summer in Oslo. Sonja had her contract arranged so that she could take her show out during the wintertime, and have two months away from the studio during the summer.

Belle didn't take Sonja seriously. "She made the statement and walked away. Just like that. I wondered if she was pulling my leg. I completely forgot it by the next day."

130

Meanwhile, the film was completed without mishap. Sonja's running battle with Zanuck continued, her affair with Tyrone Power went on—or rather she shared him with several others—and sometimes found herself wishing that her father were still around to guide her. Her activities were varied and demanding. Few people could have juggled so many careers. There were films, independent skating exhibitions, the tours for Arthur Wirtz, and promotions. She learned that there was money to be made in endorsements, so she endorsed products she never thought of using. Her name meant something. Colgate ran ads featuring a girl on ice. Never before in the history of advertising had ice skating been considered a selling tool. Just as Sonja's white shoe skates revolutionized the shoe skate industry, everything and anything Sonja was seen wearing or endorsing was sure to bring big profits to the manufacturer.

Back in Norway, Leif Henie had some ideas of his own to help Sonja make money. He looked forward to her summer visit to discuss business as well as family affairs. Sonja missed Leif and wanted him to be part of her new life, to live in Hollywood. That would take some doing, but she usually got what she wanted.

12

S ONJA'S status rose in Norway when news of *Happy Landing* reached the continent. *The American Scandinavian Review,* a prestigious publication in the Norwegian communities around the world, featured Sonja in an article. Purists, who felt that Sonja should never have become a commercial entity were somewhat taken to task by the writer who said, "... the accessories [of commercialism] regardless of expense are a measure of her immense drawing power, and they remain accessories. It is Sonja's own charm and her art of skating, more marvelous than ever, that radiate to the topmost corner of Madison Square Garden and hold 16,000 people spellbound."

Following the completion of *Happy Landing,* Sonja also took out her first real show in fulfillment of her contract with Arthur Wirtz. Sonja's dice were hot and it seemed that nothing could pose any obstacle for her. The only sadness in her entire life had been the loss of her beloved father. The rest of the family was intact and closely knit. As for squabbles with her mother, Sonja was immediately sorry for any hurt she caused her, and Selma just as quickly forgave Sonja. Sonja believed that new vistas were about to open when her show took to the road.

Jack Pfeiffer remembers that first outing under the Wirtz banner. "We didn't play a full tour—maybe three or four cities. I was the musical director on that show and our theme song was "Hooray for Hollywood." A little bit corny, perhaps, but very showy considering all the problems that were part and parcel of fielding a new show like that. Ice skaters were difficult to come by. We had skaters from Sonja's films and recruited skaters from ice hockey because that's about the only place skaters had been trained in the United States—out of the eastern rinks to play ice hockey."

Quite a number of the ice skaters from Hollywood were gay, and combining them with the rather rough types who came out of ice hockey created a real comedy of errors with lots of indignant vocalizing on both sides.

"It was more like a circus," recalls Jack Pfeiffer's wife, Liz, also a skater in the show. "It was a lot of fun, of course. We soon had our own train just like Barnum and Bailey, with our own dining car, club car, and all the baggage cars to carry equipment and personal belongings. The stars and principal skaters had their own rooms and the chorus kids were in bunks. At night everyone stayed up. The way we traveled depended on so many intangibles beyond our control. For instance, when we closed the show and prepared to go on to the next town, most of the kids had checked out of their hotels before going to the arena to perform. The show was usually over by eleven-thirty. The train then had to be loaded, which meant waiting for the equipment to be broken down and loaded in the cars designated.

"On this particular tour we opened in Chicago—and it was wintertime and damned cold. The show always played the coldest cities at the coldest times of the year, it seemed, and a lot of us from California had difficulty adjusting to the temperatures every winter on the road."

Jack adds, "Wirtz's general manager out of Chicago was a fellow by the name of William H. Burke—everybody called him Billy—and he made all the arrangements and would relay instructions to all of us. For instance, he would come backstage before the last show and say, 'The train will be loaded immediately after curtain. I want everybody aboard before three A.M.'

"We had all that time to kill after the show, so the kids would skate on an empty stomach. Sonja did the same. After the show everyone would go out and have a big meal. Sonja never liked to eat until after midnight. Almost always there was a party somewhere, usually at a nightclub or at the hotel—and the tab was picked up by the establishment in return for the favorable publicity. They would set up a big table for Sonja's party where everyone could see Sonja. It attracted business for them to present their star at a party and besides, it was all written off the establishment's income taxes as 'promotion.'"

Sonja had a clear idea of what her ice revue provided. "It offered the people what they had shown in Chicago they wanted," she recalled. "Dancing on ice combined with skating entertainment and a Hollywood star. We got together more than sixty skaters, which wasn't an easy task then. I remembered when I first came to Hollywood what a rat race it had been to find *anybody* who ice-skated. Through my films, I built up a reservoir of skaters whom I could call on. I insisted, when we had exhausted the ranks of trained skaters, that we should look for people with dance training above all else. I trained dancers to become skaters for our ensembles."

From her point of view, she saw a great deal of adventure in undertaking an unprecedented road show to the hustings of America. There had been ice shows prior to Sonja's, but nothing so elaborate or exciting. It had to be timed to the minute. Everything had to be done quickly if it was to succeed.

"To assure speed and finesse," Sonja recounted, "large sums of money

134

had to be advanced on chance." That money was provided by Arthur Wirtz. "In order to open Christmas night in Chicago, for instance, we chartered four giant twenty-one-passenger planes to fly the troupe East from the Coast."

The show had been rehearsed in Hollywood at the Polar Palace while Sonja completed her third film. Her days and nights ran together, and she slept when she could. It was the first time in her life that she was unable to get her rest at appointed hours and for specific periods of time. Not only was Sonja doubling in brass between Fox and the Polar Palace, but she also had Harry Lossee keeping the same schedule she kept. Harry directed and choreographed Sonja's skating scenes at Fox by day and directed and staged the Sonja Henie *Hollywood Ice Revue*'s rehearsals at night.

Leaving nothing to chance, Sonja recruited other Fox experts to be sure that her show was totally professional from the lowest chorus boy to the top echelons of production personnel. Other Fox employees incorporated into the Henie hierarchy included Lossee's assistant, Robert Linden; musical director Jack Pfeiffer; Royer, who created her costumes; Arthur M. Levy, who executed her costumes; and Reeder Boss, wardrobe manager. Arthur Wirtz provided the publicity director, and "Fashion Show Costumes" were designed and executed by Leif Henie in Oslo. Sonja's personal hairdresser, Ann Barr, accompanied the star when she was away from Hollywood.

Sonja could not have been more delighted with the end result. She told the story again and again. "Things I had wanted to see done all my life came into being on that tour. The show became dancing on ice, the fusion of skating and ballet I had fervently imagined since my days of regarding Pavlova as a goddess. It was theater, involving spectacle of lights, costumes, music, and big patterned movements. We delivered a really diversified program, with the numbers ranging from Liszt to the Susi-Q."

At the Boston Garden appearance, the program notes reflected previous commentary about Sonja's show:

> The lights dim, the leader's baton is raised, then come the sweet strains of the violins, the melodious surge of the wood-winds, the symphonic ensemble of a haunting, lilting waltz. The brilliant beam of a spotlight, and fifteen thousand persons are poised expectantly. Then suddenly in the bright circle of light, the little maid of Norway. There comes a spontaneous ripple of applause, hushed almost as it starts. Slowly, blonde curls bobbing, this elfin figure glides with infinite grace upon the smooth mirrored surface of ice. Faster, then faster, the tempo quickens, then with the capricious abandon of a wood nymph, she dances, this Golden Girl, glides, floats, and pirouettes as does the fresh

young breeze on a frozen lake in the depths of some mystic wood, as on the circling shore the swaying reeds and trees lend their fantastic refrain. No longer are there fifteen thousand watchers, the multitude has become as one. One who has mystically been transported from this modern adult world of mortals. One who sits, seeing once more, as those eyes once saw in the joyful dreams of happy childhood, the realm of fairyland. There is it all. The sweet and mystic music, the shimmering rays of rainbow light, the flashing jewels, and—the fairy queen. Queen indeed, for no other possesses that incomparable skill, that supreme grace, that dainty rhythmic beauty. The music rises to crescendo, the lights flare their brilliance, the spell is broken, then a tumultous outburst of applause, and Boston once more acclaims that Champion of Champions—Miss Sonja Henie!

The maiden tour under the Wirtz banner was both a financial and artistic success. From the opening night of that first annual tour, rarely was there ever a vacant seat for a Sonja Henie ice show.

While playing Washington, D.C., prior to closing in New York, Sonja was presented with a medal and made a member of the Order of St. Olav. The Knighthood of St. Olav had been established in 1847 by King Oscar I of Norway and was considered the highest honor Norway could bestow upon one of its citizens. On the only piece of Norwegian soil in the United States—the Norwegian Embassy—King Haakon, through his minister to the United States, Wilhelm Morgenstierne, made Sonja a member of the order. During the ceremonies Morgenstierne, speaking in soft Norwegian, said "Miss Henie is the youngest person who has ever received this decoration." It was an honor usually conferred in later life, when a career could be better evaluated. Morgenstierne further stated, "in recognition of your unique contribution as a sportswoman, an artist, an interpreter of the ideals of Norway's youth, and one who has upheld the honor usually conferred in later life, when a career could be better evaluated. Morgenstierne further stated, ". . . in recognition of your unique contribution as a sportswoman, an artist, an interpreter of the ideals of Norway's youth, and one who has upheld the honor of the flag of Norway."

It would not be too long until the Norwegians would wish they had not been so effusive in praise of their native daughter. Sonja occasionally entertained and was entertained by pro-Nazi elements in America. It never occurred to Sonja that her good friend Adolf Hitler posed a threat to the freedom of the world. After all, she had always felt she enjoyed perfect freedom in Germany. Sonja was enjoying the luxury of a dangerous naivete.

Madison Square Garden with its nightly throngs of sixteen thousand cheering spectators was anticlimactic after the regal proceedings in Washington, but the tour ended more successfully than even Sonja could have imagined. The media could not have been more kind. Heywood Broun said, "I think it is safe to say right now Sonja Henie is the greatest single box-office draw in America." He said she had "theatrical sense," and that she knew how to "put her stuff over." Willy Boeckl, the skating expert, added that Sonja was "in better form than ever," and that her "great reception has made thousands of new followers of figure skating."

Concurrently Hollywood was lauding her in other ways. Although Shirley Temple had been the number one box office attraction the previous year and was again in 1938, Sonja jumped from eighth place to second place behind the curly-topped moppet in box-office popularity.

There was one crack in the serene surface of Sonja's life: Tyrone Power had strayed. Sonja was telling everyone that Power had asked her to marry him but she had declined for career reasons. "I don't want to marry until I am thirty," she cooed. If Ty Power ever asked Sonja to marry him, which is doubtful, he never mentioned it to anyone else. While Sonja was on tour, the French actress Annabella, being touted as one of the hottest finds Hollywood had come across in years, was named in columns as Ty's new flame. Once again, Power was latching on to a new European star (although he preferred Europeans, he never hesitated to allow his name to be linked with any woman's if it garnered space in the fan magazines and gossip columns).

Annabella was not just another fling. In late fall, she announced her engagement to Power. Sonja didn't believe it. "It is just a publicity stunt," she told inquiring reporters in Chicago. "Ty would not do a thing like this without telling me first. I don't believe it is true."

It was true and, for Sonja, quite painful. One writer explained Sonja's feelings; "Perhaps," Molly Castle wrote in a fan magazine, "if there had been a real deep love between them she might just once in her life have altered her direction . . . it was not the love of a lifetime and when a few months later he fell in love with someone else nothing was hurt except her pride and that, not because he loved another girl, but because he was scared to tell her so."

Fan magazine writers had the ability to make star romances sound like high school crushes.

Sonja revealed to Molly (and her fans), "We were such friends. Why did he not tell me all of this instead of letting me hear it from other people and read about it in the newspapers. If only, as you say in America, he had just put all his cards on the table he might have found me so sympathetic." Sonja was anything but sympathetic. She was devastated and outraged. The hurt went very deep. Of all the men who ever entered and left her life, only one ever held her heart—Tyrone Power. Even in

137

those days, there were whispers that Ty might be bisexual. If that presented a challenge to Sonja, she never said so and she never expressed her feelings about his possible dual sexuality to anyone. Many of the gay skaters in her troupe thought he was bisexual, but then, as Sonja would giggle to one of her confidantes, "You think *everybody* is that way."

Even before the tour was completed, Sonja was preparing routines for the next one. When she returned to Hollywood, she and Harry Lossee were busy putting together new numbers. Harry, a teacher of ballet, had never seen a pair of ice skates before he saw Sonja and hadn't been interested in them, but, he got things from Sonja that nobody else ever did. Selma told a friend, "It never ceases to amaze me. Harry accepts no compromise. Sonja shakes her head when he says, 'Get out there and do it!' 'It cannot be done on ice,' she screams. It doesn't matter. Harry has a stubborn streak as long and as wide as Sonja's. I think sometimes they will kill each other, but when the practice is finished, they are both satisfied—laughing and hugging one another."

Sonja would berate her chorus when a number was badly performed. "You are all lousy," she would yell at them, and then in a hushed, embarrassed tone, she would whisper loudly, "I was the worst of all." She demanded professional perfection of her troupe, but even more of herself. She let each professional do his or her job with no lip from herself, but God help those who botched it. "I would no more tell you how to run your job," she told a writer during an interview, "than tell President Roosevelt how to run the country."

Sonja was never inhibited by the audience. "Whoever is in the audience," she said, "it is all the same to me. When I begin to skate I think of nobody. The great ones are just people. This man may have been born a king, that man a carpenter. Each comes to be entertained. And," she added, "I think they all get their money's worth from Sonja Henie."

"Money's worth" was a phrase Sonja savored. She always wanted her money's worth and more. The January 1938 issue of *Motion Picture Magazine* carried a story by-lined Roger Carroll that asked the question on everyone's lips at the time: "Is Sonja Henie Money Mad?" It was figured that she was making a conservative $250,000 annually from films, not counting her percentage of the gross, which was written into her contract after *One in a Million* skyrocketed her into the top income bracket. Her film income was more than most stars made and she, unlike most big stars, limited her working time to twenty weeks, which allowed thirty-two weeks in which to multiply that income manyfold through skating engagements. In addition there were endorsements and invest-ments (at which she was becoming more and more adept, thanks to the financial wizardry of Arthur Wirtz). Her film salary alone was an astro-nomical twelve thousand dollars per week. Never in the history of films had anyone risen to such heights so quickly.

Sonja believed in one real vacation a year, and then, after a couple of months in Norway, it was back to the money mills. The skating tour of 1938 had a guarantee of $800,000. She already had renegotiated her contract with Arthur Wirtz and it would reportedly gross her $2 million for the next year's tour. From that amount she paid her expenses, costumes, hotel bills for the troupe, and salaries. Chorus boys and girls received $75 a week. A few of the featured skaters received more. Her movie income was peanuts compared to the net profits from her ice tours. Also, by now, Leif was manufacturing Sonja Henie ski outfits and literally dozens of other promotion gimmicks that made Sonja's coffers overflow with gold.

Many stars took payment for personal appearances, endorsements, and radio shows in merchandise valued higher (at retail) than a cash salary. Sonja wouldn't do that. "I take the cash and buy my own *tings*," she would say with a giggle. A questioner asked, "Doesn't she know that the more she makes the more taxes she will have to pay?" Again Sonja would giggle. She never declared anything that couldn't be traced. In that sense, she was no different from anyone else in Hollywood.

Her tours were well orchestrated to take place either just before, during, or right after a picture in which she starred. On the road she had her own people watching the box office constantly, counting cash and empty seats. There were always plenty of the former and few of the latter.

But rarely did anyone see Sonja spending any of the millions she was making.

In the film capital she rented a house from Lana Turner, on a lease that ran for only three months at a time. She had not as yet purchased the elegant home on Delfern Drive that would become her showplace in America, but only rented cottages—one of which did not even have a swimming pool. Her attitude, at the time, was "no pool, no extra rent."

One critic of Sonja's declared, "Sonja's funds are the same place as her brother's furs—cold storage."

She did not, however, slight those who were supportive of her career and worked with her, nor her lovers. She showered Tyrone Power with expensive gifts: items of jewelry from Bill Russer's exclusive jewelry salon. Chorus boys, directors, bit players—all received generous tokens of Sonja's appreciation for making her look good on the screen. Waitresses and waiters in elegant cafés and night clubs, however, were not the recipients of such generosity. People who served her in the *Café de Paris,* the Fox Studio commissary, complained that Sonja never tipped. Not "almost never," but "never!" In London they were still complaining that she was a cheapskate who stole the sheets off the bed and the towels from the bathroom, but left not so much as a thank-you note.

On her last trip from Europe aboard the Normandie, the steamship company's representative phoned Twentieth Century-Fox offices in New York and diplomatically suggested that perhaps Sonja's failure to give anything to anyone had been "an oversight" and he inquired whether perhaps through the studio she would like to express appreciation for the "unusual" personal service she and her entourage had been given on her recent trip to America. An embarrassed studio publicity representative rushed over with several hundred dollars in cash to accommodate the irate crew members who had been slighted by Sonja.

When apprised of the situation, Sonja ordered the studio to explain that "When Sonja's father was alive, he took care of all such matters. Sonja was not aware that they were not still being taken care of."

Another story about her financial acumen was told by someone who overheard a conversation between her and an agent in a nightclub one evening. He was discussing with Sonja the offer of a radio show and the prestige that might go with it.

"What," she asked, "will they give me?"

"I think we can get maybe $2,000," he said, sounding proud that he could get so much for his client.

About that time into the club walked Robert Taylor and Barbara Stanwyck (then husband and wife). Sonja watched until the couple was seated at a nearby table. Then she turned to the agent and asked, "How much does she get when she goes on the radio? I will not accept less."

During the summer hiatus from making pictures in 1938, Sonja had traveled to Norway for her summer vacation. Landoya was progressing slowly and she urged Leif to watch the contractors more closely. "I don't want to be charged for work they are not doing," she said, more frustrated than angry. "I am so far away. How do I know what is going on. I never hear from you."

In the same breath she again attempted to prevail upon Leif's obligation to family. "I cannot understand why you insist on staying in Oslo when both mother and I need you so badly in Hollywood. It will not be as though you have nothing to do. You can become an officer in my company and help me manage things. You know ice skating and costuming. You can be such a help to me. Let someone else run the company. The fur business will take care of itself." She argued that he could return to Europe from time to time and take care of any pressing matters that required his attention.

Although her pleas were poignant and sincere, Leif still had his bride-to-be to consider. An incident took place, however, while Sonja was in Oslo, that had the opposite effect of what Sonja desired. Leif had made up half-a-dozen fur coats as a wedding gift for Gerd. Sonja, upon hearing that Leif was lavishing such a present on Gerd, couldn't wait to see the coats. When she did, they only represented diminishing profits for the family business to her.

Leif had brought the furs home to show both Sonja and his mother, leaving them at the house until his wedding. Sonja complained bitterly to Selma that "Leif is a fool! He will wind up giving away the family business." Selma, as always, attempted to soothe Sonja's ruffled feathers. It broke her heart to see her children at odds with one another.

Not satisfied with her mother's diplomacy, Sonja devised a scheme. She promptly absconded with the coats and left for America with Selma before Leif discovered his loss. Although he was furious with Sonja, it was temporary anger. He, like his mother, could not stay angry with his sister for long. Passively, he replaced the furs, but Sonja and Selma were in Hollywood when Leif and Gerd were married in August of 1938.

There are several versions of why his mother and sister did not attend the nuptials. Both were certainly invited. According to Gerd, "It was impossible for them to come. Sonja was in Hollywood making a picture when we got married." Gerd admitted, however, it was quite a while before she broke the barrier the Henie family had surrounded itself with. "There were tensions in the beginning," she said, "but we eventually became the best of friends."

Leif remembers that his mother and sister flatly refused to have anything to do with that woman "who will strip us of all the family fortune." It was certainly some time before either of the two women began to accept Gerd as part of the Henie household.

It was a time of rapid movement for Sonja, and she developed an ulcer. Not trusting American doctors to treat it, she was fanatic in her insistence that "whatever is the matter, it will wait until we go to Oslo for the summer."

Sonja's fourth film, *My Lucky Star,* was produced by Zanuck, with Roy del Ruth handling directorial chores. Although Zanuck assigned top writers to do the screenplay, it was once again a very flimsy story with Sonja's flings on the ice rink the only thing that Zanuck cared about. The cast surrounding her included Richard Greene, comic Joan Davis, Cesar Romero, Buddy Ebsen, Arthur Treacher, Billy Gilbert, and Gypsy Rose Lee (then appearing under her real name of Louise Hovick). The picture made money, but was not as successful as her previous films. The ice skating craze had diminished somewhat.

Hollywood was in the throes of transition. Storm clouds hovered over Europe. England was girding for what was sure to be an onslaught from Hitler's Germany. Sonja didn't share the opinion of those who felt her friend Adolf Hitler was a monstrous force bent on world conquest. "I know many people in the German government," she would argue. "They are men with families and ideals. If there is anybody to fear it is the Bolsheviks."

While Zanuck and Sonja battled over scripts, color instead of black and

141

white, and leading men, David O. Selznick was about to launch a new era in motion picture viewing with his forthcoming production of *Gone with the Wind*. Sonja was one of the few Hollywood leading ladies who wasn't considered or tested for the epic production.

The musical was still an important part of Hollywood during the late thirties, but it was gradually being replaced by more dramatic films. In addition, MGM was replacing Fox as the home of the musical, as well as launching "an ocean of faces" that would dominate the screen for years to come.

Shirley Temple, America's darling, who helped bring a smile to a nation in depression, although still number one at the box office, was enjoying her last year in that position. Musicals, at Fox, would henceforth be focused on the big bands and popular songs. Led by Glenn Miller, the "swing era" was coming into full bloom. Thanks to an improved economy that was gearing up for the war to come, kids had more money to spend on pleasure. The Andrews Sisters, Benny Goodman, the Dorsey Brothers, jitterbugging, and jukeboxes were "in."

Sonja's fortunes in the future would lie more with her ice shows than in films, but she still had one blockbuster coming that surprised her as much as it did everyone else. That, however, was a couple of years away.

In the meantime, Sonja visited Oslo for what would be a long, last look at her native country until after the war.

13

ONE day on the set at Fox, Sonja came over to Belle Christy following the shooting of a difficult production number. "Do you have your passport?" she asked.

"What?" Belle asked, not quite understanding the question.

"Your passport. I take you to Norway next week."

"I don't have a passport."

Sonja giggled. "That's all right. Dixon will take care of it." Dixon was Sonja's chauffeur.

Sonja, Selma, and Belle, along with loads and loads of baggage, arrived in New York aboard a TWA passenger plane that took most of the day to cross the country. They sailed from New York on the *Queen Mary,* spent a week in England, and then went on to Paris.

"Muhr," Belle's name for Sonja's mother, did not stay with the girls. "She went on to Norway," said Belle, "to see what was happening with Sonja's new home and hoping to be able to convince Leif that he should move to America. By now he was married. I'd never met Leif before, nor his wife."

Sonja had a very good friend in London, Clifford Jeapes. Jeapes was a British moviemaker who had given Sonja an unsuccessful screen test in 1936 when she traveled through London en route to America for her first tour, during the time she was romantically involved with Jackie Dunn.

"In Clifford's father's office in London, I saw the first television set I'd ever seen," said Belle. "I don't think Sonja had been exposed to television either and we both just went gaga over such an invention, although neither of us saw it as any threat to motion pictures. It was just another toy for men to play with."

Jeapes insisted on chaperoning the girls in Paris and showing them "Paris at its best." Sonja had been there many times, but for Belle it was an eye-opening adventure. "I was someone that Sonja had fun with. Like a child that she could do things for and show things to. I thought at the time how nice it would be when she got married and had children to do those things for. Of course, she never had children and that was a shame. I think she would have made a great mother."

The two were like schoolgirls on an outing. In Paris they stayed at the Hotel George V. They went to see the Folies Bergères and everybody immediately recognized Sonja and applauded when she entered. Most of their activities were of a nighttime variety because Sonja was a night person.

Belle remembers, "When we were on tour our nights didn't start until after eleven o'clock. Often it was daylight when we finally went to bed. We continued the same routine in Paris." On tour it was a later night for Belle than for Sonja because she was also secretly dating Bob Christy, one of the skaters in the chorus of Sonja's show. Secretly, because Sonja was very possessive of her close friends, as well as her employees. It wasn't just Leif whom she didn't want to get married—she didn't want anyone who worked for her to be married unless they already were when they came into her employ. She realized, of course, that once someone got married and had children, she would no longer be the most important single element in their lives. Being an outsider while others raised families would, of course, emerge as a major factor in her life later on.

"You think Paris is something," Sonja said to Belle, "just wait until you see Oslo!"

Upon their arrival in Norway Sonja found Landoya complete enough to live in, and the elegance of Sonja's taste overwhelmed Belle. "It was something right out of *Gone with the Wind*. I couldn't believe it," she recalls. "All those beautiful white columns in front and furnishings that reflected an almost royal touch in decorating."

Soon after their arrival, Belle was embarrassed by her own ignorance. "We had been there two days and on the second night I heard all kinds of noises outside Sonja's home. I ran to the window and looked out and saw firecrackers and rockets going off all over the place. The sky was filled with the glow of bonfires. How wonderful, I thought, for them to do that in Sonja's honor. I called for Sonja to come and see. She looked out and said, 'Oh, yes. They do that every year. It's to celebrate the longest day of the year.' She was amused with my excitement. I didn't have the heart to tell her I was so dumb."

The highlight of the vacation was a tour up to the northernmost part of Norway. The group included Sonja, Belle, Mother Henie, Leif and Gerd, and Sonja's theatrical agent, Vic Orsatti.

"It was fantastic," Belle recounts, "just a fairyland revealed, mile by mile. We went by train from Oslo across Norway to a big city called Bergen. The railroad in and of itself was an event, built right through the fjord. It took thirty-five years to build and the trip from Oslo to Bergen was eight hours filled with such beauty one did not have time to think of time.

"From Bergen we flew up to a place called Chonyan and then it got hairy. We were furnished with two cars with drivers and we set out

144

motoring all the way up the western coast of Norway, stopping from time to time and fishing along the way. I've never known anyone who loved to fish more than Sonja. I remember one place we stopped, and I'll bet no one ever fished there before, and Sonja was catching one fish right after another and yelping and screaming with delight like a child discovering Christmas."

Their destination was Nordcup, the most northern inhabited part of the globe, Sonja explained. Belle had expected ice and freezing cold, so close to the North Pole, but found the weather quite pleasant. "It was still summertime," she explains, "and still daylight almost all night long. It was the land of the midnight sun that I had always heard about and couldn't believe in. Sonja wasn't happy just being in Nordcup. She rented a boat and we went quite a way out on the water, always bearing north. We watched the sun come down and just tip the horizon and then start back up again. It was fantastic—and comfortably warm. Sonja was an imp. She squealed with joy at my disbelef. Oh yes, Sonja was a real pistol. Really, a little girl herself. I don't think she showed that mischievous nature to most people. It was the unguarded moment she shared with me and I'll never forget it. She was so perceptive. I would start to say something to her and she would nod her understanding even though I hadn't said anything. It was sort of an eyeball shorthand that we shared.

"I remember one particular incident from that trip," says Belle. In what we called 'civilian life' Sonja wore little curls right behind her ears where the hair wore thin from wearing wigs all of the time. She put these little patches in those sparse areas for public appearances, as well as private, away from work. Sometimes her hair would become separated from the patches of curls and if I saw it I'd casually pull my own hair down about the ears and she'd pick up on it and quickly blend her patches into the hair—she knew exactly what I meant and it worked for us.

"Sonja never asked favors. It seemed as though she felt she had to give rather than receive. Only one time did she ask a favor of me and I failed her. I was devastated. These little curls had to be put on a little wood block at night and left to dry. She asked me if I would do that for her on one occasion while we were in Oslo, and I forgot. She was dressing to go to a big function and asked, 'Bay-ul, would you bring me my curls, please.' It crushed me that I had forgotten to do them but Sonja only giggled, fluffed her hair over her ears, and bounced out the door as if nothing had happened."

Belle laughingly recalled that Sonja was the only person she ever knew who made two syllables out of her name.

Sonja dated while they were in Oslo, but Belle never knew who the men in her life were. "She was very secretive about that. She would go out, spend the evening and half the night and the next morning would discuss what she did, but never with whom. She fixed me up with a date once and it ended on a strange note. Strange in a sense that the eeriness came about on the day we departed Norway. He was a handsome man whose last name was Heyrdahl. He took me to dinner at the Grand Hotel in Oslo. He asked to see me again and I said, 'Sure, why not.' The following day he sent me orchids—those lovely green orchids—in a huge vase. Sonja promptly put them on display in the entranceway to her home. Those flowers remained as fresh and crisp as the day they were cut until the day we left. As we walked out of the house, I turned to take one last look and gasped. 'Sonja,' I said, 'look. The orchids are dead!' They had been brilliant pastel green that very morning, and now they were dead—almost an omen of our departure."

Leif had been manufacturing ski costumes, which were being distributed in the United States, and had, on a couple of occasions, made trips to America to meet with his distributors. Selma Henie's persuasive powers over her son had obviously been effective, since Leif left Gerd in Norway and returned to the United States with Sonja. Sonja had also promised Leif that if he would come and live with her and Selma she would make him an officer in a company she was forming. "My lawyer says I must be a corporation," she explained, "and I can have all my family as officers. You will be an important man and we will make millions of dollars together."

Gerd Henie, Leif's wife, remained in Norway. She seems to have had some doubts as to how the relationship between Sonja and Leif would work out. She never felt that Sonja had any real difficulty in accepting her as Leif's wife, but, rather, resented intrusions by outsiders into her family and that she also was concerned about Leif's maturity at the time. "Sonja and her mother both had some apprehensions about whether Leif was ready for the responsibilities of marriage and children," notes Gerd. "I don't remember that Leif ever got along well with Sonja. There were always differences between them, but I think Leif looked up to Sonja's accomplishments." As the son, and elder offspring, Leif felt some resentment over the fact that it had been Sonja, not he, who had captured the world's glittering prizes; but he pushed such feelings out of the way as he embarked on the mission of furthering Sonja's career. If he had been able to see the future, he would have hesitated to have any part in her affairs.

It was unclear what would happen in Europe in 1939. Everybody wondered whether or not Germany would invade the Scandinavian countries. In a personal conversation with Joseph Goebbels, Sonja was assured that her native country had nothing to fear from Hitler. It was the Russians, now poised to strike at Finland, who were not to be trusted. Sonja left Oslo feeling that her country and her home were safe from harm. Czechoslovakia, already occupied by Hitler's forces, was of no concern to her.

Sonja's party returned to the United States aboard the *Normandie* the last week in August of 1939. She was the only celebrity aboard, and Belle Christy sensed a strange uneasiness among the passengers. There was not the air of gaiety that was normal on an ocean liner.

"I couldn't understand what was going on," Belle recalls. "Almost the entire passenger list was Jewish, and they seemed a very somber group. Even the nightly dances were less frivolous. One read certain things in the papers, but they were usually blown out of proportion—something to make headlines and sell papers. We truly did not know that war was that imminent. We knew about Hitler's march into Czechoslovakia, but that had been by agreement at the meeting in Munich between Hitler and England's prime minister, Neville Chamberlain, who had promised 'peace in our time.'

"Two days before we landed in New York on the return trip," remembers Belle, the captain ordered all windows blacked out. No lights were to be shown on deck after dark. We knew something was wrong, but still did not know that our precious cargo was Jewish immigrants escaping from Poland at the last minute before Hitler's invasion of their country. It was only after we arrived in New York that we learned of the invasion and the fears that German U-boats were patrolling the Atlantic and that we were subject to being sunk by them to prevent the fleeing Jews from reaching America and freedom.

"The Jews had seen the handwriting on the wall. They knew what Hitler had done to their counterparts in Germany, and they evacuated only a few days before their fate would have been sealed in the same fashion. It was the first harsh lesson for any of us as to what the Nazis were up to—and so hard to believe. Germany was supposed to be a civilized country having some territorial differences with its neighbors."

The funereal atmosphere of the ship was quickly left behind as Sonja appeared the following day, after arrival in New York, at the New York World's Fair. Then it was time to go back to Hollywood to begin a new film and start rehearsals for her next tour.

Having Leif with her seemed to give Sonja a sense of security—she felt more comfortable having a man around the house. She had much to do with Leif's decision to leave Gerd in Norway—"for just a little while until all the details are completed at Landoya." Thus, Gerd received the left-handed compliment from Sonja of being important enough to be trusted to oversee the completion of Sonja's home in Oslo. At the same time, she was being separated from her husband. Sonja seemed to be having everything her own way. That was no accident.

Belle Christy was well aware of the realities of this brother-sister relationship. "I felt sorry for Leif. He got the bad end sometimes, but I think he allowed it to happen to him. He absolutely idolized Sonja. Later on, when she tried to take his ranch away from him, he was terribly hurt.

From the day I first met him, anything she wanted he would jump to do. She was quite indulged by her family. Her mother, especially, was very possessive of her and Leif."

Sonja was in love again. This time it was Stewart Reburn, her new skating partner, a two-time member of the Canadian Olympic skating team. She was rebounding from Tyrone Power, who had replaced Jackie Dunn in her affections. Not long after she decided to "turn off" her romance with Jackie Dunn, he met with a tragic end, which absolutely devastated Sonja. After leaving the ice show, he traveled to Texas where, one day while hunting he picked up a rabbit and then rubbed his eye. An innocent gesture, which caused him to contact tularemia (rabbit fever). The disease caused his death shortly afterward. Sonja's feelings of personal guilt drove her into seclusion for several days.

Stewart Reburn was there, as handsome as Tyrone Power, and apparently was a comfort to Sonja. She tried to erase the memory of Dunn by denying that she had ever been his skating partner. When her *Hollywood Ice Revue* was premiered in 1939 at the Polar Palace prior to going back on the road, the star-studded, jam-packed audience got a good look at Sonja's latest paramour and skating partner. The announcer stunned the crowd with his announcement of the fifteenth event on the program:

> Ladies and gentlemen! For the first time in her life, in the next number, Sonja Henie will skate with a partner! Allow me to present her in a pair-skating tango with Mr. Stewart Reburn of Toronto, winner of countless Canadian championships.

During an interview following her opening night with Reburn, Sonja emphatically denied that she had ever had a skating partner (specifically omitting Jackie Dunn's name). She may have chosen to forget the past because of the hurt, but as always she was there in the wings protecting the present on opening night; checking out every detail of the show when she wasn't on the ice herself. She took notes, gave advice, and made suggestions. Her voice was filled with the strength of authority and the knowledge of what she was about. Sonja was never a fool when it came to staging an ice show although she, like any number of her Hollywood sisters, was not always so smart about the men in her life.

Stewart Reburn, new to Hollywood, was not new to Sonja. She had known him from Lake Placid in 1932 and Garmisch-Partenkirchen in 1936. Reburn was, at the time, skating with a Canadian girl, Louise Bertram. "I never forgot him," Sonja declared, "and when he was free and I wanted a partner, I chose him."

One Hollywood lady writer, upon being introduced to Reburn, promptly went to her typewriter and recorded her impressions:

> He has the clear complexion and clipped speech of a Richard

Greene. His hair is light brown, thick and slick; his eyes are gray and smiling; his mouth full, yet finely chiseled. When he speaks, he looks at you with engaging directness; when you speak, he listens with flattering attention. He is of medium height and finely proportioned.

Sonja found the chemistry satisfactory, and immediately all other men were out of her life.

Second Fiddle, Sonja's next film project at Twentieth Century-Fox once again paired her with Tyrone Power. Power, now committed to Anabella, became "just a friend," but deep in her heart, Sonja still loved him—would always love him. She never got over learning that Ty Power had used her, and—more to the point, for Sonja the deepest hurt of all—thrown her over for another woman.

Sidney Lanfield directed *Second Fiddle*. It was produced by Gene Markey for Darryl F. Zanuck with songs by Irving Berlin—although they were not the numbers Berlin is remembered for. Much to Sonja's chagrin, it was another black-and-white production, that glittered as much, if it glittered at all, from the stars supporting Sonja as from the ice upon which she skated. Besides Power, Sonja's co-stars included Rudy Vallee, Edna May Oliver, Mary Healy, Lyle Talbot, Alan Dinehart, Minna Gombell, Spencer Charters, Charles Lane, the Brian sisters, John Hiestand, George Chandler, Irving Bacon, Maurice Cass, and, last but certainly not least in Sonja's heart, Stewart Reburn. Sonja never missed an opportunity to flaunt her new lover and skating partner before her former boyfriend. Power was only amused by Sonja's endeavors to make him jealous.

The picture was a spoof on the much-publicized search for a female lead in *Gone with the Wind* and involved Sonja, cast as a Minnesota schoolteacher, being selected as candidate number 436 to star as Violet Jansen in a Hollywood epic to be entitled *Girl of the North*. A put-up romance between Sonja and Rudy Vallee (concocted by Ty Power as a Hollywood press agent) falls through, and the John Alden-ish press flack wins the charming miss from Minnesota and everyone lives happily ever after. The greatest revelation in the film was Hollywood's poking fun at itself during a time when that was not the most popular thing to do.

While making *Second Fiddle,* Sonja had another one of her run-of-the-film conflicts with Darryl F. Zanuck. One of her skating sequences involved a scene in which she did a big production number with Stewart Reburn. When she went to view the rushes, she discovered that the big production number featuring her and Reburn had been cut short. When the viewing was finished and the lights went up in the projection room Sonja asked, "Where is the rest of the skating number?"

Lanfield explained that "it was felt this number worked better if it wasn't so long."

"Bullshit!" She screamed, startling everyone within earshot. "Zanuck do this. Only Zanuck would have the nerve to meddle with Sonja's skating numbers. Get me Zanuck—right now. I tell him a ting or two!"

When advised that Zanuck was down at Santa Monica playing polo at the old Will Rogers ranch, she exploded with a vengeance. "You tell that sonofabitch Zanuck to get his ass off the polo ponies and meet me on the set. I show that sonofabitch he don't fool with Sonja!"

Much to the surprise of everyone involved, not only did Zanuck leave his polo game but he agreed in essence to Sonja's demands. Surprising, due to the fact that Zanuck hated Sonja as much as she did him, and other Fox stars were now making films that brought in even more money than Sonja's. Yet, in a peculiar twist of appreciation, Zanuck acceded to his star's ultimatum—replace the footage or find a new star for the picture.

The reviews of *Second Fiddle* seemed certain to give her a shove in the wrong direction. *Time* (July 17, 1939), commenting on Sonja's desire to become a serious dramatic actress, said:

> Judging from the acting Trudi Hovland (Sonja Henie) does before her glass with heavy dramatic lines like "Let me go, Aye tall yu," this ambition will take some realizing. But so have all Sonja Henie's ambitions. And as she herself has remarked: "Most always I win."

The magazine also let it be known that Sonja, contrary to studio publicity, was not popular in the Hollywood community.

> Although most of the stories told about her tightfistedness and her snobbishness are apocryphal, it is true that Sonja Henie has few of the traits that make for Hollywood popularity.

A celebrity in her own right, she was pictured as one who disdained other celebrities, was ostentatious and showy, and rented a house with a pool for fifteen hundred dollars a month that could be described only as "California-Moorish."

Although she was professing undying love for Stewart Reburn, during the year she managed to have a brief fling with fellow actor Lee Bowman. That flame flickered but died suddenly when Sonja suggested he buy a toupee to cover his receding hairline. Mr. Bowman's vanity was more important to him than Sonja's company.

Sonja was also involved in a very brief affair with a young man who earned fifty dollars a week as an extra at Fox. Zanuck intervened and Sonja promised not to see the boy again, on condition that Darryl not fire him. "He is a nice boy," Sonja told her boss. "It is not his fault he is in love with me. It is the irresistible lure of making love to a star that has him under my spell." Zanuck, enjoying Sonja's casual approach to the whole matter, roared with laughter. It was a rare occasion when Sonja made him laugh.

It was now estimated that Sonja's income was around two million dollars a year before expenses. Motion pictures contributed to that income, mainly by putting her before the public and providing free advertising for her ice show. By now even Sonja knew that she would never be a great actress, so she set out to become one of the wealthiest women in the world. If she could not be the first lady of the screen, then she would be the first lady of finances. Oddly enough, this athlete-turned-movie-star was more acceptable in society circles than in the film industry. Nonetheless, she used her Hollywood connections better than anyone before or since. Her ability to produce stars for charity affairs was unequaled, starting with the initial Marion Davies fund-raiser at the Polar Palace which had been her introduction to Hollywood.

On September 2, 1939, Sonja and Arthur Wirtz rewrote their contract. Under the terms of their new agreement, Sonja agreed to "render personal services consisting of exhibition and fancy ice skating at ice revues to be held at suitable arenas such as Los Angeles . . . Houston . . . St. Louis . . . St. Paul . . . Minneapolis . . . Toronto . . . Montreal . . . Boston . . . Chicago . . . Detroit . . . Cleveland . . . and New York City." The tour was to begin on November 1, 1939, and terminate on March 15, 1940. Sonja was required to perform "a minimum of three routines at each performance arranged and at such time as may be designated" by Arthur Wirtz. Sonja agreed not to perform on ice, except in films, for anyone else from October 1 through April 30. Sonja's personal compensation was to be $150,000 with escalation clauses based on attendance, and she was always sold out. Additionally, she was making a mint selling miniature skates, programs, photographs, and souvenirs, plus having the sole right to film her show for future motion picture exhibition.

It was pure irony that Sonja's next picture at Fox cast her in the role of the daughter of a Nobel Peace Prize winner on the run from the Nazi Gestapo. Her skating was minimized. She had begged Zanuck for more drama and less ice, and when she got it she discovered that skating brought her more plaudits than emoting. The picture was described as a "rather jaded spy comedy," in spite of a cast that included Ray Milland, Robert Cummings, and Fritz Feld. Irving Cummings directed and Edward Cronjager was in charge of photography. Sonja complained to Zanuck that the picture would have been more successful if "peoples could see me in color!"

Sonja's ice show played Chicago at Christmas with Harrison Thompson replacing Stewart Reburn, who was returning to Canada to enter the military service of his country. The romance with Sonja was over, and it

151

was becoming apparent that Sonja's shoe skates outlasted her skating partners, as well as her lovers. Bert Clark was still with the show (which was now enlarged to include sixteen full production numbers). It was without peer. No other ice show boasted such lavish costumes, numbers of skaters, or elaborate musical arrangements—plus Sonja Henie. Jack Pfeiffer handled the musical chores while Harry Lossee continually demonstrated his masterful choreography. Sonja made personal changes only when she had to or when she felt someone was either not doing his or her job—or upstaging her. She tolerated no skaters infringing on her spotlight. To look better on ice than Sonja was the kiss of death and, unless a skater already had a more lucrative offer from another show, it was best to keep a low profile.

On the day Sonja's new show opened at Madison Square Garden, playing to packed houses for the run of the show, an item appeared in *The New York Times* announcing the arrival in America of Miss Marit Henie, "14-year-old cousin of Miss Sonja Henie," to display her talent as a "figure skater." She received little recognition from Sonja and no help. One Henie from Oslo was enough.

Sonja had received "some papers" from an attorney in New York a few weeks previously, informing her that she was being sued by Dennis Scanlon for monies due him as her "former representative." She had ignored the notice. "I owe that sonofabitch nothing," she declared. "He is only trying to get publicity for himself."

During her current appearance at the Garden, she received a setback in her "unwanted" battle with Scanlon. Supreme Court Justice Louis A. Valente denied her motion to dismiss the lawsuit brought by Scanlon and set the case for trial. Sonja was bitter about the loss of her appeal. "I will fight that sonofabitch to my grave. Not one penny will I pay that lying scoundrel," she declared in an emotional outburst during a break in rehearsals at Madison Square Garden.

If she was unhappy with Scanlon, she was elated with the advance sales, which had totaled $175,000 before she ever set foot on the ice. Although that amount of money was a large sum for the time, Sonja was carrying a heavy weekly overhead, which included not only costumes, craftsmen, and equipment, but a troupe of one hundred. Sonja was featured in three ballet numbers: "Les Sylphides" to the music of Chopin, a picturesque Rumanian Mazurka, and a portion of the "Scheherazade Suite" by Rimsky-Korsakov. The ballet numbers were skated with Harrison Thompson whom New Yorkers remembered as the partner of Vivi-Anne Hultén, the former American skating champion.

Sonja and her group had arrived in New York after a record-shattering appearance in Cleveland, a trip well remembered by Belle Christy. "Any of those tours had pretty much the same elements of fun and mischief," she recalls. "Of course, our special train had a big sign on the rear end that said SONJA HENIE SPECIAL. We left Cleveland and partied all night on the train. You should have seen some of those drunks coming in after the show. We had one little guy who was very funny. He boarded the train with two gals, skates tossed over their shoulders, feeling no pain, and asked, 'Is this the train to Azusa?' We all broke up. We were a real conglomeration: all nationalities, vegetarians, nonalcoholics, alcoholics, nonsmokers, chain-smokers—but a fun loving group."

The trip was not unlike any other night after the show closed and the party was going strong before all the equipment was aboard the train. Belle was in the middle of that party even though currently somewhat estranged from Sonja, and that needs to be explained. "We had a long breakup in our friendship at one point, Sonja and I," Belle explains. "Before I was married I had roommates—a girl and her boyfriend. The three of us shared a very small apartment and I can distinctly remember the day they got married we were getting ready for the wedding and arguing over whose turn it was in the bathroom when the phone rang. I said, 'Alyce, if that's Sonja, I'm not here.'

"Sonja used to call me every day of her life when she wasn't working. I mean she never missed a day. She really didn't have anything to say, just wanted to chat and it was the same old nothingness every day. You couldn't hang up on Sonja, and she could talk for hours. Sometimes the receiver made my ear ache. So occasionally I'd tell Alyce Goering, when the phone rang, 'If that's Sonja, tell her I'm not here.'

"It was as if Sonja felt she possessed me and I, after all, wanted to live my own life, too. So I would make up stories as excuses. I'd have Alyce say I had a date or something."

One day Sonja phoned and Belle answered the ring. Sonja didn't wait for any excuses. She was furious and pounced on Belle with the ferocity of a bird of prey on a ground squirrel. "Listen, Bay-ul, I know that when I call you, you say you're not there. I know that." Slam! She hung up the receiver before Belle could say a word.

"I didn't try to explain, really," Belle laughs about the incident today. "It was really a relief not to be at her beck and call twenty-four hours a day, but it bothered me that she was so angry and I wondered what caused her to explode the way she did."

Belle began to think about it and came to the conclusion that it could only have been her roommate who told Sonja that she had been avoiding her calls. Sonja didn't limit her venom to one phone call. She called a number of times and spouted off and then hung up before Belle could respond. One day she didn't hang up but asked, "Well, what have you got to say for yourself Bay-ul?"

Belle blurted out the only thing that was on her mind. "Alyce Goering is a snake!" she yelled into the phone. Sonja slammed the receiver down in her ear. "It's funny now. But it wasn't funny then. And that's not the end of the story. When Sonja and I had been in Paris, she had bought dozens of satin sheets with fabulous satin pillowcases to match. She loved sleeping on satin. On the tours, she hated the sheets that were put on her bed on the train. I might have been a lousy skater, but I was a top-notch seamstress. Stitching was right down my alley, and before this telephone business had occurred I began sewing sheets for Sonja—as a surprise gift. I bought some peach satin material to make pillowcases and sheets with matching satin ribbons to attach to the pillowcases, all hand-hemmed. They were beautiful, but when the breakup came I was sitting there with all that lovely handiwork wondering what to do.

"I was still on the tour, but Sonja wasn't speaking to me. Very cold and very aloof. We definitely were not close secret-sharing girl friends as we had been previously. Although I didn't feel like putting in all those hours for Sonja and her not speaking to me, I decided to go ahead as planned. I finished the sheets and when we boarded the train I had the porter show me where her compartment was and went in and made up her bed. I then joined the others in the club car where a party was already well under way. I was facing the entrance of the car and looked up just in time to see Sonja storming through the door, like someone from the Gestapo. She marched right up to me, very militaristically, directly and positively. When she got right in front of me she crisply said, 'Thank you for the sheets!' Never batted an eyelash. Just turned around and stalked out. I was about to cry and nobody knew what was going on. That was Sonja's way of making up. The fight was over and all was forgiven. I was crying out of happiness."

Sonja's possessiveness overwhelmed those who "belonged to her," whether it be family or friend. In her own mind, Belle was her property as much as Leif, her mother, or her ice skates. She had the same problem with the men in her life. She tried, but couldn't own any of them.

14

S ONJA had a spy system within the confines of her show troupe, but its most eagle-eyed member was her mother. Liz Pfeiffer used to sit with Selma when she was not skating in the show. "I was always amazed that she could catnap and never miss a beat of the show. She would doze off and applaud in her sleep. She did it all by instinct. Her eyes would open up for a couple of seconds and then she'd go right back to sleep. If there was something amiss in Sonja's performance, she would say under her breath, using Norwegian, 'Very *fersichte,* Sonja. Be careful darling.'"

If Selma saw something she didn't like, a skater trying to get more than his or her share of the skating pie, she met Sonja backstage after the finale and told her that so and so "is acting like a star." Depending on Sonja's mood at the time, that skater might be warned or dismissed.

Sonja loved gossip of any kind and made it a point to invite members of the chorus to dinner after the show so she could hear all the juicy items they either knew for fact or invented for her enjoyment. When they were on tour, she often tried to prevail upon Belle Christy to help her plan the events following the show.

"She used to call me in at every intermission when we were on the road and ask, 'Who do we have tonight to go out with?'" says Belle. I never would suggest anybody. She would ask, 'How about this one?' I'd say, 'That's fine, Sonja. Whatever you think.' I would always agree with her. She would then pick out whomever from the show she wanted along to amuse her that night. She always invited me, but I never felt it was my place to select her company. I found myself becoming more and more alienated from the rest of the kids in the show. I wasn't one of them anymore. Before Sonja took me under her wing, I was part of the crowd and used to go out with them and drink and have fun. Being so involved with Sonja came about inadvertently."

Belle had the same problem with living accommodations on the road. Sonja wanted her to stay at the same hotel she lived in. "I finally had to tell her, 'Sonja, I would like to stay with the rest of the gang at our next stop.' She couldn't understand why I'd prefer to be with the other skaters when I could be with the star. I argued that I never saw her during the daytime until after she woke up in the afternoon, so there was no need for me to stay at the same hotel she lived in. Even after she got up, she had to see her masseuse, her hairdresser, and all the people who take care of a star.

"'Go ahead and stay with the chorus at the next stop,' she would say, and I did. But then it was back to the same old routine of being with Sonja again at the Waldorf-Astoria and all those places. She knew I couldn't afford the Waldorf so she only had me pay what I would have paid at another hotel and she made up the difference."

Belle was dating Bob Christy and it was beginning to be a serious relationship. Sonja ignored Bob. Because Leif had been with them in Norway and was now around all the time since he moved to California, he spent a lot of time in the company of Belle, and some people assumed there was something going on between the two of them. "Leif and I were the best of buddies," states Belle. "It worked out great because he was married and I was engaged and we were ideal company for one another, without any strings. Just fun.

"One didn't tell Sonja one was engaged and going to get married. She wasn't the least bit interested in anything if it didn't involve her personally. When we were in Oslo Bob had heard that Sonja's handsome brother was with us, so a little jealousy popped up. He sent me a little toy icebox and on the inside there was a fortune cookie that read: 'Two proposals soon to come. The darker one loves you best.'

"In any event—and I'm not sure if Sonja was responsible for this or not—when we were at one of the dinners Arthur Wirtz used to host in Chicago, he had this entertainer who made up lines about people and put them to music. He would go around to the people in the show and dig up dirt, and then the night of the dinner party he was armed to the teeth with information on everyone. On this one night he sang about me and Leif, a one-liner that was a zinger. 'Leif came all the way from Norway just to see if he could ring a Belle.' I nearly died. Bob was there and right away our eyes met. I wondered if he believed anything was happening. I could see Sonja's mischievous grin.

"The next night while Sonja was standing in the wings talking to the guys who supported her in a doll house that carried her out onto the ice for a number—and Bob was one of those six tallest in the chorus—she was talking to everyone except Bob. Absolutely ignored him. The first time she ever acknowledged his existence, she looked him squarely in the eye and said, 'You sent Bay-ul an icebox in Norway.' That was it, but she made her point. I hadn't shared the meaning of the gift in Norway and I think that hurt her."

Sonja had a penchant for hats, any kind of hat. While she and Belle were in Paris, she took Belle on a shopping spree and loaded up on hats. When they got back to the hotel she put Belle to work removing the New

York labels from her old hats and inserting them in the new French ones. That way she didn't have to pay duty on them. Her generous side came to the fore when she purchased a very expensive hat that Belle had admired. "I didn't change my label," Belle remembers with a laugh. "I was too damned proud of it."

Sonja's money was always a good topic of conversation, both in skating circles and in Hollywood. If she skimped to keep from paying taxes and import duty, she invested whatever she managed to hold back. Her money was as juicy an item for columnists as her latest romance. Sonja, in an attempt to squelch rumors that she did not give to charities or that she was "greedy about money" gave an exclusive interview to Kay Proctor of *Movie Mirror* magazine. In speaking with her, Sonja convinced the lady she was indeed a generous star, prompting the writer to deduce that, "I'll bet my bottom dollar you can count on one hand the times you have read anything about how much she *gives away!* And those figures, if they were available, would be pretty extraordinary, too." Kay Proctor was never shown any figures. She took Sonja's word for the facts.

Sonja's stock answer, when the subject of charitable contributions came up, was "I would fire anyone who told of my personal donations to charity. It is personal and I don't want anyone to know. I donate anonymously."

One so-called "anonymous" incident was related by Miss Henie to *Movie Mirror*. She supposedly gave a Fox publicity representative a gold watch for not revealing that she had treated three hundred orphans to one of her shows in Los Angeles.

Sonja topped off the story with an explanation of her feelings about *her* money and how she used it:

> The real fun I've had from it has come from the little things I have been able to do for others with it. I am happy when I can give somebody something *whenever* I want to, without having to think if I can afford it, and to give them things they might never have had otherwise. Foolish things, sometimes, judged by some standards, but things they wanted with their hearts rather than their heads.

There can be no doubt that Sonja was generous with gifts, but she gave them only to those who had something to offer in return. Skaters in the chorus who made her show glitter were often the recipients of her unexpected generosity, as were choreographers, directors (although less often), musicians, and makeup people. She once gave a platinum bracelet she was wearing to a studio wardrobe lady simply because the woman admired it.

157

Stories could get twisted. As already mentioned, upon the completion of one film Sonja gave cashmere sweaters to the chorus. The story out of Twentieth Century-Fox was that during production the skaters got cold and she insisted on buying them all sweaters so they could stay warm. The gift was the same, but the implications of the Fox story suggested a compassion that didn't exist in Sonja's personality.

One of the biggest farces ever perpetrated in the name of Sonja Henie had to do with the Sonja Henie Junior Olympic Club. It had a membership that grew to fifteen thousand, and originally, Sonja paid the postage for mailings, but when she found it was costing ten thousand dollars a year to maintain the club, she tried to get the studio to foot the bill. When they didn't, she abandoned the project. "It has served its purpose," she sighed. Sonja could have deducted from her taxable income through charitable gifts and publicity promotions many thousands of dollars that otherwise went to the government for income taxes, but she didn't. The government took. Charities politely asked. It was no contest.

Sonja never stinted on anything that involved her ice shows. After visiting South America or Hawaii, she might come back with ideas for the show that would cost hundreds of thousands of dollars to stage. She never batted an eyelash about spending that kind of money to improve the show, to buy costumes, or to recruit talent.

Stewart Reburn left the show to wear a military uniform. Before the United States became involved in World War II, Canada, as part of the British Empire, was. Reburn went home and enlisted in the Royal Canadian Air Force. Harrison Thompson, handsome in the Tyrone Power image, remained with the show as one of Sonja's skating partners. Another addition was Michael Mikeler, who had known Sonja since she was a child in Europe.

"Sonja came to Vienna where I lived when she was maybe ten or eleven years old," recalls Mikeler. "Even then she was fantastic; what we called a *wunderkind*, or wonder child. The European skating coterie was like a small village. Everybody knew everybody else and so I followed Sonja's career with a much greater intensity than anyone ever would in America. I had seen her perform the Dying Swan at the Palais des Sports in Paris and we saw each other again in 1936 at the Winter Olympics. We often danced together on skates when there was no competition and I do believe that she was a born dancer. If there had been no ice skates, Sonja would have rivaled Ginger Rogers or any of the other great American musical dancers."

Michael Mikeler's first trip to New York in 1938 had been less than auspicious. Because of Sonja's success in pictures, someone had suggested bringing Belita, an English figure skater, to America and turning her into a movie star. Mikeler was asked to come over and appear in films with Belita. Although he would later appear in a picture with her, he did not on that first occasion because the deal fell through. Instead, he and Belita skated together at the Paramount Theater in New York. The Paramount was part of the Fanchon and Marco circuit, famous from the old days of vaudeville and continuing to book acts into their chain of theaters in support of the big bands (the current craze), which played between movies. The theater put in a small ice rink, and the skaters made do.

"Sonja saw me at the Paramount," says Mikeler, "and remembered. Meanwhile, I returned to London and did not come back to the United States for another year. I was living in Hollywood when Sonja needed a new skating partner, and she offered me a job, and I accepted. We had little time to rehearse together because she was getting ready to leave for New York where she was involved in a lawsuit with Dennis Scanlon and had to make an appearance. She arranged for me to go over to Twentieth Century-Fox where I watched her films every night to learn her routines so I could go on the road with her that winter.

"When Sonja returned to Hollywood we had four or five days to practice the tango duet and we did quite well with it."

Michael ran into a problem on the road, which reached its culmination in Detroit. "We had encores and Sonja wasn't one who just came out, took a bow, and skated off the ice. Never. She would do an entire number as an encore and of course the public knew they were getting something extra and cheered her on. The problem between Sonja and myself hovered about the fact that we were both blonds. The show was playing Detroit and Sonja invited me to come along afterward to a party someone was hosting for her. During the evening she suggested that I do something with my hair.

"'What do you mean?' I asked. I didn't understand. No one had ever complained about my hair before.

"'I mean, I prefer to skate with brunettes,' Sonja said. 'It makes for better contrast—don't you think so?' I hadn't thought about it, but for Sonja I would try. The following morning I went to see the hairdressers at the Bok Cadillac Hotel where we were quartered and had them fool around with the color of my hair. It was darkened, but only a little bit. Sonja was not pleased with the new color and ordered someone to find a wig for me to wear in the show.

"Because of the tango number, the public was getting to recognize who I was and when I skated out on the ice with that hideously out-of-place wig plopped on top of my hair, nobody knew who I was and people voiced their objections to what they thought was Sonja's 'new skating partner.' The following night Sonja relented and I was back to being my normal self. We continued to receive standing ovations for our numbers together and Sonja never again mentioned hair dye."

Michael Mikeler cleared up one point about Sonja's career. Although

159

the tango number was danced by Sonja with numerous partners over the years and became known as "Sonja's Tango," it was not her original idea. "The tango," Mikeler explained, "belonged to Stewart Reburn. He brought it with him. It was nothing that had ever been performed in the Olympics by Sonja or anyone else. It was strictly a Reburn innovation."

Having had tremendous success as Sonja's partner, Mikeler expected to be signed for the following year. After the tour season, he returned to Hollywood where he was in great demand as a teacher at the Pan Pacific ice rink. His reputation had preceded him from Europe, and he was not short of money, but the combination of free-lancing and being an alien wasn't a good one. One could stay only so long in the United States without a contract for work.

The new situation created problems for Mikeler. "It was difficult for me to work. I was not an American citizen. If I went to Mexico and wanted to come back into California, I couldn't do that. The people who engaged me as a teacher wanted me to go to Mexico and come back in as a resident alien, which would certainly be easier than going back to Europe. The government had some crazy regulations that differentiated between contract labor and artistic talents. People like Greta Garbo, for instance, had to get out of the country every six months and then reenter the States on a special visa."

Mikeler expected that Sonja would get in touch with him and offer a contract for the next season. She did not. Instead, she sent her lawyer to see him with some papers to sign. What Sonja did, probably on the advice of her attorney, was take advantage of Mikeler's noncitizen status by putting pressure on him to sign an agreement which, in effect, stipulated that he would not insist on being resigned for the show. Obviously, there was a loophole in the regulations covering aliens that gave him that right. He didn't know the law and was therefore coerced into the signing.

Michael met Sonja's attorney at the Brown Derby on Wilshire Boulevard. "He promised if I would sign there would be a little present for me," reports Mikeler. "I had the feeling I was being strong-armed, but in my position I didn't think I had a choice. I later found out what it was all about. If I went into the military service (which I had expressed an intention to do if I was not re-signed, rather than return to my native Austria), I would have the right to demand my job back after the war. That was the law; a law that was never explained to me, otherwise I would never have agreed to sever my service agreement with Sonja. What I did was relinquish my rights under the War Labor Act."

In Europe Mikeler had known and had been a friend of Sonja's father. "He was so different from the rest. Everybody loved him. I remember how he used to gamble every night when Sonja was skating in the amateur ranks," says Mikeler. "He used to come out on the rink and say, 'Sonja thinks that the ice is too soft.' And Sonja thinks this, and Sonja thinks that. What he really meant was *Wilhelm Henie* thinks these things. He was a marvelous promoter, with his turned-up nose, looking facially so much like Sonja. She was certainly her father's daughter. I had the impression that Sonja Henie would have succeeded at anything she tried in life. She was that kind of person. People didn't count as much as objectives. She had a tremendous drive, whether it would be flying an airplane or swimming or whatever."

Mikeler remembered, as did his wife, Gloria (also a skater in the show), Selma Henie's being Sonja's number-one spy and watchdog. Gloria sometimes would sit with Selma when she was not skating. "Talk about skating mothers, like stage mothers, Mrs. Henie was probably the best one of them all. She would sit up there rinkside like a sphinx, and she knew everything that was going on. She never missed a moment, but you couldn't tell it by looking at her facial expressions. She didn't show any emotion at all. I remember once she said to me, 'Remember, if you skate with Sonja don't smile too much. It's Sonja's show!'"

The Henies were very fond of Michael and Gloria Mikeler. Gloria never worried that Sonja might have designs on her husband because the skating star was not known to be interested in married men.

Michael Mikeler never knew why Sonja rejected him for a second season, and years later, when she needed his advice and counsel, she never once mentioned the shabby treatment she had bestowed upon him. Mikeler had difficulty dealing with Sonja's penchant for tossing people aside or putting them on standby until she needed them again, but he was willing to help her nonetheless.

As for the war, Sonja had the best of all worlds. If the Allies won, she would be the same star she was. If Hitler and his cronies succeeded, she might be an even bigger star. She was in the unique position of being adored by both sides. That, many feel, was the reason she found so little fault with Germany's Nazi leader. She insisted that Hitler wanted peace as much as anybody else.

Her sister-in-law, Gerd, felt different. She was still holding down the fort in Oslo, although Leif had sold the fur business and made a permanent move to Hollywood. By February 1940, Gerd knew that a German invasion of Norway was in the wind—no matter how many times Sonja told her not to worry. She wrote to Sonja and warned her that unless she wanted to lose everything she had, then steps must be taken to get the family art—old masters worth a fortune—out of Europe, as well as other personal and expensive possessions. "An invasion is inevitable," she assured Sonja.

Not one to like the loss of anything, Sonja okayed the shipping of dozens of crates of Henie valuables to America. Gerd followed shortly thereafter, and in April the Nazis invaded Norway.

Sonja was in Honolulu at the time, stirring up some trouble of her own.

After returning to Hollywood from an extensive ice tour, she was scheduled to go into production for her next film, *Sun Valley Serenade.* Exhausted from the long skating season, she announced to Leif and Selma that they were leaving for Hawaii—immediately. "I really need the rest and sunshine," she declared.

Leif was surprised to discover that Dan Topping was also aboard the S.S. *Lurline.* Topping, the New York sportsman, heir to millions on both sides of his family, had hosted a party for Sonja when the show was playing Madison Square Garden and had been an occasional dinner guest with the family. Leif had no idea, nor did his mother, that Sonja was having an affair with Topping.

In Honolulu the Henie party checked into the Royal Hawaiian Hotel on the beach at Waikiki. Topping rented a large house elsewhere on the island of Hawaii. It soon became obvious that Sonja had not come to the islands to rest, but to party. Dan Topping hosted several lavish parties for Sonja. On one particular evening Dan picked Sonja up early and took her to his home. Leif and his mother arrived later. They were shown into the living room, which had been converted into a ballroom for the party. A good-sized Hawaiian orchestra was playing island music. Sonja and Dan were nowhere in sight. Leif asked the bandleader where he might find the host and his sister. The leader, violin still tucked beneath his chin, pointed toward a door with his bow. Selma and Leif, opened the door, expecting a library or cocktail bar. Instead, they found Dan and Sonja, nude on a bed, in the throes of lovemaking. Leif escorted his furious mother from the room and closed the door behind them.

The entire band looked knowingly at them, and a few thinly veiled sniggers humiliated Selma further. This was more than she could handle, especially since her daughter and Dan had been so indiscreet that even the musicians knew what was going on.

Sonja refused to discuss her actions and suggested pointedly to her mother that if she was so concerned with proper decorum she should know that the basic elements of etiquette required one to knock before entering a room with the door closed. She hardly spoke to either her mother or Leif on the trip back to Los Angeles, and Topping avoided Selma.

Before reporting to the studio to begin *Sun Valley Serenade,* Sonja called a family meeting and announced that she and Topping would be married during the summer. Leif felt some relief. Sonja would have another man to take over where her father had left off. Perhaps now Leif could have a life of his own. Selma Henie's feelings were mixed. Dan Topping had been married twice before. His most recent wife had been actress Arline Judge, and the ink was hardly dry on their divorce papers. Certainly he couldn't take marriage very seriously if he was remarrying after such a short time. Topping also had a son, Dan Junior, by Miss Judge. Selma didn't consider him good husband material.

Topping, like Sonja, was an athlete. In college he had played baseball, golf, football, and ice hockey. He was never professional sports material, but he liked sports and throughout his life was involved in professional sports activities. At the time he became engaged to Sonja, he was the principal owner of the old Brooklyn Dodgers football team of the original National Football League. He was generally recognized as one of the top amateur golfers in the country as well as a playboy and, on paper anyway, extremely wealthy.

Playboy he was. Wealthy he wasn't. He came from wealth. He was the grandson of millionaires. One grandfather, John A. Topping, made a fortune in steel and was at one time president of Republic Steel Company. His mother's father was Daniel G. Reid, the tinplate king at the turn of the century. Seemingly he was wealthy. There was one little catch. His mother controlled the family fortunes, and he received a monthly check from a trust set up for him at birth.

None of that mattered to Sonja. She was once again "madly in love" and that was that. The Toppings were in the New York Social Register, and in Sonja's opinion that was better than being a member of the Academy of Motion Picture Arts and Sciences.

The Topping money meant nothing to Selma Henie either. The Henies had always had money. What bothered her was that Dan Topping seemed to be a playboy who was more interested in being married to a movie star than in making her little girl happy. Selma let Sonja know that she was not pleased with her choice of a husband.

"You will love him, just as I do, when you get to know him, Mother. He's so much fun, and he *does* love me."

There were problems enough in Sonja's life at this time. She had developed a serious throat ailment while in Hawaii and on the voyage back, the ship's doctor had to perform emergency surgery to open an abcess. The usual problems with Zanuck, which always arose prior to the beginning of a film, had to be dealt with. The importance to her personally of Hitler's invasion of Norway was beginning to hit home, and finally, she and Leif almost became the victims of a million-dollar fur heist.

When Leif sold the fur business he kept twenty thousand Norwegian silver fox fur skins, which he brought to America with him. Leif explains what happened:

> One day a man by the name of Miller telephoned me at the house Sonja was renting from Lana Turner and said he had heard of my fox skins and might be interested in buying them. I invited

him over to the house to look at them and he promised to get back to me. Two days later he called again and asked if he could pick up the furs. He wanted to examine them more closely and suggested that if they proved to be satisfactory he might even buy them all. I told him he could take all he wanted provided he brought a cashier's check to cover their value. That ended my dealings with Mr. Miller.

That very same week there were several large fur robberies in Beverly Hills and the Wilshire district of Los Angeles. A half-dozen furriers were involved. One morning, a few weeks later, I opened the morning paper and nearly fell off my chair; there, on the front page, was a large picture of my so-called customer, Mr. Miller, described as a major fur thief. He would enter stores with helpers carrying large laundry bags, lock the doors, have all the people lie down and tie them up, while his assistants stuffed furs in the bags.

He was arrested in New York where he took the furs to sell them. He was caught when the police discovered the furs in his possession had stamps on the back of the skins which matched the furs that had been stolen in California.

It was the first of a string of robberies and attempted robberies of homes, hotels, and apartments occupied by Sonja. The reputation she had acquired as a collector of jewelry, art, furs, and money fell upon the ears of the wrong, as well as the right, people. The trappings of fame and fortune acted like a magnet.

15

S ONJA made some positive decisions in 1940, one of them being the purchase of a lovely home at 243 Delfern Drive in Holmby Hills, just beyond the Beverly Hills city limits. It had previously been owned by director Norman Taurog and consisted of a large house on five acres of gently rolling hills, with an Olympic-size swimming pool, and tennis court. She purchased the house prior to her marriage to Dan Topping because, as she explained to him, "I like to keep things straight. What is mine is mine."

She arrived in Chicago to meet with Arthur Wirtz and renegotiate her contract with him. It was another one-year deal with new clauses and new escalations for Sonja. Wirtz tried to have her sign a long-term contract, but she refused. "Who knows what will happen in the future?" she reasoned.

There were subtle changes in her new contract. Wirtz agreed to "designate" Sonja as the leading star in a show to be known as *Sonja Henie with Her Hollywood Ice Revue* to be held in "suitable arenas and stadiums properly equipped with an ice surface suitable for staging a show of this nature, throughout the United States and Canada as may be determined by Arthur Wirtz." Specific cities were eliminated from the language because Sonja was also taking a show of her own on the road whenever time allowed, which in no way conflicted with the Wirtz schedule. Sonja was obligated to appear in approximately sixty performances with the usual three-number minimum on her part. Although it was to be an exclusive contract, Wirtz gave Sonja great latitude as to "prior commitments." Sonja would receive 20 percent of the gross receipts from ticket sales on the first $600,000 and 30 percent on income in excess of $600,000.

Thanks to Arthur Wirtz, Sonja began what was to become a large portfolio of stocks, bonds, and real estate investments, including Chicago apartment buildings, an interest in the Walgreen Drugstore chain, and in a liquor firm.

Leif, through the merchandising of Sonja Henie items, was also adding measurably to Sonja's annual income. For instance, there were the miniature silver skates that could be worn as a pin or brooch. Leif got the idea for selling them to the public when some gold ones he made for Sonja became very popular and everyone in the chorus began to ask where she got them. The silver skates alone accounted for nearly $300,000 in revenue—revenue she did not share with Wirtz. She did, however, split part of the profits from other promotional items with him. Eventually, greed over these items would bring the Wirtz-Henie dynasty of skating down, and Sonja would be the big loser.

Sonja was so pleased with Leif's ingenuity with the tiny skates that she finally kept her promise and installed him as vice-president and treasurer of her company. As an officer in the company, Leif became Sonja's willing servant. She disrupted his family life by insisting that he be on the road with her, and she always found excuses to have him "doing things" for her. If Gerd objected to the time Leif spent with his sister, she didn't do it very loudly, and Sonja, of course, couldn't have cared less what Gerd thought.

None of that mattered as the group set out for Chicago, for the Fourth of July wedding date that Sonja and Dan had selected.

Before the wedding, Sonja took the time to form a new corporation with Arthur Wirtz, to be known as Sonart Productions, whose initial function would be to stage an elaborate ice revue in New York the following winter. Sonja would be coproducer but would not appear in the show herself. It was another of those lucrative ventures that Arthur Wirtz, like a good magician, seemed to have up his sleeve.

Sonja and Dan exchanged their vows in the living room of Arthur and Virginia Wirtz's elegant Lakeshore Drive apartment in Chicago. The Reverend Josua Oden, pastor of the Irving Park Lutheran Church, performed the ceremony before a very small gathering: Selma Henie, Leif and Gerd, and John (Shipwreck) Kelly, a former football star and a current employee of Topping on the Brooklyn Dodgers football club. Fewer than half a dozen others were in the room when they said their "I do's."

Topping immediately borrowed $100,000 from his new bride, which he claimed to need to bolster his football club. The money wasn't repaid until the two were divorced five years later.

Sonja's desire to have a husband and companion was frustrated from the beginning of her marriage to Topping. A playboy heir all his life, he had no intention of changing his habits to please his wife. He had been a come-and-go husband for Arline Judge, and so he was for Sonja. Still she was determined to make her marriage work, even if the effort was one-sided. When Sonja was in love, it was always madly.

Dan's favorite sport was golf, and he played daily. Many times Sonja, who waited for no one, found herself at home waiting for her errant husband to return from the links to escort her to a party. She would be all dressed up for the evening while, as often as not, Dan would still be at the country club playing cards and drinking with his sports buddies.

166

When he finally arrived home, usually in a less-than-sober state, a battle royal followed. Selma discreetly stayed in her own room, but Sonja could be heard throughout the house as she dug into her sailor's vocabulary to let her husband know what she thought of him. Fortunately, the big house on Delfern was large enough for the two of them to retreat in opposite directions, until Sonja cooled off. Topping usually shrugged his shoulders and ignored his wife's complaints. "I should have known," Sonja screamed at him. "Three wives in seven years!" Before he was through, Dan Topping would make the march down the aisle three more times.

Sonja certainly couldn't look to Arline Judge for any advice. Arline despised Sonja. When their son went to visit his father on weekends, she advised him to "let Sonja have it in the face with her ice skates!"

Sonja busied herself with the two major projects that would be facing her for the next eight or nine months. One was the enormous task of putting together an ice show that would be on the road again in November, and the other was her next film, *Sun Valley Serenade.* Sonja's contract at Fox had been altered by mutual agreement, and she was now working less on films and more on the ice. No Sonja Henie films came out in 1940. *Everything Happens at Night* was released in 1939 and *Sun Valley Serenade* would not be seen in theaters until late spring of 1941.

Once again Sonja found herself filming during the daytime and rehearsing for the road at night. How she kept up the torrid pace she set for herself, nobody could say. Her unhappy marriage seemed to be in limbo. The trip to Honolulu had given her new ideas for the show. Having become exceedingly interested in hula dances, Sonja had gone to see Hilo Hattie dance and had admired her very much. She even convinced the Hawaiian chanteuse to give her lessons while she was there. When it came time to prepare for the new season, she brought Hilo Hattie to Hollywood, taking lessons from her at her home on Delfern and practicing the hula motions by her swimming pool. She even put together a Hawaiian orchestra and used an authentic Hawaiian singer to accompany her when she performed the big hula production numbers. She did three Hawaiian numbers on ice: "Hilo Hattie Does the Hilo Hop," "Sweet Leilani," and "Lovely Hula Hands."

Her old nemesis Dennis Scanlon popped up again, and Sonja found herself in a New York courtroom on October 31, 1940. The trial began before supreme Court Justice Aron Steuer and a jury in the $92,000 suit against the star. Since there was no written agreement, the jury was being asked whether it believed the famous movie star or the man who claimed that he was being victimized by an ungrateful protégé, who had discarded him once he had helped her on the road to fame.

Sonja did not testify the first day of the trial, but she sat passively in the courtroom, taking notes and smiling demurely at the jury, with an occasional scowl aimed in Scanlon's direction. At the same time Sonja was battling in court, Tyrone Power's name was emblazoned across the marquee of the Roxy Theatre with his co-star Linda Darnell, in *The Mark of Zorro*—and doing SRO business.

On November 4, Sonja took the stand for the first time in the trial. She was questioned by her own attorney, Lowell Wadmond. She admitted that Scanlon had taken her to one film company executive who had described her as "too short for motion pictures. He said my face was too round and that I wouldn't photograph well." One bit of damaging evidence against Sonja was the introduction of her pretrial deposition in which she had admitted that "I did not repay Mr. Scanlon for the tickets he purchased," for herself, her mother, and father. Sonja was not a good witness. She didn't care for all the courtroom bickering. She felt she was right and Scanlon was wrong, so it didn't matter who paid their transportation to America. Everybody in the courtroom could see Sonja's annoyance with the proceedings, and she played right into the hands of Scanlon's attorney. The jury couldn't possibly miss the implications. Sonja, in their minds, must have appeared as Scanlon portrayed her—a wealthy movie star trying to cheat a poor working man.

The jury's sealed verdict was opened before Judge Steuer on November 11. The trial had lasted six days, and the jury had deliberated six hours. The verdict was not unanimous. Two jurors voted to dismiss the suit. Ten jurors, which is allowed in New York in a civil action, voted to give Scanlon the $67,614 he sought, but scaled down the interest from $22,000 to $9,499. It was a clear victory for Scanlon and a bitter loss for Sonja.

Outside the courtroom Scanlon said, "Miss Henie is a wonderful skater and a wonderful person. I am glad the world saw my foresight and made her a star." Sonja chose not to be in the courtroom when the verdict was handed down, but her lawyer notified the assembled press that there would be an immediate appeal. Judge Steuer denied a motion to set the verdict aside due to a "reversible error" in the summation by Lloyd Thanhouse, Mr. Scanlon's attorney.

Scanlon departed immediately for Chicago to "work on perfecting" the iron lung he had invented, which was being used several hours a day to keep famous polio patient Fred Snite, Jr., alive.

Sonja's *Hollywood Ice Revue* of 1941 was more resplendent than ever and played to packed houses every performance.

The battles between Sonja and Dan Topping were a hot item of gossip on the show tour. In Hollywood, Louella Parsons assured everyone that Sonja and Dan were the ideal couple and their marriage was one of those that was "sure to endure." With a marriage in name only and a film career that was nowhere near what it had promised to be at the outset Sonja was in a bitchy and temperamental mood.

She jumped into the production of *Sun Valley Serenade*, torn by feel-

168

(right) Leif and Sonja Henie in Oslo as children. Leif was approximately seven and Sonja two years old. *(Leif and Sally Henie)*

(left) Sonja, the child champion of Norway, at eleven years old. *(Dorothy Stevens)*

(left) Wilhelm Henie making music for Sonja, 1914. *(Dorothy Stevens)*

(right) Wilhelm escorts his daughter to the ice rink in Oslo where she learned to skate. *(Leif and Sally Henie)*

(left) Sonja as a teenager in Oslo. *(Dorothy Stevens)*

(below) The Henie family home where Sonja and Leif spent their childhood weekends and summers. *(Leif and Sally Henie)*

Adolf Hitler, surrounded by high Nazi officials, greets Sonja Henie at the 1936 Olympics. Sonja, at an earlier exhibition in Berlin, had given the Nazi salute. She dined with Hitler at the Berchtesgaden and accepted an autographed portrait of the Führer. *(Dorothy Stevens)*

(left) Hitler greets Sonja at a skating exhibition in Berlin. *(H. Hoffmann and Dorothy Stevens)*

(below) Crowds line up at the Berliner Sports Palast to purchase tickets for a Sonia Henie ice show. *(Pips Plenik and Dorothy Stevens)*

Sonja—
esctasy on ice.

(Max Wagner and Dorothy Steve

Sonja with her mother and father before their arrival in Hollywood in 1935. *(Dorothy Stevens)*

(above) Sonja and Wilhelm Henie, 1935. *(Dorothy Stevens)*

(below) Arthur Wirtz, Sonja's business partner and mentor for most of her professional skating life. His Chicago Stadium is pictured in the background, with cut-outs of Sonja Henie and other skaters who performed there. *(Ralph Walters and Leif and Sally Henie)*

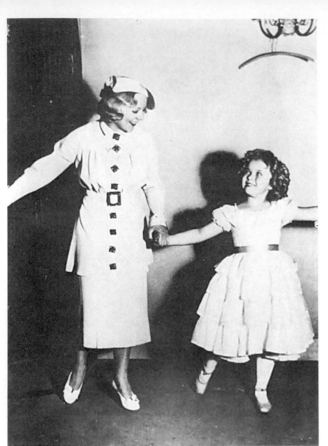

(left) Sonja Henie and Shirley Temple, two of Twentieth Century-Fox's biggest stars during the thirties, cutting up together. *(Leif and Sally Henie)*

(below) Sonja and Tyrone Power dining out together at the height of their romance. *(Leif and Sally Henie)*

Sonja with her mother, Selma, during the star's early years in Hollywood. *(Leif and Sally Henie)*

(above) Don Ameche doesn't appear to be pleased by the conversation between Sonja Henie and Adolphe Menjou in a scene from *One In a Million* (1937). It was Sonja's first picture. *(Twentieth Century-Fox)*

(below) Sonja watches in anticipation of a fight between suitors Caesar Romero and Richard Greene in *My Lucky Star* (1938). *(Larry Edmunds, Twentieth Century-Fox)*

(above) Breaking for lunch at the Twentieth Century-Fox commissary, the stars of *Second Fiddle* (1939) make a handsome quintet. From the left: Mary Healy, Tyrone Power, Sonja Henie, Rudy Vallee, and Edna May Oliver. *(Twentieth Century-Fox)*

(left) Sonja and Robert Cummings relax on the sound stage while appearing together in *Everything Happens at Night* (1939). *(Twentieth Century-Fox)*

(above) Sonja performs in a major production number on the most successful film she ever made, *Sun Valley Serenade* (1941). Notice the "black ice" used to create a mirror effect. *(Milton Sperling, Twentieth Century-Fox)*

(below) Cornel Wilde, Carole Landis, and Sonja Henie in a scene from *Wintertime* (1943). *(Twentieth Century-Fox)*

(left) Sonja and Leif at the Stork Club in 1939. As yet there was no hint of the feuds to come. *(Stork Club and Dorothy Stevens)*

(below) Sonja with her first husband, Dan Topping, before the fighting began. *(Dorothy Stevens)*

(left) Sonja at her home in Holmby Hills in the mid-1940s, giving an impression of ideal domesticity that was far from the truth. *(Dorothy Stevens)*

(below) Sonja with her trophies in her home on Delfern Drive. *(Dorothy Stevens)*

Sonja and second husband Winthrop Gardiner cut the cake. His alcoholism was to lead Sonja into some heavy drinking of her own. *(Phyfe and Dorothy Stevens)*

(left) Sonja playing tennis on her own court in Holmby Hills, California. She had won several tennis titles in Norway during her amateur skating days. *(Leif and Sally Henie)*

(right) Sonja's long-time secretary, Dorothy Stevens, Kjell Holm with Sonja riding piggy-back, and unidentified friend during a vacation at Kjell's country home in Norway. *(Dorothy Stevens)*

(left) Sonja coming out for her opening number in a 1946 ice show. *(Bauer-Toland Studios and Dorothy Stevens)*

(below) Sonja's famous Hawaiian number. *(Bill Doll and Dorothy Stevens)*

Three portraits of the Sonja whose jewels were so important to her that she wanted them, after her death, to be displayed under glass, like the Crown Jewels of England, for all the world to stare at and admire.
(Bernard of Hollywood and Dorothy Stevens)

(left) Sonja and Niels Onstad at their wedding in June 1956. *(United Press Photo and Dorothy Stevens)*

(right) Sonja at the Pickwick Ice Rink in Burbank, California, in 1968. One of the last photos taken prior to her illness. *(Dorothy Stevens)*

Sonja and husband number three, Niels Onstad, with a small portion of their magnificent art collection on the wall behind them. *(Dorothy Stevens)*

Sonja in the mid-1960s. *(Dorothy Stevens)*

ings that ranged from vitriolic contempt for others, to self-pity—and she absolutely detested self-pity in anyone. To Sonja, feeling sorry for yourself was a sign of weakness. She subscribed to the theory that the weak ones in the litter should be eliminated. Her lack of compassion was not something she picked up in Hollywood. It could be traced to her earliest childhood. She was never required to be compassionate.

There were two facets to the filming of *Sun Valley Serenade,* the location filming and filming at the studio. Sonja was involved in both. The production personnel, as well as her supporting cast, were the best Fox had available. Zanuck pulled out all stops to give her a chance to be the biggest money-maker at the studio. Shirley Temple had dropped out of first place at the box office.

Sonja was among friends again. Milton Sperling was producing. He knew Sonja, having written several of her previous films. Sonja liked him. Edward Cronjager, her favorite cameraman, was on the picture. Hermes Pan, one of the top choreographers in Hollywood, replaced Harry Lossee. The Mack Gordon and Harry Warren tunes as played by the great Glenn Miller Orchestra topped off a cast that included Sonja's new leading man, John Payne, Milton Berle, Lynn Bari, Joan Davis, Dorothy Dandridge, and the Nicholas brothers. Bruce Humberstone directed.

Sun Valley Serenade had been described as Sonja's last good film and "possibly the very best she ever did."

Milton Sperling was present for both the location and studio filming, and even Darryl Zanuck used the location sites as an excuse to ski and practice his French, with a lovely French lass in tow. Sonja was not romancing her leading man since he was reported to be having a fling with Lynn Bari, who was quite a beautiful woman. It was a very romantic season. Milton Sperling has great memories of it.

We went on location for the ski scenes in Sun Valley, Idaho. Weather and transportation plagued us. It was the goddamnest place to get to because everything had to go in by train. The line ran from Salt Lake City, and then we took what everyone called the *Pony Express,* an overnight train, and so it took two days to get there. The train itself was a rattler and the roadbed was terrible. It was just a long way from every place.

Actually Averell Harriman created this resort in the middle of nowhere, way the hell out in the low hills and the ski lifts were still being built when we got there. It was the opening season of Sun Valley and everything sort of sprang out from this beautiful resort hotel. The secluded compound, modeled after a Swiss village, featured some of the fanciest people and food you ever heard of. Society folk and so forth. Skiing was like polo, the sport of the wealthy.

The Union Pacific Railroad had built a special spur line into this hidden paradise. All of our exteriors were shot there and some of the interiors. The balance was shot on the Fox lot. Sonja didn't do any skating or skiing for the film in Sun Valley. That was all done on the set in Hollywood with controlled conditions which, in those days, cost a fortune.

The place was overrun with handsome young blond ski instructors from Austria and Germany. All good-looking men, and I'm sure that Sonja knew all of them—*intimately*. I think she ran through the whole bunch of them, one at a time. They all spoke highly of her. I'm sure she was very good in the sack, she had such enormous enthusiasm. Nothing had cooled down since we worked together in Washington. She was always hungry for sex.

One morning Zanuck and I were sitting at a counter having breakfast with Gregory Ratoff, an actor and director of inestimable wit. Ratoff was a great friend of Darryl's and he used to take him around wherever he went. Sitting directly opposite us were four ski instructors. The paperboy brought around the morning papers and there in the headlines was the news that the British had sunk the German battleship *Bismarck*.

Right away Ratoff said, "That's good!"

The Germans, in unison, moaned, "That's bad!" Sonja was frolicking with these guys every night, and they all looked it the following morning, and still her country had been invaded by Germany. Although we weren't in the war yet, I thought it very strange that she seemed to find nothing wrong with the Nazi ski instructors who were, by the way, picked up shortly thereafter and later interned until after the war was over. I went into the service right after the picture was completed. So did Darryl— *Colonel* Zanuck!

Milton was tremendously impressed with Glenn Miller.

He was one of the finest, nicest men I ever met. Modest, intelligent, and understood what he was doing. When he was called in at the end of the picture to record "Chattanooga Choo Choo" it was on a soundstage that had been redesigned for various purposes and not what one would expect a great bandmaster like Miller to accept. He was the total professional. I remember being on the set day after day listening to Miller recording his numbers. There had been a fake track, and at the end of it all the great songs were recorded. The sound was wonderful—terrific! Glenn Miller added immeasurably to that picture.

There's a hell of a PS on the story of "Chattanooga Choo Choo." During the late fifties I was appointed to the American delegation to the Moscow Film Festival. When I arrived in Moscow we were met by the official greeters while "Chattanooga Choo Choo" was being played on the loudspeakers at the airport. I said, "These people are really on. They knew I made *Sun Valley Serenade* and they're playing the song for me." I thought that was very good public relations. I discovered later that everywhere I went "Chattanooga Choo Choo" was being played. The picture had just opened for the first time in the Soviet Union. It was a smash and that song was a big hit and being played everywhere. Talk about a generation gap!

The weather was totally unpredictable. Snow land is always that way. No one knows when it is going to snow or when it is going to stop and this was especially true when *Sun Valley Serenade* was being shot. The weather forecasting wasn't anything like what we have today. Nobody could tell you when the sun would be coming out. The skis were like planks, no light equipment. The boots were big and heavy. "I remember," says Milton, "those poor bastards carrying lights and props and everything else wading through the snow and slush—no snowmobiles like we have now—and the trucks would get bogged down on mountains. Getting up those mountains with heavy equipment to catch skiing was tough as hell. Additionally, it was all indoor equipment since nothing had as yet been developed for snow country.

"People were freezing. The equipment was freezing. The sun was never coming out. Ten minutes of sun and then overcast. We had all kinds of sickness, people coming down with colds and flu. It was a tough situation putting all of this together, trying to make a picture. Sonja wanted no part of the bad weather, so she waited back at the hotel until we were prepared to shoot her scenes. The weather was the primary reason Sonja didn't do any of her outdoor work up there. A lot of money would have been saved if we had known what the weather was going to be and simply built the sets at Fox, which we ultimately had to do anyway. We got very little good footage in Sun Valley."

Zanuck, for once in his life, wasn't worrying about the budget. Milton recalls that he and his little French number were "having the best time in their lives—especially Darryl. He loved the French girls. Darryl was a man of varied tastes in women and I've often wondered whether he ever had anything to do with Sonja. I think he probably did. He took them all to bed. I'm sure he did. Why would either of them be an exception to the other?"

Selma accompanied Sonja on the set and on locations, always there with a bit of advice or admonition, and gossip of what was going on. Milton remembers vividly:

> She treated her mother terribly in Sun Valley. She didn't need a stage mother. She was her own stage mother. I believe Leif was up there with her, but he never butted into Sonja's affairs. He did pretty much what Sonja told him to do. She ran that family like somebody with a whip. When she wanted to have one of her escapades with a ski instructor, she would send her mother off on a tour or excursion somewhere. She knew how to manipulate her family. And one should also remember that she got the star treatment wherever she went. Everyone was willing to cooperate if Sonja wanted to be a little bit naughty. She demanded attention—and especially from the press. They were very accommodating.
>
> Sonja got away with a lot simply because she was a star and making money. Even her worst films made money. That's all the studio cared about. Zanuck was so ecstatic about the success of *Happy Landing,* the second film I did with Sonja, that he gave me a $25,000 bonus—and Boris Ingster, too—because in a show of paternalism, he was sharing the wealth that was pouring in because of Henie. It was marvelous.
>
> I can tell you this about Sonja Henie. Everytime that studio reached the point of having financial troubles it was always women who brought them out. Shirley Temple looms large, of course. But Sonja did. Jayne Mansfield did it for a while. Alice Faye and Betty Grable, too. The "Fox Girls" they have been called. I worked with both Grable and Faye and compared to Sonja Henie they were pallid people. Henie, for all her lack of classic features, was the most vital of all those women. Of course, they all had the same proclivities as Sonja, except that her appetite was greater. Hollywood has the reputation of being the sex capital of the world and it is. They accepted the sex revolution thirty years ahead of the rest of the world. That's why the moguls didn't want their stars to be married and have children. People who are married and have children don't screw. The girl next door was not the idea until Doris Day came along."

Bruce "Lucky" Humberstone, today a garrulous, seasoned veteran director who's been to the wars in Hollywood and had his shares of wins and losses, has fond remembrances of working with Sonja on two films. He also had good reason to know that Darryl wanted to dump Sonja at the first opportunity. This was during the filming of *Sun Valley Serenade,*

172

and Zanuck had no way of knowing what an impact Glenn Miller's first appearance in a film was going to have on the music loving youth of the country. Sonja was on her way out and he had no plan to renew her contract. Humberstone tells it like this:

> Zanuck rarely if ever came on the set of a film—certainly the ones I did and I imagine it was the same on all the others, so when he showed up on the set of *Sun Valley Serenade* it was a nervous event. I couldn't imagine what had happened and expected that he might have come down to replace me as the director. He was well known to do that on occasion. He tried it on me once, but it backfired.
>
> But anyway, he came over to me on the set and said he would like to talk to me privately. Now I knew there was bad blood between him and Sonja. That was no secret. They hated each other and he was looking for any reason in the world, legitimately, so he wouldn't have to worry about renewing her contract since this was her last picture under her current contract.
>
> "I hate this broad," he said, "and I want to know if you find any reason that I can use to dump her." I assured him that she had been most cooperative and I wished all my stars were as good to work with as Sonja. I believe Zanuck truly wished I had something to tell him so that he could get on her about it, but I didn't.

Humberstone had been working on another picture just before *Sun Valley Serenade*. Zanuck approached him one day and said, "Lucky, Virginia and I are going up to Sun Valley. You've been doing a fine job and I'd like to reward you. How would you and your wife like to come with us—all expenses paid—and we'll just have a nice time?"

"I agreed," Humberstone says, "and so we all went up there together after I finished the picture I was working on, which was only a few days down the line. We had a fun time and Darryl and I played cards almost every night. He loved to gamble and so did I, so we blew a lot of money and drank a lot of booze.

"While we were there, just before returning to Los Angeles, Darryl said to me, 'You know Lucky, this would be a great place to do a picture with Sonja Henie—what do you think?'"

Humberstone agreed and when they returned to Hollywood he began making preparations to go on up and scout locations.

Sun Valley Serenade was a film filled with stars, trivia, and great music of the day, which has managed to outlive a great many things that have been popular since. The songs, "Kiss Polka," "You Say the Sweetest Things, Baby," "It Happened in Sun Valley," "People Like You and Me,"

"I Know Why," and "Chattanooga Choo Choo," were all popular hits immediately. Two interesting trivia items stand out. Pat Friday did the vocals that were mouthed by Lynn Bari, and Dorothy Dandridge and the Nicholas brothers danced to "Chattanooga Choo Choo." Miller's big recording was done later at RCA Victor Studios with Tex Beneke, Marion Hutton, and the Modernaires providing the vocal magic.

There are purists today who will always believe that *Sun Valley Serenade* was a Glenn Miller film, not Sonja Henie's. Another great Glenn Miller recording was originally recorded for *Sun Valley Serenade,* but used in another picture. "At Last," which went on to become one of the all-time Glenn Miller ballad hits with Ray Eberle singing, was cut from the film because Zanuck thought it was overkill. "Jesus Christ," he said, "one more song like this and we'd have the Hit Parade. No, I think I'll save this one." And he did. It went on to be part of Miller's second and last picture, *Orchestra Wives,* which also starred Lynn Bari (singing "At Last," as dubbed by Pat Friday), sans Sonja Henie.

Sonja was lucky to have Bruce Humberstone as a director. He understood temperament, having worked with difficult stars before, male and female. Known as an actor's director, Humberstone would fight for the artists, knowing that happy actors made things easier for him as a director. *Sun Valley Serenade* was for the time a high-budget picture: $1.3 million. Zanuck wanted nothing but the best on this one.

Eddie Cronjager had worked with Humberstone on several "B" films; Humberstone wanted him for this film and submitted his name to Zanuck. "You're out of your mind," Zanuck roared. "A 'B' picture cameraman on this high budget picture? The answer is no."

Humberstone didn't budge. "Look, Darryl, a cameraman, if he's good at all, can be made or broken by a director. I happen to know that Eddie Cronjager is a hell of a cameraman, and he should be. His uncle was a cameraman, his father was a cameraman, and his brother is a cameraman. Eddie is just one hell of a cameraman, and I know what I've done with him in low-budget pictures, so let me have him in this big-budget film. I know what I'm going to do with him. In the first place, we're going to do a thing with black ice."

"What the hell are you talking about," Zanuck asked. "Ice ain't black."

"Well, it can be, and we're going to do it. That's why I need Eddie."

Zanuck, always interested in new ideas, relented and gave his director the go-ahead. Black ice is created by putting black ink into the mixture before it is frozen.

"When you're fooling around with black ice," Bruce explains, "it becomes a mirror and that mirror is a reflection of all the spotlights that are up in the rafters and the ceiling and it reflects on the black ice. If you don't have a good cameraman you're in trouble.

"So I had Cronjager, and he did one hell of a job on Sonja because there is not one in a million who could have photographed it the way I wanted it done when Henie was skating around. We had to get head and toe shots all of the time. If I couldn't have had someone like Eddie I would have reflections in the mirror of black ice, which is all wrong.

"Sonja was a wonderful gal. Absolutely great to work with."

It was assumed that *Sun Valley Serenade* was going to be Sonja's last film at Twentieth Century-Fox, and Zanuck never missed an opportunity to get in his digs about that. One day Sonja, in a tiff over the way she thought she looked, went home right after appearing on the set with her mother. Zanuck was delighted. "Shoot around her, if we have to," he said. "She'll be back to finish the picture, and then I'll be done with that bitch!"

Humberstone continued with the rest of the cast and felt that Sonja would calm down and be back. Sure enough, Sonja sneaked in to see the rushes the next morning and left before anybody saw her. She phoned Humberstone and asked him if he would meet her for lunch at Romanov's, a popular Hollywood restaurant. He said, yes, of course, and informed Zanuck that Sonja had called.

"Go ahead," the studio head agreed. "Maybe we can get rid of her now. Let me know what she says."

Sonja confessed that she had been wrong, admitted to sneaking into the studio to see the rushes, and told Bruce how pleased she was with what she saw. The following morning she arrived on the set early, and when Humberstone came to her dressing room she gave him a Longines watch with a gold and platinum band. "Sonja was a bad girl," she cooed. "I'll try to be better."

Zanuck, meanwhile, having had an opportunity to view what had been shot, knew he had a winner. Now he had the problem of getting Sonja to sign a new contract, because he knew that the minute *Sun Valley Serenade* reached the public Sonja would be in big demand. The picture was sneak previewed and of course the audience cards were all filled with glowing comments about the picture, Glenn Miller, and Sonja.

Sonja refused to take any of Zanuck's calls. "I'll show that sonofabitch Zanuck he can't play with Sonja," she said, slamming down the receiver in his secretary's ear. "He treats Sonja like bullshit and then he expects me to come running to him. That Jew sonofabitch not play games with Sonja." After all those years at Fox, Sonja must have been the last person left who hadn't learned Darryl Zanuck wasn't Jewish. She assumed that if he was the head of a studio he must be.

Frustrated and trying to keep the other studios from finding out that Sonja had not as yet re-signed with Fox, Zanuck went to Joe Schenck, president of the studio, and explained his unenviable situation. "Look, Joe, I can't do anything with this dame. She doesn't like me, and I don't like her, but we have a hit. A sensational smash and we've got to sign her and do another picture quick before someone else grabs her up and we look like the laughing stocks of the industry."

Sonja was in New York at the time and Schenck assured Zanuck that he would take care of the matter for him. Joe Schenck was one of the great moguls and his influence pervaded the entire movie industry. When he spoke, people listened and Sonja was no exception.

In due time Joe Schenck did go to New York and had a long conversation with Sonja and convinced her to sign another contract with Fox. It was her last with the studio that made her a famous star, and it was for only three pictures. None of them would ever equal *Sun Valley Serenade* or her previous successes, but they all made money.

Meanwhile America was about to be plunged into World War II. For the moment, however, it was the time to toast success.

16

S ONJA was developing two kinds of fans who came to see her ice show. The real skating critics came because they had followed her amateur career for many years and often were upset that she was "becoming more a show woman and less a skater." On the other hand, she had developed an even larger following among film fans who waited breathlessly for the release of every new picture and stood in lines several blocks long, in New York at least, waiting until the box office at Madison Square Garden opened with the advance sales for her annual appearances. These differing attitudes toward her professional career only helped to perpetuate the Sonja legend.

Her fourth season with Arthur Wirtz had brought her far from the four or five towns and the skimpy show she had started out with. Lincoln Werden wrote in *The New York Times*, "Those who regard skating as mere entertainment should be pleased with this revue." Sonja, as the dominating figure, had built the show up with unbelievable costuming and choreography. Her ability to stage an extravaganza was only equaled by MGM in some of its big-budget musicals of the '40s and '50s. She tried each year to bring something new and unique to the ice arenas. From the "Dying Swan" through "Little Red Riding Hood," "An Invitation to the Dance," "The Hula," "Bolero," "Waltz," "Tango," "Rhumboogie," "Intermezzo," and "Glow Worm," Sonja put her mark on ice skating forever. By this stage of her career, she had produced the combination of dance, drama, and ice skating that originally only she had been certain would succeed.

Her last tour had played to 800,000 with gross receipts from the gate alone set at approximately $1,250,000. That covered Houston, St. Louis, Buffalo, Chicago, Detroit, Cleveland, New York, Indianapolis, and Omaha where the show closed its run. Had she included Boston, Philadelphia, Washington, and the major West Coast cities, she would have easily gone over the $2 million mark. For 1941 those figures belonged to baseball, not ice skating.

Although Sonja and Arthur Wirtz focused public attention on the ice rink, they by no means discovered the ice carnival. Eddie Shipstad and Oscar Johnson, famous for their *Ice Follies,* were the innovators of the traveling ice show. They were just a couple of young kids from St. Paul, Minnesota, who, being experts on the ice themselves, put together a small show in the twin cities of St. Paul/Minneapolis in 1932—a show that flopped. But they never lost their enthusiasm nor their belief that an ice revue could be made profitable. By 1935 they were in Chicago with what became *Ice Follies,* and played sixteen months.

It was still a local attraction, although the boys did go out on the road to a few places. The real promotion of ice shows came about when Sonja Henie teamed up with Arthur Wirtz. Wirtz, who had made millions in real estate, saw "ice" as the financial salvation for the empty sports arenas across the country that had all but closed due to the Depression. His genius put "ice" on the map, and before long other attractions and shows, not ice related, were coming into arenas that now had an easier time supporting themselves.

Sidney M. Shalett, in a lengthy article entitled "Theater on Skates," made the point of crediting Wirtz and Sonja:

> While even the most enthusiastic, "ice" backers are astonished by what has happened and do not attempt to explain all the reasons for the rapid climb in popularity, none of the producers—even the rival producers—will attempt to filch from Sonja Henie, the comely Norwegian figure-skating champion who spurted from Olympic to cinematic fame, the credit that is rightly hers for enkindling ice-consciousness in this country.

Ever the business woman, by 1941 (thanks to gross profits percentages) she was making millions in pictures, the same on ice show tours, and garnering a hefty stipend from the dozens of Sonja Henie skates, pins, costumes, skis, and sweaters that were sold by the hundreds of thousands. *It Happens on Ice,* the New York show that she and Arthur Wirtz were coproducing at the immense Center Theater of Radio City, was the only profitable show that had ever graced that large arena. The few ice rinks that existed when she turned professional in 1936 now numbered over two hundred in the United States and more than 30 million customers were going through the turnstiles to see ice skating every year. If Sonja had walked away at the beginning of World War II, her impact would still have been felt for decades.

To build the organization, Sonja became the undisputed queen bee of ice. She had ridden roughshod over whoever was in the way, in order to accomplish that feat. In the process, she took her lumps, some of them physical. Twice she fell during an exhibition before the British royal family. Both falls were caused by foreign objects on the ice. During the 1940-41 tour she took another tumble in Kansas City, which left her banged and bruised, but she went right back on the ice. She might give a chorus girl expensive bracelets or trips to Europe, but at the same time, she would fire a skater for a loose screw on the bottom of his skates or a chorus girl whose sequins were not sewed on tightly. Hairpins were forbidden and would always draw a pink slip.

Sonja examined the ice with a fine-tooth comb before setting foot on it. Even so, an occasional incident occurred. At one performance some young men in the balcony heated pennies and tossed them onto the ice where they promptly melted into the hard surface, creating a hazard for skaters. In the middle of a production number, Sonja stopped the orchestra, asked for the lights to be turned on, and gave the culprits a dressing-down that would have made an Irish mother proud. It brought the loudest applause of the night. On the ice she was the leader.

She was just as meticulous when making a film. The story went around that while working on one, director Sidney Lanfield had a difficult time getting Sonja to come on the set. She was busy completing her makeup and would not come out of her dressing room until it was up to her specifications.

After what he considered a more-than-lengthy-enough period of time for any star, he knocked on the dressing room door and said, "Sonja, this is Sidney. Hurry up, dammit. You take longer to be made up than Garbo."

Sonja, not to be pushed, responded, "Yes, Sidney, but Garbo can't skate!"

Wirtz advised both Sonja and Leif to continue investing in real estate. With the war in Europe certain to involve America soon, he felt that real estate was sure to boom when people started leaving farms to work in the big defense plants in the city. "They will need some place to live, and apartments are the best buy today."

He convinced Leif to go in with Sonja on an apartment in Evanston, just north of Chicago. The building could be had at what he considered a bargain forty thousand dollars, so Sonja and Leif each put in twenty thousand dollars as an investment for the future. Leif would come to regret being involved with his sister in this or any other business venture because, as he discovered, to his chagrin, Sonja's idea of a partnership was for each side to put in the same amount and for Sonja to reap the profit. The Chicago investment, along with sixteen hundred acres Leif would later buy near Oceanside, California, would be important factors in breaking up the relationship between Sonja and her brother, and it would also cause family bitterness and squabbling that would endure until only one of them was left alive.

Sonja had almost a year off from the studio after finishing *Sun Valley Serenade,* and she basked in the sunshine of her freshly resurrected popularity. The resurgence at the box office brought even more people out to see the exhibitions she staged in California and Texas, as well as to see the next Wirtz tour. Sonja was even hoping to devise a means to keep other ice shows out of the towns she was to play. She had a small bit of success in Houston, Texas.

Leif went into Houston, spoke with the manager of the ice arena there and offered him several thousand dollars if he would book only Sonja's show into that stadium for a fixed period of time. The fellow accepted the cash and the deed was done. Whether or not he reported the money to the Internal Revenue Service was not Sonja's concern. She wrote it off as an operating expense and could prove it was.

With time away from the studio, Sonja was in a position not only to go to parties but to plan some of her own, and they were fabulous events. Everybody who was anybody came. On one occasion that summer, she spent almost fifty thousand for a bash at her Delfern Drive home that brought gasps from even the most hardened party goers. The usual tent was erected over the tennis courts and the party was catered by Chasen's—a must for "A" group hostesses, of which Sonja was the unchallenged leader.

Errol Flynn, ever the ladies' man and always in the news romantically, whether on account of his conventional love affairs or because of his trial for rape, was in and out during the night. By the early morning hours, the party had dwindled down to a few people some of whom were barely on their feet. Flynn had returned in a happy-go-lucky, not completely sober, mood and was looking for a drink. The bartenders had departed, but Dan Topping opened up the bar himself to accommodate the handsome actor. After pouring champagne, Flynn asked if he might see the trophy room. There had never been any suggestion of monkey business between him and Sonja, and Flynn had been well-behaved all night.

Sonja volunteered to show him the trophy room herself and explain what some of the trophies were for. For some reason, Dan Topping became jealous and, when Sonja and Errol were leaving the room, he blindsided Flynn with a wallop that sent him sprawling. Leif, now behind the bar, looked up as Flynn staggered toward him screaming at the top of his lungs, his head torn and blood spurting in every direction. Topping had used brass knuckles.

Flynn was trying to stem the flow of blood with his hand, but it continued to pour profusely between his fingers and down his sleeve, dripping on Sonja's expensive carpeting. "Who did this?" He screamed. "Where is the sonofabitch? What did he hit me with?"

Leif, knowing Flynn's reputation for getting into barroom brawls, figured that Errol had started a fight with someone at the party. He looked around and saw only a few people there, not one of whom looked even remotely mussed. Dan Topping was conspicuously missing.

Before Leif could respond, Sonja screamed and fainted dead away. Meanwhile while Selma Henie was hustling Dan up the stairs the enraged Flynn took a swing at Leif, who first ducked away and then

180

finally got Errol against the wall with his arms pinned behind him. Leif was as athletic as Flynn was rambunctious.

"You sonofabitch!" Flynn screamed at Leif. "You did it!"

Another party guest got into the act at this point and pulled Leif off Errol, and while someone held Leif's hands Flynn picked up a chair and flung it at Leif's head. The chair missed, but suddenly Errol realized he was picking on the wrong man.

Selma had safely escorted Dan Topping, brass knucks and all, to an upstairs bedroom out of sight of the irate actor. She was now downstairs trying to revive Sonja who was sprawled out on the floor moaning. With Errol continuing to bleed like a stuck pig, one of the other guests volunteered to transport him to the hospital. First someone wrapped a Turkish towel around his neck to catch the splashing blood.

Leif had no way of knowing that Errol Flynn had at one time been a boxing champion in Europe. "Otherwise," he laughs, "I wouldn't even have tried to hold his hands."

As things settled down and Sonja was revived, someone suggested perhaps everyone had better have another drink to settle their "nerves." A little bit later the doorbell rang and in walked a more subdued Errol Flynn, filled with some remorse over his behavior toward Leif. "I'm sorry, old boy," he said. "I apologize for making an ass of myself with you. I know it wasn't you, but Dan. I know he doesn't want to see me right now and I don't blame him, but I'd like to meet him tomorrow at one o'clock." He named a place where the two of them could discuss Topping's behavior. Then he added, "And he'd better be there!"

They did meet, but whatever transpired between the two of them was never openly discussed.

Sonja's feelings for Adolf Hitler were certainly put to the test in December of 1941, following the Japanese sneak attack on Pearl Harbor when, on the eleventh day of that month, President Franklin Delano Roosevelt declared that a state of war existed between the United States and Germany as well as Japan. As a resident alien, Sonja had to be very careful how she spoke of "the other side," because it wasn't only her native Norway that was embroiled with the Nazis. Now it was the entire free world.

Her problems with Dan Topping were put to rest temporarily when Topping enlisted as a lieutenant in the Marines and, shortly thereafter, was promoted to captain and shipped off to easy duty in the Hawaiian Islands, his old playground. He rented a beautiful home there and continued to throw parties and entertain the military brass. On one trip back to the states, he and Sonja gave a dinner party at the apartment they maintained at 400 Park Avenue in New York. They loved small dinner parties and had always given them. On this particular occasion, Arthur and Virginia Wirtz were there as was Pat DiCicco. He had been married to the late Thelma Todd, who had been a major film star. Thelma's mysterious death by carbon monoxide in December 1935 has never been solved and DiCicco was believed (by some) to have not told all he knew about his estranged wife's demise, but he was still a very popular party guest and was often at Sonja's affairs.

At this particular party Sonja said something to Topping about drinking too much and being too loud and boisterous. Captain Topping looked at his wife and grinned. "I'll show you how to be loud and boisterous," he yelled. He then angrily began to throw pots and pans from the kitchen out into the dining area. Before the night was over he and Sonja had exhausted themselves both physically and verbally and collapsed in their respective beds. The following day Topping returned to the Islands where his brand of partying was more in style.

Topping gave another demonstration of his temper one night at his club. Sitting near the fireplace, having drinks, he got mad at some remark he took to be a slur and grabbing a handful of hundred dollar bills out of his pocket tossed them into the flames. "You see," he screamed, "I don't really give a damn!" A waiter was badly burned salvaging several of the charred bills. Sonja's temperament was well known at the studio and backstage at her ice shows, but in Dan Topping she met someone who could match it and then some. In the grand tradition of the spoiled rich kid, he had to have his own way or he would throw a tantrum. Sonja was much the same, although she possessed as well the steel-hard ambition and perfectionism that made her a champion.

Sonja's first film under her new contract with Twentieth Century-Fox was *Iceland*. William LeBaron produced from a script by Robert Ellis and Helen Logan, who had worked on Henie films in the past. Bruce Humberstone directed but did not have the services of Eddie Cronjager behind the camera. Instead, the director of photography was Arthur Miller (no relation to the playwright). Mack Gordon and Harry Warren, after so much success with *Sun Valley Serenade,* furnished the songs. With the nation at war, there was a military flavor to the music. The most memorable number from the film, now a standard, was "There Will Never Be Another You." Others that received a great deal of jukebox play included "You Can't Say No to a Sailor," "Let's Bring New Glory to Old Glory," and "I Like a Military Tune." The first two were sung by John Merrill.

It was an early sampling of the hundreds of wartime films to come, both musical and dramatic. The story line was typical of the times. The Marines land in Iceland and run into more romantic battles than military ones. The film was an entertainment bone tickler and no more. "What matters," a critic stated, "are the skating routines by Henie (although no explanation is given for such lavish productions being staged in a Reykjavik nightclub) and the songs by Harry Warren and Mack Gordon."

Sonja's co-stars were John Payne (again), Jack Oakie, Felix Bressart,

182

Osa Massen, John Merrill, Fritz Feld, Sammy Kaye and his orchestra, Sterling Holloway, Adeline DeWalt Reynolds, Ludwig Stossel, and Duke Adlon. It was as Zanuck had designed from the beginning. Get good actors and any kind of a story, sprinkle Sonja's skating production numbers throughout the picture, properly mix with comedy and music, and *voila!* A money-maker.

Zanuck's desire to rid Fox of Sonja prior to *Sun Valley Serenade* almost cost him a bundle he hadn't counted on. So certain was he that she was doing her last film at Fox that he sold the ice-making machine that had been put in especially for her in 1936. Sonja was one of a kind, as MGM found out in 1939 when, in order to cash in on Zanuck's success with the ice films, they cast Joan Crawford, one of their biggest stars, in the most disastrous film she would ever make, a copycat of Sonja's pictures, called *Ice Follies.* Even James Stewart, her stouthearted co-star, couldn't pull that turkey out of the oven. Herbert Yates, head of Republic Studios, which was better known for its "they went thataway" westerns, felt the ice bug and put Vera Hruba Ralston under contract. Yates had a skating star but no machinery for making ice. When he heard that Zanuck was dumping the ice machine he quickly purchased it for a fraction of its original cost and proceeded with his studio's version of Sonja. Like Louis B. Mayer at Metro, Yates discovered there was only one Sonja and Zanuck still had her.

So, when it came time to shoot *Iceland* somebody forgot to let the people shooting the picture know that Fox no longer owned an ice machine. Sonja knew it but never said a word to anyone. Sonja thought only of how nice it would be if it took them three months to find a new machine. She had figured down to the last penny how much she would make because of delays, and it was a pretty penny to be sure.

Such was not to be the case, however. The day before Sonja's big ice scenes were to start being shot, Lucky Humberstone realized there wasn't going to be any ice. It nearly gave him apoplexy. Sonja had been rehearsing at the Polar Palace and now suddenly he was faced with the reality of his situation. In Jack Oakie's book, *Jack Oakie's Double Takes* (which was published after his death by his devoted widow, Victoria), he recalled being on the set with Humberstone on that fateful occasion.

The director was bemoaning his fate when Oakie told him he was more concerned with the weather on the set that day. "Can't you turn that air conditioner down?" asked the affable comedian who, in spite of being bundled up in winter clothing, was freezing as was everyone else there that day.

About that time an electrician approached Humberstone and said, "Mr. Humberstone, we've got the air conditioner under control now." Lucky grumbled an unintelligible acknowledgment. "About that ice-making machine," the electrician continued, "we don't need it."

Humberstone looked at the man as if he belonged in the Looney Tunes cartoons instead of on a Sonja Henie extravaganza.

"No sir," he stammered, "I'm really serious, Mr. Humberstone. We've got it figured out how to have ice."

"Yeah?"

"Yes sir. We can make ice with the air conditioner."

"I'll buy that," Oakie quipped, pulling his collar up higher.

It turned out that pipes could be laid from the air conditioner to the stage, covered with a layer of water and then another layer and another, freezing each thin layer before pouring the next. It worked. Lucky Humberstone had his rink but unlucky Sonja lost her overtime bonus.

Even if Zanuck wasn't always physically present in Hollywood, Sonja still managed to retain the quality of their relationship. During the filming of *Iceland* she was approached by one of the executive assistants from the front office. Sonja listened to him placidly. She was advised that there was a budget problem on the picture and they would have to cut corners on one of the scenes and turn it into something of a Mickey Mouse number. When the man was finished with his spiel he took Sonja's serene silence to be agreement. "I gather that will be okay with you then, Miss Henie."

Sonja stared him down icily. "I thought Zanuck took all that bullshit to war!"

He didn't seem to understand her meaning. "Then it will be okay?"

Still coldly staring at the front office man, she said, "The answer is NO! NO! NO! Is that plain enough for you?"

The guy went off talking to himself. Sonja, being patted on the wrist by her mother as a token of her agreement with her daughter's decision, turned to Jack Oakie and, beaming at him like a child, said, "Oh, Jack, if they make me do something I don't want to do just to save some money I'll just die. I mean it Jack, I'll really get mad."

Oakie, making a joke, looked down at a big bag she was carrying with the initials S.H.T. (Sonja Henie Topping) and pointedly commented, "Sonja, honey, if you get mad enough, just dot that I!" She thought his humor hilarious and broke into a loud roar of her own. But, of course, Sonja still refused to do the scene as suggested. Anxious to get their new picture out as quickly as possible to capitalize on the last one, the studio relented and Sonja got her way.

Humberstone once again had an excellent relationship with Sonja while they were making *Iceland*. "We never shot a single scene of this one on location," he recalls, "and I don't think personally it was as good a film as *Sun Valley Serenade,* but, because of that film's big success, *Iceland* made a hell of a lot more money. It has always worked. Follow a hit with another film quickly and clean up. So *Iceland* made a bundle."

Following *Iceland,* Fox wanted Humberstone to direct Sonja's next picture, *Wintertime*. He turned it down. "I read the script," he says, "and it was a terrible story. I went to Zanuck and told him I was sorry, but I just couldn't do it, and as much as I loved Sonja and wanted to do another film with her, I couldn't make this one. Another director was assigned to do it, and it still ended up awful. A terrible, lousy picture that Sonja shouldn't even have been in. She was certainly too good for that kind of writing."

Humberstone saw Sonja often after *Iceland* and they remained friends. "I'd run into her at the Palm Springs Racquet Club, where she loved to go play tennis. Other times I'd be invited to the parties she had at her house. She used to give the greatest parties in Hollywood. She was the girl who really started the great parties of Hollywood. Let's face it, a millionaire even before she arrived in Hollywood, Sonja was a gal loaded with money, so she knew how to entertain well and she did.

"She had a hobby collecting cat's-eye gems. Someone could call her from Cairo or any other place and say, 'Miss Henie, we've got a beautiful cat's-eye—ten carat—probably the most perfect cat's-eye around.' She'd be on the next plane to Cairo, or wherever, to pick up that stone. One night she took me upstairs to her bedroom at one of her parties and said, 'Lucky, I want to show you something.' Digging back into her closet she came out with a dusty old shoe box and said, 'Look. What do you think?' Inside it was filled with nothing but cat's-eyes. But that's the way she was. If she liked something she wanted only the best and as much as she could get.

"Her art collection would strangle the most devout connosieur. She had it all. Her walls were packed with the great artists, past and present. She was a great gal, that Sonja."

Humberstone's comment about Sonja's being a "millionaire" before she came to Hollywood has been substantiated by numerous others who had known Sonja and her father in the old days when Sonja was an amateur and known as "the richest amateur in the world."

One old-timer recalled, "Old Wilhelm did everything Sonja told him to do. Everybody thought he was the heavy. Not at all. He was a softie for Sonja. When Sonja said 'Daddy' he jumped. He used to roar when he would drink with us and tell stories about 'my Sonja.' She would send him, for instance, to Berlin or Paris where they wanted Sonja for an exhibition. Wilhelm, with orders from Sonja, would arrive on the scene and give them the treatment. 'You want an exhibition here? Fine. How much—or no show!'" It was also rumored that he banked every single penny in Sonja's name in Swiss bank accounts that were untraceable and that Sonja indeed did arrive in America a very wealthy woman, if not a millionaire.

In spite of all the nice things people were saying about her and all the money she was raking in, Sonja was a very unhappy wife. She loved

Topping, but he was proving to be the greatest challenge of her life. The one redeeming factor that probably, more than anything else, kept her from calling it quits much earlier was the fact that he stayed out of her business affairs. Everything between the two of them was kept on a social level, and Topping went about collecting his monthly checks from his mother, and Sonja had Arthur Wirtz tally up her annual take.

Although Lucky Humberstone could find no redeeming qualities in the film *Wintertime,* Jack Pfeiffer had recollections about the film and about Sonja during the period of time that picture was being made.

"Sonja," he declares, "had to be the way she was. When one reaches the category of big movie star and big skating star that she did, everyone wants to take advantage, and it all falls to the star to be responsible. She had to be tough. I believe she tried to keep her married life out of the business end of her life. Topping never interferred. She kept her problems with her husband very secret. She had other problems to contend with. She didn't always get a proper accounting of funds from the people she had to deal with, and she was not the kind of person to take anything sitting down. She was a tough lady and would fight when she had to, and she had to more often than she really wanted to. She fought with Zanuck and the studio. Sure she did. So did every other star in the business."

Zanuck, the military man, was still the head of Fox and running things as always. "I was on the stage," Jack remembers, "when they sent word down to the set that the picture was to be shut down. One of Zanuck's men, a real heavy guy, came down with the bad news. Zanuck didn't like to come on the set himself. Anyway, this guy comes down and makes his announcement. 'You're gonna shoot today and tomorrow and then we're gonna close dis picture down!' The picture was finished whether Sonja or anyone else liked it or not. Sonja had wanted another number. Zanuck was worried. The picture hadn't gone well from the beginning, and there were problems with the costumes, and Sonja was demanding more rehearsals. She was still fighting with the front office for her pictures to be shot in color, as were Alice Faye's and Betty Grable's. She wanted equal treatment and was, in fact, entitled to it. Consequently she was being handed an ultimatum. Either finish the picture off in two days or have it edited into a piece of nothing. Sonja did her best.

"There was something else about *Wintertime.* They used black ice. A drape was hung the full length of the ice rink at the studio. As Sonja came out onto the ice the curtain snaked right beside her. We practiced it over and over and over and had the music set for it and the ice would be smoking and all that. When it came time to shoot the actual scene, they pushed the button, just as had been done at every rehearsal. Only this time, when it counted, it didn't work. The curtain was frozen solid into the ice. The vapor had come up on the curtain from the ice and created an upright icicle and frozen the curtain in place. That cost about $150,000 because it had to be completely redone."

186

Technical difficulties were only a part of the problems Sonja encountered while making motion pictures. With the advent of World War II, professional skaters became ever more difficult to come by and not every dancer converted to ice managed to survive as Belle Christy had. On one of her films, probably *Iceland* because of its military setting, there was a military production number. Jack Pfeiffer recalls one instance of the consequences of diminished professionalism among the skaters:

"They had all these boy skaters who were dressed like soldiers and Harry Lossee calls out, 'Guide right!' Meanwhile, little Sonja is out in the middle of the ice, spinning. At a certain cue in the music she was supposed to stop and be the center of attraction as the skating line cut by her. She knew the music and was one who paid attention to cues, so she was ready when the music hit the right notes.

It was always a tricky business with the black ice. Anyway, the skating line was guiding right, Sonja was still spinning, and the lead skater brought the entire line right into Sonja. They all went down and everyone, including Sonja, was a mess of moisture and black ink. You have never heard such a barrage of Norwegian swear words in your life. She was furious, and rightly so. The lead skater was supposed to watch Sonja out of the corner of his eye, and he wasn't paying attention. Sonja detested that type of unprofessionalism and that particular skater, if he finished the picture at all, was not given the lead again."

It has been said that Sonja never missed a performance, which is probably the truth because she would go on as long as her skates would carry her out on the ice. She had that kind of tenacity of purpose. But Sonja had her share of accidents on tours.

Sonja's professionalism on skates saved her from what might have been career-ending injuries. In one auditorium the ice was inaccurately put down. Usually when the pipes were laid to freeze the rink, sand was spread between the pipes to support them. For some reason Sonja's regular crew was not in charge of icing the rink, and sawdust was used instead of sand. Jack Pfeiffer remembers that "The rink was full of air bubbles, which weakens the ice. So instead of having solid ice, what we had was a rink filled with air spaces. The first groups out on the ice were not allowed to do jumping or acrobatics, only smooth skating in order to keep the ice clean for Sonja. So, when she came out in her opening number, which was a very fast Olympic routine she did a leap and a split jump and several other intricate and exciting executions. When she came down from one of the leaps, she hit the ice and there was nothing underneath it but air space. Her skate simply dug into the softer ice and she was stopped cold. Luckily, being the athlete she was, she knew how to fall. She could have broken an arm or leg—or even her back. It was bad enough, however, because she did break a couple of ribs."

The show was rearranged, and other acts came out on the ice while Sonja went backstage to have her ribs taped and a couple of numbers later was back on the ice—more careful than before and without the leaps and jumps she was famous for—but back on the ice nonetheless. She had the heart of a lioness when it came to her work.

On another occasion she took a tumble backward during the Hawaiian Hula number due to the black luminescent lights, which limited her vision to the immediate area. She had inadvertently skated too close to the hockey corner and went sailing backward over the border right into the first row of spectators. She screamed, "Don't touch me! Don't touch me!" then got up, shook herself like a fighter that had been hit, got back on the ice, skated off, and took a bow.

Sonja was aware that everything depended on her. She was a one-woman show. There were supporting acts, and novelty and comedy acts to provide some variety, but the name that brought people in by the thousands was Sonja Henie. If she broke a leg, there went the show. So Sonja had a right to be demanding of everyone on her payroll, especially since the demands she made on herself in a professional and athletic sense were more stringent than those she set for any other skater.

17

THE early war years were turbulent ones not only for Sonja but for everyone in the entertainment industry. Leading men were difficult to keep in pictures—many of the established male stars were off fighting in the war. Sonja's male skaters were to a large degree recruited from the ranks of gay dancers, men who had either declared themselves homosexual to keep out of the military or who had been turned down by some second lieutenant psychiatrist who thought he saw "homosexual tendencies" in a prospective recruit. It was from these men that choruses, ice shows, and dance shows were recruited.

Sonja's skating partners changed frequently. During the winter of 1941-42 she skated with a new young man, Gene Turner, from California who had been the men's national figure skating champion for two years running. A touch of the times was inserted into her ice show when it opened in Madison Square Garden. Following the playing of the "Star Spangled Banner," a military drill was quite effectively staged, parade fashion, timed to the musical tempo of a John Philip Sousa march. Such a patriotic number brought the crowd cheering to its feet. Sonja knew every trick for milking an audience and used them all.

She also gained some beneficial publicity when she donated the proceeds of a Wednesday afternoon matinee performance at Madison Square Garden to the American Red Cross. The four hundred people associated with the ice show, right down to the janitors and ushers, also worked free at that performance, but it was Sonja who was honored at a luncheon given by the Red Cross representatives. Ten thousand people had attended the show and $17,740 was raised for the cause. There were grumblings among members of the Norwegian community in New York because Sonja, like Kirsten Flagstad the Metropolitan Opera diva, was not contributing to the Norwegian underground.

The truth was, that Sonja did not want to do anything to upset the Nazis. After the war was over, on a brief USO tour to Scandinavia, Sonja declared that the Germans had looted her home. That was not the case at all. When the Germans entered Norway, they occupied whatever houses and apartments they needed for quartering their officers and enlisted men. The German occupation of Norway was easier for the Nazis due to the support they received from the Norwegian traitor Vidkun Quisling, a politician who became the puppet head of occupied Norway.

Certainly the vast majority of Norwegians looked upon their invaders with detestation. When the Nazis first arrived, their warships steamed up Oslo's fjords. In the middle of Oslo Fjord, not far from the capital itself, there was a little fortress called Oskarsborg. As the German fleet passed the fortress, one of the two troopships in front was hit midship and sunk by a load from a very old cannon located at the fortress. The old cannon hadn't been fired for years, and there was great jubilation among the citizenry of Oslo and all Norway. The people of Oslo refused to eat mackerel from the fjord for a long time afterward because they supposed the fish were nibbling on German soldiers.

Many of the German officers spoke Norwegian fluently, because as small children they came to Norway after the first World War as homeless refugees. The Norwegians had fed them and taken them into their homes as their own. The Henies remembered the poor starving children who could devour enormous portions of food, such was their hunger. When the Germans returned during World War II, it was as soldiers and officers. They looked up their old homes where they stayed as children and with a smile they told everyone they were there to "save you from the English." Doors were slammed in their faces by their former benefactors.

The German officers were looking for the nicest places in and around Oslo as their headquarters. In addition to Landoya, Sonja's new home, the Henies had a beautiful estate in Landoën, about fifteen minutes from downtown Oslo. It was the country home where Sonja and Leif had been children and had first begun to enjoy skating. One day, a carload of German officers drove onto the Henie property in their limousine, running down and killing Leif's favorite watchdog. They came to a stop in front of the main entrance to the house; they demanded that the caretaker open the doors for them.

The colonel in charge, after a cursory examination, decided that this was the place where they would set up headquarters. His mind was suddenly changed when he entered a parlor and saw Mussolini and Hitler's autographed pictures sitting on the grand piano, with intimate inscriptions written by hand to Sonja.

Clicking his heels, the colonel turned and ordered his men to follow him out. They left in orderly fashion and never returned. None of the Henie properties were ever confiscated by the Germans, and orders were handed down from the German high command in Berlin that "Our little white rabbit's estates shall be preserved." Such was Sonja's prestige with the leaders of Nazi Germany. Clearly it was not in her interest to speak out vigorously against the Nazis, and she never did.

By the end of 1942 Sonja's show had drawn over a million spectators to

Madison Square Garden in a five-year period. It was a record set by a woman used to setting records, whether in skill or at the cash register. She was exceedingly proud of this record, although there were no trophies to commemorate it, and she kept the newspaper clippings lauding the event until they turned brown and crumbly with age.

When the next season came around, Sonja was skating with two new partners, James Hawley and Geary Steffen, Jr. (who later became Jane Powell's husband). Her new military opening had Sonja stepping onto the ice from an airplane in a routine appropriately called "To the Colors." It was a very powerful and popular scenario. The press more than adequately covered her current visit to New York. In spite of the lavishness of her show and its definitely theatrical atmosphere, the *Sonja Henie Revues* were always written up in the sports section of *The New York Times*. It showed a lack of insight that annoyed Sonja. She was entertainment and should be in the entertainment section of the paper along with the Broadway shows and the movies.

Consequently, she was elated when Lewis Nichols, under "News of the Theater" devoted a column to "The Winter's Ice" and Sonja. A few excerpts from that article are indicative of New York City's love-affair with Sonja:

> To many right thinking people, it is only the fact that Sonja Henie brings her ice show to town which makes New York at all habitable by Winter. . . . It is a familiar marker for the period between the Dodgers' dispersal from the sports pages and the annual arrival of the circus to herald the fact that Spring slowly is ambling its way up from the South. It carries a slogan of "Hollywood," which is a little startling to an effete East brought up on a legend of all-year-round swimming pools and oranges out there, but if Hollywood wishes to become known for Winter sports, that is fair enough, too.
>
> The right thinking people who turn out to see Miss Henie year after year do not quarrel about titles, for so long as she is present they will fill almost any stadium in the land. They will crowd into the lower seats and will climb into the dim distances of the topmost balconies where, almost above the lights themselves, they just get a jovelike feeling of studying tiny puppets—Miss Henie being the blonde one amid all the brunettes. . . . On the way out they may get Sonja Henie souvenirs for the children, who all quite naturally wish to be like her some day.

The columnist also had praise for Sonja and Arthur Wirtz's magic which "made a white Christmas from what had been mainly a white elephant called the Center Theater," and which was now boastful that two and a quarter million people had seen either the *It Happens on Ice* or *Stars on Ice* presented there.

Had Sonja chosen to make New York her home instead of California, she would easily have been adopted as Manhattan's favorite Norwegian refugee. Only the Norwegians would have had doubts.

Stars on Ice was making so much money the skaters in the chorus decided they weren't getting their fair share of the take and threatened to walk off the show unless they received an additional ten dollars a week in salary. Sonja and Arthur Wirtz at first refused to budge. Sonja was particularly adamant because: "I am paying them more than they would make anyplace else." The skaters wanted the basic salary raised from fifty dollars to sixty dollars a week, or no show.

Closing notices were flying back and forth like paper airplanes in a windstorm. Both the skaters and Wirtz issued closing orders. After receiving a wire from the skaters that "We rescind our closing notice. We would like to talk to you when you come to town," Arthur Wirtz canceled his own closing notice. In what was described as an "amiable atmosphere," Sonja (however reluctantly) and Wirtz ended two years of bickering with their chorus by signing a basic work agreement with the American Guild of Variety Artists (AGVA). The final outcome of their negotiations with AGVA brought unionization of not only *Stars on Ice* and *It Happens on Ice,* but also Sonja's own *Hollywood Ice Revue.* The powerful artists union achieved total bargaining rights for all the show's employees.

The settlement came just before rehearsals were to begin in the spring of 1943 for the show that would open in Chicago in October. Insiders at Wirtz's Chicago offices, as well as AGVA officials, were caught by surprise at the rapidity of the agreement since both Wirtz and Sonja had steadfastly refused to negotiate with representatives of AGVA in the past. Times were changing for Sonja and the cost of putting an ice show on the road would soon begin to spiral.

There was some reason for smiling, however, by October when the new 1944 *Hollywood Ice Revue* was scheduled to start out on the road. *Stars on Ice* celebrated the opening of its fourth year at the Center in New York, already having been seen by over three million people. It was the only permanently based ice production in the country and, without the excess overhead of travel expenses, was profitable beyond Sonja's and Wirtz's wildest dreams. They could well afford to pay the salary increases demanded by their skaters and still earn a handsome profit for reinvestment.

To Sonja's credit, throughout the war years no military man was ever charged admission to her shows. The USO centers gave free tickets to all her appearances to any military personnel on active duty. Sonja supported the American war effort in that generosity as much as any star performing. What she didn't do for Norway, she seemed to be directing toward the American military and related wartime drives and causes.

One of the great events in Sonja's life took place in the spring of 1943 while she was rehearsing her show for the next season. A young woman named Dorothy Howes was managing the coffee shop adjacent to the ice rink. Sonja had seen her, but they had never really talked. As it happened, Sonja was planning a large party for the following week, and her secretary had suddenly quit. As an emergency fill-in, she asked Dorothy if she would mind coming over to the Delfern Drive house and helping her with some invitations and phone calls. "It isn't much," she explained, "and I'll only need a couple of your afternoons." Those two afternoons stretched into twenty-six years. Dorothy Howes gave Sonja a devotion and loyalty that are rarely found in Hollywood or elsewhere, and if Sonja did not always treat her new girl Friday with the same respect she received, Dorothy understood. "That was just Sonja," she explains. "Her entire world centered within herself and one had to understand that or not be around her. It's just the way she was. I understood and loved her very much for just who and what she was. She had many wonderful qualities."

Sonja had not only just lost a secretary, but for all intents and purposes, a husband as well. Rumors had been coming in to her about the "other women" in Dan Topping's life, but Sonja, no pillar of fidelity herself, wasn't bothered by the word "women." However, when it boiled down to "a woman," she became concerned.

Sonja knew Topping's maid and paid her for information on Topping's life in Hawaii. The maid told her that Topping was not only seeing someone, but the woman, Kay Sutton, was living with him. Sutton was also an actress, but in passing the news on to her mother and Leif, Sonja had her say about that. "Actress!" she snorted, "Actress my ass. The only acting she ever did was on her back!" It was the end for Sonja and Dan Topping, but she did not immediately file for divorce. It was wartime and divorcing a serviceman was not the best publicity for an actress. "I'll wait," she confided to her mother. "The war won't last forever."

One of the first things Dorothy noticed when she went to work for Sonja was Selma Henie's possessiveness of her daughter. "She had just separated from Topping, and I thought her mother was being supportive because of the breakup. I came to realize that she lived only for Sonja. She would allow her own dinner to get cold rather than eat before Sonja came to the table."

Dorothy worked out of Delfern Drive and did not accompany Sonja on the road during the early months of her employment, although she became her constant companion in years to come. Sonja surely needed someone outside her family to whom she could turn for matters that were personal, but which she chose not to discuss with her mother or brother.

Sonja was big business, and rumors that mingled fact with fancy constantly circulated regarding her wealth and income. She was believed to be a major investor in a steamship line (this supposition probably came out of a business arrangement Leif was involved in), and in Sonja Henie skates, dolls, sports clothes, paper dolls, coloring books, and jewelry. One writer described her financial involvements as being "so vast that its high priestess has become on the one hand a glamorous screen star and on the other an institution." That institution was Sonja Henie, Inc.

Her traveling entourage had grown in number. She toured with a complete office staff, consisting of a secretary, an accountant, and several office workers. With a cast of over one hundred and weekly expenses running in excess of $55,000, she needed all the help she could get.

Sonja needed help in other areas, too. With all the millions she was making, not one penny went to the Norwegian underground, and Sonja was becoming unpopular with the Norwegians. They had asked her for $50,000, which, with Sonja's annual income, was not that much, although certainly it was worth seven or eight times as much as $50,000 is today. Dorothy, a lady who still has almost total recall, was well aware of Sonja's political dilemmas.

"She was making wonderful money and I saw requests in letters that came in from Norway."

Sonja ignored the letters and did nothing to help. In German-occupied Norway, the Norwegians were allowed to read about her great Hollywood parties in the course of which she spent fortunes on decorations and orchids from Hawaii. Sonja was very conscious that the Norwegian people were against her and that she would one day have to come to grips with her country of birth.

During the spring of 1943, Leif's wife, Gerd, became pregnant and this created minor chaos in the family. When Selma Henie was informed that she was to become a grandmother her first words were, "Don't say anything to Sonja. She'll be upset." Sonja never wanted to hear about babies being born, but when Leif's first son, Billy, arrived, Sonja presented him with expensive baby gifts and doted on him like a childless godmother.

Leif and his family lived in the house on Delfern Drive with Sonja and her mother. If Sonja did not gush over Gerd, she accepted her as part of the family, and Selma Henie was ecstatic at having both her children under the same roof united as a family. It was what she wanted most out of life. Dorothy gradually meshed into Sonja's world. "When I met Sonja, I knew she was a movie star, but that didn't really impress me," she remembers. "I wasn't impressed by movie stars in general. I never read movie magazines, and not being a fan, I had no particular favorites.

When I was sending out invitations for Sonja, in the beginning, I didn't know a producer from a director or who anybody in Hollywood was. It was all just a bunch of names and quite an experience for the first time, because Sonja had a very heavy accent and half the time I couldn't understand what she was saying. She seldom sat down and went over the names with me. She might be running up the stairs and holler out another name and I would try to catch it flying through the air. I spent a lot of time scanning previous party lists and Sonja's telephone directories."

Eventually Dorothy discovered such short-cuts as agents' offices and central casting.

Sonja's last picture on the three-picture deal with Fox was *It's a Pleasure*. The studio finally relented, since color was being used more and more, and allowed Sonja to go out in a blaze of brilliance. Color, and Sonja's skating, was about all the picture had going for it. Sonja couldn't stand Michael O'Shea, her co-star, and the feelings were pointedly mutual. The cast was rounded out with Iris Adrian and Marie "The Body" McDonald.

After playing opposite leading men like Don Ameche, Tyrone Power, and John Payne, Sonja found O'Shea a big disappointment. The story was even more of a disappointment; weak and insipid. Sonja knew in her heart that soon she would no longer be a big film star, but a personality, performer, and impresario in the world of entertainment. There was a funny aftermath to *It's a Pleasure,* pleasantly remembered by Jack and Liz Pfeiffer. The following season, while the ice show was appearing in Detroit, an item of publicity came out on the wire services about Don Loper, who had choreographed the movie. The release praised Loper for designing Sonja's costumes, dancing with her, and choreographing the picture. It stated that he had also written music for the picture. Sonja, whose handwriting was a beautiful script, sent a handwritten note to Jack to which was attached a clipping of the Don Loper item. She wrote, "You better watch your step because you can be replaced by the great one." Sonja had a better sense of humor than many people gave her credit for.

Selma Henie shared her daughter's sense of fun. Liz Pfeiffer spent a great deal of time with Selma on the road and they often went shopping or nightclubbing together. "I flew to New York with her once and she was like a sixteen-year-old kid," recalls Liz. "We went shopping and she said, 'Let's change this routine. Let's do something wild. This is boring.' We ended up going to the Stork Club for dinner. She was great fun on those occasions, as was the entire Henie family. Of course, I only met Leif's second wife a few times, so when I think of Sonja's family, I usually think of Gerd and Leif together. They were warm and fun. They had eye contact and would laugh like they had secret jokes from everybody else.

Mother Henie and Gerd were like sisters in those days and obviously had a great deal of respect for one another.

Ice skaters keep pretty much to themselves when they tour and make their own fun as they can. Outsiders have a difficult time entering the private circle they create, and it is not unusual for them to play harmless practical jokes on one another. Sonja, herself, did not escape some of the roasting that went on within the show.

When Sonja did her Hawaiian number she usually came on in a large float. It was a strobe-light number with beautiful Hawaiian costumes. The chorus would come out on the ice, do their bit, and then fade to the edges of the rink while Sonja mesmerized the audience with her Polynesian gymnastics.

When Jack Pfeiffer had the orchestra rehearsal, Sonja wasn't there. He just went through the music for the kids in the chorus, and they went through their paces. One of the girls in the show was described by Liz Pfeiffer as "a real party girl, one of the funniest kids you'd ever want to know on a show. Her name was Terry and everybody loved her."

What Terry did, when she went backstage, was get inside a big carton with no bottom in it, take an old broom, and come rolling out on the ice doing Sonja's musical entrance. The whole place fell apart; it was the kind of humor that prevailed throughout the group that traveled with Sonja's *Hollywood Ice Revue.*

There were three distinct facets to Sonja's life, and she played each one differently. She had the ice show, which was the fun part of her life; the studio where she did battle constantly with the father figures who ran the big dream factory; and her own family, which she dominated, tolerated, or indulged as the mood dictated, just as a plantation owner in the old South might have done with bonded charges. Sonja became a different person according to which of these situations she found herself in. Her moods varied. She could go from room to room and as she passed through a door, her demeanor would change from charm to shyness or to angry violence in a split second. It was almost as if she had three different brains.

Dorothy came into Sonja's life before the three personalities became indistinguishable, and they surely did merge into one erratically complex personality after a while.

So ecstatic was Sonja over the fact that she was doing a Technicolor picture, that she planned an enormous party to celebrate her final victory over Zanuck and Twentieth Century-Fox studios. Invitations were, of course, sent out to the press, since Sonja always had an eye on publicity and on taxable deductions for promotion. She made her parties pay off with the sort of good press coverage that helped at the box offices of both movie houses and ice arenas.

She rented a huge tent from United Tent Company, put it completely

196

over her tennis courts, and (since this particular soiree was to have a Hawaiian motif) she chartered a plane to go to Hawaii and bring back a load of little orchids. Dorothy rounded up some artificial greenery and it was wound around all the poles holding up the tent and then the tiny orchids were pinned into the greenery. Inside the tent, the roof was a sea of hundreds and hundreds of multicolored, helium-filled balloons.

She ordered ice carvings of every kind and dimension. One was a huge pyramid in the entranceway to the Delfern Drive house. Opposite the entrance, through the bar, was a very large bay window, which overlooked the pool area and created quite a view for anyone entering the front door of the house. Just outside the bay window Sonja had a second pyramid carved in ice and in the top was the largest arrangement of gladiolas ever assembled. The scene was further beautified by special lights in the trees that focused on the pyramid. There were additional ice carvings with flowers frozen right in the ice. It was very lavish, even for Hollywood. And there were the swans. Sonja loved having live swans in her swimming pool for parties, and this was many years before Hugh Hefner and his Playboy Mansion West. Quite possibly Hef got the idea from Sonja. When one of the swans got out of the pool, which was afloat with dozens of water lilies, the gardener came running through the gathering of guests screaming at Dorothy, "The swans—the swans are loose." It was hysterical but fun.

Sonja never cheated on music. For this party she had three bands: a dance band with a dance floor down in the tent area; and two bands up front, one was Hawaiian, which played authentic Hawaiian music as the arriving guests entered the foyer. It was strictly a black-tie, sit-down dinner, catered by Chasen's. Although Chasen furnished the food, it was Sonja's other loyal employee, her cook, Carrie, who made the rolls and many of the salads.

Dorothy recalls that, "It was Hollywood as everyone thinks of Hollywood. Those were the beautiful years and I'm glad I saw it at that time." It was an era of stars who always dressed to the nines for world premieres, the ladies wearing beautiful gowns and boasting breath-taking hair styles. And, in that era, Sonja Henie was one of the magicians who convinced the world that Hollywood was truly a magic factory.

18

WHILE Sonja traveled, Dorothy continued to work in the coffee shop at the skating rink and also at the Delfern Drive home, where she took care of Sonja's household bills, letter writing, hotel reservations, airline reservations, and the never-ending stream of requests from fans for photos. "I often sent out as many as five thousand fan pictures a month. She was that popular and very much in demand as a pinup girl." Dorothy simply wrote a check for postage and Sonja signed it. Fan photographs were her personal responsibility, not that of Fox studios, although the fan mail department of the big studio had its own mailing section and thousands more autographed pictures were sent from there, as well.

With the people who worked inside her own home, Sonja was warm and gentle. Because of the ice show she spent many months away from home, leaving in November (sometimes mid-October) and not returning until March of the following year. Although Dorothy came into Sonja's life while she was making her last film at Fox, she heard many of the stories about Sonja's legendary battles with Zanuck. Even in the telling Sonja occasionally became angry. "Oh yes," Dorothy says, "and the angrier she got, the thicker became her accent, with her eyes flashing and snapping. She was never satisfied with her films. Sonja wasn't really, in my estimation, an accomplished actress. She displayed only two emotions over all the years I knew her. Either giggling or anger. Some actors can absolutely be the person they're portraying, but you didn't feel that with Sonja. She was too shallow in her roles. That's probably why Zanuck didn't give her the opportunity she wanted. Too much superficiality, and it showed up on the screen."

Sonja worked long, hard hours both in Hollywood and on the road. On tour she stayed up all night and slept half the day. At home, working on a picture, she went to bed early, got up at five in the morning and, after putting in a twelve-hour day, came home to dinner and an early bedtime. Her diet made others cringe. Raw eggs were a staple, and she sent shivers down Dorothy's spine when she took her little nephews, said, "Open your mouth!" and popped down the raw eggs.

"She would just crack the eggs with her fingers," Dorothy explains, "hold the shell open and plop the eggs right in like raw oysters—every day."

Sonja also loved steak tartar with raw eggs. The cook would take a little package of meat and grind it three times as a snack for Sonja in her dressing room. That was her between-shows meal.

"It gives me energy," she averred.

Sonja was not a heavy eater, but nibbled a lot. She ate a light breakfast, with juice, and sometimes a little cereal. Surprisingly, for one so dedicated to healthful foods, she ate few vegetables. Half a baked potato, with a piece of steak, was a very common thing in her diet. Sonja loved steaks. At dinnertime, she preferred them broiled or barbecued. On her visits to Norway everything was boiled, from fish to potatoes.

Sonja had one rather unpleasant habit. In order to prevent weight gain, after she had eaten, it was not unusual for her to go into the bathroom, stick her finger down her throat and throw up her meal. In no time she would be nibbling in the kitchen again.

Sonja was very fond of dogs, but not of cats. Over the years she had a beautiful boxer, several tiny poodles that she absolutely adored, and, her last two dogs, the gorgeous Norwegian elk hounds, Tonja and Heika. Sonja did have cats at one point, and they proved to be more nuisance than pleasure. Since her poodles had done little to keep the rats out of her garbage cans, she decided that perhaps a pair of cats would take care of the problem. They did, but created another one. First there were two cats, then a few, and finally around twenty-five. The animal control people were called in to pick them up, but the cats proved to be quicker than their nets.

Carrie got the idea of sedating them. "Why don't we just put some sleeping powders in their food," she suggested. "I don't want to kill them," she explained to Dorothy, who was a great lover of cats, "all I want to do is put them to sleep so we can get rid of the lot." They went to sleep all right, but the animal control man was late, and they were wide awake again by the time he showed up. The whole process had to be repeated. It finally worked, but Carrie had several sleepless nights thinking of what might have happened. She was not an anesthesiologist.

While Sonja was prospering in life, making millions, Leif also was pursuing interests outside his relationship with his sister. He had grown up in Oslo with Niels and Haakom Onstad. Their family had started a taxi business in Norway but were not in the same financial category as the Henies. Wilhelm and Selma had always thought the family was from the wrong side of the tracks. Leif played hockey with the Onstad boys when they were all young, but that was the extent of their social contact. Later, the Onstad family went into the shipping business and, thanks to the brains of Haakom, became immensely wealthy. When Niels Onstad came over to the United States during the early part of World War II—his first trip to America—he was unable to bring any money with him, and he had left his wife in Norway, where she died shortly thereafter. He had little but found a mistress in Florida and set up housekeeping with her in Palm Beach. German submarines were being spotted frequently off the Florida coast, but due to government censorship that was not common knowledge.

Niels had no money here, but quite a fortune in Norway. He had an idea, however, and proposed it to Leif.

"You know, Leif, there is a big demand for tankers right now because of the war, and I know where we can pick up one for about $50,000. It's a great oil tanker and we can make a bundle with it. My problem is, I have no money in the States."

Leif agreed to loan him the money. It was the old story: My brains and your money. Niels promised fabulous profits, so Leif didn't charge any interest. They purchased the tanker and discovered there was a shortage of oil, so they began to haul molasses from the United States to Cuba, and soon they were making excellent money. In a few months they'd made a bundle. One day Niels called Leif and said, "Leif, we've been offered a million dollars for this boat. What do you think?"

Leif, having never been in the steamship business, said, "Niels, you're the one who knows about these things. What do *you* think?"

Niels replied, "I think we should keep it longer."

"Then, let's do that."

Hearing about this at second hand, Sonja went through the roof. "How could you be so dumb as to do business with that sonofabitch. I wouldn't trust him at my front door with double locks."

"But Sonja," her brother protested, "we've been making money. If Niels thinks we can make more he probably knows what he's talking about."

"Just you wait and see. You can kiss your fifty thousand dollars good-bye."

Leif didn't think so. He knew Sonja shared Selma's feelings that Niels Onstad came from a family of rather vulgar *nouveau riche,* and he assumed she disliked him because of it.

Whatever the reason for her dislike, her business judgment was sound. Because it was wartime, it was difficult to get more than a minimum amount of insurance. The ship went out with a convoy in the Atlantic, and the Germans blew it up en route to Cuba.

An irate Sonja told her brother how dumb he was, and this time Leif didn't bother to argue. He and Neils were both losers in the venture, but it hadn't been his own money Neils had been gambling with.

Sonja took her show on the road again for the 1944–45 season. One of her new numbers was a magnificent choreographed extravaganza called

"The Four Seasons." Sonja appeared first as Summer, performing more gracefully than ever and then she went through her elaborate exercises as the other three seasons. Her new partner was Gene Theslof. Fritz Dietl, a big favorite with audiences the previous year, was back with the show. Sonja had her show so refined at this time that there was no such thing as a "bad number." She had, over the years, culled out the bad or so-so acts, kept the good ones, and added better ones as she went along.

No matter how many times she'd been around the block with it, her hula still was the biggest attraction of the show. Sonja also introduced a samba with the very popular Carmen Miranda song, "Tico-Tico."

While the show was in New York, she consented to give show business columnist Earl Wilson an interview. She babbled on for quite a while about her "seventeen-hundred-acre cattle ranch."

"Your what?" Wilson asked, somewhat startled.

"Oh yes, my cattles," Sonja bubbled, giggling her own inimitable giggle. "They call me and say we want to dig oils, so I tell that I am flying to Europe on February 13th because if I fly on that day I will have the plane all to myself. If you find oils send me a wire collect and I'll buy Europe and never do another spin."

She explained that she was only increasing her assets to match her liquor industry in Illinois. "When you own liquor," she giggled again, "everybody loves you. I was never so popular before I had whiskey."

Wilson asked her how old she was. "You kidding? I am celebrating the fifth anniversary of my tenth anniversary of skating. I've been lying about my age for so long I didn't know how old I was myself. My God, I was two years older than I thought I was." Her sense of humor was accurately captured by Wilson in his column and tickled a lot of funny bones along his syndicated route.

The seventeen-hundred-acre cattle ranch was sixteen hundred acres and not hers, but Leif's. Leif dismissed it as a slip of the tongue or Earl Wilson padding his story. It never occurred to him that Sonja could consider the ranch hers, since she hadn't put a single penny into it. Leif had paid for that piece of property with his own money.

When Sonja returned to Hollywood after the winter tour, she had been separated from Dan Topping for almost a year and still had never publicly acknowledged the separation, even though she was asked often enough by inquiring columnists. Louella Parsons, not one to be put off, insisted that Sonja come to her house for one of her "get togethers over a cup of tea." Sonja marched to Miss Parsons's tune just as did every other major star, producer, director, or anyone else who wanted to stay on top in the film business. Louella and her hatchet-wielding competitor, Hedda Hopper, were powerful entities in Hollywood, with an extraordinary amount of influence in high places. Both were backed by powerful newspaper empires, Hedda by the local *Los Angeles Times* and Louella by the omnipotent William Randolph Hearst, giving her the edge in the gossip sweepstakes.

When Sonja seated herself in Louella's parlor, she was getting ready to embark on preparations for her last American film, *The Countess of Monte Christo,* which would go through some rough waters before its final release three years later. But that's not what Louella wanted to hear about.

"Look Sonja," she began, "I don't like to fool around so let's get down to brass tacks. What's going on with you and Dan Topping—and I want the truth."

"Well, Louella, let's put it this way. It's true that we are sort of separated, but remember Dan's been away with the Marines and there's bound to be gossip, like the Dick Haymes thing." Sonja had been reportedly having an affair with Dick Haymes, then married to actress Joanne Dru. "I don't know where some of these people come up with such stories. I have never even met Mr. Haymes. Dan raised holy hell with me when he heard about that. I only laughed and told him I would like to meet that Dick."

"Then there's no official separation or divorce in the wind?" Louella asked.

"How could there be," Sonja said, playing on Louella Parsons' well-known feelings of patriotism. "Dan's away at war."

The subject turned to Norway and the occupation. Sonja advised Louella that the crown prince and princess of Norway had visited her in New York the previous winter and said the Nazis were living in her house, but only in the summer. Sonja expressed sadness that so many people were hungry and added, "I have made many records to send back through the USO with messages of cheer. I talk to many Norwegian flyers who escaped and are now in Canada. They say they eat only fruit and other things that come from the trees. The Germans have all the potatoes and fish."

Sonja, a recently naturalized American citizen, assured the queen of gossips that she would "do anything I can to help the Norwegians to rebuild their country after the war." Parsons was far too smart a cookie to fall for all the plugs Sonja was making for herself. She knew that the Norwegians were very down on Sonja at the time, but she went along with her because Sonja was Hollywood and Louella loved Hollywood first, gossip second. Her article on Sonja was glowing and written right out of the fan magazine manual of positive stories.

Further evidence of Sonja's personal popularity came the following month when *Look* magazine featured Sonja as photographed by Nicholas Muray. She was presented as "Mrs. Daniel R. Topping, wealthy young matron." Very heady stuff. She wore a red, two-piece, short-sleeved cocktail dress with a red peacock beaded on it. Her hair style was off the

Lana Turner rack as she posed before an original Rembrandt in her home on Delfern Drive. As usual Sonja dripped with jewelry, sporting a large emerald ring, diamond and emerald bracelet, diamond and emerald pin attached to her shoulder, and diamond and emerald earrings. She looked like a Christmas tree and the decorations cost almost half a million dollars.

Sonja was called, "International queen of the ice with a Midas touch."

With the war nearing its end and the Germans already routed in Europe, Sonja began to mend her fences as best she could in Norway. A Norwegian "sportsman and journalist" announced that Sonja had sent him $45,000 for Norwegian patriot relief during the occupation of Norway. That announcement was made in May 1945. The following month Sonja, in Oslo as part of a USO tour, hoped the story might take some of the edge off the fact she had done nothing for Norway during the war.

Looking very patriotic in her USO uniform and sporting an overseas military cap, Sonja announced how pleased she was to be back, but quickly added, "I plan to make my home in America." She thought Norway looked better following the German occupation than France from where she had just come. It was difficult for Sonja to say the Nazis had damaged her properties in Norway because everyone knew that wasn't true. She weakly presented her case as a victim of Hitler's tyranny, accusing the Nazis of "stealing my dog," (which was Leif's and had been killed accidently by the German staff car examining her home as a possible headquarters) and of stealing two of her automobiles. Sonja had no real defense and everybody knew it. But so deep was their love for the Henie family, and so fond were their memories of the great joy Sonja had brought to them in the past, that the press did not attack her personally during the time she was there with the USO group.

By September, it became obvious to everyone that Sonja's marriage was finished. The war had ended in August with atom bombs being dropped on Japan at Hiroshima and Nagasaki by American B-29s. In an exclusive interview with the *Los Angeles Times,* she finally admitted there was something missing in paradise. "I do not feel too good about our future together," she announced tearfully. "Dan is to arrive in San Francisco October 10, and we will discuss the matter then."

Would there be a divorce? "I don't want to say anything prematurely, out of fairness to him." It was, of course, a publicity situation, staged to show Sonja as the faithful wife waiting for her man to come home from the wars before she let him have it. No "Dear Dan" letters from Sonja.

Sonja was already dating Van Johnson, idol of the bobby-soxers, under contract at MGM. They had met at a Hollywood party. Both denied there was anything serious about their relationship, claiming only to be "good friends." Van's studio emphatically denied any romance. The publicity department issued a statement announcing that, "Sonja is a nice girl, but her friendship with Mr. Johnson could not possibly be construed as a romance."

That didn't prevent the two from making plans to spend the Christmas holidays together in Chicago when Sonja's show played there for the opening of the new season.

Sonja said in her own announcement, "You really couldn't call our friendship a romance, because I haven't done anything about my divorce from Dan Topping as yet." It was her first public utterance to the effect that a divorce was in the works. To her family and coworkers it was only a formality. The marriage was not only dead, but the coffin holding the remains had already been sealed and awaited burial.

After spending Christmas with Van in Chicago, near the end of December Sonja, arm and arm with him, formally announced that she and Marine Major Dan Topping had definitely agreed to a divorce. Sonja's attorney, J. Arthur Friedlund, (who also represented her partner Arthur Wirtz), again denied reports that Sonja was engaged in a romance with Van Johnson.

That afternoon Van and Sonja were accosted by reporters as they returned to their hotel. "Will we get married?" Johnson exclaimed with what appeared to be astonishment. "Are you kidding? We're just in Chicago on business. I'll be returning to Hollywood in a few days."

Sonja told the newsmen, "I will get a divorce eventually. Right now I am too busy with my show."

While her show was in New York at Madison Square Garden the next month, Sonja filed suit for divorce in Chicago, charging Topping with desertion. On the surface she appeared not to be concerned, but privately she was quite depressed that another relationship had failed. Again, it was another woman. Why, she asked, did the men in her life seem always to find solace in other women? Perhaps Sonja was wearing too many male "hats" in her life to be the completely feminine woman that most of the men of her era expected in a wife or lover. Sonja was a woman living in the wrong time.

Sonja's romance with Van Johnson was doomed from the outset. Their short time together in Chicago had to suffice. Louis B. Mayer, the iron-willed head of MGM, did not want Van Johnson to marry Sonja. He was considered, at the time, to be Metro's hottest property, and Mayer was not about to jeopardize Johnson's standing with his fans by permitting him to do anything so unpredictable as getting married. He would later change his mind, but for other reasons. When Mayer heard that Sonja was returning to Hollywood, he conveniently managed Van's schedule so that he was out of town when she arrived. He was photographed in New York and Florida with Jacqueline Dayla, whose name had been romantically linked with his in the gossip columns.

Sonja was hurt by the big studio's attitude, but as always, she held her head high. Her explanation was, "Van is too grateful for what his studio has done for him to annoy them too much—if he can help it."

Meanwhile, there was some question in the mind of the Illinois courts as to whether Sonja was a resident of Chicago, where she filed for divorce. If it turned out she wasn't, then she either had to establish residence there or take her divorce suit elsewhere. Judge Edwin A. Robson of the Illinois Superior Court asked her to wait while he made a decision in the matter of jurisdiction. Under questioning, she admitted that she had never voted in Cook County, where the matter was filed, and couldn't remember if she had ever filed personal tax reports there. Anything to do with taxes made Sonja feel uncomfortable. She gave her permanent residence as the Belmont Hotel in Chicago. However, she had chartered a plane and flown in from New York for the hearing and was currently registered at Chicago's Drake Hotel.

The power of celebrity won the day and the divorce. A few days later Judge Robson made a display of outrage over easy divorces by crying out in open court, "Shame! Shame! Shame on society for its lack of respect for marital obligations." He assured Sonja that his words of condemnation did not apply to her but to society as a whole. He then awarded her the uncontested divorce and the restoration of her maiden name. It had all taken place within nineteen days of her original filing, a record for speedy divorces in Cook County. J. Arthur Friedlund, her attorney, had succeeded in having her case set above 1,086 petitions ahead of her on the docket waiting to be heard. Judge Robson, explaining the exception, allowed that he had judged the *Henie vs. Topping* case on its "individual merits." "It is my duty," he further stated, "to protect Miss Henie against public promotion and prejudice." After taking the matter under "advisement," he determined that Sonja was, of course, a resident of Chicago and entitled to be divorced in the windy city where she had been married.

Sonja, upon arriving back in Los Angeles, was questioned by reporters on the judge's comments about the laxity in American morality. "It is a shame there are so many divorces," she said, "but it is best to get it over with, I suppose."

When Sonja's ice revue opened a few days afterward in Los Angeles, it was at Sonja's own Westwood Village Ice Rink, which she had purchased for her shows in the movie city because *Ice Follies* and *Ice Capades* had contracts with the larger, more popular Pan Pacific Auditorium. On opening night Van Johnson filled her dressing room with dozens of orchids.

The turnout for Sonja's show in Westwood was a glittering one. Hollywood was making a declaration of homage to one of its own. In the audience she saw Gary and Rocky Cooper, Dick Powell and June Allyson, the George Brents, Shirley Temple and John Agar, the Harold

206

Lloyds, the James Dunns, Jimmy Durante, Jane Withers, Van Heflin, Jerry Colonna and Sabu—and these were merely a "few" of her inner circle of acquaintances. Sonja's partner was Geary Steffen. One of the new highlights of the show was entitled "Hearts Are Trump" and featured Sonja as the Queen of Hearts.

Florabelle Muir of the *Hollywood Citizen News* compared her business abilities with those of Mary Pickford, Constance Bennett, and Paulette Goddard, who were the reigning financial queens of the movie industry. "Ability and an iron will," wrote Miss Muir, "have carried her far."

Her recently divorced spouse Dan Topping, she learned, had married Kay Sutton. It did not come as a surprise to Sonja, and she acidly commented, "Dan is the kind of man who needs to be married in order to feel secure, but he doesn't need a wife. He has his mother."

As if she didn't have enough problems, the Norwegian press once more criticized her position of "neutrality" in the recent war. It seemed she would never live it down. Also, they questioned the "$45,000 donation," which had been reportedly sent to a journalist in Oslo. No one seemed to have any record of receiving it. That was most appropriate since no one in Sonja's accounting department recalled her having made it. As Dorothy explained it, "Sonja simply did not like to part with money."

When her new ice revue opened at Madison Square Garden in January 1947, the Norwegian "factor" was felt. Her Norwegian-American friends were not so friendly, and it was exhibited at the box office where the usual sixteen thousand patrons of previous opening nights dwindled to twelve thousand. That was in spite of the lavishness that was exhibited in her tenth annual visit to the city with her show. *The New York Times's* John Kendel said, "It was a show in the grand manner, of course, with this one possibly a bit grander than the usual because of a lavishness of costuming that was neither possible nor desirable during the war. Moreover, there were many accomplished male skaters, otherwise engaged in the war years, to point up the charms of the girl from Norway." Geary Steffen continued to be her number-one skating partner, but by now she had added two more for other routines.

Added to her diet of raw meat and raw eggs were daily vitamin shots in her arms and legs. She also received massages twice daily to keep in shape. At thirty-two she was well aware of how quickly an athlete's body is used up in competition. Performing, as she did, was competition of a kind. She was, first of all, competing against time. She questioned her own ability to continue the horrendous schedule she had set for herself as far back as 1924 and the first Olympics competition she had entered. For almost twenty-five years she had worked as hard as any coal miner in the bowels of the earth in order to accomplish an idea, that of combining the classic dance with classical music and flawless ice skating. In that endeavor she had been most successful.

However, the two things she wanted most of all—a devoted, responsible husband who could be depended on to fill her emotional needs, and children of her own—seemed to be eluding her. She had never been pregnant. The idea that she might be sterile certainly must have occurred to her, yet she never discussed it. She dismissed her childlessness by saying, "Who would want to bring children into the world I live in? If I had children, I'd want them to have a home with a mother and father who were there with them. In my case that would be impossible."

She, nevertheless, gave endless hours to and showered thousands of dollars upon her three nephews: Billy, Bobby, and Tommy.

When their mother would ask her, "Sonja, don't you think you're overdoing it with the children?" she would answer, "They're only kids once," or "What's wrong with children having a good time." When little Billy mentioned a saddle for his pony, Sonja found the most expensive one available and gave it to him.

She was never accused of trying to buy the children's love, but she certainly purchased their attention. Sonja always needed to have someone with her; she had an incurable fear of loneliness, a dread of being "left out." That dread would gnaw at her during the coming years more than it had in the past.

Sonja had peaked, and when you are at the top of the mountain, there is only one direction in which to travel. Sonja's descent was about to begin.

BOOK
THREE

Descent

19

$\mathcal{B}$Y 1947 it was estimated that during the past ten years some fifteen million customers had paid $25 million to see Sonja skate. Her income from other sources was, at a minimum, triple that amount. Her ice show ran smoothly, staffed by veterans who had been with her for years: Jack Pfeiffer, the musical director; Billy Burke, managing producer; and Catherine Littlefield, choreographer.

Sonja wanted to have some fun and during the spring of 1947 she slipped off to Europe simply to play. She did not keep cash in French banks, so when she went to the French Riviera or Paris she always smuggled in American dollars, which she used while on vacation. Someone, perhaps a discharged skater with a grudge against Sonja, alerted French customs that the skating star would be arriving at Le Bourget Airport in Paris en route from Brussels with "hidden American dollars." When Sonja landed she was taken into custody by the customs officials, and a French female agent strip-searched her. They found two $100 bills secreted away in her wallet which she had failed to declare. "It was just mad money I had carried for years in case of emergency," she explained. "I had forgotten all about it."

She complained bitterly that, "they made me take off everything including slippers and when they found nothing they strewed the contents of my suitcases all over the place, and I had to put everything back again. It was embarrassing. Plus which, my money was not returned. All I got was an apology from the chief customs inspector. I hope he had a good time on my two hundred dollars."

In New York, on her return trip, she joked with columnist Earl Wilson who asked, "Would you say, Sonja, that while you were traveling over there you were so *nudely* interrupted?"

Eyes twinkling, grinning impishly, Sonja said, "Hmmm—anyway, they went through me." She laughed. "I think I set, what you call it—a new president? Anyway, all my friends get undressed now. There's so much smuggling they undress everybody. But they're so apologetic— after they take your money, of course. You're almost glad for them to have it." She had expected the same treatment in London when someone approached her at the airport and said, "Miss Henie, the police want to see you."

"I thought, oh boy, another strip. I could include this in my show and make a million. But it wasn't a strip. All they wanted was to stamp my passport, darn it."

However, it was time to get down to business again, movie business. The long delayed *Countess of Monte Cristo* had to be completed. Sonja was nervous. She hadn't made a film in several years. She knew she would have to expect close scrutiny of anything she did, and from the first day of shooting, nothing went well. Sonja was dissatisfied with the director, and the studio was dissatisfied with everything. The film was a Universal International production that starred, in addition to Sonja, Olga San Juan, the Puerto Rican singer and dancer. The supporting cast included Dorothy Hart, Arthur Treacher, Hugh French, Freddie Trenkler, and Arthur O'Connell. Sonja's current (but not for long) skating partner, Michael Kirby, was also part of the cast. He was just another in a long list of men who accompanied Sonja on the ice—some of whom also accompanied her to the bedroom.

In an effort to salvage the project, Universal International head William Goetz, who was producing the film, called in Fred de Cordoba to take over the directing chores. Fred was just off Deanna Durbin's last picture, which the studio executives felt was pretty good film fare.

"Look, Freddie," Goetz said, "what we have is a picture that's sort of completed and sort of not completed. What we've seen put together is not something I'd like to present to the public. I wonder if you would be interested in taking this project on and completing it so we have a picture to distribute?"

De Cordoba and a writer, Bill Bowers, put their heads together. Freddie explains: "Bill Bowers was a very well-known writer, very glib, very facile, and quite prolific. Goetz told us to go away for a couple of weeks together, after we'd viewed the assembled film, and see what we could do about it. We were told to keep the same cast, same sets, to retain all the ice footage which had been shot, and then rewrite a totally different script to fit into those categories.

"While that seemed monumental and absurd, we went away as suggested and put our collective minds together. We figured between this number and that ice number and that set and these people we might come up with something—and when we were done with the skull session we had recreated the picture with a new story, retaining Sonja's skating sequences which were the best part of the material we inherited. We redid all of the dialogue and a great deal of the story."

Fred de Cordoba has been producing the Johnny Carson "Tonight Show" for NBC Television for a number of years and recently the producer of *The Countess of Monte Cristo,* John Beck, visited de Cordoba in his office at NBC Studios in Burbank on another matter, and they began to discuss the problems of the picture.

"We came to the conclusion, considering all that had happened in the making of the picture, that it came out to be a rather successful film. It wasn't a world-beater, but there was nothing about it that you'd have to be ashamed of, and it was fun to do. Sonja and Olga San Juan, along with the young man who skated with Sonja, could take credit."

De Cordoba had no problems with Sonja, in any respect. "I had nothing to do with her skating scenes. Those were already filmed, and I believe Sonja pretty much directed herself on ice. She was the expert. I remember the press tried to create a feud between Sonja and Olga San Juan, but it was mostly a publicity ploy. I don't think they spent their time together, but on the set during the making of the movie itself there was nothing like that.

"Sonja never claimed to be a threat to Garbo, nor do I think anybody else ever claimed that for her. But she had a combination of factors that worked for her. Even if you look at her older pictures, as far back as *Sun Valley Serenade,* she had great personal charm that came over on the screen. The dimples, the smile, the insouciance. Those kinds of things. She was, I think, a surprise to people the way a great sports star is who turns out to be considerably more than adequate in motion pictures. That's what she was.

"I think she contributed something to films. Oh yes. There was a sexy—a terrible word—but a sexy wholesomeness about Sonja, or a wholesome sexiness. I think she turned you on on the screen and certainly did off, because I found her enormously appealing as a person. We dated. We went out. We were not one of Hollywood's great romances, but we had dates and she was delightful to be with. We'd go to dinner and then the night clubs—Mocambo, Ciro's—and everybody looked up when we walked in. She was certainly an international star. Wherever we went there was an enormous reaction by the patrons or the press and I always knew I was out with a big star.

"I must emphasize, however, that I never found her to be a temperamental or troublesome actress—or date. Darling is perhaps a strange word to use for her, but that's exactly what she was. Darling. Darling and appreciative."

Fred was often a guest at Sonja's elaborate parties. "There were many lavish parties in those days as opposed to the kind of company parties now. Sonja held hers at the lovely house on Delfern. I recall that she always had exquisite gifts for her guests. No jeans and stringy hair for Sonja. She was a star when it came to entertaining and being the hostess. She was always beautifully dressed and coiffed and extremely tasteful and talented as a hostess. An interesting note, perhaps, is the way that both men and women liked her. It was not a case of the men saying, 'Oh, boy, is that a dish, but I think she's tacky,' or the wives saying, 'What a lovely, wonderful woman she is,' and the husband responding, 'but she

213

has no charm.' None of that was true of Sonja. Everybody liked Sonja. Many were envious of the outstanding men she married. She had quite a group going there."

As shrewd as he was, Arthur Wirtz once confided to Freddie that, "Sonja is shrewder."

"Sonja, like Marion Davies—who started the whole gift-giving thing—was part of an era when at the end of the picture the star used to give gifts to everybody and have a cast party," Fred recalls. "It was during the time of the star system, which doesn't exist today, which required the star status and people would ask, 'Did you see what Marion gave me at the end of the picture?' and would mean, 'What did you get from whomever?' From Sonja or Crawford or what did Flynn give you this time. Interestingly enough, many of these people who were extremely lavish in that area were tightfisted when it came to picking up a check for lunch. I think some of that still exists in Hollywood."

For all the personal good will and Sonja's cooperative spirit, the picture was generally panned.

One song, sung by Olga San Juan, "Count Your Blessings," became a popular hit of the day and later a standard.

Although the differences between Sonja and Olga were slight, the fight in the media between Sonja and new skating sensation Barbara Ann Scott from Canada spilled over into reality. *Time* magazine got into the fray with what could only be called "tabloid sensationalism," pitting the two skating stars in an unfair arena. Barbara Ann was nineteen, Sonja thirty-five. If the champions were both nineteen, the magazine opined, "the contest would be a thriller of fire *(Sonja)* v. femininity *(Barbara)* and the betting about even money." *Time* accused Sonja of being "a butterball" in her Olympic days. Sonja was also accused of disguising an unclean exercise "so expertly that the people never saw the difference."

The one thing Barbara Ann and Sonja had in common was that they were both "daddy's little girls." Each had a father who gave his full support to the ambitions of his skating daughter. Whatever the advantages, real or imagined by the press, favoring Barbara Ann, she was never the box-office champion that Sonja was. As for the axiom about records being made to be broken, it does not apply in Sonja's case. Her amateur records, especially the ten straight world championships and the three Olympic gold medals, will probably never be broken because of the nature of the Games and the changes in athletic breeding. She was Babe Ruth, Mickey Mantle, and Ted Williams all wrapped up into one little blonde bundle of joy on ice.

But if Sonja's gold medals were secure, her personal gold was often subject to the ambitions of crooks. Throughout her life she was plagued by robberies and attempted robberies. One day Leif was at Twentieth Century-Fox studios with Sonja and his mother when he received a phone call that Sonja's house was to be robbed later in the day. The tipster was an undercover police officer who had fallen into the plan quite by accident.

Leif immediately gathered up his mother and sister and drove to the house. Sonja had house guests who were thoroughly enjoying the intrigue of real Hollywood cops and robbers. Carrie fixed an early lunch for everyone while they sat at the table, draperies tightly drawn, and discussed the anticipated robbery attempt.

Several plainclothes men were hidden in the house itself and in the bushes around the grounds. Two men were posted on top of the roof, secluded from the street.

The criminals had planned well. Several days before the chosen time, a man representing himself as being from a utility company came to the house. "There's a leak somewhere in this neighborhood," he explained to Carrie, "and we're checking every home to see if we can find it. I'm sure Miss Henie doesn't want to be paying for something she isn't using." Carrie agreed to that and permitted him to check out the house.

He made a complete diagram of the home as he roamed about from room to room, putting down notes indicating where entrances and windows were located, to assist in making the heist an easy one. The undercover detective was thought, by the perpetrators, to be an out-of-work burglar, and he was invited to come along and share in the plunder.

When the crooks arrived, the police were waiting for them. The two would-be robbers were arrested on the spot. Leif felt let down.

"I was young at that time, and felt disappointed that there hadn't been any real action. I was waiting on the second floor with my Leica camera to take pictures of the whole thing."

As it turned out, the district attorney's office declined to issue complaints on the ground of insufficient evidence. A deputy district attorney added, "If the police had allowed this thing to go through there would have been no joke and these guys would have been doing time." The two men were later booked on suspicion of vagrancy, the old California catchall law when all else fails. Sonja felt she was never in any real danger. "Besides," she said with a giggle, "I keep my jewels in a vault and only I have the combination. I would die before I tell anybody."

Sonja was dating a number of men now that she was a free woman. One of those was a very handsome Norwegian, Kjell Holm, who visited her in Hollywood. Louella Parsons, who was always on the lookout for a new romance, pinned Sonja down on the issue one day. "Are you in love with Kjell Holm? I certainly believe you are."

"I am not getting married," she told Louella. "But I am very much in love with both Kjell and his brother Axel. They are not strangers. I've known them both all of my life. Still, I am too busy with my work to think of marriage."

Sonja was dressed in smart black and white, and Louella asked her why she had changed her image. "You know, when I first met you, Sonja, you were a plump little girl with a baby face who wore blue hats and dresses and was desperately in love with Tyrone Power. You were an ingenue. Now you're a smart and fashionable woman."

Sonja giggled. "I love clothes and jewels. I love to be glamorous. Don't you think all women like glamour?" Louella did. "And," Sonja continued, "when an actress tells you she wants to slip into town and not be met by the press and the newspaper people, she isn't telling the truth. I would never want to travel anywhere without being recognized."

Sonja was recognized and by no one more than the Internal Revenue Service. She paid $600,000 in Federal income tax on her 1947 earnings. Considering her penchant for hiding her money, one can only conjecture how much larger her tax bill might have been had there been a thorough investigation into her financial shenanigans.

Sonja's life, now, was work and party. There were no film offers. The days of musicals were largely past, and postwar pictures leaned more toward realism. Television, with its serials and soap operas, had cut heavily into the average viewer's outside entertainment time. Sonja never saw live television as an avenue she wanted to pursue in her career. She argued that "If people see me on television, they won't come to my ice shows."

Television was still a novelty, but it did result in the closing of hundreds of movie theaters around the country. The major film studios were selling their old movies to television to make up for the losses caused by a diminishing box office. The cost of making movies crept up.

During the month of January 1949, while Sonja was in New York playing Madison Square Garden with her ice show, she lived at the Pierre Hotel. She was in a hurry to get to the Garden for the show one night and didn't have time to put her jewelry in the safe downstairs or lock it in her trunks, which were stored in the massage room in her suite. She simply crammed everything into the masseuse's suitcase, which was made of cardboard and which even a child could have opened.

Upon returning from her performance, Sonja did not realize at first that someone had been in her apartment, but when she dressed for a late supper party, she could not find her black Russian broadtail fur coat. She noticed, then, that the bed pillows had been rearranged. She ran to the massage room to find that her trunks had also been ransacked. But there, on the floor, untouched and unopened, was the little cheap cardboard suitcase with over a million dollars worth of jewelry in it.

The thieves did make off with $28,000 in fur coats. Sonja seemed, to the police, unimpressed by the loss. "I have many more furs worth lots more money," she said. She admitted that only $18,000 of the loss was covered by insurance. "I suppose," she sighed, "my insurance rates will go up again."

Sonja continued on her tour and returned to New York early in the summer. During the first week of June she was back in the headlines. She had met a handsome young man, again someone from the society set, Winthrop Gardiner, Jr. Winnie and Sonja dated constantly, and the press quickly surmised that she was headed for the altar once more. Selma Henie read the columns with a sense of disgust. "How can they get away with this sort of trash," she asked Sonja. "Why don't you do something about it?"

"Oh, Mother, it's nothing. You know the papers. They love to stir up dirt. If you call them up or complain, all they do is print another story worse than the first one. It's nothing. Winnie and I are just friends. You know that."

Selma was no longer sure what she knew or what Sonja was up to. There was an unspoken breach between mother and daughter, and it bothered her terribly. Leif and Sonja were her life and she could listen to their sibling bickering with a mother's understanding, but for Sonja to be secretive with her mother—that was something to consider.

When Sonja decided to toss a big bash, with Winnie Gardiner the unofficial guest of honor, the press fell all over its typewriters to cover the party. Sonja put out the word that she intended to let New York "know what a Hollywood party is like," and she did just that. Earl Wilson reported in the *Daily News* that it was "such a wonderful party," some people didn't get over their headaches for several days. He expressed disappointment that Sonja did not announce her engagement to Winthrop Gardiner, Jr.

"Darling," she giggled, "I simply can't do that. How can I talk of something so serious as marriage when we are having so much fun. What do you think?"

The press thought they were being conned out of a June bride story.

Sonja blended her Hollywood friends with those she counted on her side in New York. The party was sprinkled with class "A" stars: from Hollywood, Jane Russell (accompanied by her mother-in-law) who wore a black, slinky, low-cut gown with full-length satin gloves, revealing almost more than she did in her famous debut film *The Outlaw*—and upstaging Sonja as much as anyone ever could, Harold Lloyd, Richard Widmark, and Joan Blondell. From New York, Ethel Merman stood out.

Sonja was immediately dubbed "the Norwegian Elsa Maxwell—with money." It was a very expensive doing and done with style and taste right down to the last finger bowl and toothpick.

There was also a less cheerful reason for Sonja to be in the papers. The next day she reported the theft of $35,000 worth of sables and other

217

clothing items from a truck. As usual, she joked with the press about her losses. "Why I've lost a whole new wardrobe and all those lovely sables." Winking, she added, "Luckily, I've got a few doodads left."

The truck driver transporting the bags to the airport for shipping to California explained to police that he had locked the door to his truck but somebody had tampered with it while he was making another pickup. Her suitcases were insured for $5,000; the furs for full value.

If Sonja was trying to keep secret any plans that she and Winnie Gardiner had, she let the wrong people know about them. A friend, Ross McLean, who operated the Roosevelt Field Inn in Garden City on Long Island, let slip to the press that Sonja and Winnie had discussed their impending marriage with him the night before, August 25, and added, "They're trying to decide where to fly tonight."

The skater and the socialite already were flying out in his private plane to visit his mother and two sisters in East Hampton and obtain his family's official blessing. It was not until early September that the announcement was made, through a public relations firm. The press release stated that both had been married before and said:

> Miss Henie recently has been engaged in the promotion of ice shows. Gardiner who has homes here [Manhattan] and in East Hampton on Long Island, inherited Gardiners Island. He became the 14th owner of the Island settled by his ancestor, Lord Lyon Gardiner in 1622. He is in charge of the aviation department of the Industrial Tape Company of New Brunswick, New Jersey.

There was a minor hang-up in their plans when Winnie, unable to produce his divorce papers from Frances Lattimer, was denied a license to marry Sonja. However, the following day he produced the required document and the license was issued. Sonja and Winnie were married in a private ceremony at the Park Avenue Methodist Church on September 15, 1949. Only sixty invited guests attended the rites, but outside the church the crush was so great that police had to clear a way for Selma and Mrs. Alexander MacArthur (Sonja's matron of honor, Arthur Wirtz's daughter) to get out of the church.

Sonja was escorted down the aisle and given away by Leif. Winnie's best man was his sister's husband, Olney B. Mairs, Jr. Winnie Gardner gave his age on the marriage license as thirty-six; Sonja, already thirty-seven, listed her age at thirty-three. Nearly three hundred bobby-soxers squealed and "oh'd" outside the church during the double-ring ceremony. Sonja's gown was of ice blue net and lace, designed by Carrie Munn. She carried a bouquet of peach spray orchids and faced a barrage of photographers both upon entering and leaving the church after the ceremony.

At Sonja's request, the word "obey" was eliminated from the traditional marriage vows. Sonja might love a man, but she found it difficult to acknowledge that she "obeyed" anyone. Darryl F. Zanuck would have certainly said, "Amen!" to that.

The tears Sonja shed during the reading of the marriage vows turned to bright sunshine smiles at the Park Plaza Hotel, where an elegant reception awaited the newlyweds. The happy couple danced alone under a spotlight while the orchestra serenaded them with "I Love You Truly." The four hundred society guests downed canapés and gulped champagne for hours after the bride and groom had disappeared.

Selma Henie was disappointed and heartbroken that her daughter had chosen another of those "society bums" for a husband. From the moment she set eyes on him, Sonja's mother never liked Winnie Gardiner, and she never missed a single opportunity to show her disapproval of the marriage.

Fortunately for Sonja's peace of mind, she had no idea of how right her mother was. Her wedding to Gardiner would bring her to her knees emotionally and financially. She would rue the day she married him. But she would get her revenge.

20

$\mathcal{W}$ INNIE Gardiner broke tradition at their wedding reception. While the men were lined up to kiss his bride, he formed his own line of women and gave them a sample of what Sonja was going to receive. Ethel Merman went through his kissing line twice.

Each of Sonja's marriages had been to men who were married twice before. Being brought up in a strict, orthodox Norwegian atmosphere, one would have thought that that was a mistake she would not have committed a first time, much less a second.

But Sonja was in love again, and, as usual, it was "madly." She vowed that there would be "no more divorces." Once again she was married to a socialite who was more socially than financially sound. His famed Gardiner's Island, which had been in the Gardiner family since the sixteen hundreds, had nearly slipped through his irresponsible fingers just prior to his marriage to Sonja. It was only the financial intervention of an aunt that allowed him to retain control of the island, which had been just about to be auctioned off for unpaid taxes.

To prove her love, Sonja began to deluge her new husband with expensive gifts, including a new Cadillac and a private airplane. Unlike Dan Topping, who cared nothing about Sonja's business affairs, Gardiner immediately began to give Sonja advice. Instead of pursuing his own career, he traveled with Sonja on her tours and generally had his finger in everything financial that she was involved with. He made enemies within her close circle. Leif found him pleasant company socially, but obnoxiously uninformed about the business of ice skating. Winnie Gardiner was a drinker, and after a few cognacs he became a know-it-all.

Selma and Sonja, thanks to the intrusion of Winnie into the Henie family, were having difficulties they had never had before. "Isn't he just the most handsome man you've ever seen, Mother?"

"It depends on what you call handsome," her mother replied. "I don't see anything handsome about a man who never washes his hair and always looks like his head is plastered with pomade. Not my idea of the ideal man. No, not at all."

If Winnie's personal hygiene left something to be desired, Sonja matched him when it came to litter. She could mess up faster than any maid could straighten up. The combination of Sonja and Winnie must have driven Selma Henie right up the wall, because she was an immaculate woman who wanted everything in its place at all times.

Sonja must have kept Carrie, her cook, busy—for she was in and out of the refrigerator ten or fifteen times an hour, strewing particles of food on the floor, table, or stove as she walked around nibbling. She lived her personal life right out of the court of a French king.

Dorothy Howes was a firsthand witness to the relationship between Selma and her son-in-law. "Mrs. Henie," she says, "was always around the house. When I came to work for Sonja she and Dan Topping were already separated and I had no idea just how possessive Mother Henie was of her daughter. I knew she was always willing to be at Sonja's elbow when she needed something, but that didn't involve a man. That was a mother being helpful to a very busy daughter. When Sonja married Winnie Gardiner I saw a different situation. Mother Henie could hardly stand to see Sonja and Mr. Gardiner retire at night.

"There were other ways she showed her dislike of the man. For instance, if they had steak for dinner, she would cut the tail off her steak and the tail off Sonja's steak and put them on his plate. Not exactly throwing out the welcome mat for her daughter's new husband. Winnie put up with quite a bit there and I think it was definitely Mrs. Henie who caused that breakup. He and Sonja had a good time together, and I believe at the time of the marriage Sonja thought he had more of a financial background and more money than he turned out to have. He seemed to receive only a meager quarterly income from the Gardiner estate. But as far as them having fun times together, they did. I believe the marriage would have lasted longer had it not been for Mother Henie's interference, but eventually it would have soured because money would have become a big factor. Sonja needed a lot of money."

Sonja did not particularly like women and had few female friends. Perhaps her amateur days had given her the habit of looking at other women in competitive terms or perhaps it was a direct consequence of having had romances with womanizers like Tyrone Power and Dan Topping. Whatever the reason, like many female stars before and since, she cultivated friendships with the gay boys in her show. Dorothy says, "I think she felt safe and secure around them. She saw them as people who were no threat to her marriage and as men who genuinely liked her and wouldn't use her as some others might. For instance, I can still hear some of them coming up to Sonja and saying, 'You look gorgeous today. What did you do to your hair? Just gorgeous!' Sonja ate that up."

Sonja's home was not a place where people would drop in unannounced to chitchat and relax. Dorothy says, "Very seldom did any children come to play with Leif and Gerd's children. Billy was frightened to death of those other kids the day I took him and enrolled him at school for the first time. He just wasn't used to seeing any other kids except his young brothers. The Henies lived so closely—just family. But Sonja had a few friends who were women. Kay Gable was one of her friends. They talked on the phone a lot and shopped together occasionally. Sonja was great on the phone. That's where she did her chitchatting. Belle Christy was one of the very few who got close to Sonja as a friend. She was exceptional in that she was her only female friend who did not come from stardom or money. They had a special relationship."

Frances Hommes, a socially prominent lady in Beverly Hills and on the West Coast, was also one of Sonja's closest personal friends over a period of years. Although she made few friends with women, those she did make were preserved in concrete. They were all loyal to Sonja and, in general, she returned that loyalty.

During the first year or so of Sonja's marriage to Winnie Gardiner they appeared to be happy with each other. Winnie made a pretense of taking care of his business affairs in New York, but whatever activities he had going on the East Coast were really taken care of by his family and the family accountants. Winnie spent most of his time with Sonja. He was in New York when Sonja and Arthur Wirtz purchased the Cole Brothers Circus. Sonja knew nothing about circuses, but Wirtz assured her it was a great investment. In April 1950, the circus opened in Chicago and Sonja was there. "I wouldn't miss the opening of anything," she said as she and Leif deplaned on their arrival from Los Angeles. Winnie flew in from New York to meet them. Would she appear or travel with her new circus? she was asked by reporters.

Sonja giggled. "No, I don't think so. I don't think I have any place with such agile performers, so Winnie and I will leave in ten days for Europe. We're going to spend June and July in my Beverly Hills home and then go to East Hampton for a month."

She further explained, "I was in Los Angeles only for a short time. I wanted to see my new baby nephew, Tommy, my brother's third son. Actually," she added, "I'd hoped for a little Sonja this time. But he's a beautiful baby and I love him the same as the other two."

This season's ice show would be the last she would perform in under the Arthur Wirtz banner, thanks to the meddling and intervention of her husband. During the time the show was playing at Wirtz's Chicago Stadium, at Christmas, Sonja and Winnie were frequent visitors at Billy Burke's Cameo Restaurant, one of Chicago's top gourmet establishments. Burke was an employee of Arthur Wirtz and naturally reported to Wirtz. Night after night, when Sonja and Winnie came to eat after the show, Winnie was belting the cognac, one drink after another. The more he drank the more he bad-mouthed Arthur Wirtz.

Burke reported what he heard to Wirtz, who was most unhappy with

Winnie's interference in not only Sonja's business, but his own. There was much more to it than butting in. He was trying to convince Sonja that Arthur Wirtz was a crooked business partner who was cheating her out of her fair share of the profits. Nothing could have been further from the truth. Thanks, in large part, to Arthur Wirtz and his guidance, Sonja had become a multimillionaire, reputed to be one of the richest women in the world.

Sharing Sonja's pillow at night, Winnie was in a position to influence her greatly, and, for the first time, Sonja had begun to drink. Perhaps it was to be a companion to her husband who was becoming more and more of a falling-down drunk, or perhaps it was just that the pressure of her life had finally gotten to Sonja. Sonja's drink of choice was scotch; under its influence she became profoundly aggressive and unpredictable.

According to Gardiner, Sonja should receive all of the concession money, not just 50 percent. It came down to a face-off with Arthur Wirtz to see if he would meet Sonja's demands. She and Winnie flew into Chicago. Wirtz had been expecting a visit, but he had no idea that Sonja intended to sever their relationship. Actually, he had already made up his mind to concede a larger percentage of the subsidiary income to Sonja, if that would make her happy. Wirtz was enormously wealthy, so the money was never an issue with him. He was crazy about Sonja as a person and had always respected her business head. "She's tough," he often told other business associates, "but she's got a soft interior. She's a little girl battling in a man's world. You've got to respect her for the way she competes with men."

Winnie Gardiner, however, had persuaded Sonja that she should have it all. Sonja's greed made her easy to convince. Arthur Wirtz could not, in principle, concede everything, and this Chicago visit marked the beginning of the end of their long and profitable association. It was one of the darkest days in Sonja Henie's life, but she didn't realize that for quite some time.

It is ironic that, given Wirtz's attitude toward her, she could probably have restored their relationship with a single phone call. Sonja, however, didn't like to turn back, and she certainly never apologized for anything she'd said or done. Mistakes were for lesser mortals. Sonja had made her own bed, and now she proceeded to sleep in it.

Returning to Los Angeles, she began to plan her production for the following season. She dreamed of making even more money during the coming year, since she would not have Wirtz taking 50 percent of the subsidiary income, and she opened the summer party season with one of the splashiest events the Hollywood community had seen in many moons. She and Winnie hosted the dinner dance at Delfern on a Saturday night.

Sonja wore white lace graced with a million dollars worth of diamonds and emeralds, her favorite jewels. Sonja's own Hawaiian orchestra provided music for dancing, and she had imported Polynesian girls to dance the authentic hula. Louis B. Mayer and his wife, in an Orry Kelly original gown—also loaded with diamonds—danced every dance. Louella Parsons sat with the Mervyn LeRoys, along with Loretta Young in a gown by Adrian and Marion Davies wearing a gown with "a white lace top that would cause any style conscious woman's heart to miss a beat." Davies also adorned herself in rubies worth, as Louella reported it, "a king's ransom." The eighty-eight guests included: Anita Louise and her husband, Buddy Adler; Gregson Bautzer with Evelyn Keyes; Mrs. Gary Cooper, Dan Dailey, Pat DiCicco (a frequent guest at Henie affairs) with Gussie Moran, Barbara Stanwyck, and Nancy Sinatra, Sr., unescorted but soon surrounded by unattached males, Kirk Douglas and Irene Wrightsman, the Huntington Hartfords, Richard Egan with Ann Sothern, Charles and Jean Feldman, Ann Sheridan, the Gordon MacRaes, Joseph M. Schenck, George Jessel, Tyrone Power with Linda Christian, Mrs. Ray Milland, Mitch Leisen, the Arthur Lakes (Marion Davies's niece and nephew) with their houseguest Captain Horace Brown (later, Marion Davies's husband, following the death of William Randolph Hearst), Mildred and Harold Lloyd, and Charles and Mary Morrison, the owners of Mocambo, the popular Hollywood night spot.

The following week, she announced that her new show would "have many changes and unusual effects." "I believe most sincerely this is going to be one of the most exciting of all our shows." She planned to open in Milwaukee and close in Madison Square Garden. In between she vowed to take her show to "one hundred key cities." Even for Sonja that was an almost impossible task. She let it be known that, "If just the right story could be found for me, I'd love to do a motion picture at this point but it would have to be a story with character and depth. I think a skating picture in color would be delightful, but it would have to have a good strong story before I'd do it."

A good dramatic role and color were still uppermost in Sonja's mind when talk came to motion pictures. She also spoke of allowing her ice extravaganza to be televised from New York, something she had never been too enthusiastic about until Winnie Gardiner began to tell her how much money she might make from it. "We could televise from Madison Square Garden," Sonja explained, "and then show the film only in motion picture theaters."

Sonja had great plans for her future, all with the idea of building up her financial war chest for new ventures. Leif meanwhile, was beginning to look after his own nest, spending weekends and any other free time he could on the ranch at Oceanside with his wife and three boys, hoping to create a unique community surrounding a golf course. It was a major undertaking, but he had the ambition and wherewithal to bring it off. His only obstacle seemed to be Sonja and the demands she made upon his time. Now that she was putting together her own show those demands were accelerated. She was a frequent visitor at the ranch when she wasn't working.

The one thing Sonja hadn't reckoned with when she decided to part with Arthur Wirtz was his position in the sports world. He controlled most of the major rinks in the country and she found when she went into the larger cities that all too often she was competing with an Arthur Wirtz ice show.

But before getting down to business Sonja, with Winnie, Leif and Selma, embarked on a European vacation. Throughout the trip Selma did everything possible to bring Sonja and Leif closer even if that meant excluding Winnie Gardiner who, by this time, was finding more companionship in his cognac glass than the marriage bed.

While they were in Oslo, Winnie ordered an expensive yacht, especially designed by a top designer of boats and built by Berg Olsen, the finest builder in Tonsberg, Norway. Olsen was an old and dear friend of Leif's. They had raced together at the time Leif won the Norwegian championship and two King's Cups (two years running) in the Norwegian speedboat competition.

Winnie ordered the yacht but didn't pay for it. The statements of the unpaid account continued to come into Sonja's Delfern Drive home and became such an embarrassment to the family that Selma Henie paid off the balance from her own personal bank account in Den Norske Creditbank of Oslo. Winnie promised to pay Mrs. Henie back, but never did.

Returning from Europe, Sonja took time out in New York to be interviewed by columnist Igor Cassini and told him, "If you're wondering when I am going to quit—I will tell you. I'm skating better than ever. My legs don't get as tired as they used to and I don't even breathe as heavily after a solo. The day I cease to enjoy my work is the day I quit."

Sonja, without Arthur Wirtz to do the financing, put almost $1 million of her own cash into the 1951–52 season. Although she hired a choreographer, she did most of the choreographing herself. She was also the producer and director as well as the star.

As vice president and treasurer of Sonja's large organization, Leif had a heavy responsibility of his own, and Sonja's loyal secretary and assistant, Dorothy, found herself with the responsibility for managing the everyday affairs of the show, booking accommodations for the skaters in advance, handling the payroll, and doing other jobs too important for a mere "secretary." But a secretary she was and so she was treated. It was only because of her intense loyalty to and love of Sonja that she continued in the role she was given.

A new ice show had to begin by solving very basic problems. *Variety*, the show business bible, itemed Sonja's upcoming venture:

226

Sonja Henie is set to produce her own ice show. She's currently lining up a crew on the Coast to open at the Cow Palace in San Francisco, November 1st. Miss Henie already has asked the American Guild of Variety Artists for a minimum basic agreement and is seeking to line up further dates. The new ice show will carry its own equipment. Miss Henie has two portable tanks that can be set up in various arenas and thus will be in a position to play in many towns that haven't seen a major blades display for some time. The big difficulty with an operation of this kind is that to play a week's stand in any town she'll have to rent the auditorium for a minimum of 12 days. It requires 3 days to install the freezing machines and two days for over-all dismantling. Just how her schedule will conflict with other major ice shows cannot be determined until she lines up all her dates. It is conceded that it's difficult to snag sufficient time in arenas that already have ice shows carded. Most spots have been booked for the entire season. Open time in key areas is scarce. Another factor is the possible stands of arena managers who may be fearful of ruining the box office status of packages that have played their spots for years.

One of those packages was the Arthur Wirtz production, which had featured Sonja for a dozen or more seasons. Meanwhile, she was trying to set up dates in Europe, having been turned down already by Wembley Stadium in London, which was booked up for the current year. Ice shows, like circuses, book two and three years in advance.

Sonja sailed into San Francisco, happy as a lark, like a leaf floating in the breeze. She was determined to show the world, and especially Arthur Wirtz, who was now Mr. Bad Guy, that she could succeed on her own. She followed the county fair. "We had to be very careful where we walked," Dorothy remembers, "because those animals from the fair hadn't been too neat with their toilet duties. It was a mess."

Nothing seemed to deter Sonja, however. She was down at the arena early in the morning to supervise things. She stood with William Webster, her refrigeration engineer who designed all her rinks, and made decisions on how things would be laid out. She brought a new skating partner to San Francisco, a handsome young brunette named Bobby Harris. Winnie was around but more an annoyance than a help. Leif sent him on advance promotion on several occasions, but instead of doing what he had been asked to do, he found drinking buddies and spent the time in bars, totally ignoring meetings that were important to his wife's career. Leif found it was better not to expect much from his brother-in-law. It was a big enough problem trying to compete with Arthur Wirtz.

Sonja was questioned as to why she was producing the show without

Arthur Wirtz. Was there a split between them? the reporters wanted to know. "Oh, no. Never such a thing," she explained with a nervous giggle. "I *like* to do it alone. That's all."

Declaring that her first night would be a charity event with the proceeds going to the Damon Runyon Cancer Fund, she received excellent press coverages. Walter Winchell, longtime chairman of the Runyon fund, lauded her as a real champion "in every possible meaning of the word." Sonja was pleased.

Sonja had a show, but no manager. Madame Karinska, one of her designers in New York, recommended a gentleman she knew, an older man named Hugo Schaff. His credentials included two New York plays he had managed in their out-of-town runs before they came into New York. He had never managed an ice show. He arrived in San Francisco, and Dorothy was required to work quite closely with him, inasmuch as she helped check the box office after each performance, counting tickets and making out box office reports. Sonja always wanted an accurate count after the show by the time she was in her dressing room.

Dorothy had no days off. No holidays. Sometimes she was at the Cow Palace box office with Mr. Schaff after everyone else had gone home for the night. Occasionally Mr. Schaff would ask Dorothy, "Would you like a cup of coffee and a doughnut before we get back to the hotel?" Usually they stopped at a restaurant and had their coffee before returning to the hotel. It was some distance, since the Cow Palace was the edge of San Francisco and the hotel was downtown.

Sonja's young men from the chorus were always on the lookout for gossip to transmit to Sonja. Dorothy explains, "There was a couple who seemed to delight, not only with me, but with everybody in carrying tales to Sonja. They seemed to believe that it would put them higher up on the totem pole with her. And she loved to hear the gossip about anybody in the troupe. This particular duo made a beeline to Sonja to inform her that I had been out with Mr. Schaff."

Sonja was quite upset, but kept silent. She was very formal in her discussions with Dorothy. "Oh, I knew there was something wrong because she wouldn't talk to me. There was a big chip on her shoulder whenever I appeared. I still couldn't understand what I had done wrong. Sonja was like that, however. She loved to leave you dangling with a guilty conscience over something mysterious she was holding over your head. I'd been with her long enough to know that the best thing to do was let it ride."

Instead of coming right out and asking Dorothy if she was dating Schaff, which really wasn't any of Sonja's business in the first place, she hired a private detective to follow her secretary.

An old friend of Dorothy's who owned the Westwood Ice Rink was coming to San Francisco and wanted to get tickets for the show. He was coming with his wife and a four-star Air Force general, who happened to be a friend of Dorothy's also. She told him there would be no problem with the tickets. She'd leave them at the box office.

Mr. Downs, the ice rink owner, said, "Dorothy, we'd like to have you come to dinner with us if you can get away."

"Yes," she said, "I think I could get away long enough for dinner. I'd love it."

When they arrived, Dorothy went out for a quick dinner with the group before the show and then back to her room. She dressed and met them again after the show. This occurred the very night Sonja's private detective went to work tailing Dorothy.

"We went out for drinks and a light supper. I'd made reservations for the group at the Huntington Hotel where we were staying. Sonja was on the tenth floor, the general was staying on the ninth and Mr. Downs, his wife, and I were all located on the eighth.

"The detective came back to Sonja's room about nine o'clock the next morning, and she was waiting for a full report. I doubt she slept, worrying what I was up to. Sonja loved cat-and-mouse games."

The detective handed Sonja his written report, which stated that the subject met a gentleman and another lady and a general in front of the Cow Palace at such and such a time. They proceeded to such and such a restaurant, had something to eat, and then took a taxi to the Huntington Hotel. There they entered the elevator and went off to their separate rooms for the night.

Sonja recognized the famous general's name and asked "What the hell is this?"

"Those are my observations of your secretary's activities last night," he responded, somewhat startled by Sonja's attitude.

Sonja went into an absolute fit, yelled and cursed at the detective, and flung the report to the floor. "You dumb sonofabitch, you followed the wrong woman. I'm not going to pay you one red cent. Now get out!"

The detective began to argue and Sonja threatened to throw him out bodily if he didn't leave. He left, promising to sue Sonja for his fee if he had to.

Shortly thereafter, Sonja said to Winnie and Carrie, "Let's go down to breakfast, I'm hungry. Can you imagine that sonofabitch trying to take my money under false pretenses." Carrie declined the invitation, and Sonja and Winnie entered the elevator on the tenth floor.

Dorothy picks up the story. "The timing was such that when Sonja's elevator stopped on the ninth floor the general entered and tipped his cap to Sonja. She smiled knowingly. On the eighth floor I got on the elevator. Winnie already knew the general because they had flown together during the war. He had introduced the general to Sonja between floors. So I got on the elevator and there was no one else there except the four of us.

Sonja, Winnie, the general, and now—me. The general tipped his cap to me and said quite pleasantly, 'Good morning, Dorothy.' If I ever wanted to fade out, that was the time. Sonja's eyes nearly popped out of her face. I couldn't understand why she had such a strange expression on her face because I had no idea about the detective business. But I was quite embarrassed. Sonja did not like me to date or anything like that and I was just certain she would be upset with me even more than she already was."

Instead of anger, as Dorothy expected, Sonja seemed quite pleased that her secretary knew someone so famous.

Later, when Carrie explained all the details to Dorothy, she understood, and Sonja was again her good-natured self with Dorothy. "She could be the sweetest person in the world," Dorothy says, "unless she was drinking scotch."

The person drinking scotch was somebody else. A very mean and nasty individual who had nothing to do with dimples and curls and charm took over control of Sonja's mind then.

21

*D*ESPITE the findings of her hired detective, Sonja dismissed the manager of the show after the San Francisco run. She had made up her mind that Dorothy was seeing him and that was that.

The show moved out of San Francisco to Texas, first Dallas and then on to San Antonio where Dorothy began secretly to date Ken Stevens, the emcee and vocalist with the show. Two of Sonja's spies in the chorus dished out the news to Sonja the night the show closed and was getting ready to move on to Houston. Dorothy noticed an immediate coolness in Sonja's attitude. She had no idea why. After the debacle in San Francisco she wrongly supposed that Sonja would leave her private life alone.

When they got to Houston, Sonja and her entourage, including Dorothy, moved into the Shamrock Hotel. Ken Stevens was quartered in downtown Houston at the old Rice Hotel with the rest of the cast.

Sonja had sent the word out to her spies. "Keep your eye on Dorothy. I want to know what she's up to." The show opened in Houston and the reviews were good, all things considered. Dorothy waited in the wings for Sonja to accompany her back to the dressing room. Sonja didn't say anything in particular, but was quite curt with Dorothy as she changed clothes.

"I knew something was eating her," Dorothy says, "so I asked Carrie what was going on."

Carrie shook her head solemnly. "I don't know what's the matter with her, but just watch your step. Just watch your step." Then she added the damning words, "Don't be going out with anyone on the show."

"I knew then she had heard I was going out with Ken Stevens, and I knew eventually it would all come to a head."

It happened much more quicky than she anticipated. Later that night, after everyone had retired, Dorothy's telephone rang in her room. She looked at the clock as she switched on the light and wondered who would be calling her at three o'clock in the morning. It was the first night out and Sonja had gone to bed earlier than usual, as had everyone else. Opening nights are always tiring. She picked up the phone and sleepily answered, "Hello."

"Dorothy!" It was Sonja, voice firm and blunt. "I want you to call Ken and tell him to get out here. I want you both to come to my room. I'll unlock the door. Call him right away."

Dorothy said, "Well, it'll be at least half an hour, Sonja, before he can come from downtown Houston—even by taxi. Is there anything I can do?"

"No. I want you both here." She hung up.

Dorothy didn't want to alarm Ken, but she had to do as Sonja requested. "Ken," she said after he answered, "I don't know what Sonja is up to but she wants you to come up right away to the Shamrock."

"But Dorothy, it's three in the morning."

"I know, but she insists. Just hurry up." She didn't mention that Sonja wanted to see both of them together until he arrived half an hour later.

"What's this all about?" he asked Dorothy.

"She wouldn't tell me, but she wants to see the two of us together." With some trepidation, Dorothy had made up her mind that no matter what Sonja had to say, she was going to continue to see Ken Stevens and that was that.

They knocked on Sonja's door and she said, "Come in. It's unlocked." She was propped up in bed with her night cream and curlers in place. "Dorothy you sit here by me on the bed. Ken, sit over there on that chair." They both obeyed, as if mesmerized by their employer. Sonja directed her brief remarks to Ken Stevens. "Ken, I just want to tell you one thing. Dorothy is under contract to me for life! And don't you *ever* forget it!"

Dorothy and Ken sat stunned and speechless.

"That's all," Sonja snapped. "Goodnight. You can both go." And they were dismissed. Neither of them said anything to Sonja. They walked out as quietly as they had walked in and did not discuss the meeting again.

"But we continued to date," Dorothy said. "Sonja was just going to have to deal with that, in spite of her spies from the chorus."

By the time they arrived in Denver, the next stop on the tour, Sonja had devised a plan to break up whatever was going on between her secretary and her announcer. "Dorothy," she ordered, "I don't need you here right now. I think you better go on back to Los Angeles and see how things are going at the house. If I need you I'll let you know." She sent her home to get her away from Ken, hoping that absence would not make the heart grow fonder. Dorothy spoke daily with Sonja on the telephone, as well as with Ken Stevens.

Sonja's personal entourage, sans Dorothy, included Winnie, Leif, Selma Henie, and Doris Haines, her hairdresser. While they were on the tour Sonja had sent her mother to New York by plane to have her skates sharpened by Eddie Peck, the only person she trusted to hone her blades.

Selma had rejoined her in Dallas in time for the opening there. Even her mother became a "gofer" when Sonja demanded it.

The tour was a major undertaking for Sonja. Problems arose that she didn't even know existed. Problems that had previously been taken care of by Arthur Wirtz out of his Chicago offices. Sonja's was a shoestring operation compared to the well-oiled organization she had previously been a part of.

Her seven-car train was expensive to operate and, including both workers and cast, she was supporting two hundred people, seven days a week. In the South she ran into racial segregation problems, especially in the Atlantic seaboard states, in cities like Atlanta and Raleigh. In Houston the "colored" acts (which included Cuban) stayed in "colored" hotels or with private families. In the more hard-core segregationist states, the acts had to be removed from the show. The local people did not want a mixture of black and white working together. That didn't seem to bother Sonja. It certainly did bother Leif and some of the others who had difficulty understanding such racial intolerance. But there was little anyone could do about it unless Sonja made it an issue, and she was having too many other problems to deliberately put herself in hot water in the South.

In Denver Sonja realized she needed Dorothy, so she swallowed her pride, phoned her secretary, and asked her to rejoin the show. She hadn't changed her mind about Ken Stevens and Dorothy, but she depended on Dorothy just as she relied on her right arm. Over the years Dorothy had stored away knowledge it would have taken a computer to duplicate. Things that she could easily handle, others fumbled around with. She'd been in the ice business with Sonja a long time, and she knew how to get things organized efficiently. Sonja desperately needed that kind of help.

"It was a terrible season for Sonja," Dorothy recalls. "She wasn't handling bookings in the proper manner. I can still see us all around the table with a map of the United States in front of us and someone would pinpoint a city and say, 'Give them a call and see if we can get in.'" For instance, the Coliseum where we had played in Denver the year before was booked by another show and we went into a less desirable and smaller place, the Denver Armory. We did not do well and the reviews were only so-so. There wasn't the excitement a Sonja Henie show usually generated with the critics. The people were sort of drained with ice shows, and some of the cities could not handle that much traffic with that type show. We had interim managers who didn't know what they were doing, and Winnie Gardiner was still trucking around with us, although he and Sonja were getting close to the end of their marriage.

"I think Sonja's greatest heartbreak came in Chicago when she couldn't get into Arthur Wirtz's Chicago Stadium and had to take her show into the Amphitheatre on the South Side in the stockyards."

Wirtz booked his own show into cities in direct competition with Sonja. He was starring Barbara Ann Scott in his revue, so Sonja was now in direct conflict with her.

"The newspapers didn't play favorites. If they ran an article about Barbara Ann, they gave Sonja equal time," Dorothy recalls. "In Chicago, Mother Henie had some of us running constantly over to the Chicago Stadium to count the house—to see how many people Wirtz was getting. Wirtz was leading, but there was great competition. Nerves were frazzled and tempers were high. Sonja was quite upset, of course, to think that Barbara Ann was with Wirtz, being as possessive as she was. In her mind, only Sonja should play in an Arthur Wirtz stadium."

Sonja's difficulties got worse. From Indianapolis, where she did a bad show, they went into the Carolinas. "Our jumps," Dorothy says, "were, for the most part, quite long ones." Wirtz's shows were booked for transportation very wisely, and his hops between cities were short ones. Sonja had to go wherever she could get into an arena. She had the fortitude of granite, however, and never once thought of calling it quits. "I will beat this thing," she repeated, over and over. "No one will ever best Sonja."

Thus the struggle went on and was going on when Sonja's weary troupe, aboard her special train, rolled into Baltimore, Maryland, in early March 1952. The show was due to open at the Fifth Regiment Armory and, to accommodate what was expected to be a record crowd, temporary bleachers were being built. They were barely finished in time for opening night. It looked as if Sonja might have reached the turning point in her efforts to compete successfully with Wirtz. Advance ticket sales had been the best anywhere on the tour. At the preopening press conference and cocktail party, Sonja was bubbly and effervescent, joking with reporters. She even parodied her Norwegian accent, which amused and delighted the press people. It really did look like a new beginning for the lady with the strong heart and even stronger will.

She still was having trouble finding a suitable manager for the show, and things were being handled by committee, which meant they weren't really being handled at all. She had recruited a man by the name of Muchmore, prior to coming to Baltimore, to act as an interim manager. Mr. Muchmore had been selling programs, and according to Dorothy, "He was a good barker and could sell programs like crazy. But he didn't know anything about managing a show."

Jack Pfeiffer was still Sonja's musical conductor and Ken Stevens her announcer and singer. The group was pretty well intact. She had some new acts because some of the old ones were under contract to Wirtz, but essentially Sonja had the same show she had always taken on the road. The only real problem had been finding arenas without conflicting schedules.

234

"I remember that opening night better than any other in my life," Jack Pfeiffer says. "People were still coming in. It was somewhere around eight o'clock in the evening and I usually started the orchestra anytime between eight-fifteen and eight-thirty. I waited a few minutes. The place was obviously going to be packed and we were pleased with that. I knew it would make Sonja happy. I was just about ready to begin the overture. We were tuning up when I heard this terrible crackling. Being from California, my first thoughts were of an earthquake because that's what it sounded like, the snapping of wood. I turned and looked toward the back end of the armory where the sound was coming from, just in time to see the temporary bleachers disappear. Straight down—people and all. There was terrible screaming. People in the seats on the other side were so frightened they panicked and began to scramble down on the ice where it was slippery. They were sliding and falling all over the place."

Ken Stevens, sensing a disaster if someone didn't step in and take some control of the situation, grabbed a microphone and announced, "People! Please do not run on the ice. Stay where you are. This is a state armory. There are nurses and doctors on duty here. Everybody will be taken care of. Just be calm and everything will be all right."

Jack immediately lifted his baton and the orchestra began to play music, hoping to help calm down the mass of disorganized humanity. It helped to prevent what would almost certainly have been total chaos. Nearly four hundred people were buried in or under the debris. Within seconds every available ambulance was called to the armory to transport the hundreds of injured to the various hospitals in the area.

There was no show that night. The next morning's papers were filled with somber details of the disaster. Jack Pfeiffer and Ken Stevens were singled out as big factors in preventing an even worse catastrophe, and probably saving lives. Officials at the scene were amazed that no one was killed.

It is often said that people are attracted to the scene of disasters, and that may well be true. Sonja's show opened the following night to an overflow seven thousand people. The debris from the fallen bleachers had been removed and 350 extra chairs had to be brought in to accommodate that many counterfeit tickets presented at the turnstiles. Rather than make an issue of the phony tickets, Sonja insisted that the people be seated. "They paid good money for those tickets. It is not their fault they were cheated," she said.

Baltimore, in spite of the accident, was a tremendous success for Sonja. The show was sold out every night. Sonja alone made the decision to stay in Baltimore with the show although the accident had devastated her. Nothing of this sort had ever happened to her in her career and she felt deep pain for the victims and their families.

The reason for the disaster was that the construction company had employed some carpenters who reported to work intoxicated and who failed to install enough bar beams for support. Six investigations were launched and within eighteen hours after the accident, the lawsuits began to be filed. Sonja knew she was in for a rough time but felt she could ride it out. She was insured. Leif had famous Hollywood attorney Jerry Geisler fly into Baltimore to represent Sonja during the initial onslaught.

By the end of the run, lawsuits totaling almost $1 million had been filed in Maryland State Court. People were suing, it seemed, who weren't even at the show. The defendants included Sonja, Winthrop Gardiner, Jr., The Sonja Henie Enterprises, and Edward Coronati, Jr., the contractor who built the stands. The armory was not sued since it was a military facility merely rented out to lessees who assumed full responsibility for any accidents.

The day before the closing in Baltimore Leif was informed privately that there was a movement afoot to put a lien on all the show's equipment to prevent its removal from Baltimore until the suits were settled. Leif had gone to the bank every day during the run, taking out money— as much as possible without arousing suspicion—knowing that the bank account would be attached as soon as someone thought of it.

"What we did," says Leif, "was hurriedly load the show out in moving vans instead of going our normal method by rail. The marshals were watching the train, waiting for us to load up before they served the papers. We exited the city by means of a back route so we didn't look conspicuous. We were just more trucks traveling a truck route and nobody noticed."

By the time Sonja and the show arrived in New York the lawsuits had grown to over $5 million. The show was scheduled to open at the Kingsbridge Armory since Arthur Wirtz prevented her from going into Madison Square Garden. The fallout from Baltimore had preceded her. The commanding general of the armory was demanding a million-dollar bond be posted before the show could go on. Sonja's bond, already in place, was for only three hundred thousand dollars. It was ironic that the same contractor was to be employed to put in bleachers at the Kingsbridge Armory.

Unable to put up the bond, Sonja had to cancel her New York appearance, and that left her heavily in the red financially and in a state of depression. She and Winnie were fighting. He was downing a quart of cognac a day, and Sonja was doing some drinking of her own.

She called a press conference to announce cancellation of the New York engagement. Before the news assemblage at the Plaza Hotel, where she was staying, she said, "Of course I'm concerned with the public safety of my fans. I am as distressed over the accident in Baltimore as anyone else. I am calling off the New York show because we simply

236

cannot meet the bonding demands on such short notice. We're talking about a lot of money here."

Sonja told the press that "My plans for the 1952 *Ice Revue,* at this point, are somewhat indefinite, but I think we will continue the tour for six or seven weeks in other cities. Believe me, it breaks my heart to cancel out New York because I do so at great personal financial loss." She assured everyone that she would continue to pay her two hundred people and vowed to refund all advances made for the New York show—which she did, and immediately. In parting she said, "We'll be back another time." The news people applauded her courage.

Although there would be no show in New York, Sonja did not cancel her own appearances at various restaurants and nightclubs. She ran into Earl Wilson at a party, and he later commented that, "Sonja Henie wears so much jewelry when she dresses up to go out in New York that some folks mistake her for the aurora borealis."

Sporting a twenty-five-carat diamond ring, she told Wilson, "I plan to produce a very big ice show next season. You can say I told you so."

The $200,000 Leif brought out of Baltimore barely covered expenses. Something had to be done to fill in for the lost date. One of the chorus boys suggested she take her show into Cuba. "They will love you there," he assured her.

Meanwhile, Muchmore, the manager, had departed. Dorothy remembers it well. "He got so cockeyed scared when the seats fell down in Baltimore. He was afraid he was going to be sued so he simply disappeared without notice—just got lost. So when Sonja decided Havana might not be such a bad idea she came to me and said, 'Dorothy, I want you to get on a plane and go to Havana and book the show in there.'"

She told Leif to prepare to move the train to Miami where they could rearrange the show to accommodate whatever sized stadium or arena they could secure in Havana. The train was parked on a siding in Washington, D.C.

In Cuba Dorothy contacted an old friend, Pedro Mendietta, who was very close to the dictator, Batista. Pedro took her out to look for a suitable and available site for the show.

It would have to be a stage production because the Havana Sports Palace hadn't as yet been completed. Dorothy finally decided to recommend that Sonja accept a booking into the Blanquito Teatro.

"I explained everything to Sonja. We would have to restage our four-sided show to accommodate the theater stage. I gave her the seating capacity and logistics, which I worked out before calling her."

Sonja was agreeable, and the show moved out en masse to begin rehearsals in Havana, a city under martial law.

The Blanquita Teatro boasted of having an ice stage. When Jack Pfeiffer saw the theater, the "ice stage" was composed of a terrazzo floor with pipes underneath, which could be frozen—an idea copied from the Roxy Theatre in New York by a wealthy and influential Cuban senator.

When Sonja arrived in Cuba she had in tow a new manager by the name of Colligan, who immediately took command. He never seemed to like Dorothy. She couldn't understand why. "Maybe it was because I knew too much," she says. "He wouldn't let me get into the office to work. After we were there for a while I could see certain things going on that I thought were not in Sonja's best interests. Ticketwise and moneywise. I believe he knew that I knew and finally he went to Sonja and convinced her to take me away from working on the payrolls and from involvement in any of the hiring."

Along with a lack of compassion, Sonja lacked loyalty. She had shown that lack to Wirtz and to Dorothy, and, in years to come, she would show it to her longtime attorney and, finally and most incredibly, to her mother.

"It's true," Dorothy reiterates, "that she was cold in that respect. She was not loyal no matter how loyal you were to her."

By now she listened to whoever had her ear. Sonja was floundering around trying to get her life and her career back on an even keel, and failing miserably at both. "So insecure at this time," Dorothy states sadly. "Her world seemed to be collapsing and it all started when she allowed her husband to influence her into splitting from Mr. Wirtz."

Sonja and Winnie had split up. She didn't want him to come to Cuba. She had to find someone to blame for the fiasco in which she found herself, and for a change she blamed the right party. Winnie was left in New York where, as Sonja soon found out, he was boozing regularly and changing female partners almost daily. Again, other women were the burr under Sonja's saddle.

As for the new manager, Sonja had found him and wasn't going to admit that he might not be the right man for this job. She certainly wasn't involved with the man romantically. Disgruntled over her own marital situation, she put men very low on her scale of priorities. She was too busy trying to save the show and her own career.

She rode herd on everyone, but particularly on her secretary.

"She called me day and night. I never had any life of my own," Dorothy says. "Ken Stevens was in Cuba with us. We were still quietly seeing each other but being very careful because by now Sonja was drinking more than she should have been and was given to rages that were unbelievable."

Sonja's rampages took place in the middle of the night, never during the daytime. She was too busy rehearsing then. One evening she had gone out with Jack and Liz Pfeiffer to a nightclub where they saw a wonderful dance team—Alexander and Martha. Sonja perked up immediately. "I want to learn to do that kind of dance on skates," she said. It was a dance called the *Zamba*. Sonja the perfectionist took over. Every morning she had Jack out to accompany her and the four young men she recruited to play the bongos, working hard to learn to do on ice all those things that she'd seen on the dance floor. Sonja incorporated the dance into her show and when she left Cuba even took the couple with her to make sure she kept the dance authentic.

Batista's government, eager to please Sonja, provided a very good though somewhat unusual orchestra for Jack to direct. "The first day I came to rehearsal I noticed the wood men," Jack recalls. "The flute player and the clarinet players were in uniforms. Police uniforms. The sax players carried .45s on their hips. I had no idea what was going on. I'd never seen an armed orchestra before. So I asked one of them what it was all about. They said, "We're in a state of martial law and have to carry the guns."

They were from the police and navy and army bands. Jack didn't ask any more questions. He'd brought along a nucleus of five key men and would build the band around them: first sax, trumpet, drummer, violinist, and pianist. Jack played piano, so there were two pianos. He sometimes conducted from the piano, especially when Sonja did the "Claire de Lune" or "Liebestraum" numbers.

After a couple of days the orchestra manager, a young woman who played violin, approached Jack and said, "We're going to have a rehearsal tomorrow."

"I'm very happy. Everything is fine," he said. "We don't need any further rehearsal."

"No, no," she insisted. "We have to *have* a rehearsal. We are going to have a lot of substitutes tomorrow."

Pfeiffer was confused and his expression showed it. She explained. "Most of the players who won't be here must be part of a special symphony concert that's been arranged. There's nothing anyone can do about it."

Batista had ordered the benefit to help replace the orchestra's funds, which had been embezzled by the former manager. Jack had to start fresh with a number of new musicians.

One day there was no show at the Blanquito, and the entire cast, except Sonja, went off on a tour of the countryside and the Hershey Chocolate plantation and factory. Dorothy went with the group. "I assumed I also had the day off," she said. "Sonja wouldn't be up until sometime in the afternoon. At least that was what I thought."

It was a chance for Dorothy and Ken to be together, and they had a great time. When Dorothy returned after the outing, she ran into Carrie. "What's new, Carrie?" she blithely asked.

"I'll tell you what's new," Carrie cautioned. "Sonja's madder than hell. She's been trying to get you all day. Where've you been?"

"I went with the show to the Hershey mill."

"Well, I can tell you she's really mad this time."

Dorothy went to her room expecting a phone call from Sonja at any time, but none came. Dorothy was quartered in a small apartment down the hall from Sonja. When Sonja hadn't called by ten o'clock in the evening, Dorothy went to bed.

About three o'clock in the morning she was awakened by a loud banging. "It sounded like somebody was tearing down the building," she says. "There was this terrible bang, bang, bang on the door. I wondered who it could be as I got up and slipped on a robe. 'Just a minute,' I called out."

She went to the door and before opening it asked, "Who is it?"

"Sonja, goddamit! Open the door!" Dorothy undid the latch to let Sonja in. "Get him out of here, goddamit! And I mean right now!" She was raging.

Sonja's behavior stunned Dorothy. "Get who out, Sonja? There's no one here but me. What are you talking about?"

"Don't give me that bullshit. Get Ken Stevens out of your room and I'm telling you I want him out right now! Do you understand? Right now!"

"There's no one here but me, Sonja. Come in and look for yourself."

Sonja, roaring drunk, wasn't having any of it and refused to come in to look for herself. She stalked off in a drunken stupor, calling back over her shoulder, "You heard what I said. Just get him out!"

Sonja and Dorothy were the only occupants in their apartment building. Originally Sonja and her close associates had been staying at the Hotel Nacionale. Batista's people decided that Sonja would be better accommodated in an apartment building that had just been completed and not yet occupied. Sonja had plenty of privacy at the new place, but the electricity worked only intermittently and the water pressure was frequently low. Not even Sonja, however, argued with the Cuban dictator.

When she moved, Sonja had cleaned out the hotel suite she occupied at the Nacionale, and the management wouldn't put up with that, even for a star of her stature. The hotel sent an emissary to Sonja with the message that all towels, silver, and bed linen had to be returned to the hotel immediately or charges would be filed against her. Stealing was a very serious offense in Batista's Cuba. The lifted articles were returned by Dorothy. "I had to pack everything into big pillowcases, and I shiver every time I look back and see myself dragging those pillowcases full of Sonja's stolen articles across the lobby of the Hotel Nacionale with everybody giving me dirty looks. I expected to be arrested myself."

The show closed after a moderate run, in spite of what was an excellent production. Sonja might rant and rave through the hallways at night, but she was Miss Perfection when it came to her shows, and this

240

one was no different from any of the others. She was offered suggestions whereby she might cut corners to save money, but refused. The show was the thing and she felt it should be done to the best of everybody's ability.

The skaters and support group were flown into Miami by chartered plane and from there they were given railroad tickets to their various hometowns. The season was over. Mr. Colligan was handing out train tickets, and Dorothy stood in line with the others and waited. When the tickets had all been given out she asked, "Mr. Colligan, where is my return ticket to Los Angeles?"

He said, "You don't get one. You don't belong to the union. You'll have to find your own transportation home." In all her years with Sonja this had never happened. Sonja might get angry and she might berate Dorothy, but she never left her stranded. This time she did.

Some of the skaters had their automobiles in Florida and were going to drive home. Word quickly spread that Dorothy was stranded and one of the skaters, who lived in Los Angeles and was going there by car, gave Dorothy his train ticket.

Sonja never once apologized for treating Dorothy in such a hostile and ungracious manner. Dorothy says, "She never apologized to anybody for any reason."

So ended a season in which Sonja not only didn't make any money, but lost considerable amounts of it—something she didn't take lightly.

"Next year will be better," she stated. "I'll reorganize. You'll see. Bigger and better than ever."

And she sincerely believed what she was saying.

22

ONJA returned home to Los Angeles for a well-deserved rest, only to be faced with further litigation. An attorney whose services she had engaged in 1951 sued her for "failing to pay for professional services." Although the original bill had been for five hundred dollars, the suit was for six thousand. Jerry Geisler, accustomed to multimillion dollar suits and scandalous accusations against his Hollywood clients, must have felt at best uncomfortable, as he sat beside Sonja in the courtroom as "an observer."

A couple of weeks later she was already starting to recruit skaters for her new show. She tried to replace as many skaters as possible because bringing in newcomers cut costs. Their salaries were much less than veterans.' She held auditions at the Polar Palace to fill out the skating vacancies on her show. Sonja attributed the need for skaters to the fact that, "We lose about 20 percent every year. Most of them marry and retire from skating altogether."

The old days were gone. Now, while Sonja was planning her show, Leif was trying to get "Henie Hills, his ranch, going; and Dorothy realized that she was out of work. "I hadn't been fired by anyone, but Colligan was in charge and he made it plain there was no job for me. He told me that, not Sonja." Dorothy then took a job in Los Angeles as a bookkeeper with the Goodyear Tire and Rubber Company.

When Sonja was preparing for the next tour and all, the lawsuit from the lawyer she hadn't paid came up. Dorothy hadn't seen anyone in Sonja's family since leaving Florida. Hadn't been near Sonja's house. "I was minding my own business, trying to get my life back together and enjoying a freedom I hadn't had for some time" she recalls. "Then one day I was subpoenaed to appear in court. I was served at work."

Dorothy showed up on the day requested and sat in the courtroom alone. "No one seemed to notice me or know me. Sonja was there with her mother and Leif. Colligan was certainly in attendance. None of them spoke to me. I sat and waited patiently until Sonja's attorney called me up to the witness stand."

Dorothy was asked questions, and she answered them very precisely, just as she remembered the events that had occurred during the time referred to. Sonja's lawyer thanked her and the judge dismissed her as a witness.

It had taken Dorothy's entire day. During lunch, she ate alone. No one invited her to join them. She was there to help Sonja, yet Sonja ignored her completely. The attorney for Sonja, Amos Scudder, approached Dorothy as she was leaving and said, "I'm going to have certain documents ready. Do you want to pick them up at my office and take them over to Delfern Drive?"

"Mr. Scudder," she said, "I don't work for Sonja anymore."

He was dumbfounded. "What!"

"No. I haven't worked for her since we finished the tour in Cuba last spring."

Sonja hadn't even informed her own attorney that Dorothy was no longer her secretary. "I am sorry to hear that," he said, somewhat embarrassed, "because you have been an excellent witness. If you ever consider becoming an expert witness on a professional basis, I'd like to know." Dorothy thanked him and left. She was never reimbursed for her time. She returned to her job at Goodyear.

In August Sonja took her skaters into San Bernardino where they rehearsed at the Orange Show Hall. Colligan was still managing the show, so there was obviously no room for Dorothy. The show took off without her. She was saddened by the turn of events, but it was, after all, Sonja's show.

Sonja was still estranged from Winnie Gardiner but took consolation with her new skating partner, Marshall Beard. Marshall was a sharp cookie who knew the ropes. He'd been skating for a long time with Morris Chalfen. Marshall was young and handsome and brunette—one of the best skaters in the business. He complemented Sonja's blondeness, both on the ice and in her hotel room.

The show opened in Denver. Before breaking camp in San Bernardino, she phoned Dorothy, as if nothing had ever happened between them. "What are you doing, Dorothy?"

"Bookkeeping and working," she said.

"Well, I can tell you things are in a hell of a mess up here."

Dorothy's heart did a sentimental flip-flop. "What happened?" she asked.

"I've got to let this Colligan go."

"I'm not too surprised."

"He hasn't paid any of the bills at home and they've cut off the gas and electricity. Carrie says it is impossible to keep the house going the way things are there." Without a second breath she continued, "You've got to get back here and get this all straightened out. We're closing here in San Bernardino. You get ready and meet us in Denver."

Just like that, Dorothy quit her job, dropped everything, and flew into Denver. As she says, "I was back again."

Although Sonja and Winnie were unofficially not together, he kept showing up from time to time at the show.

Marshall Beard has great recollections of that fatal tour. "Winnie Gardiner kept popping in, but he didn't have anything to do with the show. He'd come and visit and Sonja couldn't wait until he was gone so we could pick up where we left off before he arrived. He was a joke, really. I was divorced then, and Sonja and I horsed around. It was no big thing, just a convenience thing for both of us. I mean, I wasn't her paid stud. Nothing like that. I don't think anybody ever occupied that position. Sonja was too tight. She was miserably greedy. Unbelievable. You wouldn't believe the things she would do.

"I'd heard about stars taking a towel or two from hotels, but Sonja was the best. She could strip a place bare. I've seen her go into a hotel and take not only the bath towels, which she used for taking off makeup or to walk on down at the arena, but the silverware, thermos bottles, bathmats—even toilet paper. She was the pro to end all pros in that department. She was Sonja Henie, that's who she was."

Beard remembers Sonja's drinking as well. "She had an interest in Black and White Scotch and would fill 7-Up bottles with scotch so nobody would know what she was drinking. She took that 7-Up bottle into restaurants with her. She was never without it, and it was always scotch. She was developing a sort of paranoia, too. She wouldn't even come out on the ice with the other skaters when we were rehearsing in San Bernardino. She had her own private ice time and had nothing to do with the rest of the cast. And another thing the bitch used to do. I say 'bitch' because it took a bitch to be so cruel. When we were in Chicago she'd make the other skaters wait outside in the cold while she was rehearsing. She didn't even want them in the building. She would never just tell them to be quiet while she rehearsed, she simply let them stay outside and freeze.

"One thing I remember so well was her vocabulary. She talked like a stevedore. 'Mother fucker' was her favorite expression, and she knew how to talk to the union people. She could get down and dirty better than any woman I ever met in my life. She was a hard-nosed bitch and maybe you think I'm putting her down. Not at all. She had the balls of a brass monkey and worked harder than anybody on the show. You had to respect her. It's easy for me to see why so many men loved her. She was the kind of woman who knew how to challenge men. Men love the challenge. We all do. Sonja was the greatest challenge I ever ran into."

The show was on the road, still hopscotching about the country with road maps and thumbtacks. The troupe pulled into Raleigh, North Carolina, and found the building wasn't large enough for a Sonja Henie show. They still had a $20,000 a week payroll to crack.

"We simply picked up and moved into Washington, D.C.," Dorothy recalls. "One of the other shows had just played Washington. Either *Ice Capades* or *Ice Follies*—one of the larger shows. And we went creeping in behind them. The timing couldn't have been worse. There just wasn't any business. The show was in trouble. We couldn't meet the payroll and for a change even Sonja was worried."

After Washington the show was scheduled to play the Shubert Theater in Boston, but Sonja's cash flow was no longer a trickle—it was a dry creek. In order to move on to Boston some money had to come in to pay the skaters. Otherwise there would be "no Boston." Sonja had her train and all the heavy equipment that was necessary to put the show on. If anyone had suggested she was fighting against odds that couldn't be beaten, and why didn't she find a man with money to take care of her, she would have responded, "I am Sonja Henie. No man has ever paid my way. I take care of Sonja. I'll be back bigger and better than ever. You'll see. I don't need anybody else. Just Sonja."

She was not feeling so sure of herself when she sat down in her Washington hotel suite with Leif, Dorothy, Selma, and Winnie, who had popped up out of nowhere again. "I can remember sitting in the sitting room of her hotel," says Dorothy. "Mother Henie, Leif, Sonja, Winnie, and myself. Sonja had some of her jewelry in her lap and was trying to decide which set of jewels to sell to cover the payroll for the skaters who would have to be cut before we went into Boston. It broke her heart to have to dismiss her skaters, but they had to be paid. Right now we were talking about severance pay, not Boston. She simply couldn't afford to take a full complement into Boston. She was flat broke.

"Someone, maybe it was me—I don't know—suggested that she could borrow on one of her insurance policies. What we did, I think, was borrow $35,000 on a Sun Life policy that pulled Sonja through the payroll crisis, and we were able to move on to Boston. I think that was one of the most courageous moments in Sonja's life because, next to her life, her jewelry was her most treasured possession, and yet, for the sake of the show, she was ready to relinquish her gems to maintain her integrity and honesty with her skaters. A rare quality in anyone, no matter their other failings. I felt very close to Sonja that day."

Another disappointment, which would have caused lesser mortals to fold up their tents and sneak away, hit Sonja while she was in Washington trying to reconcile her finances. An advance report from Boston indicated that the stage of the Shubert wouldn't accommodate Sonja's show. Sonja shrugged. "Something will happen. Don't worry." Still, she worried more than anyone else. Winnie's presence didn't help any. Winnie drank and Sonja drank with him. Sonja wasn't yet ready to deal with her husband, but his comeuppance wasn't too far off.

Sonja had heard about a fellow by the name of Gorman who was a show manager in Canada. She said, "Let's get this fellow on the phone and see what he has to offer. I hear he would like to bring an ice show up north."

Gorman was reached by phone. He told Sonja that "I can take you into St. Andrews by the Sea in Newfoundland for three performances and we can go from there. What do you say?"

Sonja said yes. She had never heard of St. Andrews by the Sea, but working anywhere was better than sitting in the nation's capital crying over bad luck. She sent Leif back to California, where he busied himself with his ranch, staying with his wife and children at Sonja's Delfern Drive home during the week and spending weekends in Oceanside.

On November 10, 1952, Sonja called a press conference. She intended to be in the public eye, no matter what happened. "If I have to give up a few things for my principles," she announced, 'I want my fans to know I haven't quit." Her meeting with the press was short. "I am canceling my current tour. It is with much sadness that this must be done. Because of the prohibitive costs of playing in arenas with limited capacity, and seat restrictions due to the Baltimore disaster of last season, I have decided to discontinue my arena-type production for the time being." She even indicated that television might be something to look into.

Before going into Canada she announced that she was challenging Barbara Ann Scott to an ice match for a $20,000 purse and the "World's Professional Championship." In an exclusive interview with the *Ottawa Citizen,* Barbara Ann's hometown newspaper, Sonja said, "There is simply not room for two world champions in our business, and this is as good a time as any to decide who is tops."

"I suppose," Barbara Ann said, "she meant figure skating. I'd be delighted to meet her."

It was November and frigid when Sonja took her now thoroughly overhauled and reduced show into St. Andrews by the Sea in Newfoundland. They arrived in what appeared to be, according to Dorothy, "the middle of nowhere." Ice, snow, and mud were everywhere. The town had been closed for the season. It was a fishing village and there were no hotels. Sonja was quartered in a private home, arranged for by Mr. Gorman. She took with her into the home her hairdresser and Carrie. Dorothy stayed in another home with Louise Stewart, a lady who did secretarial work for Sonja, and Janet VanSickle, one of the skaters who worked on payroll now and then.

The trip was not without humor, as Dorothy recalls. "Four of our gay chorus boys stayed with a widow and the poor dear didn't know there was such a thing as gay boys, and she was so frightened at having four men in her house that every night when she went to bed, she put a chair against the door to keep from being attacked. Everybody in the troupe, including the boys, had a good laugh over that."

There was only one taxi available in the town and Sonja commandeered that immediately. After all she was the star. The rest of the group had to wade through mud and snow in order to get to a Quonset hut where the show was to be presented. The Quonset hut seated only six hundred people. The seats were wooden planks with a lot of slivers in them. There were no toilets in the building, no dressing rooms, and no ordinary creature comforts. Dorothy and some of the backstage people arranged the large wardrobe cases so that areas could be blocked off to give a little bit of privacy for the boys and girls and for Sonja. The bathroom was a block down the street at an oil station. The building had no heat. It was a long way from Delfern Drive or Madison Square Garden, but Sonja never uttered a word of complaint.

Dorothy chokes with emotion. "This was the setting. Can you imagine the scene? Here is what I mean when I say that Sonja was a fighter. Here was the greatest ice skater in the world, who had performed before kings and queens and other crowned heads in the largest ice arenas in the world ... Madison Square Garden ... thousands of cheering people ... at St. Andrews by the Sea in a Quonset hut with a seating capacity of six hundred. Sonja did not fold her tent and steal away. She faced it. She went out in that Quonset hut, freezing cold, and performed with the heart of a champion."

Sonja wore her coat until the curtain opened. She tossed the coat to Dorothy and dashed out on the ice. She was Sonja Henie, the most celebrated ice skater in the world, and she did a smashing good show, putting on her numbers in the worst possible circumstances on the worst possible ice. She was now the dedicated pro. She had left her bottle in Washington with Winnie. She was determined to be the winner she knew she was.

The townspeople loved Sonja. She had won the hearts of the fishermen who saw the effort she put forth for them. They gave Sonja and her group a dinner party one night upstairs in one of the club halls. It was freezing cold and they all sat around in their fur coats and parkas trying to keep warm as they ate their dinners.

Sonja had everybody pitching to win. Selma Henie in her fur coat stood at the door and sold programs. Selma Henie was proud but a trouper. She sold programs without protest. After all, it was for "my Sonja."

The six hundred seats were filled for the three performances at St. Andrews by the Sea. Fisherman and sealers came from all around to see the legendary Sonja Henie. Gorman was totally awed and impressed by Sonja, that a star of her stature would play tank towns before she would quit. He respected her. Everyone did, and she deserved respect. Seldom in the annals of show business has a star been subjected to such a buffeting and stayed around long enough to survive.

Gorman asked Sonja if she would like to try another booking in New Brunswick. "Whatever you say," she beamed. "Just show me how to get on the ice and we'll do a show." Amazing. Sonja was booked into Frederickton for three performances, in another small building. Sonja was managing to handle the small payroll—barely. The performing line had been reduced to twelve boys, twelve girls, and Sonja. The bedraggled group moved from Frederickton into St. Johns and on to Halifax. Sonja came out of the wilderness into Ottawa on December 8 for a week's engagement in Canada's capital.

Marshall Beard privately had been in touch with Morris Chalfen, the genial proprietor of the European edition of *Holiday on Ice*. Beard informed Chalfen of Sonja's gallant efforts in Newfoundland and New Brunswick where Sonja performed before six hundred just as she would have before sixteen thousand in Madison Square Garden.

Chalfen was not unaware of Sonja's exploits. He admired her greatly and felt that a skater of her talent should not be squeezed out for lack of a place to skate.

Wirtz was also in competition with Chalfen, and for that reason Chalfen had chosen to take his unit to Europe, where no other shows had gone up to that time, and he was doing fantastic business. By adding a star like Sonja to his tour, especially in Europe where Sonja was so well known and loved, he figured to do even better business, plus helping the great star back on her artistic feet.

Chalfen approached Sonja for a meeting, and one was scheduled in Ottawa. This meeting shows that Sonja could be flexible. Marshall had asked Chalfen to come and see Sonja when her show was having a rough time in Indianapolis. She had turned down an invitation to meet with him then. Now, several months of rough sledding had softened her attitude. She would listen to his proposal.

The meeting took place in the living room of Sonja's hotel suite. Present were Sonja, Chalfen, Selma Henie, and Dorothy, who took notes. Chalfen was a small man with a wonderfully warm face. He chain-smoked big cigars and was known for his honesty. He was a man whose handshake was more valid than most written contracts. If he promised to do something, it was done. He was a self-educated man with a mind as sharp as a Harvard law school graduate's.

After the preliminaries, he made his proposition to Sonja. He said, "I've got excellent buildings in Europe, and you have a beautiful show. We'll build it back to where you had it when I saw it in Indianapolis. You bring the show, and I'll have the buildings, and we'll work on a percentage deal." Sonja was to receive 40 percent and Chalfen would take 60

249

percent. Out of his percentage he would take care of the local stage hands, advertising, and promotion. Sonja would pay the skaters. She would bring the show to the door, so to speak. Chalfen agreed to pay for setting it up and taking it down, which was a major cost and which had been a big problem for Sonja since she left Arthur Wirtz. Chalfen said he would pay for Sonja's hotel accommodations and those of her immediate staff. The skaters would pay their own. It appeared to be a nice working agreement.

Sonja tried to hide her excitement. She had always operated from a position of strength, and she put up a strong front. Chalfen respected that. He knew her situation, but he never spoke down to her or implied that he was rescuing her from the depths of despair.

Finally Sonja said, "I'll have to think about this, Mr. Chalfen. But I thank you for coming. It is an intriguing offer."

"That's all right, dear," he said. "You don't have to give me an answer today. Tell you what I'll do," he said, "I'll get this typed up so you can read it and go over it at your leisure. I'll have my secretary get it back to you right away." He promised to call the next day for another meeting.

After Chalfen left, Sonja sat for a long time with Dorothy and her mother, discussing it pro and con. She had actually made up her mind to accept his offer before he even came to the hotel, but she had to maintain her image and that meant pretending to be a little bit reluctant.

By the time Chalfen came back to the hotel the following day, she had agreed in principle to his offer. Right away he began to detail a European tour. "We'll play London during the coronation of Queen Elizabeth, we'll go to Germany, to Berlin. They loved you in Berlin." Chalfen was aware of Sonja's standing with the Germans. "And from Berlin we'll go directly into Oslo. What a homecoming that will be for you."

Sonja blanched. "Oh, no! No! No, Mr. Chalfen. I can't take the show into Oslo."

"But Sonja," he protested, "that'll be one of your greatest performances on the tour."

"No," she said. "They don't like me in Oslo. I can't go there. I should have done more for the Norwegians during the war. They don't like me for that. The newspapers said terrible things about me. No. I can't go to Norway."

Not wanting to upset his star, Chalfen patted her hand and said, "That's all right, dear, but let me go to Oslo and feel them out. In the meantime we'll play Paris and London and Germany, maybe even go into Sweden and a few other places. If I feel there's any anti-Sonja sentiment in Oslo I'll never bring the subject up again. All right?"

It was all right. He and Sonja shook hands and they had a deal. The signed contract that came later was a mere formality.

Sonja continued the Canadian tour, filling her commitments to Gorman. It was a struggle and she was barely meeting her weekly payroll, but Sonja did not welsh on commitments.

The European tour would begin during the summer of 1953 in London, so there was time for other things. She had a long jump from Canada to her next stop in Fort Worth. In between engagements she flew into New York to star in an episode of "All Star Revue," an NBC television comedy and variety show that alternated guest hosts. Sonja rarely did television, so this was a treat for her fans.

Dorothy was busy lining up skaters for the coming European tour. Sonja would not be able to take the full show with her. Under the European laws a show could bring all of its principals, but was required to hire 50 percent of the chorus from local talent.

After Canada, the show went back to hopscotching around the States, going into whatever city had an open date. Sonja's advertising left a lot to be desired. Often the first knowledge the populace had of her show was a week before it came. This was a terrible way to promote, and it was only the Henie name that made it possible to go on this way.

Sonja played Fort Worth and Houston, skipped over to Albuquerque, then did a small run in San Diego for a few days and at last traveled up to San Francisco and the Cow Palace for her biggest engagement of the tour. Sonja was beginning to feel better about herself since meeting with Chalfen. She was drinking less and becoming easier to get along with.

The show opened at the Cow Palace in mid-February, receiving excellent reviews. It was a time for interviews. Both Sonja and her mother were being very glib with the press. One story, banner-headlined "Mother Henie Explodes the Henie Myth," surprised even Sonja. "She's never been a fiend for practice as some people think. Never done more than an hour in the morning at school, at figures, and an hour in the afternoon of free skating. There is no point in hanging around the rink all day." She added that, "Sonja never had a driving ambition."

"Why she said those things, I'll never know," commented Marshall Beard, then Sonja's skating partner. "They just weren't so. Sonja had tremendous ambition. So did her mother, a very pushy lady just like her daughter."

Selma's interview was really an indication of her desire for Sonja to let up and work less. Selma wanted a happy home life with both her children around her. She never liked the road life but felt compelled to go with Sonja, wherever the trail might lead. She was an unhappy woman locked into a situation over which she had no control.

Sonja, in an interview with Will Connolly of the *San Francisco Chronicle*, explained why she stayed on the road instead of making two movies a year and settling in Hollywood year-round.

"I like the stimulation of flesh and blood shows," she explained. "I even like the headaches. I find it hard to do my best skating on a soundstage in Hollywood. The warmth of an audience and their applause makes me feel good. I get a lift from opening the show in a new city; the change of scenery is a fresh challenge. The movie isn't."

She discussed her weight. "People seem to like me better when I fatten up to 104 pounds. At 100 pounds I look drawn, they tell me. The first month on the road I lose weight, then I gain it back."

Connolly concluded his interview by writing:

> The Cow Palace PR people warned us that Henie was likely to blow her top on the slightest provocation. She came to town with a cold and wasn't feeling chipper. Anyway, Henie has the reputation for slamming the door in the face of an interviewer. We found her nice as pie—make that read "smorgasbord." Even if she had slammed the door of her plywood shack backstage— which she didn't—it is hard to be mad at her.

Winnie was back with Sonja in San Francisco, one of his come-and-go appearances. He always left with a pocketful of cash. Why Sonja was so indulgent of her husband was anybody's guess. She was not so generous in dispensing cash to anyone else.

Someone commented that Sonja had played before the king of England and now was playing before the common folk of San Francisco. "From Buckingham Palace to the Cow Palace," he said.

Sonja, quick on the uptake responded, "Yes, but there's more money at the Cow Palace. And I'm still the best cow you've ever had here." In three weeks she pulled in half a million dollars. She left San Francisco a very contented "cow," indeed.

23

BEFORE taking on a European tour, Sonja returned to Hollywood at the end of February and opened her ice revue at the Shrine Auditorium, where she always seemed to give her greatest performances and receive her largest plaudits. It was home, and the audience was heavily populated with her peers. Winnie was with her.

She gave interviews in Los Angeles and commented on her current life-style. "I used to tour only four months a year, but since I took over my own show I haven't stopped skating. I'll be taking eighty skaters with me, plus scenery, costumes, and machinery when we open our show on June 2 at Earl's Court in London—which just happens to be coronation week."

The subject of Sonja's earnings came up and she discussed her film career as well as other ventures. "It is funny, but I never stopped to figure out all of the income. I know I made nine pictures for Twentieth Century-Fox and the studio tells me they grossed over twenty-five million dollars."

Winnie interrupted to add, "Plus another thirty-five million. Sonja's ice shows have grossed a total of two million dollars yearly for seventeen years. You can add an estimated ten million to the ten years she coproduced the ice show at the Center Theater in New York. There have been countless endorsements. I'd say the figure is over seventy million dollars." Winnie always knew where the money was.

"I wouldn't print that," Sonja said, and giggled. "I haven't got it in my pocket now, you know. Producing your own ice show is some job. After I split with Arthur Wirtz I put my own show on the road. I am banker, business manager, and chief worrier. To give you an idea of what it costs, I spent one hundred and fifty thousand dollars for ice machinery alone. Costumes cost four hundred thousand dollars a year and they are good for only one year, and some of the chorus girls' dresses cost eighteen hundred each. My packing equipment includes items few girls even possess. Ten point six miles of pipe, three ice compressors totaling eight tons. It costs eighteen thousand dollars to convert the Shrine Auditorium into an ice rink. I have two hundred thirty people on my payroll and all the major problems. There is scheduling, arena percentages, advertising, equipment, and ice conditions are all on my shoulders. I also skate six numbers a day."

She had every detail in her head and it was the first time she ever publicly called the severance of her relationship with Wirtz a "split."

Winnie had the last word, however, stating, "I think when Sonja is ready to quit she'd like to find a little Sonja to take over and she'd continue to produce, but so far Sonja hasn't found that girl. They're either too old or too muscular. Or else they can skate but lack rhythm."

Once again Winnie didn't know what he was talking about. Sonja had no intention of ever becoming the "older generation of skaters." There had been plenty of opportunities to train someone new, but she declined them all.

Sonja was uneasy about her Shrine Auditorium opening. She was home and among friends, but she felt certain they knew of the difficulties she had been through. Dorothy was with her and explains.

"It made her nervous to come back and play. She knew there would be a lot of movie people in the audience and the press worried her a little bit. They were aware that she had been doing little tank towns in Canada, but she gave a nice performance with nice reviews. She did very well at the Shrine. She was feeling like a star."

Preparing to move her show across the United States and then the Atlantic ocean was no mean feat. A lot of hard work went into that effort, and a great deal of it fell to Dorothy.

"We had to ship the equipment to New York, get it on the *Liberté*, round up our skaters—and that was difficult. Here again, we had to make new contracts for the skaters."

The skaters were paid part of their salary in a dollar check, and they had to agree to take the rest of their salaries in local currency, which could be used for their meals and hotels. Some didn't care for that arrangement, but to others it was no problem.

Dorothy took the chorus skaters over on the *Liberté* with the equipment while Sonja was tied up in court regarding the accident in Baltimore. Jerry Geisler, her attorney, advised her that it would look bad if she took off for Europe with so many civil suits hanging over her head.

"I want you to remain here and face the court," he told her. "It is important to your case."

Sonja testified in the case, and the jury completely exonerated her and her company from any liability. However, Circuit Judge John T. Tucker set aside the jury verdict and held that the Sonja Henie Ice Revue Company was liable for damages in the case, but upheld that part of the verdict that the blonde skating star was "not personally liable for the mishap . . ."

Dorothy meanwhile, had arrived in Europe with the troupe and had begun to rehearse the skaters. The *Liberté* had docked at Le Havre in

France. Dorothy and her charges went by train to Antwerp, Belgium, where Chalfen had arranged with an ice rink there for the skaters to begin rehearsing. Sonja was never at any of the rehearsals.

Dorothy handled the problems in Europe. She interviewed the skaters, hired them, and rehearsed them. Chalfen's advance people had already moved into Paris where the show would open. The mechanics of staging the event were more refined under Chalfen's guidance. Instead of taking several days to put up and take down the rink before playing a date, he had one engineering crew putting it in and taking it out in one city, while another engineering crew was going on to the next city to set things up.

The show opened and played the Palais des Sports where Sonja had given some of her greatest exhibitions. She was enveloped in love and affection by the Parisians, who had always adored her.

Sonja and her show arrived in London just before the coronation of Elizabeth II, in June 1953. Her show played Empress Hall and the royal family attended opening night. If ever a sagging star bounced back, Sonja did. Thousands cheered. It was a million light years from the Quonset hut with six hundred spectators in Newfoundland only a few months earlier.

Rather than living in a hotel while she was in London, Sonja rented an apartment in the very fashionable Eaton Square section of the city. Dorothy was staying elsewhere, but Sonja had Carrie Roberts, her cook and housekeeper, with her. Around four-thirty one morning Sonja was awakened by a rustling noise at the foot of her bed.

"I sat up and saw a young man dressed in a black suit, two yards away, just staring at me," she told investigators. "I screamed bloody murder and jumped out of bed."

The startled intruder bolted out of Sonja's bedroom into the hall, leaping over a pile of Sonja's things which, as usual, were spread out all over the floor. The burglar had several of Sonja's valuable furs over his arm and she was not about to let him get away with her mink and ermine coats, so she ran after him, in her nightgown. Carrie, hearing all of the commotion, took up the chase in a long flannel nightgown. The two women pursued the fellow down an alley in the dark. Chilled and out-distanced, they returned to the apartment to phone the police. "He certainly was a fast runner," Sonja told officers. Police later found two mink coats on top of some ashcans a short distance from Sonja's apartment. They theorized that, in the dark, he had dropped them and just kept running. Sonja was insured for the loss of her ermine.

Rumors were rampant in London that Sonja was unhappy with her life, and in order to squelch what she called "total untruths," she gave a lengthy, no-holds-barred, interview to the *Daily Express*.

"I'm very happy. How could anyone say differently. I have witnesses to prove what I say—the thousands of spectators who cram the Empress

Hall each night to see my ice revue. Ask any one of them: 'Did Sonja look happy?' They cannot help answering 'Yes.'"

She cautioned anyone from getting the wrong impression, however. "Because I have enjoyed every minute of my time on the ice, don't run away with the idea that the years have treated me with special consideration. They haven't. Deep down, all the time, I must admit that I have felt a sort of odd man out just because I have had so many successes. I've had to run ahead of so many people, you see, striving to break records, to achieve things in the world of sport that are apt to be beyond all but the very few.

"I've had to defy the kings of sport, at times, the wealthy magnates of the film world and the men who own and run the vast stadiums where I stage my spectacles."

She credited the men in her personal life with helping her accomplish her goals. "My father, who died just as I was starting to make it as a professional, and then my brother, Leif, and now my husband—were always at my elbow to guide and direct my many business interests, but in the sports area, I've always fought my own battles."

A romance that began while she was in Paris was the subject of much discussion over breakfast tables in both France and England. Gossip columnists in Europe made pointed comments about her dates with Claude Terrail, the handsome owner of Tour d'Argent restaurant overlooking the Seine in Paris.

Louella Parsons was the first of the American press to pick up on Sonja's cavorting. Buried deep in her column was the question "Isn't the marriage of Sonja Henie and Winnie Gardiner near the breaking point? In Paris Sonja is seen everywhere with Claude Terrail."

Sonja couldn't have cared less at the time. She was "madly in love" again, and she always threw caution to the winds in such circumstances.

This romance, however, although it began as a torrid affair, fell off abruptly when Sonja's pocketbook became involved. Dorothy explained how it started and ended.

"Claude Terrail was very charming and invited her again and again to his restaurant while we were playing Paris. When we moved on to London, he showed up. With her marriage already irreparably damaged, Sonja would have dated Claude openly in England, but the British are a bit more staid about such things. She was still a married woman so a plan was devised to get her across the channel to France on weekends. We were in London about six weeks, so this covers a lengthy period of time.

"The cinema is closed in London on Sunday evenings. So after the show on Saturday nights Sonja would tell me, 'Dorothy, pack something. We're leaving for Paris.' She would then charter a plane, fly into Paris, pick up Claude, and we would go down to Nice and fly back to be in London in time—barely in time—to do the show on Monday night. She

256

took me along, I believe, because she felt it would be less noticeable that she was going to meet Terrail.

"Since Sonja did a lot of flying and was always chartering planes, Terrail suggested that what she needed was a private plane. Her own special plane, and he more or less intimated that he was going to build it—or supervise the building, have it all done up special for her—the interior, I mean. He talked of putting in a bar, bed, tables, and lighting. It was to be a little apartment for Sonja when she traveled. Sonja squealed with delight. Yes, she told him, she would certainly like to have her own private airplane.

"The big surprise came later. She was so happy about this and so elated to know that Claude Terrail thought so much of her that he would give her an airplane. That's all any of us around her were hearing about. She drove us up the wall talking about the plane that Mr. Terrail was going to *give* her."

The big surprise. One day Dorothy was opening the mail and gasped. Enclosed was a great long invoice, in the thousands of dollars, from the manufacturer of the airplane. "It mentioned the installation of a bar and other things—all very luxurious, including plush carpeting. It was all billed to Sonja."

Dorothy thought there certainly had to be a mistake, and took the bill to Sonja and asked, "What is this?"

"Let me see," she said, taking the bill. Her eyes snapped. "I'm not paying for that plane. He's giving me the plane."

"Well, Sonja, I'll check into it. Perhaps the company made a mistake in the billing."

Dorothy checked with the company and was advised that the billing was correct and, "Miss Henie will have to pay this."

Sonja was furious. "You get that sonofabitch Terrail on the phone," she screamed. "I'll show him who's paying for what for. I'm not supporting some goddam gigolo. Who does he think he is, anyway?" Words flew across the channel. Sonja was raising hell from England, and Claude was trying to soothe her ruffled feathers in Paris. It was the end of the fabled romance, and Sonja was no longer "madly in love."

"Sonja had loaned Claude a thousand dollars," Dorothy recalls, "for something or other. Maybe because she picked up the bill at the hotel in Nice on one of the trips down there. I don't remember exactly what it was for, but she wanted her thousand dollars and she wanted it right away."

"You get my thousand dollars back from that man, Dorothy," she ordered. "You tell him I want my money. Nobody makes a fool out of Sonja."

Dorothy made several trips from London to Paris trying to locate Claude to collect the money. "He wouldn't be there, or else couldn't be found. I'd check all over and would be told he was out of town or was in

New York or Spain. It was many months later that I finally got hold of him on the telephone. I said, 'Mr. Terrail, Sonja wants her thousand dollars.'"

According to Dorothy, Claude laughed and said, "Tell her not to worry. I'll send the money to her." And he did, eventually. No one knows what happened to the plane. Sonja didn't pay for it, and didn't get it. She didn't ask Claude to return the diamond cuff links she had given him when things were cozier, although she was capable of taking a gift back.

"Sonja gave nice gifts on occasion," Dorothy recalls. When she was first dating Winnie Gardiner, she gave him jewelry, a pair of diamond cuff links, a beautiful watch. She ordered everything from her Beverly Hills jeweler, William Russur. He made exquisite jewelry. She ordered little gold skates with her name on them, to give as gifts. She gave gifts to certain people, and to others she wouldn't give much of anything. I'm speaking of people she was close to."

Marshall Beard, although declared by Sonja to be her "very favorite skating partner" over a period of several years, was not so fortunate. "There were a couple of small things. Nothing sensational." He remembers Sonja as cold and calculating and not above using people. "She had no real traffic with people in the show. She had a line captain who handled all of the corrections and changes. Now here's an example of her coldness. If there was a girl in the line and Sonja didn't like her, that was it. Get rid of her. I remember there was one girl she refused to take to Europe. The girl was a good skater, but one of her spies said something bad about the girl and that was that. The girl was dropped. Today she wouldn't be able to get away with that kind of stuff. Her spy network was unbelievable. She had everybody in her family reporting to her and a lot of people in the show carried stories to curry favor, which is not so unusual. But she had no daily contact with her skaters. She barely knew most of them. She never hesitated to bounce anyone who got on her wrong side.

"And she was scandalous when it came to tipping. Never left a nickel. Downright cheap. Sonja was a kleptomaniac and got caught at it several times after she split with Arthur Wirtz. He used to go behind her and pay for the things she stole out of hotels. That didn't work later on. It was embarrassing for everyone because we were all on the spot. We were part of Sonja's troupe and if she was a thief—people sort of tossed us into the same category."

Sonja had long talks with Marshall Beard while they were on the first European tour, and she frequently mentioned Oslo. "It took Mr. Chalfen a long time to convince Sonja that it was okay to take the show into Norway. That's one of the reasons Oslo was one of the last stops on the tour. She told me, 'They call me their American Quisling. We better wait until last if we go to Oslo because it could ruin me in Europe and hurt Mr.

258

Chalfen if they say bad things about me now.' She was very conscious of that feeling. She knew she hadn't given anything or volunteered to help her country during the war. I understand why she didn't help. Sonja was a taker not a giver."

At some of her European press parties she would scoop up the food and take it to her own suite. Beard saw that, too. "For instance there would be a large platter of shrimp and hors d'oeuvre set out on a table for the newspeople. She made sure that a large portion of everything was sent up to her rooms for nibbling later. She didn't even like to share the food unless she had to. She always had a gofer to take care of such matters.

"I wasn't the only one of her skaters who took Sonja to bed. There was another fellow, who was married, but Sonja rewarded him with extra things like his wardrobe, and I suspect he was making a lot more money than anyone else in the show. Still, it was Sonja's show and Sonja's money, so she ought to be able to do whatever she wanted with it."

Dorothy left early from London with the equipment and chorus skaters. Sonja would meet them in Dortmund, Germany, when the show opened there. Germany was no picnic for Dorothy and her charges. There was customs to deal with. She had warned everybody in the troupe. "Please remember to have your passports with you at all time, otherwise you will not be allowed to cross international borders. They are very strict about that in Europe." The inevitable happened.

"The two Cuban dancers didn't have the proper visas and Larry Hamm, our comedian, packed his in a trunk now buried somewhere in a mountain of baggage en route to the Continent.

"We had to travel on the train through a small stretch of Holland before crossing into Germany. I managed to talk English customs into permitting us on the boat, but the official warned me, 'You're going to have real problems in Holland. They're very strict.'"

Dorothy smiled weakly at the man and said, "I'll take my chances. Come on, Larry, let's get on the boat."

True to the official's prediction, when they arrived in Holland, Dorothy, Larry Hamm, and the two Cubans were detained while the rest of the troupe began boarding the train for Dortmund. Dorothy gathered them all together on the station platform. "Make the train—all of you. We don't have a lot of time and I don't want to have to come looking for you when this mess is straightened out. So scoot."

There were some phone calls to Amsterdam and The Hague. "The man was explaining that I had these people and they didn't have the correct documents and one had a passport that he could produce in Dortmund and so on. He did a lot of talking and then put me on the phone, and I talked to the person on the other end of the line. He had very broken English but he could understand."

The result was that Dorothy had to sign a document saying she would take complete responsibility for these people, which she did readily. The important thing was to get the show to Dortmund. The other skaters pulled them aboard the already-moving train moments after the customs officials released them. More was ahead.

"Before we arrived at Dortmund the immigration people again came through the train and here we go again. They stopped the train and Larry Hamm was taken off. The Cubans were allowed to continue."

Larry and Dorothy were walking alongside the train waving good-bye to the rest of the kids. "I'll see you in Dortmund, everybody," she said waving, but seriously doubted she'd see anybody for a while. "I wasn't about to leave Larry there alone. They were going to lock him up for sure. I was running along beside the officer begging him to let Larry go. He was a strong, very stubborn German who wasn't going to budge. I have no idea why I did it, but I suddenly stopped in my tracks and said, 'Well, anyway, Larry—have a happy birthday.' Of course it wasn't his birthday at all and I don't know why I said such a thing."

Whatever the reason, the officer asked Larry, "Is that true? Is it your birthday?"

Larry picked up immediately and said, "Yes sir. It is."

The officer softened and said, "Go on. Get back on the train, and I don't want to see your face again."

While the show moved from Dortmund to Berlin where its next opening was, Sonja flew to Oslo to have some meetings with Chalfen and local ice rink officials. Her mother accompanied her and they stayed at Sonja's home, Landoya.

Dorothy was still moving the show through Germany. Sonja would be playing another of her old haunts in Berlin, the Sports Palast.

Arrangements had to be made with the Russians to get the baggage, equipment, and skaters through the Russian checkpoint in order to pass through East Germany, which was occupied by the Soviets. The equipment was okayed to pass through via truck convoy, and the personnel were to travel on a sealed train.

Dorothy was standing at the Westphalen Hall in Dortmund when a man came racing up to her with bad news: "The personnel can't go! The Russians won't let us through on the train."

A startled Dorothy asked, "What?!"

"Don't worry," he said. "We're going to work it out. We're going to have a meeting. I'm going back to Berlin now." He got in his car and drove away. Instead of telephoning ahead to let the people know they would be delayed, he had driven all the way from Berlin to tell them in person.

The train couldn't leave until the Russians cleared it. Dorothy watched the last truck loaded and gone. The rain was coming down in torrents. She got in a taxi and ran all around town to different hotels, knocking on doors, calling out, "Don't go to the railroad station. Meet me at Westphalen Hall at ten in the morning. There's a meeting."

Some of the skaters were quartered in underground bunkers left over from the war, and the rooms had no numbers, just a bunch of doors, so she banged on doors and hoped. Seven of them were in private homes and she didn't have their addresses, so she just had to wait and hope they showed up.

The seven, of course, arrived with all their luggage and were informed by Dorothy that they wouldn't be leaving. While everybody waited, Berlin was on the line saying, "Stand by! The Russians didn't give us permission yet. We're having another meeting at three this afternoon." It was now Monday, so Dorothy told the skaters to go have some fun and report back at three. At three, the word came from Berlin: No permission as yet. "Wait until tomorrow. There's another meeting in the morning."

So the whole thing was repeated again the following morning at ten o'clock, Tuesday morning. The Russians, as yet, still had not made up their minds. Another meeting was scheduled, and the troupe was asked to stand by until Wednesday morning. Dorothy was beginning to worry, because the show was scheduled to open Thursday night in Berlin and time was now growing short. Wednesday morning, same old story. "We're working on it in Berlin."

Things were beginning to look a little bleak. Money was in short supply. The kids had spent theirs, and Dorothy was down to two hundred German marks. Sonja was in Oslo, totally unaware of the situation in Dortmund. Dorothy had a meeting with her skaters. "I want you to come back at three and this time bring everything you own—all your luggage. We're going to leave this place. I don't know how, but I'm going to find a way."

She saw only one solution. "I had enough money to charter two large buses," she explains, "so when they showed up at three I loaded them all into the buses, and we started for Hanover, which was the last stop before the Russian sector. I had checked and knew that planes flew from Hanover to Berlin. . . .

"It was late when we arrived in Hanover, around midnight on Wednesday. The kids hadn't had anything to eat. Some had a little bit of money. Some had none. I had to use my few marks to pay the bus drivers." Dorothy had money in Berlin but that wasn't doing any of them any good.

The two buses pulled up in front of the terminal at the airport. It wasn't a large terminal. "Everybody wait right here," Dorothy ordered. "I'm going to talk to the people at Pan Am."

The man behind the Pan American counter was a very tall, handsome American. Dorothy thought, "Aha! I'll make my attack here."

The man looked up to find what appeared to be a teenager in blue jeans and pony tail. He smiled. "Mister," she began, "I have a problem. I have to get to Berlin."

"That's no problem," he responded. "I have a plane coming in here in twenty minutes bringing refugees out of Berlin and it'll be flying back. No trouble."

"You don't understand," she continued. "I have no money."

"Aha! You have no money."

"Number two. I'm not alone."

With that he looked up, over her head and out the window, and there were 175 kids with everything but the kitchen sink lined up on the sidewalk with all their luggage. "What the hell is going on? What is that out there?" he asked.

"That's the Sonja Henie show trying to get into Berlin. We open there tomorrow night. That's why I have a problem."

She had said the magic words, "Sonja Henie." Within seconds the agent was on the phone with Pan American public relations. It was midnight, but in no time at all the place was overrun with photographers, and a great crowd had gathered. The cameras clicked and flashed and within twenty minutes after Dorothy had approached the ticket agent the first load of skaters was boarding a plane en route to Berlin.

Pan Am had a photograph of the group on the front page of their house magazine. Dorothy left Hanover at five in the morning. She hadn't slept for almost three days, except for catnaps at Westphalen Hall stretched out on two chairs pulled together by the telephone. Meanwhile, Sonja was sleeping comfortably in the luxury of her home in Oslo, content that Dorothy was bringing the show to Berlin.

Thursday came, Sonja had a fantastic opening night, and the Berliners shouted for their "Kleine Häschen." Dorothy would have settled for a good night's sleep.

24

S ONJA returned to Oslo after closing in Berlin. Dorothy and her stout-hearted skaters traveled seven hours through the Russian Sector, again, but this time she went through the Swedish Embassy for her arrangements. The Swedes had good rapport with the Russians. Even so, the railroad cars were sealed and the windows blacked out. The military controlled the train and patrolled it throughout the journey.

Chalfen met the group on their arrival in Oslo and gave Dorothy money to make the payroll—an advance, since Dorothy hadn't had time to do payroll en route. She had been too busy trying to get from one location to the next.

"Everything was wonderful and *clean* in Oslo," Dorothy remembers with a sigh. "We played thirty-five performances. It rained a great deal of the time we were there because it was the rainy season there. We were there from August 21 to September 20. It would pour down rain all day long. The box office would be open for about twenty minutes. People were lined up for blocks in the rain, and they just shoved the tickets out as fast as they could take the money in. When all the tickets were gone for that day's performance, the box office closed until the following day.

"They had a certain number of seats, but about seven thousand of the people had to stand up all through the show. It was standing room upon a terrace—open air—and you could see the big moon some nights when it wasn't raining, as it came up over the horizon."

A strange thing happened in Oslo that originated an expression still used in Norway—"Sonja weather." It would pour down all day. The audience would arrive at the amphitheater while the rain was coming down in torrents. The curtain would open for the show, and the rain would stop. Just like that. The ice, of course, was covered with a tarp, which was rolled back for the show. Sonja would go out and do a beautiful show—it was absolutely gorgeous in the open air. She would make her exit on the last number, and down would come the rain again. *Sonja weather* stirred up a lot of conversation, both in and out of the papers.

Opening night in Oslo was Sonja's most difficult moment on ice. The place was packed. Chalfen had assured her that all was forgiven from the war, and the officials had all agreed: Sonja would be a tremendous hit. Still, she fretted, almost hesitating with every movement as the time grew nearer for her to make her entrance on the ice.

"I still remember that night," Dorothy says with emotion. "I get chills just thinking about it. I stood with her and her mother behind the curtain while the orchestra played and the act on the ice finished up their routine. Sonja was wrapped in her full-length white fur cape—and still her skin was as cold as the ice on the rink. She trembled with fear and anxiety. Finally the crucial moment arrived, the curtain opened, and she went sailing out, not knowing what to expect. The thunderous applause told us all what we needed to know. Sonja had come home and was being welcomed with wide open, loving arms.

"She made the big circle around the arena with her cape, came back and handed the cape to me, and sailed back out to the people who were more dear to her than anything else in the world—her audience. Tears ran down her cheeks. That was the most vulnerable moment of her life. Mother Henie and I both choked back our emotions."

It was Sonja weather and a Sonja night—a night to end all nights. It was the highlight of her long career.

Not all events were so emotional—not for Dorothy, anyway. Sonja had forbidden Ken Stevens to come on the tour, and she told Dorothy to forget about him. Without Ken in the picture, Sonja was as sweet as she could possibly be to Dorothy, which made life much easier. Dorothy had other problems to deal with, however.

Sonja was cleaning up financially in Oslo and had no intention of leaving any funds there if she could possibly get them out. She would go out at night after the show and in speaking to people at parties and restaurants, would always ask if they knew anyone who would convert the Norwegian kroner into dollars to take back to America with her. Whenever she heard of such a person, she sent Dorothy off with sufficient kroner to cover the dollars and the trade was made.

There were several such trips. On one occasion she and Marshall Beard took a paper bag full of kroner to Switzerland and had to turn around and bring it back to Oslo because Sonja had set a limit on how low she would go on the exchange. There were, however, some very close calls with customs—and "others." Dorothy has some hair-raising stories, but one stands out.

"I was going in all directions trying to make a trade for dollars. Sonja was stuffing kroner in her safe deposit box at the Oslo bank and everywhere. We had those large paper certificates all over the house and Sonja kept harping about getting rid of them for dollars. She would phone me up at three o'clock in the morning from a party and say, 'Dorothy. Somebody just told me where I can get some dollars. Take some kroner and go to such and such a place. I'll make arrangements for you to make the switch.'

"Well, on this particular occasion the amount of kroner we had to offer was able to buy fifty thousand dollars in American money. Sonja gave me the directions, which she had scribbled down on a piece of paper. 'I want you on the first plane out to Paris, but I want you back in time for the show tonight.'

"My hair was long and I wore it sort of in a pony tail. I certainly didn't look the part of an international money exchanger at the time I was doing all of this. I looked more like a schoolgirl then. I wasn't under any suspicion. I wore socks, instead of hose, and an all-purpose coat which hung loose."

She took the kroner and tied it to her body underneath her clothing. This enormous bundle worth fifty thousand dollars was a lot of kroner.

"I checked myself out of Oslo, caught the plane to Paris, went through customs there without any problem, and checked in at the hotel.

"On this particular run for money, I was told to go to a certain address that was way out in the worst part of Paris you could imagine—a very slimy area—cobblestone streets with sidewalks that weren't wide enough for two people to pass, one would have to step off the curb. It was a horrible area. I had the name of a club on this particular street. I took a cab and went to this place. The buildings were jammed up against one another all along the street—all dives, believe me. I had to go to the basement alone. Always alone. No one ever went with me to exchange money except for the one time Marshall Beard accompanied me to Switzerland. Sonja didn't want anyone to know about it.

"So I walked in and there were nothing but men at the bar. I was the only woman in the place. Of course, all heads turned when I entered, but I ignored them, found the stairway as I had been instructed, and went down the very dark stairwell. On the lower level there was another long bar and to the side a sort of small dining room, with checked tablecloths. We didn't use names, but somehow or other the more work I did in that area, the more I could spot my contact. I was hard to spot because they expected a man, not a girl.

"I stood waiting, and of course several of the men at the bar wanted to buy me a drink and I politely declined, feeling very uncomfortable and trying not to let it show. Finally a fellow that I thought was the one I was to meet looked at me, and I walked up and asked, 'Are you Mister B?'"

The man said, "Yes."

Dorothy said, "I've come to see you." He couldn't believe it, that a woman would come on such a dangerous mission. "I've just arrived from Norway."

That was the password: "Norway." So the man knew Dorothy was the person he was looking for. "Let's sit down and have a drink." He directed Dorothy to a small private room.

"I wasn't about to drink anything," Dorothy says with a laugh. "But he ordered drinks and I just sat there fondling the glass. Sonja cautioned me never to take chances, so I just chatted a bit. He spoke very broken English."

"I have fifty thousand dollars in kroner," she said, broaching the subject.

"I have fifty thousand American dollars," he responded. There was no way to count the money, so both sides had to rely on trust. The tablecloth hung over the sides of the table. Dorothy took her bundle of kroner and passed it under the table. Their hands met, she with her kroner, he with his dollars. The exchange executed, they sat for a few minutes in brief conversation and left, separately.

Dorothy started walking toward a large wagon-wheel intersection. It was the rush hour. The shops had closed, people were going home, and the traffic was simply vile.

"I hadn't walked very far," Dorothy explains, "before I became conscious that I was being followed. I turned just enough to see that it was an enormously tall black man. I mean, he was *big* and he was *tall* and he was *black*! The faster I walked, the faster he walked. I kept looking for a taxi along the narrow street and of course there was none to be had. I knew the man was after me and my bag full of dollars. I kept thinking to myself, what am I going to do? I knew better than to enter any of the doors along the street—I'd be trapped for sure. So I did the most sensible thing—stayed in full sight of everybody and kept walking as fast as my legs would carry me.

"I finally arrived at the wagon wheel where the streets went off in all directions with a hub in the center where there was a little round cement block with a light hanging over it. That was where the policeman usually stood and directed traffic. On this occasion there was no policeman. He had not arrived for duty as yet. I thought I'd rather get killed making my way to the center of the spokes than have the guy following me get Sonja's money.

"When I got to the corner I simply zipped out into the traffic. Tires screeched, horns honked, and Frenchmen yelled at me. But I reached the center safely."

When she looked back at the corner, the man who had been following her was standing waiting for traffic to subside. Dorothy stayed on the island, hoping for a taxi to come by.

Finally the policeman came on duty and in English asked, "What are you doing out here?" He was very angry. Waving his arms and cursing at Dorothy. She didn't dare tell him the real reason she was out there. She knew she would have been arrested on the spot. Trafficking in money on the black market was an international offense.

"I'm trying to get a taxi," she said meekly, never mentioning that she was being followed. Meanwhile the man was still standing on the corner trying to get across the thoroughfare.

The policeman hailed a taxi, helped her into it, and cautioned her to never do that again. Meanwhile, the guy on the corner was frantically waving his arms, trying to get the cabbie's attention. As the car started to swerve through the traffic in the man's direction, Dorothy began to yell in her very broken French for him to take her to her hotel. He didn't seem to understand and continued to move across the lanes. "No! No! No!" she shouted. "No one else!" She pushed a large bill in his face. He smiled and got back into the line of traffic.

"I was a nervous wreck by the time I got to the hotel, but I quickly tied the dollars around my waist and took a taxi to the airport where I boarded the next available plane for Oslo. Needless to say, I missed the show that night. I had missed an earlier plane so I got back to Oslo just before the show was over—but I had the money, and that's what counted."

When Dorothy walked into Sonja's dressing room, the first thing Sonja said to her was, "What the hell happened to you? Where have you been? Where's the money?"

"I've been standing under a street light on a little circle in Paris," she said, "but I have the money."

"Goot!" was all Sonja said. She had sent Dorothy to do a job, and the job was done.

That was the relationship Sonja maintained with Dorothy. Carrie Roberts, on the other hand, could get away with much more. "Carrie," Dorothy explains, "was another type person. She could do things, say things to Sonja that I wouldn't even think of saying. Carrie would boss her around and get away with it—like a mother. She could do it even with Mother Henie. Both of them took it from Carrie, but from nobody else."

If Sonja didn't want to eat something, Carrie would sternly point a finger and say, "You eat it! It's good for you or I wouldn't put it on the table." Sonja obeyed like a little child, especially after Mother Henie died. "Carrie really became her mother then," Dorothy says.

"Carrie," according to Dorothy, "was very loyal. She spent the same twenty-six years with Sonja that I did except for a brief period when she went to work for someone else, but she came back to Sonja and stayed with her the rest of her life. Carrie is ninety-six years old now. Carrie, as a matter of fact, was the kind of person who could save your life or cut your throat, but either way she would convince Sonja she did right. She could put someone to the ground, and Sonja would go along with it."

More speculation that Sonja's marriage to Winnie Gardiner was over appeared in the *London Daily Express* during the fall of 1953: "Since August she has been out steadily with her childhood sweetheart, handsome Kjell Holm, a Norwegian sardine king." Neither Selma nor Kjell's mother wanted these two to marry. Otherwise they would probably have done so many years earlier. Each mother had her own reasons for discouraging the match.

From Oslo the show returned briefly to France. After completing her engagement in Paris, Sonja flew back home, and Dorothy returned to the United States by ship, with more of Sonja's cash from the French run. "I brought a whole briefcase filled with Sonja's cash back from France. She had left francs in the safe deposit box at the Hotel George V and ordered me to convert them to dollars and bring them home. By now we had contacts all over Europe, and so I did as she told me and had the briefcase on board with me in my stateroom, which I was sharing with an older lady who was returning from a social trip in Europe. There was a little gas heater in our room, like you might have in your home—tall and narrow, set into the wall.

"With all the arrangements Sonja left for me to attend to, I hadn't really gotten a lot of sleep and used the voyage home as an excuse to sleep-in, mornings. I didn't even bother with going down for breakfast. On this particular morning the little lady had awakened and rinsed out her nightgown and hung it on a hanger in front of our little heater to dry. I woke up in a fright to find the cabin filled with smoke. My first expression was, 'My God! Something's on fire!' The second thought that entered my head was of Sonja's money in the briefcase. I never once thought of myself being hurt. My whole energy was directed to rescuing Sonja's dollars. There I was running down the hallway in my pajamas screaming for help. The steward put out the fire, the lady's gown burned up, and Sonja's bucks were safe. Speak of the *Perils of Pauline!*"

Back in New York, Sonja was on the long distance phone with Louella Parsons. She confirmed to the Hollywood gossip queen that it was all over with Winnie. "He does not seem to want to continue our marriage. I was very upset over legal troubles and the suits filed in Baltimore when I left for Europe several months ago. I thought sure Winnie would have come to me, in view of my nervous condition. His bags were packed, and I had bought his ticket, and suddenly without apparent reason he just refused to go. All the time that I was abroad with my ice show I expected him to join me—first in Paris, then in London, and later in my native Norway, but he didn't show. I heard he was upset because my name was linked with that of a Nassau realtor I had never even met. He never gave me a chance to tell him the truth so what is there left for me to do except to say we are separated. I will return to Los Angeles Friday, alone."

A divorce, she said, was in the offing, but "I have no immediate plans." She told Louella that she planned to "go out on the town tonight." And go out on the town she did—in a grand manner. But first of all she phoned Leif in California.

"Leif," she said, "I want you to come to New York and meet with my lawyer, and then I want you both to go out to the Long Island Yacht Harbor and pick up my yacht."

"My yacht," was the boat Winnie had purchased in Norway and which had been paid for by Selma Henie. Sonja told Leif, "It's yours. I want you to have it. You can sail it down through the Panama Canal and dock at Balboa."

Rather than become involved in Sonja's marital brawls, Leif declined the offer. Sonja was not pleased, but her real anger was directed at Winnie Gardiner, who was involved with another woman. Although Winnie had inherited the Gardiner home in Long Island, Sonja had decorated and furnished it out of her own funds. She heard, while staying at the Plaza, that Winnie was taking the other woman out one night. "Get me the biggest moving van you can find," she told Dorothy. "I want you and Carrie to take a short drive with me out to Long Island. We're going to pay a surprise visit on my soon-to-be ex-husband."

One van soon turned into two. When Sonja arrived at the gates of the estate she identified herself as Mrs. Gardiner and the new guard admitted her with her trucks onto the grounds. She stripped the place to the bare walls. The only reason she didn't lift the carpeting was because it was too difficult to get all the tacks out in time. Sonja ran through the house right at the end and grabbed all the toilet paper and supervised the removal of the drapes from the windows. She tripped on the way out and fractured an ankle and had to have it bound up the next day at Lenox Hill Hospital.

The vans pulled away from the estate at five in the morning, and as Sonja was driving her car down the highway, behind the vans, she passed the car that was carrying Winnie and his girlfriend home from a night of reveling. "I wish I could be there when he and that bitch walk into the house and find out they'll have to screw on the floor."

By the time she arrived at the Plaza, Winnie had phoned several times and when they finally spoke the conversation was anything but cordial. Sonja stashed the furnishings in a warehouse, and Winnie Gardiner never got any of them back.

It had been a remarkable year for Sonja. One of the nicest things that happened to her came in the form of a letter she received from Morris Chalfen at the end of her first European tour. It was written and delivered to Sonja's dressing room before the last show of the tour on October 26, 1953:

Sonja Henie Enterprises Inc.

Kungliga Tennishallen,
Stockholm, Sweden.
October 26, 1953.

Dear Sonja:

Tonight you will give your last performance of this current European tour and you will go on a well-deserved vacation to Oslo, and I will go back to the States tomorrow, to further coordinate the tour of the show in America. Your show will continue on for a couple of stops in France and then return to the States.

But, before parting, I want to send this little note to tell you how wonderful it was to work with you. I am not much for flowery oratory or fancy words, but I sincerely want you to know that I think you are a very grand person, aside from being Miss Ice-Skating herself.

I hope you have enjoyed the European tour as much as I have. You really were, contrary to other things that I had heard, one of the easiest persons I ever worked with. We saw eye to eye and you were flexible in doing all the things consistent with good business, like cutting bad stops short and extending the good ones and putting in extra performances when the money was there. You skated outside under hazardous conditions and in the cold in Oslo, and inside on an unfamiliar, shortened portable rink, and never once did I hear a complaint from you. I want you to know that I fully appreciate all of these things and I think you are the greatest trouper of all time.

The greatest tribute that I could pay to you is knowing that when they had you down for the count of nine you never gave up and refuse to be counted out, as any normal person would have. Instead, you gritted your teeth, kept fighting and wound up in a blaze of glory, like the true champion you are and have always been.

I hope you have a pleasant vacation and I am looking forward to seeing you in the States. Of course, let me know your whereabouts from time to time. I will be in Minneapolis through Christmas. I would like to know about your arrival in New York, so we can arrang something with the press.

As a parting word, I also want to tell you how much I admire your Mother, whom I have found to be a very admirable person.

Best wishes,

HOLIDAY ON ICE SHOWS, INC.

Rick

Morris Chalfen, President.

Plans were already being made, not only for an American tour, but for a European one as well—and a trip behind the iron curtain to Moscow. It was designed to be an exchange program. Sonja's show would perform in Russia and a top Soviet ballet troupe would tour the United States. It looked as if it was going to be a big coup for Sonja.

And well it might have been. However, when Sonja discovered she could not bring any money out of Russia and would have to spend her profits there in that country, she nixed the deal. There were no such restraints on foreign attractions in the United States, and she refused to be on the short end of a venture.

If hard work was what Sonja wanted, she was getting it. Usually her tours were through by the end of March, and she turned to movies and home. In March 1954, Sonja premiered her own American ice show, *The Sonja Henie Ice Revue,* at the Coliseum in Nashville, Tennessee. She flew into Nashville from Rome and Oslo, where she had been visiting. Continental rumors followed her. At a press party she was asked if she planned to marry Kjell Holm as soon as her divorce from Gardiner was final.

Sonja laughed. "I am not yet in the divorce courts, first of all, and second, I am so busy with work and all I have no time to think of romance."

She totally captivated Tennessee's capital city during her run. Sonja was riding high again and enjoying every minute of it. She should have enjoyed it and savored it, because it was truly her last hurrah. She had another tour with Chalfen later in the year, but it was anticlimactic.

In May 1954 Sonja's show went into Columbus, Ohio. It was a bad week from the day she arrived, on a Sunday. Sonja had scheduled an interview with thirty teenagers and kept them waiting for a couple of hours. At a press conference on Monday, she was publicly scolded for her treatment of the youngsters. "I didn't get any sleep last night," she said, bursting into tears, whereupon she dashed out of the press party being held in her honor at the Deshler Hilton Hotel.

Later she stood with her mother, after recovering her composure, and made her explanations. "I haven't eaten for three days. I had two shows on Saturday and two on Sunday, and I'm plain tired. I had to have my hair washed at eight this morning and then tried to get some sleep this afternoon. There was a meeting with Governor Lausche for pictures. I couldn't help the delay. My schedule is just so tight."

Columbus critics praised the show's "color" but added that it lacked "form." "On the debit side," Norman Nadel wrote, the show exhibited "a general lack of organization and possibly effort."

Charlotte Curtis, writing for the *Ohio State Journal* the following day said, ". . . what reporters, radio and TV people, and the teenagers didn't know was that the 41-year-old Miss Henie was a tired sick woman."

When the show closed in Columbus, Sonja was planning to fly to

Madrid and asked Dorothy to go with her. Plane reservations were made and bags packed when Dorothy received a telegram from her father telling her that her brother had died. After the matinee that day she went to Sonja with the telegram and said, "I can't go to Spain with you because my brother has just died, and I have to pick up my mother and father and go to Omaha."

Sonja offered no condolences. All she said was, "We'll talk about your coming to Madrid later." Dorothy did join her in Spain, and later in the summer the show returned for an engagement in Detroit, without Sonja. Dorothy was with the show in Detroit as Sonja's representative. "Sonja had a percentage of the show, and she always wanted to know what was going on, so she wanted me to be there to protect her interests."

While in Detroit, Dorothy took care of her own interests as well. She and Ken Stevens were married there. When Sonja phoned from Europe to see how things were going, Dorothy told her the news.

"Oh!" Sonja said. That was it. She changed the subject immediately without congratulations or anything else.

25

BY 1955 Sonja was drinking heavily. It seemed to her that all her life she had been perfect, doing all "the right things," but now when the castles began to crumble around her, she found that all of her strength was used up. The years had taken a heavy toll on her emotional life. She had no children, only money, openings, schedules, deadlines, and responsibilities.

By this time, Sonja's relationship with her brother was becoming more and more distorted by the fact that she had developed some sort of mania for his properties. It started with the apartment building on Judson Avenue in Chicago and eventually reached a point where she wanted half of the sixteen-hundred-acre ranch in San Diego County. There were some bitter fights.

An amusing prelude to that was the big but very temporary romance with Liberace. Sonja even announced that she and the glittering pianist were going to be married. Jack and Liz Pfeiffer were totally surprised by that. They remembered the time when the show had been in St. Louis, and Liberace was playing the Chase Hotel where Sonja's party was staying. According to Liz, "Liberace seemed to have a thing for Sonja, but no one took it seriously. It was amusing. He had dinner with us one evening and later Sonja complained that he wore 'such God-awful perfume.' She managed to avoid him as often as possible after that."

However, she brought him down to Leif's ranch one time during one of the numerous trips she made there with various associates and friends—always by chartered plane—and usually drunk and raving. It was a weekend. "Sonja was acting like she owned my home," Leif recalls. "This was a weekend visit, before I built her a house of her own at the ranch. They were drinking 'seventy-fives,' (a mixture of champagne with cognac) and after quite a bit of imbibing, Liberace kept admiring my antique bronze Viking ship on the mantel over the fireplace. To my astonishment, Sonja got up, took it down from the mantel, and gave it to Liberace. 'Leif wants you to have this.' I was too embarrassed to say anything.

"On their departure for Los Angeles I drove them out to the airport where Sonja's chartered plane was parked. As Liberace entered the plane, carrying my Viking ship, he crossed the plane's door, stopped and turned around toward me waving good-bye, and to my further amazement and no little embarrassment, he began to throw kisses at me, waving his arms and tossing big rainbow kisses.

"I couldn't wait until they closed the plane door and I could get away from the airport."

Nothing would satisfy Sonja until she had her own house on the ranch, so Leif built one to shut her up. He had no idea that she was in a sense establishing squatters rights on his property and would use that as a lever to force him to split the ranch with her.

While in Oslo on her second European tour for Morris Chalfen, she found herself seated at the same table with Niels Onstad at a party given in her honor by the city.

She had always detested Niels in the past but suddenly they were very close. Selma Henie took a dim view of it, if for no other reason than that Sonja was still married, and Niels Onstad was engaged to another woman. In Selma's opinion, the whole thing was disgraceful. Sonja hadn't ever listened to her mother before, so it was no great surprise that she didn't this time.

"But Sonja kept stalling when asked about the dissolution of her marriage to Winnie Gardiner. "If I don't get a divorce from Winnie, I won't make the same mistake again. Right? Two times is enough. I am finished with marriage."

Sonja was meddling so much in Dorothy's marriage that her secretary and her husband both decided to leave ice skating and move back to Los Angeles where they would try to live a normal life. It didn't work out that way, exactly. Ken insisted that Dorothy give Sonja her notice, but she kept putting off facing Sonja because she wasn't sure of her reaction.

Dorothy also wondered what she would do for a job if she left Sonja. "One of the reasons I kept putting off telling her anything," she says, "is because she didn't know anything about my personal life, my family. She didn't care. She was my family so far as her concerns were involved. There was no one else."

Not wanting to upset her on opening night in Paris, Dorothy finally did approach Sonja on their second night. She went into Sonja's dressing room before the show and said, "Sonja, I've come to the conclusion that about the best thing I can do is tell you I can't work for you anymore. I'm sorry, but I think things will work out better this way."

Sonja's expression froze. Icily she snapped, "If that's the way you want it!"

On closing night Sonja kept Dorothy packing and repacking her wardrobe case over and over again. Sonja left the arena, and Dorothy remained to complete Sonja's packing. When Dorothy arrived back at the hotel at seven in the morning, her husband had departed with the show for Switzerland, having changed his mind, and she had to take Sonja to the airport to catch a plane.

"Before you leave," Sonja ordered, "take care of my money." She had little else to say to her secretary, who obeyed her instructions to take the French francs to a black market money changer and get "as many dollars as you can for them." She did as she was told and carried the money across the Atlantic in a black briefcase.

Once Sonja was back in Los Angeles she continued her assault on her brother for the apartment building in Chicago. Now she was also asking for half the ranch. They fought constantly on the telephone, and Sonja's demands became ever more outrageous. For the first time in his life, Leif stood firm against his sister. He refused to budge. It was a difficult period for Leif, since his own marriage was beginning to fall apart.

Having placed her foot in the door by getting Leif to build a house for her on the ranch, Sonja was in a position to take the next step. The subject of the Chicago property had come up in a leisurely fashion a couple of times, but Sonja had merely suggested that sometime she might like to "buy Leif out."

Now that she was putting the pressure on Leif, Sonja's weekend visits became more frequent, more dramatic, and more unwelcome. She always chartered a plane and brought along an entourage, together with enough booze to saturate the area for some time to come.

Leif had become friendly with Ty and Sally Weihle. Mr. Weihle had been in the real estate business in Beverly Hills and had his own insurance business. He was well-versed in real estate development. Leif needed a man of his caliber to help him with the development of Henie Hills, so they worked out an agreement, and Ty Weihle came to work for Leif. It was an easy friendship to develop. Both were successful businessmen, family men with children, boys close in age.

Sonja's weekend visits were interrupted by an engagement at the Roxy Theatre in New York where she was going to be for several months. After recovering from a severe bout of pneumonia contracted in Europe, Dorothy Stevens phoned Carrie Roberts one day at Sonja's house to let her friend know she was back and that her husband had remained in Europe.

"What are you doing now?" Carrie asked.

"Nothing really, but I've got to start looking for a job pretty soon."

They chatted a while longer and hung up. About ten minutes later the phone rang in Dorothy's house, and she found Sonja on the other end. "Dorothy," she asked, as cheerful as a lark, "what are you doing?"

"I've not been feeling too well, so I'm not doing anything."

"I'm going into the Roxy Theatre in New York. Do you want to go?"

"Sure." So she was back with Sonja and Sonja, of course, was delighted that Ken was still in Europe.

In New York Sonja picked up where she had left off in Oslo with Niels Onstad. She even moved into his apartment, keeping a suite at the Plaza Hotel to cover up her clandestine affair. Niels was backstage at every performance. Selma Henie was outraged but had long since learned that the best thing to do when she disagreed with Sonja was to keep quiet. Sonja had become more and more abrupt with her mother, and Selma had begun to have some minor physical problems that would not improve.

With little to do while rehearsals were under way for the new show in New York, Sonja was quick tempered and irritable. Her drinking had increased, and she was becoming obsessed with Leif and his ranch. Leif received a long-distance call from Sonja one night. She had been drinking scotch all afternoon and evening and rambled on for quite a while before he understood what she was talking about. It turned out that she wanted to buy out his interest in the Chicago apartment house.

Leif was now ready to listen since he needed some cash for the golf course he was putting in at the ranch.

"I'll give you fifty thousand dollars," she said. "That's twice what you have invested. I think double your money ought to be a good deal for you. I'll have my lawyer draw up the papers before I get home."

Sonja's arithmetic was correct, but her sense of timing was way off. The property had been purchased almost fifteen years ago and had appreciated considerably more than double. In addition to appreciation there were improvements on the property.

"No, Sonja. What we'll have to do is have the First National Bank of Chicago send us an unbiased appraisal. They are the bank that handles our trust accounts, and I'm sure they'll be fair and equitable. I'll sell you my interest for exactly half what they appraise the current value."

Sonja agreed, hung up the phone, and went back to her glass of scotch. Leif went back to dinner and his guests and made a note to call the First National Bank in Chicago the next morning.

Several days later, Sonja called her brother again. Had he checked the appraisals and what did the bank say?

"Sonja," he began with great patience, aware that she was drunk, "I have two appraisals. One is for two hundred and seventy-five thousand dollars and the other for two hundred-eighty. I'll take half of the lesser amount."

She exploded. "You no-good sonofabitch you'll take fifty-thousand dollars and like it." They fought for several minutes and then Leif hung up on his sister. Leif eventually accepted what Sonja had offered in the first place.

While she was appearing at the Roxy in New York, Sonja and Chalfen met, and a South American tour was put together. If Chalfen knew that Sonja was now drinking on a daily basis, he said nothing to her about it.

276

She always performed when she was on the ice. Nevertheless, he kept a backup skater on call in case something happened and Sonja was unable to continue the tour.

The tour was disastrous from the day they set foot on South American soil. Sonja worked hard in Caracas, the first stop. Everyone did, but they were playing to people used to bullfights, in a converted bull ring. On opening night moths the size of sparrows stuck in the ice and the opening number had to skate through them. Large rats ran around the bullring during the show. It was an extraordinary situation, but Sonja and her troupe performed like the veterans they were.

Chalfen was very well connected politically in South America and felt that everything was going to be all right once the show settled in for the tour. The skaters, however, had only recently returned from Europe where rinks were well laid out, large enough to perform on, and clean.

Bill Webster, Sonja's ice engineer, had taken one look at the bullring when they arrived and said, "We have trouble."

"What trouble?" Jack asked.

The temperature of the water flowing through the pipes in Caracas was too high. Normally in American cities where the show played in the wintertime the temperatures of the water would range between forty and fifty degrees and was not difficult to freeze. In Caracas, close to the equator, it was much higher. So high that ordinary freezing methods didn't work. Bill had to build a large tower where the water could be precooled, and as the water dripped down through the system, layer after layer, they were finally able to cool it enough so the refrigeration machine would freeze it.

"It was an open area," recounts Pfeiffer. "No roof, just an open rink. It was covered over with canvas during the daytime so at night we could get it frozen to the right consistency for the skaters to perform on. It had to be inspected daily. That was only one of the many problems in Caracas."

Sonja, ever the perfectionist, saw some Spanish dancers doing a sort of bullfight number and decided that would be just the thing for her show in Caracas and later, Rio. She practiced like mad and kept asking the couple, "Am I doing it right? Is this the authentic way you do it?" They assured her she was and it was. The number consisted mostly of walking, or skating through and doing all the things that a bullfighter would do in the ring. The chorus skaters had a difficult time learning it on such short notice, but Sonja insisted it be ready for opening night.

South Americans preferred the bullfights to ice skating, and they didn't understand Sonja's hula, which was the mainstay of her performance elsewhere. They weren't used to ballet on ice, and the show fell flat with them.

It was hoped that Rio de Janeiro would be a better place to produce an ice show. It was May 1956, and the weather was all that anyone could want. The beaches at Impanema were crowded and it was always carnival time. A new stadium had been built in Rio, all cement with new dressing rooms. It was the home field of the great soccer player, Pelé. The stadium accommodated one hundred thousand seated spectators and there was room for another one hundred thousand to stand. There is nothing like it in North America. A great moat circled the field, like a medieval castle, to prevent the immense crowds from rushing onto the field and creating mayhem. South Americans get very emotional over sporting events. The ice rink was set up next door in the basketball arena. Seating only about eight or nine thousand, it couldn't compare with Madison Square Garden.

Unfortunately Sonja was not well received by the Brazilians. She was becoming very unhappy with the show work, and to a large extent that may have been a result of the lack of response from the fans. No big applause. No standing ovations. No encores.

Sonja was drinking heavily and not skating well, not even following her music any longer. The director had to follow her. Jack Pfeiffer did the best he could. He knew her routines and could either speed up or slow down the orchestra, but the rhythm-conscious South Americans knew what was wrong. Sonja was no longer merely drinking all night after the show. She now was belting the scotch by the glassful before the show, and becoming ever more discouraged with it, with the other skaters, and with herself.

It was usually daylight when Sonja crawled into bed or was put there by someone who often had to clean up the bathroom because she had thrown up all over it.

Dorothy and Selma Henie were with her constantly. "She had hangovers and wasn't feeling well," Dorothy explains, "and was angry at everybody and everything. Nothing could go right. Mother Henie was scared to death of Sonja when she drank, so her life was a constant state of fear."

Dorothy could sense when the little "click" was about to happen in Sonja's head and the "other personality" would take over. "She wouldn't even go out on the ice when other skaters were around. She didn't want any of the skaters to see her on the ice—not even the stagehands. Everyone had to be out of sight. When she was assured that nobody else was on the ice, she would dart out, but not a second sooner."

Everything bothered Sonja, and she would become disoriented and hallucinatory. Chorus skaters were skating better and getting bigger hands. She was merely wobbling around on the ice. When she did her three jump, she was lucky if she got six inches off the ice. And she fell. It was sad to see this great star scrambling all over the ice.

"Mr. Chalfen wanted to train a successor; let Sonja take a young skater under her wing and groom her for the time when Sonja would only produce and not skate. Sonja wouldn't hear of it," Dorothy declares. "That was the problem that came to a head in South America. The papers were mentioning her age more and more, and she couldn't deal with that. She just couldn't face getting older—not being the young Norwegian ice skating phenomenon she had been when she captivated America and Twentieth Century-Fox Studios in 1936."

Sonja's physical and mental condition were rapidly deteriorating. Not Dorothy nor Anne Fordyce (her hairdresser from England) or Vera Schaefer, the wardrobe lady, could console Sonja or please her. She was slipping into a deep depression. She began to talk of suicide. "I'm finished," she sobbed. "Look at me. Old! What's the use of going on?"

No one's reassurances could bring her out of her depressed state, and Selma Henie, fearful that her daughter was about to kill herself, insisted that she be watched twenty-four hours a day. Dorothy was elected to spend the nights with Sonja—the worst of all times because that was the period when she went into rages, which turned into crying jags before she eventually passed out.

Dealing with Sonja was a physical as well as an emotional problem. Dorothy recalls that, "Sonja was as strong as an ox. You'd never know it to look at her, but all those years of athletics gave her tremendous strength."

The nights were nightmares. Sonja had to be watched when she went to the bathroom lest she had hidden some pills or a razor blade. She was continually threatening to jump off the balcony.

Most everyone was pleased to see the show close in Rio and was looking forward to a better week in Sao Paolo, the next stop. Sonja refused to go on with the show and was replaced by a German skater, Erika Kraft, the reserve skater whom Morris Chalfen had kept on ice "just in case."

"I can't go on," Sonja cried. "Look at me. I'm old. Nobody loves me. You all saw how they treated me. I was booed. It's all over. I can't go on anymore. I'm going to New York."

Winnie Gardiner had finally filed suit for divorce from Sonja in April 1956, charging "desertion" and "mental torture." The divorce was finalized in West Palm Beach, Florida, six weeks later. He remarried shortly thereafter.

Sonja had been having long conversations back and forth with Niels Onstad, who was now in New York where he had offices for his shipping business. Selma had hoped their relationship would have ended when Sonja left him in New York, but it didn't. When Niels had visited Leif in California years before, Sonja had refused to go out to dinner with Leif and some friends if Niels were a member of the party. But times had changed.

Sonja wanted Dorothy to join her in New York, "but not until you've taken care of my money matters." The "money matters" involved returning to Caracas to withdraw money Sonja had deposited there while they were in Venezuela. Dorothy flew to Caracas and had no sooner checked into her hotel than the phone rang. It was Sonja—sober, excited, and filled with vigor. "You're the only one not here. Mother and Carrie are here. I've decided to get married, so get here as fast as you can."

"Married?" Her secretary was stunned. "To whom?"

"To Niels, of course. Who else? I want you here with me when I get married. It's to be a small wedding. Nothing fancy. We're just going to be married in the apartment. But don't forget to bring the money."

Dorothy, due to plane schedules, was unable to be there for the wedding that took place on June 6, 1956, but joined the newlyweds in Miami for their wedding breakfast.

Sonja's marriage shocked Leif, who was not present. But by that time he had already been shocked in far more serious ways, and to explain that it will be necessary to go back a number of months and trace a story that began in 1955.

As so often in Sonja's life, it all had to do with money. She had lost a good deal of it producing her own show, but she had made something of a financial recovery since then, and her actual assets were in the millions. It wouldn't have mattered if she'd had ten times as much. Enough was never enough with Sonja, and because of that she was about to become involved in some of the most disgraceful actions of her life.

One day in 1955, Selma Henie showed up at Sally Weihle's house, wringing her hands and quite upset. "Sally," she cried, "you'll have to talk to Leif about this business. Get him to sign half the ranch over to Sonja. It doesn't mean anything. She's just in a bad mood."

Sally told Selma that she couldn't talk Leif into anything like that and recalls that, "Mother Henie was crazy about my husband, Ty, and thought we had a lot of influence with Leif. We invited Leif over to our house, and his mother reiterated her conversation with me. Leif was adamant. 'I'm not about to sign half the ranch over to Sonja. It *does* mean something.'"

"But Leif," his mother begged, "she's going to sue you. We can't have all that bad publicity in the family. It will be terrible."

Leif stood firm. "I'm sorry, Mother, but I simply cannot bend to Sonja's will anymore. She has ceased being the most important thing in my life. I have children to think about." Mrs. Henie drove back to Beverly Hills in tears, not really understanding why Leif wouldn't acquiesce to his sister's demands. It was, she reasoned, all family.

Leif discussed the matter further with the Weihles after his mother left. "My sister didn't even put five cents in this property. The title to that property is vested in me 'as a married man as his separate property.' Even Gerd can't touch it. I'm not giving her anything other than the house she already has here. I've done enough. I'm through giving to Sonja."

Sally said, "Leif, Sonja will probably sue you."

"My sister's bad but she would never sue me."

The following day Sonja appeared—drunk.

Sally recalls what happened:

"She always had to make a big show. She had a man who was kind of a man Friday and served as a gofer for her. He piloted the private plane for her and did all of her important errands. That sort of thing. Carrie, the cook, was with her. Leif was at my house, and I looked out the window and saw Sonja and her entourage approaching.

"I said to Leif, 'Here comes your sister.' Sonja had already been to Leif's house, gone through dresser drawers and jewelry boxes and taken back all the jewelry she had given him over the years. Now she was headed for my house."

Sonja began by banging on the door, and, as Sally explains, "I had to let them in. She would have literally broken down the door or windows. She was raving. My husband had gone off some place on business and the help was scared to death. She stomped into the house with a stranger, a man I'd never laid eyes on before, and I knew immediately that he was a process server. Sonja was speaking rapidly in Norwegian to Leif. She wanted to know if he was going to give her half the ranch and he said, 'No!' She proceeded to call him every name in the book, and it certainly wasn't 'My dear brother.' All of a sudden this nice young man stepped forward and politely asked, 'Are you Leif Henie?'

"Leif said, 'Yes,' and he handed Leif the paper. A summons."

The radio and television newscasts as well as the newspapers carried the story. "Sonja Henie Sues Brother." The scandal that Selma Henie had tried to avoid was now wide open.

It was during this period that Leif and Gerd were arranging their divorce. Although Sonja hadn't liked Gerd in the beginning, she eventually accepted her as Leif's wife and part of the family. She was crazy about their three boys. However, when Sonja received the news that Leif and Gerd were divorcing, her only comment was, "I knew the marriage wouldn't last," although they had been married nearly twenty years.

If she had accepted Gerd, she never liked Sally.

Sally Weihle's husband died from a massive heart attack in January 1956, and it seemed natural enough that she would turn to her husband's employer and friend for guidance. Leif was not around one day when Sally's maid opened the door for Sonja. Sally had warned her servants to "never let Sonja in my house."

"She didn't want me to marry Leif. Mother Henie was the same way, but she and I never had words. She always called me when Sonja was acting up. She often would call me up to ask what to do about Sonja's drinking, or to tell me that 'Sonja has just been treating me so badly, Sally.' She'd cry when she spoke of Sonja's meanness.

"I knew Sonja did not like me and after she found out Leif and I planned to be married after his divorce, she became vicious. My maid didn't understand English but knew something was radically wrong when she saw Sonja coming. She only needed to open the door a little bit. Sonja was strong as an ox and just knocked that door open, and my maid went flying across the room.

"I hid in the closet. She was very physical after all those years as a skater. I thought if I hid in the closet she'd think I wasn't at home. She went right to the master bedroom and opened all my closets and then went into my son's room and opened all the closets and took the hangers and started hitting me over the head. I got away from her and got to the telephone. I threatened her. 'You get out of here right now, Sonja, or I'll have you arrested. You're not talking to Leif, now.'"

Sonja left but shouted drunkenly, "I'll be back."

Meanwhile, Sally was able to contact Leif, and he came immediately to her house. Not too long afterward, they heard a car coming up the driveway, and Sonja was back, with her entourage.

"I didn't get a good look at her," Sally recalls, "because I didn't wait. Leif and I went into the bathroom and locked the door. We hoped she would go away. I could hear her—the whole neighborhood could hear her. She was screaming at the top of her voice to my maid, 'Where's the butcher knife? You show me right now or I'll kill you,' she screamed. 'I'm here because nobody is going to get my money, my ranch.'

"Although Leif had signed a temporary agreement with Sonja, a final document had not been prepared by the lawyers, and Sonja was obsessed with the idea that I might in some way come into something she felt she should have. The maid didn't understand a word she was saying, and was begging her in Spanish to go away. 'I'm here and I'm here to kill everybody.' She knew we were in the house but couldn't find us. 'I know you're here and I'm going to kill you and Sally, and then I'll kill Billy, Bobby, Tommy, and Little Ty.'"

Sonja was careening about the kitchen like a mad woman. Those with her said nothing.

The "Little Ty" whom Sonja referred to was Sally's eight-year-old son whom Leif would adopt after he and Sally were married.

When Sonja mentioned the children's names, Sally tensed. "Leif, she's crazy drunk. She might go down there and kill all the kids. They wouldn't know what was happening. They'll probably say, 'Look, here comes Aunt Sonja' and walk into God only knows what. You've got to get out and I'm going to phone the police.

"He said, 'Oh, no. She wouldn't do that.' But I insisted on calling the police."

282

Leif opened the bathroom door and went out into the house, and Sonja immediately attacked him verbally and physically. Leif was trying to prevent Sonja from hurting anybody, and while he struggled with his sister, Sally went to the phone and called the police.

Sonja was screaming all the while. "That bitch will never get my property. Never! Do you hear me Leif? Never!"

Soon the Oceanside Police arrived in a black-and-white car, red lights flashing and sirens going full blast. They expected a possible homicide.

Sally recalls with a laugh that "All Leif could say was, 'Oh, there's going to be a scandal about my subdivision!'" It was understandable. He had put hundreds of thousands of dollars into the sixteen-hundred-acre ranch. The police wanted to arrest Sonja. As one officer put it, "Just until she sobers up."

"Oh, no. We could never have that," Leif told them. Leif and Sally declined to press charges, a truce was negotiated, and the officers convinced Sonja to leave the premises.

Leif and Jerry Geisler had always been good friends. So, when Sonja sued him for half the ranch he called Geisler to ask him about an attorney, mentioning that somebody was suing him over the ranch, but he didn't say it was Sonja. Geisler gave him the name of an attorney in San Diego. Leif hired him, and when Sonja came to San Diego to sit down with Leif to discuss a settlement, she was accompanied by her attorneys—Jerry Geisler and about six other lawyers. Geisler had known all along that it was Sonja who was suing Leif.

The meeting was held at the courthouse in San Diego. It was to be a pretrial meeting in an effort to prevent a public trial and more airing of the dirty family linen. Leif was adamant on the one hand that he would not surrender to Sonja, but, on the other hand, he wanted to prevent a public scandal at all costs.

Sally accompanied Leif, which further infuriated Sonja. A big argument ensued, and when Leif got up to leave, Sonja told him, "I'll break you, Leif, if I have to keep you in court for seven years. I have the money to do it." The whole conversation was in Norwegian and the attorneys understood nothing except that there would be no settlement that day.

26

THE publicity that attended Sonja's lawsuit against her brother created problems for Leif. He was in the process of selling lots and houses at Henie Hills, and when the news reached the public, sales fell. People began to wonder who actually owned the land they were purchasing.

It cost Leif half a million dollars in the first year of legal fighting. His bank accounts were attached, and there were threats of mechanics' liens against the property. Sonja spread the story that she had bought the property during the war. In her words, "I didn't want Leif to go, so I purchased the property for him because it was farmland and they weren't taking farmers in the service."

Leif held out as long as he could but in the end the financial pressures were too great. Investors were backing away from Henie Hills, and he wasn't sure if people would still have confidence in him after a public scandal. Rather than risk that he did what he felt he had to do. He was wronged, but pragmatic. In early 1956 a one-page interim letter agreement was drawn up, later to be replaced by a more formal one, which read as follows:

The settlement agreed upon between Sonja Henie and Leif Henie as of February 15 is as follows:
(a) Sonja Henie to pay Leif Henie $80,000;
(b) Sonja Henie to receive $80,000 worth of lots. The number of lots to be determined by the value placed on the property approximately 2 years ago;
(c) In addition to the above lots, Sonja Henie is to receive not less than 500 acres of ranch property located in the least hilly section of the property. This property will have approximately 3000 feet from frontage on the highway;
(d) In addition to the above lots and the acreage, Sonja Henie is to have clear title to the house on the subdivision which was paid for by her and clear title to the lot upon which this house was built;
(e) All of the above properties are to be free of any mortgages or debts;

(f) Leif Henie to assign his 50% interest in the 834 Judson Avenue Building Corporation to Sonja Henie and Sonja to assume the note now owed by Leif Henie to this Corporation in principal sum of $50,000 and approximately $6,000 interest.

Sonja had her way—but not completely. She settled for a lot less than she wanted to on the ranch.

Sonja's greed didn't stop with Leif. She swiftly followed the ranch settlement by having one drawn up for her mother's signature one week later. It was signed by Selma on February 24 and witnessed by two people, one of whom was Carrie Roberts. It read as follows:

In consideration of the sum of 1,000,000 kroner heretofore loaned to me by my daughter, Sonja Henie, and the forgiveness of said debt, I hereby agree as follows:

1. To convey to Sonja Henie upon demand, all my interest in the real property known as Landoën, Oslo, Norway, together with all furnishings in said premises.

2. To execute and deliver to my said daughter, upon demand, a bill of sale of all trophies which were won by my husband and all silverware owned by me.

3. To execute an irrevocable Last Will and Testament devising and bequeathing to my said daughter, Sonja Henie, all my estate, both real and personal, in the event she shall be living at the time of my decease.

Sonja had stripped her mother of everything. Selma didn't want to sign the paper, but Sonja had threatened to move her out of the house if she didn't.

Although the agreement with Leif stipulated that Sonja had paid for the house on the property, she in fact hadn't put a penny into it. It had been entirely a gift from Leif. She later sold some of the acreage to a university for two million dollars, which she funneled into Oslo without paying taxes on the capital gains. Leif got stuck for that at a later date when Niels Onstad broke the Chicago trust which had been set up for him by his father.

When Sonja married Niels, she insisted on a prenuptial agreement. In the pact, although she had lived at 243 Delfern Drive in Holmby Hills for fifteen years, she stated her home address as "838½ Judson Avenue, Chicago, Illinois." The first clause of the agreement indicated that in the event she should survive his death that the New York apartment and a house in New Rochelle owned by Onstad, each to be free of any mortgages and any other encumbrances, automatically become her property. And, if he should sell the properties during his lifetime, then Sonja should be compensated in the amount "for which either or both of said properties were sold."

Sonja's attorney drew up the agreement specifically stipulating that there would be no "commingling" of their property and assets. Sonja was maintaining her rule that, "What is mine, is mine."

All was not sugar and cream in newlywed land. After Sonja's marriage to Niels, Dorothy left to return to an American tour of *Holiday on Ice,* as Sonja's representative with the show, in which she retained an interest. It was playing Lansing, Michigan. Sonja had been married only a short time, but she and Niels had a big fight, and she caught the first plane out and joined the show in Michigan.

Sonja had finally met her match in men. Niels neither indulged her nor lived off her income. He was a no-nonsense businessman who did not have the time to loaf around like a playboy while his wife performed.

Onstad had an office for his shipping company on the lower floor of their apartment in New York and was very busy running his business during the daytime. Sonja wanted full-time attention and demanded it as she always had with her husbands when they were around. Niels was too occupied making money to be bothered with Sonja's temperament. It was the first time in her life she was unable to force someone to bend to her will. Niels Onstad had a will of his own. He was as stubborn as his wife and, when drinking, just as mean. Sonja had finally met her Mr. Right. After a few days of licking her wounds, she flew back to New York and her husband.

Sonja wasn't working after her marriage to Niels, and the real problem was that she had nothing to do. Niels found something for her. Sonja had always been interested in art. But her preferences had been influenced by her parents who were aficionados of the great masters: Rubens, Rembrandt, and Gainsborough. Niels was also a collector, but his taste ran to abstract art, and in the beginning he and Sonja had terrible arguments about the two styles. Perhaps the conflict was therapeutic for Sonja because, much as she loved her old masters, when she returned from New York to Delfern Drive she seriously took up the study of modern art. She even became friends with Picasso and occasionally visited him in Paris.

Slowly, over the years, Sonja managed to ship all her old masters to London, where they were sold by Sotheby. Her family, particularly Leif, was incensed that she had sold off the family art treasures, but now that she had control of her mother's worldly goods, Sonja didn't have to ask Leif's permission for anything, and she didn't.

Sonja became more and more expert in regard to art. Dorothy couldn't believe it when she walked into a room one day and found Sonja curled up in a chair with a large volume on modern art opened in her lap. "It was the first time in my life that I saw Sonja do much reading. If she read anything at all it was usually the gossip columns about other skaters. Now she was doing serious reading and it was not just a passing fad. She became extremely knowledgable. It was like the days when she used to go into the material shops and select fabrics for costumes. She was an expert. Now, she could go to an exhibition and point out a painting and say, 'One day he's going to be great.' She had a natural instinct."

Sonja's marriage provided her with the opportunity to resume her party giving. Without a heavy schedule of practices and rehearsals she had more time. She threw herself into organizing a series of lavish, eye-popping, extremely well-attended parties for the motion picture colony. Legendary were the *Dancing Waters* party (not long after her marriage to Onstad) given at her home on Delfern with the swans swimming about her pool. Another time she rented Ciro's night club and arrived on an elephant. The *Dancing Waters* party was, however, the one which is best remembered. A system of water jets was installed in the pool with timers; an impression was created that the waters were actually dancing as the jets shot spurts into the air.

Carrie was with Sonja when she returned to Los Angeles, but for the better part of two years Dorothy was only there sporadically, because she continued to travel with Morris Chalfen's *Holiday On Ice* as Sonja's representative.

In 1957 Leif's and Gerd's marriage was dissolved and, soon after, Leif and Sally Weihle were married. Gerd married her obstetrician. Leif and Sonja were still not speaking, however, and when Leif and Sally moved to Palm Springs from Oceanside, Sonja went to New York with Niels and urged her husband to phone her brother in order to facilitate some sort of reconciliation. "Leif," he asked, "why don't you come back to New York? Sonja and I are here and we're having a wonderful time. Let's be like old times again. Come back and forget everything. Sonja has already forgotten the past."

"I'll never come back, and I'll never speak to her again as long as I live, Niels. She damn near ruined me and it wouldn't have mattered to her if she had. I've finally realized that Sonja's an utterly greedy woman."

Niels did not give up and at Sonja's urging continued to call until finally he spoke with Sally. "Sally," he said, "can't you do something to have them make up? Sonja and her mother are both miserable about this mess."

Sally said, "Niels, I want you to know I've never interfered with their relationship. Sonja is his sister. It's up to him."

On other occasions Sonja would call and tell Sally, "Mother's dying. Put Leif on." But Leif stubbornly refused to speak to Sonja and would later confirm in conversations with his mother that she had been quite well.

Anytime Selma Henie phoned her son she would whisper to Carrie or

Dorothy, "Don't let Sonja see the phone bills. I don't want her to know I called Leif." Her fear of Sonja's wrath was well-founded. On one occasion while personally going over the phone bills, Sonja did discover calls to Oceanside and Palm Springs, and she hit the roof. "Who the hell's been calling Leif? I want to know right now." And, by the time she had finished her tirade, she had reduced Selma to tears.

It was not unusual for Selma to phone Sally and say, "What am I going to do, Sally? Sonja and Niels are so mean to me. Oh, how I wish we could be a family again before I die."

In the mid-fifties, Sonja had been in New York to appear on a "Colgate Special." She was belting scotch by the paper cupful and was drunk as a lord when she performed but did not miss a cue, executing everything perfectly. After the show she continued to drink until she was unconscious. Mother Henie phoned Leif and begged him to come to New York because "Sonja has had a heart attack."

Leif refused to come. It is interesting that in spite of what Sonja had done to her brother, she still considered him part of her life and did not intend to do without him.

The house Leif and Sally were living in at Palm Springs belonged to Sally, and during the time they were living there, Sonja tried a more direct approach, as Sally recalls: "Sonja and Niels came down to Palm Springs and called Charlie Farrell at the Racquet Club to obtain my address. One day we were sitting out by the pool. The property was surrounded by a very high wall, and I looked up and my God, who should be peeping over the fence but Niels Onstad. He called out to Leif, 'Take good care of yourself.'"

Leif ignored him. Not too long afterward Leif and Sally returned home from an evening out and there, parked in the driveway, they found Sonja and Niels waiting for them. They turned around and went someplace else until they felt the two had given up.

"I got to thinking," Sally says. "What the hell. This is my property and I'm not going to have this." So she hired a private detective and had him sit in the driveway. The detective advised Sonja and Niels when they returned a couple of days later that they were trespassing on private property. That ended the lookout. On another occasion while their house was undergoing repairs, Leif and Sally checked into a Palm Springs motel owned by some friends. During the afternoon the owners came to Leif's room and said, "I think you ought to know that Sonja called and made a reservation for the weekend and specifically asked if you were here. If you don't want to see them, I'd suggest you stay out of sight."

"They were just a pain in the neck," Sally recalls. "They were following us around and we simply avoided them. Mother Henie accompanied them on one trip. Funny part about it is that they didn't see us but we saw them driving around together—all three of them."

Leif was having little to do with his mother because he felt she had sided with Sonja about the ranch. And, desperate as she was to avoid confrontations with her daughter, that was, of course, essentially what she had done.

Several months went by and one day in the late spring of 1959 Leif received a phone call from the Delfern house. It was from Sonja. "Mother has had a heart attack and I think you'd better come right away." Leif was skeptical, but Sally insisted that he would have it on his conscience for the rest of his life if he didn't go see his mother. The call had come about nine at night. Sally threw some things in a suitcase and said, "Leif, we're going to up and see your mother, and that's that."

When they arrived at St. John's Hospital in Santa Monica where Selma Henie was in the cardiac wing, they asked for her room. The nurse on duty said, "Mrs. Henie is not permitted to have any guests."

"I'm sure of that," Leif said, "but I'm her son. My sister called and said she is not expected to live."

"Your sister," replied the nurse, "also forbids that you enter the room."

Sally, aghast and angered, told the nurse, "You'll have a lawsuit on your hands if my husband can't see his own mother. So you better give us the room number now."

The nurse complied immediately. Selma Henie was indeed in bad condition. However, she emerged from semiconsciousness when she heard her son's voice and began to cry. "I thought it was a dream, but you're really here. You're really here!"

Leif promised to return the following morning. When he came out into the hospital corridor he was confronted by Sonja, accompanied by Dorothy. Sonja pounced on Leif like a vixen. "Get the fuck out of *my* mother's room, you sonofabitch."

"She's my mother, too, Sonja," Leif said. "I have as much right to be here as you do."

"No you don't. What did you ever do for her? Tell me one thing. You don't care about her. You've never put one penny in on her share." Sonja was screaming at the top of her lungs. "Get the hell out of here. Do you hear me—get out!"

Leif stayed in Los Angeles until his mother was able to go home. When he checked out of his hotel he discovered that Sonja had collected all of Selma Henie's medical bills and left them at the hotel for Leif to pay. Leif didn't pay them, however, because his mother still had the trust fund, which Sonja couldn't touch until her death, and her medical bills were paid from that. It was just one of Sonja's many attempts to intimidate her brother.

After Selma Henie returned from the hospital a chair lift was installed in the house to facilitate her getting up and down from the lower floor to the bedrooms upstairs. It was paid for out of her trust, but Sonja complained constantly about "unnecessary" medical bills.

One day when Carrie was at the house alone with Selma, she called Dorothy and asked, "Please come over as quickly as you can. There's something wrong with Mother Henie."

Dorothy hurried to Holmby Hills from her home in the San Fernando Valley. She went up to Selma's bedroom and found her in what seemed to be a serious condition. She phoned for the doctor who diagnosed a heart attack and advised that "the next twenty-four hours will be the crucial ones." No one dared send her to the hospital because Sonja was dead set against that.

"Shall I call Sonja?" Dorothy asked. Sonja was away from the city at the time.

"No," the doctor said, "let us wait. But don't leave her alone at night. We'll see how it goes in the morning."

Dorothy and Carrie spent the night sitting up and watching her. The following morning the two of them went downstairs to have a little breakfast. It didn't seem likely that Mother Henie would awaken anytime soon. "Suddenly," Dorothy explains, "while we were eating we thought we heard a noise and both of us went flying up the stairs—and there was Mother Henie. Totally comatose when we went down for breakfast, she was now sitting up in bed as pert as you please. While we didn't believe what we were seeing, she acted as if nothing had happened."

"I'm hungry," she said to Carrie. "Will you fix me some breakfast?"

Dorothy called the doctor immediately, but meanwhile Selma was saying, "Dorothy, you really don't have to be here. I've got things to do and I'm sure you have, too."

She not only got better, but she got up that very same morning and was soon sitting out by the pool with the radio blasting away on a jazz station. The doctor expressed little surprise. "This happens. That's why I asked you not to call Sonja. I've seen cases like this come out either way. They either go fast, or survive."

Nonetheless Selma Henie was having serious heart problems and after each attack, small or large, she grew weaker and of less use to her daughter. She was no longer able to wait on Sonja hand and foot. She needed waiting on herself now.

"I found it strange that Sonja did not want Leif to visit his mother," Dorothy says, "but it must have had something to do about the family money. That was about the same time she had convinced Mother Henie to change her will and disinherit Leif and maybe Sonja was afraid that her mother would tell Leif what she had done. I'm sure Sonja discussed the matter with Niels, but it was mostly her own idea. Sonja loved money more than anything."

It was in May 1960, a few months before she died, that in the face of Sonja's insistence, Selma agreed to write a new will in which she disinherited Leif, and left everything she had, including her trust, to Sonja. Paragraph four of that will said, "I give, devise, bequeath and leave all of my property over which I have the power of testamentary disposition, wherever such property is situated or located." In the settlement that Selma Henie had signed in February 1956, she had promised to draw up such a will, and this was the fulfillment of that promise. Sonja had coerced her mother into signing the previous document in payment for money that never changed hands, but now that she had the will as well, she was confident she would be free of litigation.

The will excluded Leif not only from inheriting from his mother, but if Sonja should predecease her mother, it still cut him out and left the estate to Niels Onstad, if he were still Sonja's husband.

Sonja's treatment of her mother was a shock to Dorothy. "Mother Henie had been ill for about a year and a half before she passed away. She was a lady who had lived her life for her daughter and for Leif—in that order. When I say Sonja did not have compassion, I can give a graphic example. After Mother Henie was no longer able to carry her own weight around the house and do the little duties Sonja expected of her all the time, she became ill and we had her in and out of St. John's Hospital and it cost money. That's when Sonja began to turn against her own mother. That hurt me because her mother idolized her—her whole life was Sonja. She was not a cold woman, just very protective and possessive.

"Mother suffered heart failure over a period of a year and a half and I must say that Sonja started to drift away during that time. She complained about the money and scolded her mother for being ill, saying, 'There is nothing wrong with you. You don't need nurses. Dorothy and Carrie can take care of you.' Mother had her own trust account and it paid an amount sufficient for her hospital bills. However, it was running thin. The truth is, it was getting to where it wasn't going to be so much that would be left for Sonja after her mother passed on. During that year and a half Mother Henie took a lot of abuse from Sonja, both verbal and physical. At one time Niels slapped her during a heated argument between him and Sonja over her mother's condition. Sonja never said a word in her mother's defense."

Leif and Sally returned from Europe in April 1960, and Selma Henie invited them to Los Angeles from Palm Springs for lunch. Sonja and Niels were vacationing in France. When they arrived at Sonja's house, Selma was not feeling well at all, having suffered a series of little strokes. "I'm feeling just terrible today," she told Leif. "Why don't you and Sally spend the night. I don't like being alone."

Leif agreed and phoned Sonja to apprise his sister of their mother's condition. "She's not well at all," he told Sonja, "and I think you ought to be here with her."

"Oh, Leif," she said, "I don't want to come home yet. Mother's had these little things happen before. It's nothing, I'm sure. But if it wouldn't put you out, why don't you and Sally stay with mother."

"I didn't think you wanted us in your home," he said.

"Leif, let's just forget all the bad things. You and Sally won't find it difficult to stay there until we get home. Let's not keep this thing going on forever."

Leif decided it would be better to stay with his mother. God only knew when Sonja would come home. Since she had given up her skating career, she had become very jet-settish and traveled as much to Europe as she did to Oceanside.

Selma's condition worsened through the summer, and Leif continued to call Sonja to urge her to come home. But as long as her mother was alive and Leif was with her, she saw no reason to do so until she and Niels were ready.

On a Friday afternoon, Mrs. Henie took a turn for the worse. She spoke at some length with Dorothy and Sally. She kept saying she had to "talk to Sonja. I've done a terrible thing. Please tell Leif I'm sorry. But I must talk to Sonja."

The doctor said it was merely a matter of time now and Leif got on the phone with Sonja in France. "You've got to come, Sonja. Mother is dying. You'll be lucky if she's still alive when you get here."

"Oh, Leif, don't be so dramatic. I can't possibly come today. Niels and I are going across the border to Switzerland to do some gambling."

"But Sonja, she keeps asking to see you."

"You'll have to tell mother we'll be there as soon as we can, Leif."

Sonja did not leave Europe until the following day. Niels chose to stay in France, and Sonja was very annoyed that Leif was calling her back home for what was probably "a false alarm." En route she fortified herself with plenty of scotch. Dorothy accompanied Leif to the airport to meet Sonja's plane. Before they left, Selma said to Dorothy. "Oh, Dorty, I would die happy if we could just get Sonja and Leif to be friends again. My only wish is to have them friendly again."

"Mrs. Henie, I think it's impossible," Dorothy replied.

"Oh, Dorty . . . if they would only be friends . . ."

Sally stayed at home with Selma and kept assuring her that Sonja would be there soon. However, her plane was three hours late arriving in Los Angeles, and as the time grew on, Mother Henie finally looked over to Sally and said, "Sally, it's too late."

Soon after that she no longer recognized anyone and lapsed into unconsciousness. Sonja arrived about six in the evening, having had an additional three hours to fortify herself with booze. She swept off the plane, dragging a mink coat behind her, and staggered through the terminal. Leif tried to guide her by taking her arm, but Sonja kept jerking away. Both Leif and Dorothy gave a sigh of relief when they finally had their charge in the car and on the way home.

The moment she entered the house Sonja began to scream at Leif and Sally. Sally went to her bedroom, and Sonja and Leif went battling on into their mother's bedroom where she lay dying. Dorothy vividly remembers that evening.

"Oh, she was bitching and yelling at everybody. She didn't want Leif and Sally in the house all of a sudden. Even me. I can remember her mother lying there in bed. Sonja was sitting at the foot or side of her mother's bed. Leif was in a chair and Carrie and I were in the room. Leif and Sonja were arguing back and forth across their mother's body. Sonja was very drunk and said to Leif, 'You sonofabitch! You never did anything for her. What the hell are you doing here?'"

Carrie, very upset, kept begging, "Sonja, your mother is dying. Stop that."

Sonja ignored her.

One of the nurses on duty said to Sonja, "This isn't helping your mother, dear."

Sonja lunged from the bed at the nurse, wrestled the startled woman out into the hallway and, slamming her over the stair railing, attempted to throw her from the balcony to the first floor. "You sonofabitch, whoever you are, I'm not your *dear*. I'm *Mrs. Onstad*. How dare you call me *dear*!"

Carrie and Dorothy tried to pull Sonja off the nurse and, as Dorothy recalls, "Sonja was strong ordinarily. when she was drunk and angry she was almost superhuman. That poor nurse almost lost her life that night. I'm sure she knows it."

Sonja next became angry with the second nurse and called her a quack because, following doctor's orders, she had given Mrs. Henie some shots in an effort to keep her alive and conscious until her daughter arrived.

Leif finally left and went to his room to join Sally. Then, as Dorothy recalls, "The nurse went back to Mrs. Henie, and Carrie and I convinced Sonja to come into her sitting room off the master bedroom, and sit for a while. We hoped she would calm down and she did. Only the nurse was with their mother when she died."

Dorothy was with Sonja when the nurse she had tried to choke earlier came into the room and said, "Mrs. Onstad, your mother has passed on."

Sonja looked directly at Dorothy, and with no sign of emotion, said, "Go get her jewels, Dorothy."

At that moment Carrie Roberts entered the room, and Sonja looked up and calmly said, "Mother's gone, Carrie."

"I know," she responded, "and I'm sorry."

Sonja turned back to Dorothy and again told her, "Dorothy, I said go get those jewels!" Dorothy looked aghast, but sensing her feelings, Carrie said, "Come on, Dorothy. I'll go with you."

The two women went into Mrs. Henie's bedroom, where the nurse was calling the doctor to advise him of the death, collected all of Mother Henie's jewelry, and bringing it back to Sonja, placed it in her arms. She dropped it into her lap and began to sort through it. Fingering a strand of pearls she said, "I think I'll have another strand added to these and make a new necklace."

Within an hour or so Sonja was checking all of the television channels to see what was being said about her mother's death, and the following morning she sent out for all the Sunday papers to see if there was anything in them. She hadn't been to bed all night. By then Sonja was quite sober, and she called Niels to let him know her mother was dead. For whatever reason, he declined to return home until after the funeral.

Sonja absolutely refused to have anything to do initially with the funeral or the funeral arrangements. Dorothy and Sally went together to the funeral home to select the casket and make arrangements.

The family was divided at Selma Henie's funeral service; Sonja sat on one side of the aisle while Leif and his family sat on the other.

Selma was to be cremated, and her ashes were to be sent to Norway to be buried beside her husband. Nobody wanted to pick out the urn, and it fell to Dorothy to do that. One task, however, she did refuse. By the time of the cremation Niels was back, and he was discussing it with Sonja. "I want to be sure that they are Mrs. Henie's ashes," he said. "Somebody has got to be present."

Sonja turned to Dorothy. "Dorothy, you go down and be sure it is mother. I want to know that her ashes are still in the urn."

Dorothy shook her head. "No. I can't do that. I just can't do it."

Carrie spoke up, quite angrily, "Don't worry about that, Sonja. They have people down there to do that. You don't have to worry yourself with that."

The rift between Sonja and Leif was not healed with their mother's death. Leif was utterly shocked to learn that his mother had disinherited him. He could only correctly assume that Sonja had cajoled and threatened her.

27

*D*OROTHY had many memories of the Onstads' life-style.
"They fought over the simplest things. Even the drugstore bill.
They did it all the time. I wrote the checks for the different bills
that came for the house. I paid the household bills, and Niels would go
over my list to see what was his and what was Sonja's. I would then take
the stack which accumulated after the first of the month to Sonja, who
would sign her share."

Sonja would take a sheet of paper and list all of the checks: how much
and to whom. Then she would sit with Niels and decide. "I pay for this
and you pay for that." She would have already written "N.O." on those
she intended Niels to pay.

Then the arguments would begin. Niels refused to pay for toothpaste,
for instance. "Sonja, I am not going to pay for this. It's not even my
brand."

"It is so and you'll pay for it."

And so the arguments would go, often for hours, as they haggled over
the telephone bill, grocery bill, and charge accounts at department
stores.

Niels had a terrible temper and was morbidly fearful of and superstitious about birds. On one occasion they were looking at some oriental
carpets that had been brought to the house for viewing. One of them had
a bird on it. The carpet was gorgeous, and Dorothy had Carrie stand on it
so Niels couldn't see the bird. But he spotted the bird the minute Carrie
moved her foot and out went the carpet.

Sonja and Niels drank together and fought furiously when they did.
One night as they swilled cognac and scotch and fought, Niels spotted
two Dresden urns that had belonged to Wilhelm Henie. It was before
Selma's death, and she was crouched on the upper landing watching and
listening. In his drunken anger, Niels kicked and broke the beautiful
urns because they had birds on them.

Probably the worst example of his cruelly superstitious streak happened after Sonja's death. Dorothy watched in horror. "There was a
little decorative urn on the wall going down to the pool from the bar, with
a rose arbor over the passageway. A little sparrow had built her nest in

this urn because it was so protected by some roses that had grown there. Mr. Onstad, walking to the pool one day, heard 'cheep, cheep, cheep.' He promptly turned around and came back. Looking into the nest he found several baby birds which he took out and threw to the ground, crushing them with his foot. It would have devastated Sonja because she loved all animals."

If Sonja had had a superstition, it would have revolved around the possibility that a dollar might pass by and she would miss it. She hated paying any kind of taxes, and she came very close to going to jail trying to escape the duty on diamonds brought into the United States illegally. On one of her European sojourns she had seen an exquisite diamond tiara in Czechoslovakia and purchased it. The sellers reported the sale of the diamond-encrusted masterpiece and the name of the purchaser. It was a government regulation that they do so. Sonja had intended to smuggle it into the United States, but she was fortunate enough to have a friend in the FBI who got word to her that she was going to be arrested when she went through customs. The diamonds were quickly removed from the tiara and each item brought into the country separately. The duty on mounted diamonds was quite high, but on unset stones only about 10 percent. She wore that tiara in most of her shows.

It was not unusual for Sonja to carry over a million dollars in jewelry from her personal collection when she traveled. Dorothy carried a large sofa pillow with her when they toured or visited outside Hollywood. It was covered with a silk sham, was well padded, and had a large zipper that looked like another seam in the pillow. When it was zipped open, there was a big cavity in the middle where Sonja's jewelry was put. The pillow was so well padded that the outlines of the hard objects within weren't discernible.

"With all the traveling she did," Dorothy recalls, "she always packed her jewelry into this pillow. It was pretty heavy, I must say, and I can still hear Sonja saying, 'Carry it light! Straighten up!' I carried that pillow on and off trains, planes, and ships, keeping my hand on it at all times and often using it as a pillow to cushion my head. I took that thing through customs all over the world and was never once asked to open it or let someone examine it. Of course, this was before they had metal detectors. We were lucky. You'd never get by with it today."

After their mother died and Leif returned to Palm Springs, he and Sonja began gradually to resume a relationship. It would never be the same as it had been prior to the ranch fiasco, but it did improve. The first real break in the ice came in November 1961. Sally was listening to the radio one day and remembers what she heard.

"I was listening to reports of a fire in Bel Air but we didn't consider Delfern Drive as Bel Air. That was Holmby Hills. Consequently it was only from a news interest that we kept the radio on. The fire was jumping so fast it was hard to keep up with where it was from minute to minute and it did, in fact, burn all the way to Malibu, destroying dozens of very expensive homes, many owned and occupied by movie people.

"Sonja was in Europe and when the phone rang I was surprised that it was she calling about the fire. Someone had phoned her from Hollywood to tell her that her home was being threatened. She wanted Leif to go to Delfern immediately and try to save whatever could be saved. All of her and her father's trophies were in the house and could never be replaced."

Leif and Sally left immediately, and when they arrived the fire was roaring down Beverly Glen Drive, just one street over from Sonja's home. Flames were everywhere and fire equipment filled the streets as Leif tried to make his way to Sonja's home.

Dorothy recalls the events of the day and an interesting irony. "Our neighbors across the street, John Bowles and his wife, were lovely people from the South, where hospitality reigns. Sonja and Mother Henie were prejudiced against him because he might come over, tap on the door, and want to come in for a drink or chat, without announcing in advance that he was coming. Oh, they'd get so mad. But this wonderful gentleman forgot his own belongings and brought his station wagon over, parked it in front of the main door to the house, and said, 'Get all of Sonja's trophies into my station wagon and I'll drive them to safety.' He had a gorgeous collection of paintings in his own home, but her trophies were more important to him. Later, when I had a little party in Sonja's memory, after her death, Mrs. Bowles went out in her garden and brought me huge armfuls of flowers to place about the house for our memory party."

While Mr. Bowles was rescuing the trophies, Leif was busy with Carrie and Dorothy dumping all of the silver into Sonja's pool. Fortunately the flames did not reach her house, but a lot of gallant effort was exerted to preserve her treasures—by neighbors she considered "hicks" and by a brother she had tried to ruin financially.

Time heals wounds, and as the only surviving members of the family (there were Leif's children, of course) the brother and sister began to see one another socially for the first time in years. However, even those events were not without argument and hostility.

Sonja had a close friend, Alfredo de la Vega, who was also an insurance broker and handled all of Niels's and Sonja's insurance matters. Sally recalls an evening when she and Leif were guests in Sonja's home for dinner.

"Alfredo, at one time, was very much against Leif because Sonja had given him the idea that she was practically supporting Leif, which was totally erroneous. Sonja had told not only Alfredo, but all of her friends and acquaintances that the ranch belonged to her and she was permitting Leif to live there. All of which was a pack of lies. In any event, this one night we were at Sonja's house for dinner and both Sonja and Niels were stinking drunk by the time we got to the dinner table. Always when they drank they'd start a fight with us. It seemed to be some kind of game the two of them loved to play once the alcohol clicked in their brains.

"We were into dinner when Niels, quite paternally and dictatorially, said to Leif, 'I want you to give your insurance to Alfredo de la Vega. He's a very dear friend of ours.'

"'Niels,' I said, 'my son is in the insurance business and he carries all of our insurance.' Well, both Sonja and Niels went into a rage, cursing and flailing their arms in the air, sloshing their drinks all over the food, the table, and us. Simply disgusting and immature behavior. Sonja was used to lording it over Leif, but she wasn't dealing with Leif when she tried such tactics on me. She never could understand why I would defy what she called, 'Niels's better judgment.'"

After a number of such events, it was Sally who decided it was better not to see Sonja and Niels except when they had to. "Leif," she said, "I'm not going there to dinner anymore because it is the same old thing night after night. Drinking and fighting. We're not going to be their whipping boys."

So the reconciliation was brief, and the most that went on thereafter was a phone call or a meeting in the company of a lot of people where Sonja felt obliged to behave herself.

After her marriage to Niels, Sonja began to dabble in the stock market because her husband did. The only investments she had ever made prior to their marriage were when she was with Arthur Wirtz. She loved to get one up on Niels, and she looked for stocks that he dismissed and that she might make a big profit on. On her own she decided she would invest in Hilton Hotel stock.

"Oh, no, Sonja. That's not a good stock," Niels said.

"It is so a good stock," she argued, "and I'm going to get it." So she bought it on margin, and it took off and she made a nice profit. She loved to throw that up to him. Sonja loved getting one up on anybody. She never lost her competitive spirit.

Sonja's biggest investments, however, were in jewelry and art. Nobody could better Sonja's judgment about gems, and she became almost equally adept at spotting solid art investments. At her death, her art collection and her jewelry collection were each worth more than five million dollars.

After her marriage to Niels, Sonja no longer seemed to worry about aging. She no longer had to face the pressures of a career, and she apparently enjoyed being married to a man who was financially secure and to whom she could look for support and comfort. Most of the people who had known Sonja over the years did not like Niels Onstad, which didn't bother him in the least. He was aware that he wasn't winning any

300

personality prizes, but both he and Sonja were enormously wealthy and were looking forward to a great future together. Theirs was considered to be one of the truly solid marriages in Hollywood.

A very important part of Sonja's character was her inability to show love or affection. Her whole life was Sonja. Skating, film career, husband, family, money—all were secondary to herself. It is not surprising since she was consistently spoiled. From the time she was a small tot until her death, Sonja was allowed to feel that anything she wanted was hers. Certainly Leif had indulged her for years, and, in that sense, it is not surprising that she was shocked and bewildered when he refused to give her half his ranch.

To fulfill a life of collecting, Sonja had one more major ambition. She wanted to establish a museum and arts center in Norway to house her treasures, and in early 1962 she began to work toward that goal. She poured all her energy into the project. It was intended to reflect her long career in amateur skating, films, and ice shows, as well as to showplace her collections of art, jewelry, and family heirlooms.

The magazine *Show* profiled Sonja in March of that year, and in conclusion said, "Now married to Niels Onstad, a Norwegian shipping owner, she lives in the center of Oslo. Recently she and her husband gave $7 million in cash and paintings to found a modern art museum at Høbik-oden. She still skates a bit."

She managed to spirit much of her art out of the country, piece by piece, to Norway to begin her dream. Her 365 trophies were not shipped out conventionally from her Delfern Drive home. She had someone come from Norway to take the dimensions of her trophy room and an exact replica was built on a larger scale at the museum in Oslo.

To get the trophies over to Europe, she used some extremely large suitcases. Dorothy helped her pack the trophies.

"We used bath towels; most of them had been carried out of hotels from time to time. I saw many familiar names stamped on them. I did most of the packing. Sonja would come down from the attic with piles of these hotel towels and dump them on the floor. I would securely wrap each trophy, pack it in a suitcase, and then whenever anybody was going to Europe they were asked to take a suitcase full of trophies. We hauled them over in suitcases. A suitcaseful at a time, they were sent over with the luggage.

"It would be difficult to determine the dollar value. Some of them were solid gold and solid silver. Irreplaceable. They are all in the museum now."

Money for the museum was filtered through one of Niels's businesses in Lausanne, Switzerland. Sonja's assets were gradually being transferred quietly into Swiss banks and companies.

On May 15, 1963, the first ice skating Hall of Fame was unveiled in

301

Chicago, with Sonja Henie as its first entry. She was inducted, along with 84-year-old Norval Baptie, at a formal dinner the night before that was attended by more than one hundred fifty rink operators from the United States and Canada, including her old mentor, Arthur Schwartz. Sonja was near tears, showing a lack of emotional control rare for her. Only her return to Oslo with Chalfen's tour had moved her so much.

While in London in 1961, the year of the Bel Air fire, Sonja and Niels produced a motion picture, starring Sonja, called *Hello London*. She had entertained some idea of making pictures again, and she and Niels decided that if the American moviemakers wouldn't star her in a film, then she would make her own.

This, however, was no return to the screen. The skating was good, as always, but everything else about the film was amateurish at best, and it was never released.

Plans for the museum moved along and it became time for Niels and Sonja to discuss a name for this monument to Sonja's successes. Since it was a joint venture, it was decided that both names should be included, but deciding whose name came first developed into an unending battle. Niels felt it should be "Niels Onstad/Sonja Henie." Sonja put her foot down. It would be Sonja first or no museum. "We'll drop the matter right now and pull out all the funds," she fumed. "Besides," she needled him "whoever heard of Niels Onstad?"

Niels reasoned that he was putting a lot of money into the project and his name should be first. He did put more money in than Sonja. They originally thought it would cost each of them a million dollars. Sonja sold off a big piece of the Oceanside property to a junior college and another big piece to Tri-City Hospital. She took that money and deposited it in her Swiss bank account for transfer to Oslo for the museum.

However, it didn't matter to Sonja who put more money into the museum. Her name would have to come first. Eventually, of course, it did.

Sonja's greed went so far that at one time, after Selma Henie's death, she attempted to break the trust that had been originally set up by Wilhelm Henie to go to Selma at his death, to Sonja after that, and to Leif if Sonja predeceased him. Sonja wanted it to stop with her. She was totally unsuccessful, but Niels would pick up the fight after Sonja's death with more success.

She was making numerous trips back and forth to Oslo in connection with the museum, and during that time she resumed her friendship with her childhood girl friend, Lilyba. She had Lilyba doing some work for her in Oslo and even purchased a small car for her use. One day she asked Lilyba to do something for her, some errand. For whatever reason, her old friend was unable to do it at that time, and Sonja, becoming extremely angry, went over to Lilyba's house and took the car away. It was the end of their friendship. When the museum finally opened there was a great debate between Sonja and Niels as to whether or not Lilyba should receive an invitation. They finally did send her one, but she did not come to the opening. Even at Sonja's death she didn't attend the reception after the crematorium services.

Sonja thought it was a good idea to be secreting her valuables out of the country. In 1965 the last of the many robberies she had suffered took place. One night while she and Niels were having dinner at a popular Hollywood eating establishment, Sonja's home was burglarized, and the thieves made off with seventeen of her fur coats. It was only one of many fur and jewelry robberies that had tormented the Bel Air/Holmby Hills area, and the police believed there was a thread that connected them.

The furs ended up in Las Vegas and were discovered when police raided a warehouse about a month or so after the robbery. A representative of the Las Vegas Police Department phoned Sonja to tell her that they had discovered a large cache of what appeared to be stolen furs and that he believed some of them might be Sonja's. She and Dorothy immediately left for Las Vegas to claim her stolen property. Upon their arrival they were escorted to the warehouse. Dorothy describes what they found.

"There were furs everywhere. Some of them were hanging on a rack, some were on the floor. They had started to remove the linings before they were caught. Sonja had her monogram inside many of her coats, but not all." However, between the two women they were able to identify all of Sonja's furs.

One detective asked Sonja, "How do you know which are your furs?"

Sonja snapped right back at him, "How do you know which woman is your wife?"

The leader of the ring was revealed to be the maitre d' at the Hollywood restaurant where Sonja and Niels had been dining. He was sentenced to a long stretch in the state penitentiary.

It was about this time that Sonja secretly began to practice her skating again with her old skating partner, Michael Mikeler. "For the last five years of her life," he states, "my wife and I were very close friends with Sonja and Niels. She and I skated three times a week for about three years at the Pickwick Ice Rink in Burbank." Mikeler was teaching and managing at the ice rink, and initially Sonja came only to exercise. "She came once in a while. The chauffeur brought her in her Rolls Royce. She always brought along her dogs, elkhounds I believe. When I knew she was there I went out and asked, 'How are you Sonja?' We talked for a bit socially and I said, 'Why don't you skate a little instead of merely exercising?' She would rent the rink for the whole morning. This was in the beginning in 1964. It was later that she became more serious about skating again.

"She started easy, and I would put on some music and tell her what to do and she was quite willing, an excellent student. She never said, 'No, I won't do that.' Never. An amateur skater is not prepared, but she was a professional with lots of discipline. I soon discovered that she was still a very good skater. I think she was down on herself because she had made that terrible movie in London and had been drinking a lot during that period of time. I tried to lift her spirits and make her feel good about herself."

Sonja was so pleased with her first session back on the ice that when she got home she asked Dorothy to phone the Mikelers and invite them to a screening and dinner afterward.

"It was the first time I'd met Sonja," Gloria Mikeler, Michael's wife, remembers. "Michael and I drove over to their home to pick them up. We were at the showing only a short time and Sonja said, 'Let's leave here.' So we went over to the Bistro for dinner. During the course of the evening Sonja got into an animated discussion with Michael."

"'We never paid you enough for what you did in the show,' she said to Michael. She had lost a false eyelash and was trying to put it back on as she talked without looking conspicuous. She was very cute about the whole thing. Alfredo de la Vega was her escort that night as Niels was away on business.

"The thing that struck me," Gloria says, "is her manner. While she was talking to Michael about being underpaid for his work, she was trying to fix the eyelash and Michael, treating her like a little girl, kept saying, 'Eat, Sonja. Eat.' And she obeyed like a child. She always took the food home to her dogs.

Sonja was extremely generous with Michael and Gloria. There were gifts of gold bracelets, gold chains, gold cigarette lighters. And she paid for every lesson he gave her.

She still retained her fiery spirit. One night she invited the Mikelers and a Jewish friend out to dinner. They were driving by the Los Angeles Country Club off Wilshire Boulevard. Sonja said, "You know something? They won't let me join that club because I'm an actress, and they don't allow Jews there, but we're going there tonight."

Gloria remembers the night as a personal triumph for Sonja. "I thought it was an absolute tribute to her stardom, that she ignored the rules and did as she pleased. She defied them and went in anyway. On another occasion I was complimenting Sonja on a ring she was wearing. She said, 'Try it on,' slipping it off her finger. 'But it is so large, Sonja,' I said, almost embarrassed, but she insisted I try it. 'It's yours,' she said. That's the way she was. Very spontaneous."

One day at the rink she brought up the subject of the days before the war when Michael was skating with her. "I realize that I could have done and should have done more for you—but we'll do things in the future. Lots of things."

Sonja loved any kind of opening and Niels, as Sally recalls, "was a publicity hound," so they went out a lot to premiers, sports events, and first nights at plays. On one occasion the Mikelers were going with Niels, Sonja, and Dorothy to an event in Santa Monica at the skating rink. Dorothy, Michael, and Gloria were riding in the back seat and Sonja and Niels were up front. Dorothy and Gloria were chattering away in the back seat when all of a sudden Sonja, who was supposed to make a little talk on television when they arrived, turned around and snapped, "Well, if you two wouldn't be talking so much I'd be able to concentrate on what I'm going to say when I get there." Dorothy was used to Sonja's abruptness but it shocked Gloria until she got to know her better.

Sonja could be very relaxed with friends. Gloria and Michael were invited over to Delfern Drive one night. "I want you to come over to dinner and I'll cook dinner," she said on the phone. When they arrived they discovered that Niels was away on business and Sonja wanted some company. "We just took off our shoes and made ourselves comfortable," Gloria says with a laugh. "Sonja was like a little girl. A neighbor came over from across the street to join us and Sonja ran some films of when she was a little girl—diving and swimming with her father in the lake. She seemed so happy that night barbecuing steaks out by the tennis court. Again, it was a spontaneous thing. Nothing was planned. She just decided to do it."

"It was important to me in this sense," Michael adds. "I had seen this girl when she was eleven years old in Europe, she had gone through that marvelous career and then at the end, what did she come to after millions of dollars spent on her and earned and all the jewelry she could possibly have—here she comes back to the skating rink like a little girl again. Her fabulous career had come full circle. A wonderful person in spite of all the little nasty things we could say about her. As a person she was larger than all those petty things."

Word leaked out, of course, that Sonja was practicing, and everybody thought she was preparing for a big comeback, which she probably would have attempted if she hadn't been running back and forth from Los Angeles to Oslo carrying millions of dollars worth of paintings to the projected museum. It was often a funny sight at the Pickwick Rink. There was Sonja in her Rolls Royce and Jack Kent Cooke, owner of the Los Angeles Kings hockey team, with his players practicing at the rink.

"She loved it," Michael says. The hockey players were big stuff from Canada and Chicago and they always asked, 'Who's the chick?' Sonja joked with them. She would skate twice as fast just to show them what she could do."

Sonja perhaps missed the spotlight. One night at the Bistro where she was having dinner, Joan Crawford came in and sat at the next table. All eyes turned toward Crawford, who looked absolutely fabulous. Sonja said, "Doesn't she look awful?"

On the way home in the car, Niels chided her. "Don't say she looked awful. I thought she looked beautiful."

"You would," Sonja snapped. Crawford had gotten the kind of attention Sonja was used to throughout her life, and she may have resented it's going to someone else at her expense. She didn't draw the same looks that Joan Crawford did that night.

One night Sonja gave a party at her home and she mentioned that she might do a television special. The host of a well-known game show interrupted her and said, "You've had it. Don't waste your time." Sonja, feeling very good after a few Chivas Regals, let him have it in spades, and when she was through said, "And get the fuck out of my house!" The other guests applauded loudly.

Michael Mikeler believes she really did intend to do the television show and would have, except for circumstances. "She tried hard. Sonja had feelings. She could hurt, but she managed to hide it most of the time. While she was working out at the rink in Burbank she had a few bad falls. She was so anxious to get back in shape to appear in public again. One day some kind of headgear she was wearing came off and her hair wasn't done like it usually was. She was crawling around on all fours, on her hands and knees, which was quite human, very touching to see this great lady retrieving her headgear because she was embarrassed that her hair was not perfect.

"One day she kicked herself hard with the heel of her skate. She took it off and blood was gushing. She simply put the skate back on and went right on skating as if nothing had happened. The lady had great professionalism."

However, skating would have to wait for now. The museum was finally completed and its dedication and formal opening set for August 1968. En route to the opening Sonja gave an interview to the international *Herald Tribune* in Paris. She assured the writer that she was going ahead with her New York television spectacular, but first things must come first. "It takes some two months to prepare for active practice," she explained. "I went into training again last fall and was ready to appear when the scheduled show was unexpectedly postponed. Soon I shall begin limbering up again and then go to New York to select my supporting company. You know," she added, "I brought the ice revue to America and motion pictures. Now I am going to introduce the full-scale ice extravaganza to television."

Niels had a press release made up for the event, which read as follows:

> When King Olav of Norway formally opens the doors to the Sonja Henie, Niels Onstad Art Center just outside Oslo on August 23rd, some 116 paintings, valued at ten million dollars, will go on public display as a gift to the people of Norway.

306

The multimillion dollar center, also a donation from the couple, is situated on a craggy peninsula in a forty-acre park. The museum will house what was one of the richest private collections in the world. It includes Picassos, Villons, Rouaults, Miros, Matisses, Bonnards and other works amassed over the last forty years and united when the couple married in 1956. In addition to the paintings, the buildings will display the trophies awarded Miss Henie during her lifetime career as an international skating star. There will also be an amphitheatre for films and concerts, a sculpture garden, a yacht marina, parking facilities for 600 cars, a dining room and a cafeteria.

The generous contribution by shipowner Niels Onstad and his wife to the Norwegian people is envisaged as a parallel to New York's Guggenheim Museum and is expected to draw visitors from all over the world. It is the first building in Norway devoted completely to displaying modern art.

The completion of the art center is the realization of a seven year dream by the Onstads that began in 1961 with a tedious nationwide competition for the country's most qualified architects. Two young students, Svein-Erik Engebretsen and Jon Eikvar, were selected from over 100 architects who entered the contest.

Construction of the building began in 1964. The main level consists of five exhibition halls, arranged in a fan like manner with an entrance hall and stairwell as its center point. Also on the entrance level is a restaurant, a cafeteria and administrative offices. The lower level contains a library, study rooms, a lecture hall and storage space. Balconies connect the various wings of the building on the outside.

It was an immense undertaking. Sonja had triumphed again. For the first time in her life she truly gave back more than she got. For the first time she said, "What's mine is yours, too."

The event was a gala to end all galas. The entire Norwegian royal family attended, and a contingent of bejeweled and fur-coated friends from Los Angeles, Paris, and London turned up for a two-day round of parties that lit up the Norwegian skies. The opening day ceremonies were followed that night by a glittering party hosted by Sonja and Niels at their summer estate, Grandholtet.

The subject of Sonja and the Nazis came up because of a photograph from the 1936 Olympics that pictured Sonja being congratulated by Adolf Hitler.

"They're still very touchy here," observed Sonja.

At the party, Sonja swept down the white-carpeted staircase "a 5-foot

2-inch, 105-pound sunbronzed mermaid in a blue, beaded sheath that went with a sapphire clip the size of a hen's egg attached to a diamond necklace, diamond cascade earrings, a diamond bracelet and two sapphire solitaire rings," as described in a dispatch from Marylin Bender to *The New York Times.* Among her guests were the socially prominent Mrs. Jules Stein, wife of the chairman of Music Corporation of America; Mrs. Dolly Green, daughter of the developer of Beverly Hills, and Mrs. Harry Cohn, widow of the head of Columbia Pictures.

After such a blast, Sonja rested Saturday during the daytime, having arranged a boatride for her houseguests through the fjords around Oslo. She met them on their return in the afternoon wearing a blue quilted bathrobe and a white ruffled mob cap.

There was another dinner that night, a formal one, at the Center. Out-of-town guests mingled freely with Norwegian ship owners and art experts. Sonja still looked as bright as a new penny and happy as one might expect under such auspicious circumstances. For this party she wore a white, beaded, ostrich-flounced dress. Her white diamonds were complemented by large ruby stones. After dinner everyone went out on the museum terrace for a display of fireworks.

Someone commented, "For a breathtaking five minutes, it seemed as though Sonja Henie had tossed her jewelbox into the midnight sky."

When it was all over, she said to Niels, "What we need is a rest."

Little did she know how prophetic her words were.

28

_O_T began simply enough. Sonja and Niels had gone to Las Vegas sometime in September 1968 to see some shows and do a little gambling. Sonja returned home with a very bad cold and called in Dr. Robert Kositchek, the family doctor. He gave her some medication and told her to get some rest. Over the next few days, Sonja did not respond, and she became so weak that the doctor suggested she enter the hospital. There, they found she had pneumonia in one lung. Sonja spent the next few weeks in St. John's Hospital in Santa Monica.

The doctor decided to take some tests because she was not healing as rapidly as she should have. She had lost weight and complained of being very tired. The doctor ordered some blood tests but did not discuss his fears with Niels or Dorothy. Dr. Kositchek, a heart specialist, had been the family doctor for a long time and had complete charts on Sonja. He had been Selma Henie's doctor, too.

Not satisfied with the results of his first tests, he ordered new ones a few days later. Over a period of a week a pattern was observed. The red blood cells were quickly decreasing between tests. At that point Dr. Kositchek called the house and asked Niels and Dorothy to come down to the hospital and see him before going in to see Sonja.

He met with Niels and Dorothy in a little room at the hospital and said, "I'm afraid I have some very bad news to give you." Niels narrowed his eyes. "We have this week been taking blood tests, and before I brought you in for this meeting I wanted to be sure that what I feared was true. By all indications Sonja has leukemia."

"What is that?" Niels asked.

"Leukemia," the doctor explained, "is actually a cancer of the blood. The white corpuscles are eating up her red corpuscles very quickly. Very fast. Some leukemias are slow. Some are fast."

"Are you sure?"

"I'm as sure as I can be about anything."

"I don't believe in American doctors," Niels told him. "I want immediately a sample of blood to go to Dr. Moe in Oslo. He is a very brilliant man."

The doctor nodded. "Niels, I don't blame you. I certainly will prepare it but the blood must be expedited."

Dorothy went immediately to the telephone and called Scandanavian Airlines, where the customer relations representative in charge was a friend of Sonja's.

"I have a package that is of the utmost importance that must be delivered to Oslo as quickly as possible."

He assured her it would be no problem to have it on the next flight, which was the following morning. That gave the doctor time to draw blood and seal it in a canister for shipment. The doctor waited until the last possible moment to draw the blood in order to get it to Oslo in the right condition. Dorothy rushed out to the airport with the package and gave it to the representative.

She then returned to the house and called Dr. Moe in Norway. Niels also spoke with him in Norwegian. "We are sending a vial of Sonja's blood to you," he explained. "Will you please test it? The American doctors think she has leukemia and I don't believe it. Call us back after you have done your tests."

Dr. Moe received the vial of blood, tested it, and immediately called Niels and confirmed that Sonja did have leukemia. Niels turned to Dorothy and said, "We must not tell anybody. This is a secret between you and me."

She said, "Yes, Mr. Onstad. I understand."

Sonja finally recovered from her pneumonia and was home in time for New Year's Eve. The doctor told her she had to take certain medications and had to get as much rest as possible and not overextend herself. Sonja had been informed that she was suffering from anemia.

Dr. Kositchek held a second meeting with Niels and Dorothy before Sonja was released from the hospital and told them that "As far as the tests and studies are concerned, it would appear that Mrs. Onstad has about nine more nonths to live. That could vary a month or two, maybe more."

Niels was visibly shocked. Whatever the difference he and his wife had had, they had been married for almost thirteen years and were well matched. They loved one another. He had a hard time realizing that it was going to end before long. He cautioned Dorothy again. "You must never tell Sonja. We will do everything as we have always done it."

And they did. She continued working with Michael Mikeler, and Niels encouraged her to do that. Dorothy reflects on how they handled it. "We didn't change a single thing or make any mention of her illness. She would get up at seven in the morning as she was working out, planning to do her television spectacular in New York. She wanted to do it with the theme music from *Dr. Zhivago*. She had been to see the film and gave a special dinner party for Omar Sharif, its star. She thought the movie was tremendous and was crazy about "Lara's Theme," the sound-track music. She went out every morning promptly to work out.

"She returned from the rink and, as was usual for her, would do the footwork of her routine on the carpet. She would float around the room to the music from *Dr. Zhivago*. She was so filled with happiness and expectations it almost made me cry to know that it would never come to be."

She was starting to plan her costumes for the show, to have some of them made, and to select people to work in the television spectacular with her, and she had plans for an air date in January 1970. She purchased costume material for her chorus skaters.

"I knew she wouldn't live that long," Dorothy says, "but I couldn't bring myself to say, 'Why don't you hold up on buying material for costumes for a while.' We just went ahead and planned, and I tried to show as much excitement as Sonja did. It was quite an effort."

Sonja made great light of her "anemia" when she was at the ice rink with Michael. "She didn't want anyone to know that she was sick in any way," he says.

She spoke of her hospitalization lightly one day on the ice with Michael. "I went to a Beverly Hills doctor," she said, "for a checkup. The sonofabitch charged me two thousand dollars. Some fancy checkup, huh? Makes you feel good, though, to know you are all right."

But she wasn't all right. Dorothy noticed one big difference. Sonja was invited to a lot of big parties and would always plan to go, but many, many times she would be upstairs dressing and would call down the stairs and say, "Dorothy! Dammit Dorothy! I'm so tired I can't finish getting dressed. You'll have to call and say that something came up and it was unexpected and we can't make it. Don't tell them I'm tired."

Of course, Sonja was not surprised since she had been told that she would be rundown until she got her blood built up. "I know," says Dorothy, "she never sensed that she was on limited time."

Niels and Sonja returned to Europe in the spring as usual. Mr. and Mrs. Ray Hommes went over that summer and were with them on their vacation. They went fishing, visited Kjell Holm's historic estate at Sandu, and had a great time. Sonja really never looked better. She was thin, but radiant.

Just before she left for Europe she phoned the Mikelers and said, "Why don't you come and have dinner with us at Trader's in Beverly Hills? We're leaving for Europe and would like to see you."

"Niels carried most of the conversation during the evening," Gloria recalls. "He seemed so loving and attentive to her and kept assuring her that she was still as good as ever."

Sonja turned to Michael and said, "If you get me back in show business I'll give you half."

Michael and Gloria accompanied Sonja and Niels to their car. In parting, Sonja whispered to Michael, "Niels is leaving tomorrow. I'm going later. When he's gone I'm coming skating." But she didn't come.

In September Sonja and Niels went down to Lausanne, Switzerland, to

311

their apartment and spent some time there. Then in October they moved on to Paris. They'd been gone from Delfern Drive since June but had kept in touch with Dorothy by letter and telephone. Sonja also wrote to Michael telling him of all her great plans for the television special she was planning and assured him she wanted him to work with her.

From Paris, Sonja called Dorothy to tell her she was planning to fly back to America soon, and Dorothy remembers the phone call well. "She had a good friend in Paris, Margie Tucker. Sonja called me on Saturday night and said they had been out and had had one hell of a time and then had gone over to the big market where they had all the meats and vegetables."

"You remember, Dorothy, when we were there, and the bird shit all over your shoulder? God, how we laughed. Well, we had a great time tonight, too. It was late when we got home but it was worth it."

"I'm glad you had such a good time, Sonja," Dorothy said.

"Listen, the reason I called. I'm coming in on Tuesday. I don't know whether it will be the afternoon or evening flight, but I'll either telephone or wire you. In the meantime, I want you to go down to Beverly Hills Silk and Woolen and pick up a bunch of samples. I want to have some new dresses made. Call my dressmaker and tell her I'll need some fittings. Call Elizabeth Arden and set up a manicure and pedicure and my hair on Wednesday. Whew! I guess that's about it. I'll see you at the airport on Tuesday."

Dorothy said, "Okay, Sonja. I'll see you at the airport."

It was the last time she ever spoke to Sonja. "My telephone rang on Sunday morning, and I could tell by the noise on the line it was an overseas call. My first thought was, as usual, Sonja forgot to tell me something. I had actually been sitting there waiting because she always seemed to think of something she'd forgot to tell me. It had only been six hours since we talked."

The cables finally cleared and Dorothy said, "Hello."

The voice on the other end of the line said, "Dorothy, this is Onstad. Sonja's dead." Six hours earlier she had been full of excitement and life, and by eight o'clock Pacific Daylight Saving Time on October 12, 1969, she was dead.

She had been planning to fly over to Portugal for a party, but she suddenly told Niels she was tired and didn't feel up to it.

Sonja had been receiving blood transfusions in Norway. She had received the blood from Dr. Moe because Niels didn't trust American doctors. However, she had neglected to have a transfusion during their last stay in Oslo.

Niels said, "I think we should go back to Oslo and have Dr. Moe give you some blood and then we'll fly from Oslo to Portugal. I'm sure you'll feel better after you've seen Dr. Moe."

312

He chartered a plane with a pilot and copilot and they started back to Oslo. Once they were in the air, Niels settled back to read a newspaper. Sonja was sitting next to him and said, "Oh, Niels, I am so tired."

"Sonja," he said, "try to get some sleep and I'll wake you up before we get in."

He put his arm around her, and she put her head against his shoulder, and he read the newspaper. About twenty minutes out of Oslo, he went to wake her up. "Sonja, we're getting close to Oslo now. You better wake up."

There was no response. Again he said, "Sonja?" He took her hand and found it cold. He called the pilot who came back and took her pulse.

"I'm sorry, Mr. Onstad, but I think she's dead."

Niels looked at the man with disbelief. "She couldn't be. Radio Oslo and have an ambulance and Dr. Moe at the airport." When the plane landed Dr. Moe was there with the ambulance as requested. He came aboard the plane and examined Sonja and then looked up at Niels and said, "I'm sorry, Niels. Sonja is dead."

The queen of ice was dead!

Sonja's life was a grand display of talent. She had cut a path across the sky, and for such a star the last rites must necessarily be those appropriate to a queen.

Leif and Sally, now living in Mexico, received the news from a friend in London who had heard it on the radio. Shortly afterward Dorothy phoned them. The family feud was forgotten, and Leif's grief was real and genuine. He remembered the sister who tagged along after him when he went skating with his friends and the warm bubbling little girl who was so anxious to be the best at everything. He loved that Sonja and would miss her forever.

The pageantry of Sonja's funeral and burial was regal, indeed. Niels had Dorothy leave on the first available plane for Oslo. Plans had to be made. Decisions about whom to invite. The crematorium had limited seating, so it could not be merely an open funeral. The invitations read that guests must be in their seats by 2:45 P.M. because the royal family came after that hour and nobody was allowed to enter the chapel once the king and his family were seated. Dorothy describes the events.

"The little casket was there. The day dawned a very gray, dull, dark day. Very, very dark. It was so gloomy and so foreboding. We arrived in a long black limousine. It was a long drive up to the crematorium.

"The seating was in the rear, just rows of seats and an aisle down. The casket was up in front and beside the casket, on either side, was a huge bouquet which had been sent by King Olav V. The building, and I describe this for a purpose, was an A-frame in the front with a very high peaked roof which sloped down and all of this was window. Outside the window was a courtyard. As you looked out the window there were banks and banks and banks of gorgeous color from the floral arrangements. The casket was in the front of the building at the end of the aisle. The seats for the royal family were very special seats near the casket on the left.

"Mr. Onstad, Leif, and Sally and myself were sitting in the front seats on the right. When the royal family approached the bugles blew and the drums rolled as they wound up the hill to the crematorium. Everyone stood and turned to face the door as the king and his family entered and came down the aisle. No one sat until after the royal family was seated."

Hollywood's own royalty sent tributes and telegrams, but none of the film colony's giants attended Sonja's funeral. It was a Norwegian event, not Hollywood's.

The service that followed was beautifully conducted. The minister stood behind the little casket on this dark and ominous day and spoke a very lovely sermon.

A strange thing happened that Dorothy recalls as being uncanny. "The day was so dark. And as the minister was doing the final prayer, 'Ashes to ashes and dust to dust . . .' I looked through the A-frame pyramid window, and I saw the little white casket—practically plain with hardly any decoration on it. Suddenly that little box with the red roses on it lit up. The white became crystallized beneath the roses, like white enamel. My eyes followed what seemed to be a beam upward to the peak and, would you believe it, the clouds separated and the sun came through, and its rays dipped down as if a spotlight operator had focused on Sonja's casket. As the minister finished the prayer, the clouds closed again and the light went out."

Sonja weather had prevailed and the dimpled darling of the ice world had enjoyed her last spotlight on earth.

Epilogue

*A*T Sonja's death she left a will that was a surprise to most of those who were close to her. In it, she specifically disinherited all the members of her family. Carrie Roberts and Dorothy Stevens, who had each served her loyally for twenty-six years, were also left without a bequest. She bequeathed $10,000 to Vestra Gravelund, a cemetery in Oslo, "for the perpetual care of the family plot in which my father is interred."

Her jewelry was bequeathed to the Sonja Henie Foundation of Oslo.

All else went to Niels Onstad to be used by him during his lifetime and to revert at his death to the foundation in Oslo.

The paragraph of her will involving Leif and his three sons read:

"I have intentionally declined to provide herein for any of my heirs, including my brother, Leif Henie, or his sons, Wilhelm, Robert or Tommy, not because of any lack of love or affection but only for the reason that I have amply during my lifetime made suitable provision for them."

Sonja was successful in disinheriting her family, but the fate of her jewelry was not what she had designed it to be. Dorothy remembers Sonja's own words regarding the matter:

"I want people to be able to see my jewelry. They can build a permanent large concrete base with a heavy glass over it for protection, like the crown jewels in England. They should be sealed hermetically. Then people can look through the glass and see my sets of jewelry. I see my diamonds arranged together and my rubies are together as are my emeralds and sapphires—all in complete sets. Then the pearls can be fully displayed."

One day Dorothy approached Niels Onstad to ask him why nothing was being done to display Sonja's jewels.

"That's impossible," he said. "We'd have to have a permanent guard to stand and watch them."

She explained how Sonja wanted them sealed for such protection, but he insisted that he would take the jewels and use the money from their sale to go to the museum.

315

The jewels, however, were never sold. Niels's second wife received several of Sonja's gems, his daughter was given some, and girl friends received their fair share. Dorothy was given a little gold angel pin with mother of pearl wings that Sonja wore every day going to the store or running errands, and two small angel earrings to match.

It bothers Dorothy still that the specific bequest of Sonja's jewelry to the museum in Oslo was never carried out.

Niels Onstad was not satisfied with the proportion of Henie money that Leif still retained through the trust that had been set up for him by his father. Sonja had had no success in breaking that trust, but Niels found a precedent that allowed a trust to be broken into for the purpose of paying estate taxes and by complicated legal maneuvers he saw to it that almost a quarter of a million dollars was detached from Leif Henie's trust to help pay Sonja's estate taxes. It didn't break Leif, but managed to put a hefty dent into his trust fund. The actual value of Sonja's holdings when she died was somewhere between twenty-five and fifty million dollars.

It took Niels and Dorothy, along with a battery of tax lawyers, over two weeks in Switzerland to sort out her assets and determine their location and value.

A few years after Sonja's death, Dorothy obtained permission from Niels Onstad to hold a memorial party at the Delfern Drive house for Sonja. She invited old friends and skaters from all over the country who had worked with Sonja in films and in the ice shows. Over three hundred people attended. Some had not seen each other in thirty years. Belle Christy, Jack Pfeiffer, Michael Mikeler, and Marshall Beard were among those who came. There was plenty of food and drink, and the guests viewed some of Sonja's films. At four o'clock everyone gathered by the pool, and Dorothy gave a little tribute to Sonja. She asked that people bow their heads and give a little thank you to "this great lady who has brought so much into our lives."

"I just stood there, head bowed," Dorothy recalls, "and the only sound I heard was a little bird singing. When I lifted my head I saw many faces streaked with tears, but none comparable to Belle Christy's. She was wracked with sobs. I was touched by that."

Sonja Henie was one of a kind. Her equal on ice will probably never be found now that times have changed and the nature of Olympic competition has been altered. She was a champion on the ice and a champion in her heart. She was indeed the queen of ice but, alas, in her personal relationships, the queen of shadows.

ℱigure Skating ℛecords

Olympics Figure Skating Championships

1924, Chamonix
1.   Herma Planck-Szabo, Austria .... Gold Medal
2.   Beatrix Loughran, United States .... Silver Medal
3.   Ethel Muckelt, Great Britain .... Bronze Medal
4.   Theresa Blanchard-Weld, United States
5.   Andrée Joly, France
6.   Cecil Smith, Canada
7.   Kathleen Shaw, Great Britain
8.   Sonja Henie, Norway

1928, St. Moritz
1.   Sonja Henie, Norway .... Gold Medal
2.   Fritzi Burger, Austria .... Silver Medal
3.   Beatrix Loughran, United States .... Bronze Medal
4.   Maribel Vinson, United States
5.   Cecil Smith, Canada
6.   Constance Wilson, Canada
7.   Melitta Brunner, Austria
8.   Ilse Hornung, Austria

1932, Lake Placid
1.   Sonja Henie, Norway .... Gold Medal
2.   Fritzi Burger, Austria .... Silver Medal
3.   Maribel Vinson, United States .... Bronze Medal
4.   Constance Wilson-Samuel, Canada
5.   Vivi-Anne Hultén, Sweden
6.   Yvonne de Ligne, Belgium
7.   Megan Taylor, Great Britain
8.   Cecilia Colledge, Great Britain

1936, Garmisch-Partenkirchen
1.   Sonja Henie, Norway .... Gold Medal

2.	Cecilia Colledge, Great Britain	....	Silver Medal
3.	Vivi-Anne Hultén, Sweden	....	Bronze Medal
4.	Liselotte Landbeck, Belgium		
5.	Maribel Vinson, United States		
6.	Hedy Stenuf, Austria		
7.	Emmy Putzinger, Austria		
8.	Viktoria Lindpaintner, Germany		

World Championship Figure Skating Finals

1927
1. Sonja Henie
    (runners-up's names not available)

1928
1. Sonja Henie
    (runners-up's names not available)

1929
1. Sonja Henie
    (runners-up's names not available)

1930, New York City
1. Sonja Henie, Norway
2. Cecil Smith, Canada
3. Maribel Vinson, United States

1931, Berlin
1. Sonja Henie, Norway
2. Hilde Kolovsky, Austria
3. Fritzi Berger, Austria
4. Maribel Vinson, United States

1932, Montreal
1.   Sonja Henie, Norway
         (runners-up's names not available)

1933
1.   Sonja Henie
         (runners-up's names not available)

1934, Oslo
1.   Sonja Henie, Norway
2.   Megan Taylor, England
3.   Liselotta Landbeck, Austria
4.   Vivianne Hulthen, Sweden
5.   Maribel Vinson, United States

1935, Vienna
1.   Sonja Henie, Norway
2.   Cecilia Colledge, England
3.   Vivi-Anne Hultén, Sweden
4.   Hedy Stenuf, Austria

1936, Paris
1.   Sonja Henie, Norway
2.   Megan Taylor, England
3.   Vivi-Anne Hultén, Sweden

———

Miss Henie also won numerous Norwegian and European championships.

Filmography

One in a Million
Twentieth Century-Fox
Producer: Raymond Griffith
Released: 1937

Director: Sidney Lanfield
Script: Lenore Praskins and Mark Kelly
Camerman: Edward Cronjager
Musical Director: Louis Silvers

Cast:
  Sonja Henie
  Don Ameche
  The Ritz Brothers
  Jean Hersholt
  Ned Sparks
  Arline Judge
  Dixie Dunbar
  Borrah Minnevitch and His Rascals
  Montagu Love

Thin Ice
Twentieth Century-Fox
Producer: Raymond Griffith
English Title: *Lovely to Look At*
Released: 1937

Director: Sidney Lanfield
Script: Boris Ingster and Milton Sperling (from the novel *Der Komet*
  by Attilla Orbok)
Camerman: Robert Planck and Edward Cronjager
Musical Director: Louis Silvers

Cast:
   Sonja Henie
   Tyrone Power
   Arthur Treacher
   Raymond Walburn
   Joan Davis
   Sig Rumann
   Alan Hale
   Melville Cooper

Happy Landing
Twentieth Century-Fox
Producer: David Hempstead
Released: 1938

Director: Roy del Ruth
Script: Milton Sperling and Boris Ingster
Camerman: John Mescall
Musical Director: Louis Silvers

Cast:
   Sonja Henie
   Don Ameche
   Cesar Romero
   Ethel Merman
   Jean Hersholt
   Billy Gilbert
   Wally Vernon
   El Brendel
   The Condos Brothers
   Raymond Scott Orchestra

My Lucky Star
Twentieth Century-Fox
Producer: Harry Joe Brown
Released: 1938

Director: Roy del Ruth
Script: Harry Tugend and Jack Yellen
   (Story by Karl Tunberg and Don Ettlinger)
Camerman: John Mescall
Musical Director: Louis Silvers

Cast:
Sonja Henie
Richard Greene
Joan Davis
Cesar Romero
Buddy Ebsen
Arthur Treacher
George Barbier
Louise Hovick
Billy Gilbert
Patricia Wilder
Paul Hurst
Elisha Cook, Jr.
Robert Kellard
Brewster Twins
Kay Griffith

Second Fiddle
Twentieth Century-Fox
Producer: Darryl F. Zanuck and Gene Markey
Released: 1939

Director: Sidney Lanfield
Script: Harry Tugend, based on a story by George Bradshaw
Camerman: Richard Day and Hans Peters
Musical Director: Louis Silvers

Cast:
Sonja Henie
Tyrone Power
Rudy Vallee
Edna May Oliver
Mary Healy
Lyle Talbot
Alan Dinehart
Minna Gombell
Stewart Reburn
Spencer Charters
Charles Lane
The Brian Sisters
John Diestand
George Chandler
Irving Bacon
Maurice Cass

Everything Happens at Night
Twentieth Century-Fox
Producer: Harry Joe Brown
Released: 1939

Director: Irving Cummings
Script: Art Arthur and Robert Harari
Camerman: Edward Cronjager
Musical Director: Cyril J. Mockridge

Cast:
  Sonja Henie
  Ray Milland
  Robert Cummings
  Maurice Moscovich
  Leonid Kinsky
  Alan Dinehart
  Fritz Feld
  Jody Gilbert
  Victor Varconi
  William Edmunds
  George Davis
  Paul Porcasi
  Michael Visaroff
  Eleanor Wesselhoeft
  Lester Matthews

Sun Valley Serenade:
Twentieth Century-Fox
Producer: Milton Sperling
Released: 1941

Director: H. Bruce Humberstone
Script: Robert Ellis and Helen Logan; based on an original story
  adapted by Art Arthur and Robert Harari
Cinematography: Edward Cronjager
Choreography: Hermes Pan
Music: Mack Gordon and Harry Warren

Cast:
  Sonja Henie
  John Payne
  Glenn Miller and His Orchestra
  Milton Berle

Lynn Bari
Lynne Roberts
Joan Davis
William B. Davidson
Melville Ruick
Eddie Kane
Edward Earle
Chester Clute
Ralph Sanford
Almira Sessions
John "Skins" Miller
Nicholas Brothers
Dorothy Dandridge
Forbes Murray

Iceland
Twentieth Century-Fox
Producer: William LeBaron
Released: 1942

Director: H. Bruce Humberstone
Script: Robert Ellis and Helen Logan
Photography: Arthur Miller
Music: Mack Gordon and Harry Warren
Musical Director: Emil Newman

Cast:
Sonja Henie
John Payne
Jack Oakie
Felix Bressart
Osa Massen
John Merrill
Fritz Feld
Sammy Kaye and His Orchestra
Sterling Holloway
Adeline DeWalt Reynolds
Ludwig Stossel
Duke Adlon

Wintertime
Twentieth Century-Fox
Producer: William LeBaron
Released: 1943

Director: John Brahm
Script: E. Edwin Moran, Jack Jevne and Lynn Starling,
    from a story by Arthur Kober
*Photography: Joe MacDonald
Songs: Leo Robin and Nacio Herb Brown
**Musical Director: Alfred Newman

Cast:
   Sonja Henie
   Jack Oakie
   Cesar Romero
   Carole Landis
   S. Z. Sakall
   Cornel Wilde
   Woody Herman and His Orchestra
   Helene Reynolds
   Don Douglas
   Geary Steffen
   Georges Renavent

   *Some filmographies list Glen MacWilliams as director of photography.
**Some filmographies list Charles Henderson as musical director.

***It's a Pleasure**
RKO Release
Producer: David Lewis
Released: 1945

Director: William A. Seiter
Script: Lynn Starling and Paul Elliot
Photography: (Unknown)

Cast:
   Sonja Henie
   Michael O' Shea
   Bill Johnson
   Marie McDonald
   Gus Schilling
   Iris Adrian

*Sonja's only color feature film.

The Countess of Monte Cristo
Universal-International

Producer: Jack Beck
Released: 1948

Director: Frederick De Cordova
Script: William Bowers from a story by Walter Reisch
Songs: Jack Brooks and Saul Chaplin
Photography: (Unknown)

Cast:
Sonja Henie
Dorothy Hart
Michael Kirby
Arthur Treacher
Hugh French
Freddie Trenkler
Arthur O'Connell

Syv Dager for Elisabeth
A silent film made in Sweden in 1924. Production records unavailable.

Hello London
Sonja and husband Niels Onstad produced this travelogue (in color), which featured Sonja's skating abilities. It was started in 1958 and completed (final editing) over a year later. It was never shown in a public theater and was Sonja's last attempt to make a comeback in motion pictures.

Index

Raymond Strait is the author of *Alan Alda, Hollywood's Children, Lanza, Star Babies, This for Remembrance,* and other well-received books. Leif Henie was Sonja's brother and, until his recent death, her only surviving relative. He was there from the beginning and at the end.